CONTEMPORARY SUPREME COURT CASES

CONTEMPORARY SUPREME COURT CASES: LANDMARK DECISIONS SINCE *ROE V. WADE*

Donald E. Lively and Russell L. Weaver

GREENWOOD PRESS

Westport, Connecticut • London

Library of Congress Cataloging-in-Publication Data

Lively, Donald E., 1947–
    Contemporary Supreme Court cases : landmark decisions since Roe v. Wade / Donald E. Lively and
Russell L. Weaver.
        p. cm.
    Includes bibliographical references and index.
    ISBN 0–313–33514–1 (alk. paper)
    1. Constitutional law—United States—Popular works. 2. United States. Supreme Court—Popular
works. 3. Judgments—United States —Popular works. I. Weaver, Russell L., 1952– II. Title.
    KF4550.Z9L58 2006
    347.73'260264—dc22   2006015155

British Library Cataloguing in Publication Data is available.

Library of Congress Catalog Card Number: 2006015155
ISBN: 0–313–33514–1

First published in 2006

Greenwood Press, 88 Post Road West, Westport, CT 06881
An imprint of Greenwood Publishing Group, Inc.
www.greenwood.com

Printed in the United States of America

The paper used in this book complies with the
Permanent Paper Standard issued by the National
Information Standards Organization (Z39.48–1984).

10 9 8 7 6 5 4 3 2 1

TABLE OF CONTENTS

PREFACE

The power of judicial review is not specifically enumerated by the Constitution. It is a function that the Supreme Court secured in its first landmark decision, *Marbury v. Madison* (1803). Since establishing its "power to say what the law is," and thus make its interpretation of the Constitution binding on the political branches of government, the Court has rendered many more landmark rulings. This book's predecessor, *Landmark Supreme Court Cases,* catalogued more than two centuries worth of benchmark Supreme Court decisions. In both instances, the challenge is one of inclusion and exclusion.

Determining landmark status is even trickier when the focus is upon cases that have been decided in the recent past. A century ago, Supreme Court jurisprudence was defined by an emphasis upon economic rights. By the mid-twentieth century, economic rights doctrine had been abandoned and largely discredited. Short-term landmark status thus is not necessarily a precursor of long-term significance. This book identifies landmark cases on the basis of their societal impact, specifically the extent to which they adjust the boundaries of government power and individual rights and liberties. It is conceivable that the force of some of these cases will be diminished or undone by future decisions. Such a development does not minimize their significance, however, as a landmark of the time.

The use of *Roe v. Wade* (1973) as a starting timeline for modern landmark decisions is not an arbitrary choice. Many observers view the Warren Court, and its decisions concerning civil rights, First Amendment freedoms, and rights of the accused, as the twentieth Century's primary source of landmark decisions. It is against this backdrop of perception that *Roe v. Wade* becomes a compelling starting point. The decision in this case, establishing a woman's freedom to choose an abortion, is a post-Warren Court ruling. It represents a model of review that is characterized by critics as activist and that takes the Court beyond the boundaries of interpreting the Constitution and into the zone of creating a Constitution. Although the Warren Court has been the main target for such criticism, the decision in *Roe v. Wade* demonstrates a model of review that not only is a primary source of landmark decisions. It also has extended beyond a single era and has achieved a level of controversy rivaled by few Court decisions in the nation's history.

Like its predecessor, *Landmark Supreme Court Cases* (1999), this volume is divided into four primary sections. The first section, "Separation and Distribution of Powers," examines cases that have charted boundaries among the three branches of the federal government. The second section, "Power to Regulate or Affect the Economy," consists of cases concerning the federal commerce power and the states' sometimes conflicting authority to exercise their police powers. The third section, "Equality Concepts," includes cases relating to constitutionally prohibited forms of discrimination including classifications based upon race and gender. The final and largest section pertains to individual rights and liberties, including those enumerated by the Constitution and those developed by the judiciary through its interpretation of the due process clause. These substantive sections are augmented by two tables of cases (in alphabetical and chronological order, respectively), the United States Constitution, a glossary of key terms, overall bibliography, and index. Cases generally are presented in chronological order in each chapter. Exceptions exist, however, when it is more logical to group cases within a chapter by subject matter.

The authors have developed this book with the aim of making it relevant and accessible to a wide variety of audiences. Toward this end, it identifies not only the Court's rulings on "what the law is" but offers competing perspectives on "what the law should be." The hope is that readers will gain not only insight into the nation's highest law, but awareness that the Constitution is a work in progress subject to highly competitive perspectives on how it should evolve and be evolved.

ALPHABETICAL TABLE OF CASES

CHRONOLOGICAL TABLE OF CASES

I

SEPARATION AND DISTRIBUTION OF POWERS

Federal power under the Constitution is distributed among three branches of government. The principle of separation of powers is not set forth in the text of the Constitution but is evident in its structure. Articles I, II, and III of the Constitution enumerate, respectively, the authority of Congress, the President, and the judiciary. These coordinate branches function independently but also interact on the basis of checking and balancing each other's power. The consequent relationship reflects the framers' sense that authority should not be centralized and effective governance could be achieved through a convergence of their roles.

Constitutional doctrine has been driven by conflict among the branches with respect to their respective roles. Separation of powers decisions typically have resulted from conflicts between branches of government over how far their respective authorities extend. The first significant separation of powers decision was *Marbury v. Madison* (1803), which established the Supreme Court as the final authority in interpreting the Constitution. This decision resolved a conflict between the Court and President Jefferson, who had argued that the judiciary's rulings did not bind him in the exercise of his power. Boundaries of power within the federal system have been tested periodically since.

The departure point for this section is the power of judicial review which, pursuant to *Marbury v. Madison,* gives federal courts the authority to determine conclusively the Constitution's meaning. The balance of this section relates to the boundaries of presidential and congressional power.

CHAPTER 1

THE POWER OF JUDICIAL REVIEW

The Supreme Court's status as the final arbiter of the Constitution's meaning is established not by constitutional text but by the Court's interpretation of it. The usual starting point for any discussion of judicial review is *Marbury v. Madison* (1803). This case arose from President Jefferson's refusal to deliver the commission of a judge appointed by President Adams. Although the Court did not require the President to deliver the commission in this case, it declared the power to do so. More than a century and a half later, President Richard Nixon confronted the Court with a claim that raised similar issues with respect to the judiciary's power over the presidency. This case concerned whether the President, on the basis of executive privilege, was immune from having to participate in the criminal justice process. In *United States v. Nixon* (1974), the Court determined that the President was accountable to the judicial process and ordered him to comply with an order compelling production of evidence in a criminal proceeding.

United States v. Nixon

The power of judicial review was established as a general proposition early in the nation's history. Its specific implications have been developed, however, through subsequent case law. In the 1950s, for instance, some states challenged the Court's authority to order desegregation of public schools. Citing *Marbury v. Madison* (1803), the Court in *Cooper v. Aaron* (1957) reaffirmed that it had "the power to say what the law is" and ordered the implementation of desegregation. The *Cooper* decision established the Court's constitutional authority in relationship not only to the federal government but also to the states.

Citation: 418 U.S. 683.

Issue: Whether executive privilege enables the President to resist a judicial order directing him to provide evidence in a criminal proceeding.

Year of Decision: 1974.

Outcome: It is the role of the judiciary to determine whether the executive privilege claim or needs of the criminal justice process should prevail.

Author of Opinion: Chief Justice Warren Burger.

Vote: 8-0.

The next significant constitutional challenge to the scope of judicial review arose in circumstances that, like those in *Marbury*, concerned the President and the Court. It arose following a politically inspired burglary of Democratic Party national headquarters during the 1972 presidential election campaign. Two years later, in the course of a special prosecutor's investigation, a grand jury indicted several executive aides and advisers and named President Nixon as an unindicted coconspirator. The district court, at the special prosecutor's request, subpoenaed documents and tapes relating to conversations between the President and his aides and advisers. Although providing edited transcripts of those conversations, the President moved to quash the subpoena on grounds the tapes and other materials were protected by executive privilege. After the district court rejected the President's arguments, the controversy was presented to the Supreme Court.

The Constitution does not mention executive privilege in specific terms. President Nixon argued, however, that it was implicit in executive power. Without such protection, he maintained that it would be impossible for policy makers in the executive branch to engage in open and frank discussion. The Court agreed with the President, as evidenced by its observation that "government ... needs open but protected channels for the kind of plain talk that is essential to the quality of its functioning." Without the ability to keep internal communications confidential, members of the executive branch would be chilled in their discourse. If the risk of public disclosure had to be assumed, they would be less willing to assume the intellectual risks necessary for dynamic and fully reasoned policy making. Although not disagreeing with this premise, the Court ruled against the President with respect to his conceptualization of the privilege and its applicability in this case. Specifically, it rejected the contentions that (1) his claim was beyond the scope of judicial review and (2) executive privilege was an absolute barrier to the Court.

In rejecting the argument that the privilege claim was beyond its power of review, the Court restated the central premise of *Marbury v. Madison*—that the judiciary has the ultimate power to decide "what the law is." From the Court's perspective, "an absolute, unqualified privilege" would undermine significantly the "primary constitutional duty of the Judicial Branch to do justice in criminal prosecutions." Such an impediment "would plainly conflict with the function of the courts" under the Constitution. The Court, however, made a significant allowance for the presidency by finding that a presidential claim of confidentiality is presumptively privileged. What this determination means is that the chief executive could prevail upon a claim of privilege when a court finds that the interest of confidentiality outweighs the interests of the criminal justice system.

In striking this balance, the Court found that the privilege sought by President Nixon was based upon a "broad, undifferentiated claim of public interest." The Court was unmoved by this argument at least for purposes of finding a basis for confidentiality. A more precise and compelling basis for the privilege might have yielded a different result. Most particularly, if military, diplomatic, or sensitive national security secrets were at stake, the Court might have been more responsive to the President's interests. Given the criminal justice system's dependence upon pertinent and admissible evidence, the generalized interest in confidentiality was not sufficiently compelling. Another factor in support of the outcome was the judiciary's ability to review the materials privately and limit public disclosure only to those evidentiary materials relevant to the criminal proceeding. The President's interest thus was subordinated to "the legitimate needs of the judicial process."

The Court's ruling thus drew upon "the ancient proposition of law ... 'that the public ... has a right to every man's evidence.'" Although disfavoring operation of executive privilege in the specific instance, the interests of the chief executive were not entirely disregarded. Rather, the Court affirmed that the "confidentiality of Presidential communications has ... constitutional underpinnings." It follows from this premise that the President may have a protected confidentiality interest when a court finds that, under the circumstances, the need for secrecy is compelling. The interests of the judicial process also may be diminished in settings outside the criminal justice system. In the context of civil litigation, when the parties represent private concerns, public interest may be less of a factor. The need for presidential participation also may abate when the evidence is relatively inconsequential and available from other sources. The balance tilts more against the President, however, insofar as the government is suing a private party. As in a criminal prosecution, there are fairness concerns if government can use the litigation process to its advantage by denying the other party access to relevant information.

Despite acknowledging the constitutional basis of a conditional presidential privilege, the ruling is most notable for reaffirming the power of judicial review. The *Nixon* case, like its landmark antecedent *Marbury v. Madison,* represented a constitutional clash between the President and judiciary. President Jefferson, when thrust into this showdown context, threatened to resist the Court. Contrary to this belligerent tone, President Nixon promptly complied with the Court's order to turn over documents and tapes. Shortly thereafter he resigned the presidency. Nearly a quarter of a century later, the Court revisited the issue of executive privilege in *Clinton v. Jones* (1997). In this case, President William Clinton argued that the "character of the office" justified postponement of a civil lawsuit until his term in office expired. Referencing its decision in *Nixon,* the Court rejected the claim that litigation would impose an unacceptable burden upon him and impair his performance in office. It also restated the proposition "that the President is subject to judicial process in appropriate circumstances."

Bibliography

Raoul Berger, *Executive Privilege: A Constitutional Myth* (Cambridge, MA: Harvard University Press, 1974). The need for executive privilege, for the President to govern effectively, is examined.

Archibald Cox, *Executive Privilege,* 122 *University of Pennsylvania Law Review* 1383 (1974). The first special prosecutor in the Watergate controversy sets forth his insights into the scope of executive privilege.

Patricia A. Krause, ed., *Anatomy of an Undeclared War: Congressional Conference on the Pentagon Papers* (New York: International Universities Press, 1972). A critical perspective upon the motives and reliability of executive privilege claims is provided.

Charles Warren, *The Making of the Constitution* (Boston, MA: Little, Brown and Company, 1937). This contains a discussion of why the Constitution's framers considered secret meetings essential to their work and productivity.

CHAPTER 2

THE POWER OF THE PRESIDENT

The boundaries of presidential authority initially were tested in *Marbury v. Madison* (1803), when the Court determined that not even the chief executive was beyond its power "to say what the law is." The *Marbury* decision, like the Court's ruling in *United States v. Nixon* (1974), drew a line between presidential and judicial power. Turf issues also have arisen between the President and Congress. In *Youngstown Sheet and Tube Co. v. Sawyer* (1952), the Court ruled against President Truman's seizure of the steel industry. The President had justified his action on grounds that it was essential for successful execution of the Korean War. The Court determined that, absent any specific constitutional provision or congressional authorization, the President had exceeded his authority. In *Dames and Moore v. Regan* (1981), the Court revisited the boundaries between the President and Congress. This case concerned the resolution of a conflict between the United States and Iran and provided more flexibility for the chief executive to act in foreign affairs. The President's power to appoint officers of the United States was examined in *Morrison v. Olsen* (1983), when the Court upheld congressional authority to appoint independent counsel to investigate and prosecute government misconduct. Executive authority to detain "enemy combatants" was the issue in *Hamdi v. Rumsfeld* (2004). In this case, the Court determined that an American citizen in an allegedly "enemy" relationship with the United States could not be detained through the duration of a war without due process.

Dames and Moore v. Regan

Citation: 453 U.S. 654.

Issue: The scope of presidential power to make law in the context of an infringement of individual property rights.

Year of Decision: 1981.

Outcome: The scope of presidential powers depends on an assessment of a variety of factors including the President's explicit powers and those powers delegated to the President by Congress.

Author of Opinion: Justice William Rehnquist.

Vote: 8-1.

Relying on eighteenth century European political philosophy, the framers of the United States Constitution created a system of divided powers. Influenced by the adage that power corrupts, and absolute power corrupts absolutely, the framers chose to divide power between three separate and independent branches of government (the legislative, the executive, and the judicial). The framers hoped that the three branches would compete with each other for power and would thereby limit the power of the other branches. As the Court put it in *Mistretta v. United States* (1989), the Constitution created "a carefully crafted system of checked and balanced power within each Branch [to avoid tyranny in a Branch]."

The concepts of separated powers, and of "checked and balanced" power, are reflected in various provisions of the Constitution. Even though Congress has the power to pass legislation, a bill does not become law unless it is signed by the President (or unless a presidential veto is overridden by a supermajority). In the area of foreign affairs, whereas the President is given broad authority over foreign affairs and is denominated as the commander in chief of the armed forces, Congress is given the power to regulate foreign commerce, to spend money to raise armies, to declare wars, and to consent to treaties.

The clash between the President's power and Congress's power over foreign affairs has played out in several dramatic cases. One of the most famous cases, *Youngstown Sheet and Tube Co. v. Sawyer* (1952), arose during the Korean War. Facing a strike at United States steel mills, President Truman seized them in order to preserve the continuity of steel production during the war. The President claimed that a national emergency existed because "steel is an indispensable component of substantially all of such weapons and materials," and "to assure the continued availability of steel and steel products during the existing emergency, it is necessary that the United States take possession of and operate the [steel] plants."

In an opinion by Justice Hugo Black, the Court concluded that President Truman had acted illegally. Viewing the President's power formalistically, the Court concluded that the President was required to point to "express constitutional language" supporting his right to seize the mills. In other words, the President's power, if any, to issue the order must stem either from an act of Congress or from the Constitution itself. Since no constitutional provision explicitly authorized the seizure, the authority could not be implied. The Court rejected the argument that the President's explicit powers included his obligation to "take Care that the Laws be faithfully executed" and his power as "Commander in Chief of the Army and Navy of the United States." The Court ultimately concluded that the "Founders of this Nation entrusted the law making power to the Congress alone in both good and bad times. [T]his seizure order cannot stand."

The Court departed from *Youngstown's* formalistic approach in *Dames and Moore v. Regan*. In this case, which arose after Iranian students had held Americans hostage for more than a year, President Carter entered into an executive agreement with Iran that obtained the hostages' release. The agreement provided that attachments and liens on Iranian assets in the United States would be nullified, and those assets would be transferred to Iran. The agreement also provided for a suspension of claims against Iran and presentation of those claims to an International Claims Tribunal. After the Executive Agreement was finalized, the Treasury Department promulgated a regulation providing that "[u]nless licensed or authorized ... any attachment, judgment, decree, lien, execution, garnishment, or other judicial process is null and void with respect to any property in which on or since [November 14, 1979,] there existed an interest of Iran."

The case arose when Dames and Moore challenged the Executive Agreement and the regulation. Dames and Moore claimed that it was a beneficiary under a contract to conduct site studies for a proposed nuclear power plant in Iran and sought damages for services provided as well as interest. Although the trial court entered orders of attachment, the regulation required disallowance of the claim.

Had the Court applied *Youngstown's* more formalistic view of presidential power, it should have struck down the Executive Agreement and the regulation because the President's actions were not explicitly authorized. Instead, eschewing *Youngstown's* formalistic approach to presidential power, the Court relied on Justice Robert Jackson's concurring opinion in *Youngstown*. In that concurrence, Justice Jackson articulated a flexible approach to presidential power that focused on the relationship between the President and Congress. When the President acts pursuant to express or implied congressional authorization, "the President's power is at its zenith because he exercises both his own power and Congress' power." In such a situation, the President's action "would be supported by the strongest presumptions and the widest latitude of judicial interpretation, and the burden of persuasion would rest heavily upon any who might attack it." By contrast, when the President acts without congressional authorization, he enters "a zone of twilight in which he and Congress may have concurrent authority, or in which its distribution is uncertain." In this second situation, the analysis is more complex, and "the validity of the President's action, at least so far as separation-of-powers principles are concerned, hinges on a consideration of all the circumstances which might shed light on the views of the Legislative Branch toward such action, including 'congressional inertia, indifference or aquiescence.'" Finally, when the President acts contrary to Congress's will, "his power is at its lowest ebb," and the Court "can sustain his actions 'only by disabling the Congress from acting upon the subject.'"

In *Dames and Moore*, President Carter asserted that his authority to nullify attachments fit within Justice Jackson's first category because he was acting with congressional authorization. President Carter relied on a federal statute that allowed him to "investigate, regulate, direct and compel, nullify, void, prevent or prohibit, any acquisition, holding, withholding, use, transfer, withdrawal, transportation, importation or exportation of, or dealing in, or exercising any right, power, or privilege with respect to, or transactions involving, any property in which any foreign country or a national thereof has any interest; by any person, or with respect to any property, subject to the jurisdiction of the United States."

In accepting President Carter's argument, the Court concluded that, because "the President's action in nullifying the attachments and ordering the transfer of the assets was taken pursuant to specific congressional authorization," it was "supported by the strongest of presumptions and the widest latitude of judicial interpretation, and the burden of persuasion would rest heavily upon any who might attack it." As a result, the Court concluded that, "[u]nder the circumstances of this case, we cannot say that petitioner has sustained that heavy burden."

The Court also upheld the President's authority to suspend pending claims in United States courts. Although Congress did not explicitly authorize the suspension, Congress arguably approved it when it enacted the *International Claims Settlement Act of 1949*. Congress had amended the *International Claims Settlement Act* to provide for its application to settlement agreements, and the Court viewed this fact as demonstrating Congress's acceptance of the President's claim authority. The Court concluded that "[i]n light of ... the inferences to be drawn from the character of the legislation Congress has enacted in the area, such as the IEEPA and the Hostage Act, and from the history of acquiescence in executive claims settlement—we conclude that the President was authorized to suspend pending claims pursuant to Executive Order No. 12294."

Dames and Moore is one of those landmark decisions that reshape the Court's approach to a constitutional problem. The decision rejected *Youngstown's* more formalistic approach to presidential power and substituted a flexible approach that examines both congressional and presidential action. The net result was an expansion of presidential power. No longer must the President point to a specific constitutional provision that explicitly authorizes his actions. Moreover, especially when Congress has explicitly or implicitly signaled its assent to the presidential actions, the President can rely on both his constitutional prerogatives and Congress's as well.

Bibliography

Arthur S. Miller, *Dames and Moore v. Regan: A Political Decision by a Political Court,* 29 *UCLA Law Review* 1104 (1982).

Kenneth C. Randall, *The Treaty Power,* 51 *Ohio State Law Journal* 1089, 1091 (1990).

Laurence H. Tribe, *Taking Text and Structure Seriously,* 108 *Harvard Law Review* 1221 (1995).

John C. Yoo, *Laws as Treaties?: The Constitutionality of Congressional-Executive Agreements,* 99 *Michigan Law Review* 757 (2001).

Morrison v. Olson

In drafting the United States Constitution, the framers divided power between three separate and independent branches of government, but also provided for overlapping and intertwined relationships between the three branches. Examples of this intertwinement are evident throughout the Constitution. The decision to enter into a treaty requires combined presidential and Senate action. Likewise, even though Congress is vested with the power to pass legislation, the President must approve it before the legislation becomes law (unless two-thirds of the Congress override the President's veto). As the Court observed in *Youngstown Sheet and Tube Co. v. Sawyer* (1952), "[w]hile the Constitution diffuses power the better to secure liberty, it also contemplates that practice will integrate the dispersed powers into a workable government. It enjoins upon its branches a separateness but interdependence, autonomy but reciprocity."

Citation: 487 U.S. 654.

Issue: Whether an independent counsel, whose role is to investigate government misconduct, is an "officer" of the United States and thus appointable only by the President.

Year of Decision: 1988.

Outcome: An independent counsel is an "inferior officer" and thus may be appointed by department heads or the judiciary.

Author of Opinion: Justice William Rehnquist.

Vote: 7-1.

Under the appointments clause of the United States Constitution, the Constitution generally vests the appointment power in the President subject to the advice and consent of the Senate. The clause provides that the President "shall nominate, and by and with the Advice and Consent of the Senate, shall appoint ... all other Officers of the United States, whose Appointments are not herein otherwise provided for, and which shall be established by Law: but the Congress may by Law vest the Appointment of such inferior Officers, as they think proper, in the President alone, in the Courts of Law, or in the Heads of Departments." (U.S. Const., Art. II, s 2, cl. 2.)

In general, the appointments clause has been construed to place the appointment power in the President. For example, in *Buckley v. Valeo* (1976), the Court struck down portions of the *Federal Election Campaign Act of 1971,* in which Congress established the Federal Election Commission (FEC) and vested it with the power to administer federal election laws. Congress provided that commissioners were to be appointed by the President (subject to confirmation by both houses of Congress), the President pro tempore of the Senate, and the Speaker of the United States House of Representatives. The Court concluded that "any appointee exercising significant authority pursuant to the laws of the United States is an 'Officer of the United States,' and must, therefore, be appointed by the President." The Court concluded that all of the FEC commissioners were "officers" because they exercised discretionary enforcement power.

The Court has construed the President's removal power similarly. In *Myers v. United States* (1925), the Court held that the President had the right, without Senate approval, to remove a postmaster. However, a decade later, in *Humphrey's Executor v. United States* (1935), the Court qualified *Myers* in holding that the President did not have discretionary authority to remove a Federal Trade commissioner. The Court held that a statutory provision, providing that the President could remove commissioners only "for inefficiency, neglect of duty, or malfeasance in office," was constitutional. The Court distinguished *Myers,* reaffirming its holding that "congressional participation in the removal of executive officers is unconstitutional."

Morrison arose in the wake of the Watergate break-in and cover-up that ultimately led to President Nixon's resignation. The *Ethics In Government Act of 1978* provided for the appointment of an "independent counsel" with the authority to investigate, report, and prosecute governmental misconduct against the law. While a panel of three federal judges appointed independent counsels, the executive branch retained the removal power. This power was vested in the attorney general, who was required to show "good cause" for removal and report those reasons to the appointing judges.

In upholding the *Ethics in Government Act's* appointment provisions, *Morrison* held that the critical question is whether the independent counsel is an "officer" of the United States (in which case the President must retain the power to appoint) or is an "inferior officer." Under the appointments clause, Congress may vest the appointment of these "inferior officers" in the President alone, the heads of departments, or the Judiciary. The Court concluded that an independent counsel is an "inferior officer" of the United States. The Court offered several justifications. First, the independent counsel was subject to removal by a higher Executive Branch official and therefore was regarded as being "some degree 'inferior' in rank and authority." Second, under the Act, independent counsels were empowered to "perform only certain, limited duties" consisting of "investigation and, if appropriate, prosecution for certain federal crimes." Third, the independent counsel's jurisdiction was limited because it applied only to certain federal officials suspected of certain serious federal crimes, but also because the independent counsel's authority is limited by the special grant of authority authorized by the attorney general. Finally, the Court noted that the independent counsel's tenure was temporary and lasted only until completion of the assigned task. As a result, Congress could vest power regarding the appointment of independent counsels in the court.

Morrison did not hold that Congress has unlimited power to vest the appointment power over "inferior federal officers" outside the Executive Branch. The Court suggested that it might invalidate such appointments if "there was some 'incongruity' between the functions normally performed by the courts and the performance of their duty to appoint." However, the Court held that independent counsel appointments did not raise these concerns.

Justice Antonin Scalia dissented, arguing that the independent counsel's function is essentially executive in nature "in the sense that they are law enforcement functions that typically have been undertaken by officials within the Executive Branch." As a result, he would have invalidated the statute because it reduced "the amount of control or supervision that the Attorney General and, through him, the President exercises over the investigation and prosecution of a certain class of alleged criminal activity."

Morrison is an important decision because it helps define the scope of the President's appointment power. While the President is vested with the power to appoint "officers" of the United States, *Morrison* makes it clear that Congress can vest the appointment of "inferior officers" in the courts.

Bibliography

Louis Fisher, *Constitutional Conflicts Between the Congress and the President* (Lawrence, KS: University Press of Kansas, 1997).

John L. Gedid, *History and Executive Removal Power: Morrison v. Olson and Separation of Powers,* 11 *Campbell Law Review* 175 (1989).

Lawrence Lessig and Cass R. Sunstein, *The President and the Administration,* 94 *Columbia Law Review* 1 (1994).

Hamdi v. Rumsfeld

The terrorist attack on the World Trade Center buildings in 2001 triggered a rapid review and restructuring of national security. Consistent with historical experience when national security risks have been elevated, the role of the President became a focal point of debate. In this particular instance, a key issue was whether the President's power to combat terrorism included the authority to detain enemy combatants. Few doubted that the United States legitimately could take steps to improve security and to prevent future terrorist attacks. Indeed,

> Citation: 124 S.Ct. 2633.
>
> Issue: Whether the military may detain a United States citizen on enemy soil as an enemy combatant without a hearing.
>
> Year of Decision: 2004.
>
> Outcome: A citizen cannot be held indefinitely without being given the opportunity to challenge the government's conclusion that he/she is an "enemy combatant."
>
> Author of Opinion: Justice Sandra Day O'Connor.
>
> Vote: 6-3.

Congress responded to the attack by creating a new cabinet-level agency, the Department of Homeland Security, and enacting the *USA Patriot Act. Hamdi v. Rumsfeld* concerned another aspect of antiterrorism policy: whether a United States citizen, who was captured as an "enemy combatant" during the conflict in Afghanistan, could be detained indefinitely on American soil with no opportunity to challenge the legality of his detention.

Prior to *Hamdi,* the Court had rendered a number of decisions regarding governmental power to detain citizens during wartime. In *Ex parte Milligan* (1866), decided shortly after the Civil War, the Court limited governmental power by holding that United States military officers had improperly imprisoned United States citizens. By contrast, in *United States v. Korematsu* (1944), which arose during World War II, the Court adopted a more expansive view of federal power. In that case, the United States established military areas from which persons of Japanese ancestry were excluded and also provided for their detention and resettlement. Under this system, Fred Korematsu was ordered to report to a detention camp. When he refused to report, Korematsu was ultimately convicted of remaining in a military area from which persons of Japanese ancestry had been excluded. The Court upheld his conviction in a decision that was deferential to legislative authority. In another decision from the same era, *Ex Parte Quirin* (1942), the Court recognized broad presidential authority to treat enemy combatants differently. In that case, petitioners traveled by submarine across the Atlantic Ocean and landed on Long Island, New York, in the middle of the night. After they landed, they changed to civilian dress and buried their German military uniforms. After they were captured, the President appointed a military commission to try petitioners for offenses against the laws of war.

Decisions like *Korematsu* and *Ex Parte Quirin* were effectively overruled by a 1971 act, the *Non-Detention Act,* which limited the power of the President to detain individuals unless authorized by the legislative branch. Many believed that this act was passed to prohibit internment camps for citizens like the one in which Korematsu was detained.

Hamdi's inception can be traced to the World Trade Center in 2001. After that attack, Congress authorized the President to "use all necessary and appropriate force against those nations, organizations, or persons he determines planned, authorized, committed, or aided the terrorist attacks," as well as against any persons or groups that "harbored such organizations or persons." In addition, the President was given the power "to prevent any future acts of international terrorism against the United States by such nations, organizations or persons." The Act did not explicitly authorize the detention of persons. However, Congress also enacted the Authorization for Use of Military Force (AUMF), which gave the President the power to use all "necessary and appropriate force" against the al Qaeda terrorist network, the Taliban, and any nation harboring terrorists. In November 2001, the President issued an order directing the military to identify and detain "enemy combatants," those persons fighting for or supporting terrorist organizations opposing the United States.

Following United States intervention in Afghanistan and Iraq, the United States detained individuals that it believed to be members of the al Qaeda terrorist organization or the Taliban regime of Afghanistan. Within a short period of time, the United States held nearly 600 purported "enemy combatants" at the United States Naval Base located in Guantanamo Bay, Cuba. By labeling the detainees as "enemy combatants," the President endeavored to subject the detainees to a military process rather than a civilian process.

Yaser Esam Hamdi, a United States citizen who was born in the United States but who grew up in Saudi Arabia, was captured by United States military forces in Afghanistan and labeled an enemy combatant. At the time, he was fighting with the Taliban. Hamdi was first detained at Guantanamo Bay, but was later transferred to the continental United States where he was held without formal charges or access to counsel. Hamdi's father filed a habeas corpus petition challenging the government's right to hold his son without charges or an opportunity to rebut the charges.

In *Hamdi,* the United States Supreme Court held that the AUMF allowed the United States government to detain enemy combatants for the duration of the Afghanistan conflict. The Court recognized that the government has broad power to detain enemies during wartime. Otherwise, these "enemy combatants" might return to the battlefield and inflict injury on United States forces. As a result, the Court held that detention was an appropriate remedy: "detention of individuals falling into the limited category we are considering, for the duration of the particular conflict in which they were captured, is so fundamental and accepted an incident to war as to be an exercise of the 'necessary and appropriate force' Congress has authorized the President to use."

The Court then considered whether, despite the government's power, Hamdi was entitled to challenge the government's determination that he was an "enemy combatant." In other words, the government could not hold Hamdi indefinitely without the opportunity to challenge the designation concluding that the writ of habeas corpus has historically provided "a critical check on the Executive, ensuring that it does not detain individuals except in accordance with law." In reviewing the Act, the Court concluded that Congress assumed that habeas petitioners "would have some opportunity to present and rebut facts and that courts in cases like this retain some ability to vary the ways in which they do so as mandated by due process." In other words, Hamdi was entitled to contest the issue of whether he was an "enemy combatant."

However, the Court did not hold that alleged "enemy combatants" were entitled to "hearings" in the same sense as ordinary citizens. In assessing the process that was due Hamdi, the Court balanced a variety of factors and ultimately engaged in "an analysis of 'the risk of an erroneous deprivation' of the private interest if the process were reduced and the 'probable value, if any, of additional or substitute safeguards.'" In concluding that Hamdi was entitled to a hearing, the Court affirmed the "fundamental nature of a citizen's right to be free from involuntary confinement by his own government without due process of law," and balanced it against the "weighty and sensitive governmental interests in ensuring that those who have in fact fought with the enemy during a war do not return to battle against the United States." The Court concluded that a citizen-detainee must be given the opportunity to challenge his classification as an enemy combatant. As part of that challenge, the citizen must be given notice regarding the factual basis for his classification, and a fair opportunity to rebut the Government's factual assertions before a neutral decision maker. However, the Court recognized that "enemy combatant proceedings may be tailored to alleviate their uncommon potential to burden the Executive at a time of ongoing military conflict." In other words, even though hearsay might be excluded from other judicial proceedings, it can be admitted and considered in a citizen-detainee proceeding. In addition, the Court held that "the Constitution would not be offended by a presumption in favor of the Government's evidence, so long as that presumption remained a rebuttable one and fair opportunity for rebuttal were provided." As a result, the government could shift the burden to rebut the conclusion that he is an enemy combatant. Moreover, the Court suggested that the trials might be conducted before a military tribunal.

Justice David Souter, joined by two other justices, concurred on the basis that Hamdi's detention was forbidden by federal law. Justice Scalia, joined by Justice John Stevens, dissented, arguing that, when the Government accuses a citizen of waging war against it, "our constitutional tradition has been to prosecute him in federal court for treason or some other crime." In his view, this tradition can be relaxed only as demanded by the exigencies of war and then only temporarily. "The very core of liberty secured by our Anglo-Saxon system of separated powers has been freedom from indefinite imprisonment at the will of the Executive. The gist of the Due Process Clause [was] to force the Government to follow those common-law procedures traditionally deemed necessary before depriving a person of life, liberty, or property. Where the citizen is captured outside and held outside the United States, the constitutional requirements may be different."

Justice Clarence Thomas, dissenting, argued that Hamdi's "detention falls squarely within the Federal Government's war powers, and we lack the expertise and capacity to second-guess that decision. As such, petitioners' *habeas corpus* challenge should fail."

Hamdi is an important decision because it rejects the notion that citizens can be detained on American soil without an opportunity to rebut the allegations against them. The constitutional requirement of due process demands that the citizen be informed of the allegations against him and be given an opportunity to rebut those allegations. Only if the court concludes that the government's allegations, that the citizen is an "enemy combatant," are sustained can the citizen be detained for the remainder of the conflict.

Bibliography

Ryan H. Beery, *Modern Use of Military Tribunals: A Legal "Can" and a Political "Should"?* 28 *Ohio Northern University Law Review* 789 (2002).

Peter Berkowitz, *Terrorism, the Laws of War, and the Constitution: Debating the Enemy Combatant Cases* (Stanford, CA: Hoover Institution, 2005).

Jenny S. Martinez, *Availability of U.S. Court to Review Decision to Hold U.S. Citizen as Enemy Combatant—Executive Power in War on Terror,* 98 *American Journal of International Law* 782 (2004).

John E. Nowak and Ronald D. Rotunda, *Principles of Constitutional Law* (St. Paul, MN: Thomson/West, 2004), 114–16.

CHAPTER 3

THE POWER OF CONGRESS

Mistrust of centralized authority was an overarching influence upon the nation's founding and has been a significant factor in the Constitution's evolution. Early constitutional case law focusing upon congressional authority reflects this concern. In *McCulloch v. Maryland* (1819), for instance, the Court addressed the issue of whether congressional power should be limited strictly to what the Constitution specified or allowed for action that enabled Congress to exercise its authority more effectively. In ruling for a broader definition of congressional power, the Court set a principle and tone that favored development of a national identity. Separation of power controversies typically arise from disputes over which branch of government should exercise authority in a particular context. Separation of power concerns are not limited, however, to conflict between branches. As federal powers have expanded over the course of the twentieth century in particular, Congress has initiated efforts to increase the efficacy and efficiency of governmental operations. Its ability to delegate legislative authority to administrative agencies, charged with responsibility to manage increasingly complex social and economic problems and needs within Congress's scope of responsibility, generally has been upheld since the middle of the twentieth century. Other structural efficiencies, such as the legislative veto reviewed in *Immigration and Naturalization Service v. Chadha* (1983), have not survived constitutional scrutiny.

Immigration and Naturalization Service v. Chadha

Since the constitutional crisis of the 1930s, which led to a dramatic shift in the United States Supreme Court's approach to federal power, federal administrative power has grown so dramatically that some now refer to the administrative bureaucracy as a "veritable fourth branch of government." Not only has there been a significant increase in the number of administrative agencies, but those agencies now create a large quantity of law in the form of administrative regulations. Although Congress has searched for ways to rein in administrative power, none has proved effective.

Immigration and Naturalization Service v. Chadha involves one attempt by Congress to rein in administrative power through the use of the so-called one-house veto. The case arose in a deportation proceeding involving Chadha. Although Chadha conceded that he was deportable because he had overstayed his visa, he applied for a suspension of deportation. An immigration judge agreed to suspend the deportation. Under the governing statute, which allowed either house of Congress to overturn the

Citation: 462 U.S. 919.

Issue: Whether Congress may authorize one house to veto administrative regulations.

Year: 1983.

Outcome: The "one-house veto" violates the concept of separation of powers.

Author of Opinion: Chief Justice Warren Burger.

Vote: 6-3.

suspension order, Congress reversed the decision of the immigration judge. Thereupon, Chadha challenged the law on constitutional grounds.

Ultimately, the United States Supreme Court agreed with Chadha. The Court noted that the Constitution requires that all legislation be passed by *both* houses of Congress and that it then be presented to the President for signature or veto. The Court regarded this "presentment" power as extremely important: "The decision to provide the President with a limited and qualified power to nullify proposed legislation by veto was based on the profound conviction of the Framers that the powers conferred on Congress were the powers to be most carefully circumscribed." The presidential function "in the lawmaking process also reflects the Framers' careful efforts to check whatever propensity a particular Congress might have to enact oppressive, improvident, or ill-considered measures."

The Court also rejected the one-house veto under the bicameralism requirement of Art. I, § 1, cl. 7. That clause requires that, in order to pass legislation, it must be passed by both houses of Congress. The Court concluded that the one-house veto was exercised in a "legislative" manner and that it could act only bicamerally: "Neither the House of Representatives nor the Senate contends that, absent the veto provision in § 244(c)(2), either of them, or both of them acting together, could effectively require the Attorney General to deport an alien once the Attorney General, in the exercise of legislatively delegated authority, had determined the alien should remain in the United States." The Court concluded that, when the Constitution authorizes one house of Congress to act unilaterally, it stated that power explicitly. The Court concluded that the Constitution provided for unilateral action in only four situations: "(a) The House of Representatives alone was given the power to initiate impeachments. Art. I, § 2, cl. 6; (b) The Senate alone was given the power to conduct trials following impeachment on charges initiated by the House and to convict following trial. Art. I, § 3, cl. 5; (c) The Senate alone was given final unreviewable power to approve or to disapprove presidential appointments. Art. II, § 2, cl. 2; (d) The Senate alone was given unreviewable power to ratify treaties negotiated by the President. Art. II, § 2, cl. 2." Otherwise, the Court concluded, Congress must act in a bicameral manner and must present the legislation to the President for his signature or veto.

While the Court agreed that the one-house veto provided a "convenient shortcut" by which Congress could assert authority over the Executive branch, and thereby share power with it, the Court held that "the records of the Convention, contemporaneous writings and debates, that the Framers ranked other values higher than efficiency."

Justice Byron White dissented noting that the Court's decision "strikes down in one fell swoop provisions in more laws enacted by Congress than the Court has cumulatively invalidated in its history." He went on to express concern that "it will now be more difficult 'to insure that the fundamental policy decisions in our society will be made not by an appointed official but by the body immediately responsible to the people,' *Arizona v. California,* 373 U.S. 546, 626 (1963) (Justice John Harlan, dissenting). "I must dissent."

Chadha is an extremely important decision because it invalidates Congress's attempt to gain control over the administrative bureaucracy through the mechanism of the one-house veto. After *Chadha,* Congress will be forced to find alternate methods for reining in the growth of administrative lawmaking.

Bibliography

Stephen Carter, *From Sick Children to Synar: The Evolution and Subsequent De-Evolution of the Separation of Powers,* 1987 *Brigham Young University Law Review* 719 (1987).

Abner S. Greene, *Checks and Balances in an Era of Presidential Lawmaking,* 61 *University of Chicago Law Review* 123, 126 (1994).

D. Lively, P. Haddon, D. Roberts, R. Weaver, and W. Araiza, *Constitutional Law: Cases, History, and Dialogues,* 2nd ed. (Cincinnati, OH: Anderson Publishing, 2000), 428.

II

POWER TO REGULATE OR AFFECT THE ECONOMY

The primary driver for the United States Constitution was the need to create a viable economic union. This imperative was a shared concern that had been generated by experience under the Articles of Confederation. The initial postcolonial experience with self-government had broken down pursuant to interstate rivalries and frictions that made the confederation a sum less than its parts. The efforts of states to gain advantage over others, by means of tariffs and other trade barriers, were primary incidents of this syndrome. Framing of the federal constitution reflected a legacy concerned with centralization of power. Lessons learned under the Articles of Confederation, with respect to the essential requirements for a successful economic union, were applied in the framing of the federal constitution. Foremost in this regard was Congress's power to regulate commerce "among the several states." The commerce clause of the Constitution gives the federal government primary authority over interstate commerce. This power at times intersects state police power to regulate health, safety, and morals. To the extent it does, the Court must determine whether state or federal powers or interests should prevail.

CHAPTER 4

FEDERAL POWER

Federal power to regulate interstate commerce through the early twentieth century was interpreted narrowly. As the nation plunged into a national economic crisis in the form of the Great Depression, however, case law became highly deferential toward federal power to regulate any activity that might affect the national economy. For half a century thereafter, the Court consistently upheld regulatory initiatives that expanded federal power into areas traditionally reserved for state control. Expansion of the federal commerce power slowed in the 1990s, as the Court began to insist on a more demonstrable relationship between federal concern and national economic impact. The Court's decision in *United States v. Lopez* (1995) was a front-wave ruling in this regard.

United States v. Lopez

In the Articles of Confederation, the governing document that preceded the United States Constitution, the founders of the United States gave the states broad authority, including the power to regulate commerce. Over time, it became clear that the Articles were fatally flawed. The states used their power over commerce to protect their own economies and to discriminate against interstate trade. As state economies floundered, the states ultimately found it necessary to replace the Articles of Confederation with a new governing document, the

Citation: 514 U.S. 549.

Issue: Whether the federal power to regulate interstate commerce gives Congress the power to regulate gun possession in school zones.

Year of Decision: 1995.

Outcome: Congress lacks the power to regulate guns in school zones because of an insufficient relationship to interstate commerce.

Author of Opinion: Chief Justice William Rehnquist.

Vote: 5-4.

United States Constitution. The Constitution gave the federal government the power to control commerce "among the several states," as well as commerce between the United States and foreign countries. However, aside from delegated powers, like the commerce power, the framers sought to create a federal government of limited, enumerated, powers and to reserve other powers (including some limited power over commerce) to the states or to the people.

Until the 1930s, the federal government struggled to define the scope of the federal commerce power and to clarify the dividing line between federal power and state power. In a number of cases, the Court concluded that Congress had exceeded the scope of its power. For example, in *Hammer v. Dagenhart* (1918), the Court struck down a prohibition on the interstate transportation of goods manufactured in violation of child labor laws. In other cases, the Court suggested that Congress did not have the power to regulate such activities as "production," "manufacturing," or "mining." For example, in *United States v. E. C. Knight Co.* (1895), the Court found that "[c]ommerce succeeds to manufacture, and is not part of it." Finally, in *Carter v. Carter Coal Co.* (1936), the Court distinguished between "direct" and "indirect" effects on interstate commerce and concluded that Congress did not have power to control the latter.

The Court's attitude towards federal power changed dramatically in the 1930s. Following the 1929 stock market crash, the country settled into a prolonged period of economic depression. More than 2,000 banks failed, "one-fourth of the nation's work force was unemployed," the price of wheat dropped by "nearly 90 percent," and industrial output fell by 60 percent. In 1932, President Franklin Delano Roosevelt was elected on the promise of a "New Deal," and he took office demanding "action, and action now." One of his first acts was to call an extraordinary session of Congress to begin just five days after his inauguration. During his first 100 days, Roosevelt pushed through Congress a host of bills regulating financial markets, creating federal works programs, and regulating prices and wages. These acts were hostilely received by the federal courts. Decisions like *Panama Refining* and *Schechter,* coupled with the Court's restrictive interpretation of the commerce clause in cases like *Carter Coal Co.,* angered President Roosevelt, who viewed the Court as an obstacle to his New Deal.

Following his landslide reelection victory in the 1936 election, President Roosevelt developed his infamous "Court Packing Plan," which would have altered the Court's membership (and, presumably, its decisions) by adding additional members to the Court. The Plan provided that, when a judge or justice of any federal court reached the age of 70 without availing himself of the opportunity to retire, an additional justice could be appointed by the President. At the time, six justices were age 70 or older. If the plan had passed, the Court's membership would have expanded to 15 members, giving Roosevelt a majority of members sympathetic to his position.

Despite the popularity of both President Roosevelt and his New Deal, many opposed the legislation. Even though Congress was constitutionally authorized to control the number of Supreme Court justices, many believed that FDR was trying to manipulate the Court's membership in an obvious effort to control the Court's decisions. In the midst of the controversy over the Court Packing Plan, the Court decided *NLRB v. Jones and Laughlin Steel Corp.* (1937) and adopted a more deferential attitude towards Congress's commerce clause authority. Many believe that the Court's more deferential approach resulted from the pressure conveyed by the Court Packing Plan. Regardless, *Jones and Laughlin* ushered in a half-century during which the Court upheld essentially every assertion of federal regulatory power under the commerce clause.

This post-1937 deferential approach came to an end with the holding in *Lopez,* which concerned the *Gun-Free School Zones Act of 1990,* in which Congress made it a federal offense "for any individual knowingly to possess a firearm at a place that the individual knows, or has reasonable cause to believe, is a school zone." Lopez, who was then a 12th-grade student, arrived at Edison High School in San Antonio, Texas, carrying a concealed .38 caliber handgun and five bullets. When he was arrested and charged with violating the federal enactment, he defended on the basis that Congress had exceeded its power to regulate commerce. The Court agreed and reversed Lopez's conviction.

In deciding the case, the Court reaffirmed the notion the Constitution created a federal government of "enumerated powers." The Court quoted James Madison's statements in the Federalist Papers: "[t]he powers delegated by the proposed Constitution to the federal government are few and defined. Those which are to remain in the State governments are numerous and indefinite." In addition, the Court recognized that decisions like *Jones and Laughlin Steel* had greatly expanded Congress's authority. Then, for the first time in more than half a century, the Court held that Congress's power to regulate interstate commerce is "subject to outer limits." The Court concluded that Congress may regulate commerce in three different situations: it "may regulate the use of the channels of interstate commerce; it may regulate and protect the instrumentalities of interstate commerce, or persons or things in interstate commerce, even though the threat may come only from intrastate activities; & Congress' commerce authority includes the power to regulate those activities having a substantial relation to interstate commerce, *i.e.,* those activities that substantially affect interstate commerce." In *Lopez,* the Court concluded that the latter category requires proof that the regulated activity "substantially affects" interstate commerce.

In striking down the *Gun-Free School Zones Act,* the Court found that the first two categories of authority were absent because the Act did not regulate the channels of interstate commerce and did not prohibit the interstate transportation of a commodity through the channels of commerce. As a result, if the Act was to be upheld, the Court would have to find that it involved regulation of an activity that substantially affects interstate commerce. The difficulty was that the Court found that the law had "nothing to do with 'commerce' or any sort of economic enterprise, however broadly one might define those terms." The Government argued that possession of a firearm in a school zone can "result in violent crime and that violent crime can be expected to affect the functioning of the national economy" because insurance spreads the cost of crime throughout the nation, and because violent crime reduces the willingness of individuals to travel to places that are regarded as unsafe. The Government also argued that the presence of guns in schools presents a substantial threat to the educational process by threatening the learning environment and resulting in "a less productive citizenry" with a consequent impact "on the nation's economic well-being."

The Court refused to accept these arguments, noting that such arguments would allow Congress virtually unfettered authority to regulate the day-to-day lives of the people. Under the government's "costs of crime" rationale, Congress could "regulate not only all violent crime, but all activities that might lead to violent crime, regardless of how tenuously they relate to interstate commerce." Moreover, if the government's "national productivity" reasoning were accepted, Congress could regulate any activity that it found was related to economic productivity including family law in general and issues like marriage, divorce, and child custody in particular. It could also regulate the entire educational process mandating curricula for all schools. The Court rejected these possibilities, noting that the "possession of a gun in a local school zone is in no sense an economic activity that might, even through repetition elsewhere, substantially affect any sort of interstate commerce." The Court emphasized that there was no proof that either Lopez or his weapon had been involved in interstate commerce. "To uphold the Government's contentions here, we would have to pile inference upon inference in a manner that would bid fair to convert congressional authority under the commerce clause to a general police power of the sort retained by the States."

Justice Anthony Kennedy, joined by Justice Sandra Day O'Connor, concurred, arguing the Act "upsets the federal balance to a degree that renders it an unconstitutional assertion of the commerce power." Even though he doubted that any reasonable person would argue students should be allowed to carry guns on school premises, he believed that states should be allowed to experiment and use their expertise "in an area to which States lay claim by right of history and expertise." Justice Clarence Thomas also concurred, arguing that the Court's commerce clause jurisprudence has "drifted far from the original understanding of the Commerce Clause."

Justice John Stevens dissented, arguing both that guns are "articles of commerce and articles that can be used to restrain commerce." In addition, he argued that the possession of guns is a "consequence, either directly or indirectly, of commercial activity." Justice David Souter also dissented, arguing that the practice of deferring to rationally based legislative judgments "is a paradigm of judicial restraint," and he speculated about whether the Court was returning to its now discredited pre-1937 jurisprudence on the scope of the commerce clause.

Justice Stephen Breyer, joined by three other justices, also dissented, arguing Congress could have found that guns in school zones significantly undermine the quality of education in the country, and "that gun-related violence in and around schools is a commercial, as well as a human, problem." He also worried that the Court's holding raised questions regarding the validity of other federal criminal statutes premised on the commerce power. He noted that more than 100 sections of the United States Code are premised on the commerce power, and he wondered whether they would be upheld or struck down.

Lopez is an extremely important decision because it ends half a century of judicial deference to congressional assertions of power under the commerce clause. In subsequent decisions, the Court has required a more substantial nexus between a regulated activity and interstate commerce than it had previously required. However, the Court has struggled to find a proper balance between its prior deferential approach to congressional power and *Lopez's* more rigorous review.

Bibliography

John P. Frantz, *The Reemergence of the Commerce Clause as a Limit on Federal Power: United States v. Lopez,* 19 *Harvard Journal of Law and Public Policy* 161 (1995).

William E. Leuchtenburg, *The Origins of Franklin D. Roosevelt's "Court Packing" Plan,* 1966 *Supreme Court Review* 347–94.

D. Lively, P. Haddon, D. Roberts, R. Weaver, and W. Araiza, *Constitutional Law: Cases, History, and Dialogues,* 2nd ed. (Cincinnati, OH: Anderson Publishing, 2000), 514–24.

Robert S. McElvaine, *The Great Depression* (New York: Times Books, 1984), 137.

Grant S. Nelson and Robert J. Pushaw, Jr., *Rethinking the Commerce Clause: Applying First Principles to Uphold Federal Commercial Regulations but Preserve State Control over Social Issues,* 85 *Iowa Law Review* 1 (1999).

V.F. Nourse, *Toward a New Constitutional Anatomy,* 56 *Stanford Law Review* 835 (2004).

Clinton Rossiter, ed., *The Federalist No. 45* (New York, NY: New American Library, 1961), 292–93.

CHAPTER 5

STATE POWER

Although the commerce clause vests the federal government with exclusive authority over the national economy, the states retain an interest in regulating matters of health, safety, and public welfare. A state law that prohibits smoking in restaurants, for instance, accounts for public health but also affects interstate commerce. Regulation of this nature is allowable, however, so long as it does not unduly burden federal interests in efficient interstate commerce. Dormant commerce clause issues are not contingent upon congressional enactment of a conflicting regulation. Such controversies are resolved pursuant to the supremacy clause and associated preemption principles, discussed later in *Pacific Gas and Electric Co. v. State Energy Resources Conservation and Development Commission* (1983). The seminal dormant commerce clause case arose in the mid-nineteenth century when, in *Cooley v. Board of Wardens* (1851), the Court upheld a state law requiring ships to use local pilots for navigation to and from the port of Philadelphia. This outcome correlates with modern standards providing that, absent protectionist methods or an undue burden upon interstate commerce, state regulation is permissible. The Court's ruling, in *Philadelphia v. New Jersey* (1978), exemplifies the Court's intolerance for state regulation that would secure an economic advantage and undermine the premises of a national economic union.

City of Philadelphia v. New Jersey

Following the American Revolution, the 13 colonies adopted the Articles of Confederation and retained for themselves the authority to regulate commerce. Under the Articles, the economy did not function well as the individual states established trade barriers and imposed protectionist measures, and it eventually became clear that the Articles must be amended (or some other action taken) to provide the federal government with greater power over commerce. Ultimately, a decision was made to replace the Articles with the United States Constitution and to vest control over interstate commerce in the federal government. Under the Constitution, the states retained the "police power," which gave them the right to promote health, safety, and welfare issues. However, the Court placed

Citation: 437 U.S. 617.

Issue: Whether the State of New Jersey violates the constitutional ban on discrimination against interstate commerce when banning the importation of out-of-state landfill waste.

Year of Decision: 1978.

Outcome: A city may not discriminate against interstate commerce by prohibiting the importation of out-of-state garbage.

Author of Opinion: Justice Potter Stewart.

Vote: 7-2.

limits on the states' power to discriminate against, or impose burdens on, interstate commerce.

City of Philadelphia v. New Jersey involves the ongoing conflict between Congress's power to regulate interstate commerce and the state's police powers. *City of Philadelphia* involved a New Jersey law that prohibited the importation of most "solid or liquid waste which originated or was collected outside the territorial limits of the State...." The law was challenged by private New Jersey landfills, as well as by cities in other states that had contracts with the landfills, on the basis that the law involved an unconstitutional discrimination against interstate commerce. The New Jersey Supreme Court upheld the law on the basis that it advanced "vital health and environmental objectives" and imposed no economic discrimination against, and with little burden upon, interstate commerce.

In reversing, the United States Supreme Court recognized that many aspects of commerce escape congressional attention "because of their local character and their number and diversity" and that the states may retain authority to regulate these subjects. When a state seeks to advance legitimate health and safety interests, and there is no attempt to discriminate against interstate commerce, the Court suggested that it would evaluate the restriction under a less restrictive level of review. However, the Court held that its prior decisions generally prohibited state and local governments from imposing "economic isolation" and protectionism and that "a virtually *per se* rule of invalidity has been erected" against isolationist measures.

In evaluating the New Jersey law, the Court quickly concluded that it was a "protectionist" measure. Although the state was concerned about the environmental effects of waste, the state sought to preserve its landfill sites exclusively for New Jersey citizens. The state thus determined that the best way to extend the life of its landfill sites was by excluding out-of-state waste. The Court concluded that, "whatever New Jersey's ultimate purpose, it may not be accomplished by discriminating against articles of commerce coming from outside the State unless there is some reason, apart from their origin, to treat them differently. Both on its face and in its plain effect, ch. 363 violates this principle of nondiscrimination."

In rendering its decision, the Court recognized that "not all laws which facially discriminate against out-of-state commerce are forbidden." The Court noted that it had upheld quarantine laws even though they single out interstate commerce for special treatment. However, the Court concluded that quarantine laws should be distinguished from the New Jersey landfill laws, noting that quarantine laws banned the importation of articles such as diseased livestock that "required destruction as soon as possible because their very movement risked contagion and other evils." In addition, the Court noted that quarantine laws did not discriminate against interstate commerce, but instead "prevented traffic in noxious articles, whatever their origin." In this case, although New Jersey sought to justify its landfill law as a health measure, which would reduce the exposure of New Jersey residents to the harmful effects of landfill sites, the Court held that there was "no claim here that the very movement of waste into or through New Jersey endangers health, or that waste must be disposed of as soon and as close to its point of generation as possible." Any harm results after the deposit of waste in landfill sites, and New Jersey waste is no different from out-of-state waste in that respect. "If one is inherently harmful, so is the other." The Court concluded that New Jersey's "legislative effort is clearly impermissible under the Commerce Clause of the Constitution."

The Court concluded with the observation that the "Commerce Clause will protect New Jersey in the future, just as it protects her neighbors now, from efforts by one State to isolate itself in the stream of interstate commerce from a problem shared by all." In this regard, the Court observed that "cities in Pennsylvania and New York find it expedient or necessary to send their waste into New Jersey for disposal, and New Jersey claims the right to close its borders to such traffic. Tomorrow, cities in New Jersey may find it expedient or necessary to send their waste into Pennsylvania or New York for disposal, and those States might then claim the right to close their borders."

Justice William Rehnquist, joined by Chief Justice Warren Burger, dissented, arguing that problems with the sanitary treatment and disposal of solid waste is growing and that "landfills present significant health risks because they produce noxious liquids and pollute ground and surface water." He disagreed with the Court's conclusion that New Jersey could not prohibit out-of-state waste from being deposited in New Jersey landfills and pointed out that New Jersey was free to prohibit the importation of items "which, on account of their existing condition, would bring in and spread disease, pestilence, and death, such as rags or other substances infected with the germs of yellow fever or the virus of small-pox, or cattle or meat or other provisions that are diseased or decayed or otherwise, from their condition and quality, unfit for human use or consumption." On the same basis, he concluded that "New Jersey should be free to prohibit the importation of solid waste because of the health and safety problems that such waste poses to its citizens. The fact that New Jersey continues to, and indeed must continue to, dispose of its own solid waste does not mean that New Jersey may not prohibit the importation of even more solid waste into the State."

City of Philadelphia is an important decision because it reaffirms the long-standing principle that the states may not enact protectionist measures and may not discriminate against interstate commerce. Even when the "commerce" involves sanitary waste, which presents potential safety and health risks to a state's citizens, the state has no power to discriminate.

Bibliography

Jonathon A. Adler, *Waste and the Dormant Commerce Clause—A Reply,* 3 Green Bag 353 (2000).

Kirsten Engel, *Reconsidering the National Market in Solid Waste: Trade-Offs in Equity, Efficiency, Environmental Protection and State Autonomy,* 73 North Carolina Law Review 1481 (1995).

Richard A. Epstein, *Waste and the Dormant Commerce Clause,* 3 Green Bag 29 (1999).

CHAPTER 6

FEDERAL PREEMPTION OF STATE POWER

Wariness of a strong central government was a central theme of the federal Constitution's framing and ratification. Although the national government was conceived as a government of limited power, the Constitution's supremacy clause provides that laws enacted "under the Authority of the United States, shall be the supreme Law of the Land." Determining whether a conflict exists is not always easy. Congress, moreover, often does not indicate whether its enactments intend to preempt state regulation. The Supreme Court, however, has developed standards for determining whether a conflict between federal and state law exists and, if so, how to resolve it. In *Pacific Gas and Electric Co. v. State Energy Resources Conservation and Development Commission* (1983), the Court applied these principles to the issue of whether a state moratorium on nuclear power plant development preempted the federal government's interest in regulating the economics of atomic energy.

Pacific Gas and Electric Co. v. State Energy Resources Conservation and Development Commission

Citation: 461 U.S. 190.

Issue: Whether Congress's regulation of nuclear power plant safety preempted a state moratorium on nuclear power plant certification.

Year of Decision: 1983.

Outcome: Federal regulation did not preempt the state's ability to regulate the economics of the nuclear power industry.

Author of Opinion: Justice Byron White.

Vote: 9-0.

The supremacy clause of the Constitution, set forth in Article VI, Section 2, establishes federal law as "the supreme Law of the Land." This provision is implicated when a state enacts legislation that conflicts with a federal law. It is reminiscent of the commerce clause, which is a barrier to state laws that unduly burden or discriminate against interstate commerce. Unlike the commerce clause, however, the supremacy clause operates only when Congress has enacted a law and an actual conflict is identified. A threshold issue in all preemption cases thus is whether, in fact, a conflict exists between federal and state law. Because congressional intent to preempt is not always manifested by explicit terminology, the Supreme Court has developed criteria for determining whether it can be identified.

Numerous activities and conditions are subject to both federal and state regulation. In many instances, dual regulation may be complementary rather than conflicting. Within the framework of dual sovereignty, case law establishes a preference for accommodation rather than preemption. Inquiry under the supremacy clause thus begins with a presumption that the state law is valid. This orientation is reflected in the Court's analysis, in *Pacific Gas and Electric Co. v. State Energy Resources Conservation and Development Commission* (1983), of a state imposed moratorium on certifying nuclear power plants. The reason for the moratorium was expressed in economic rather than safety terms. As the state explained it, the lack of effective technology eventually might force closure of nuclear power plants. This condition, if it were to arise, would have a profoundly negative impact upon the cost and availability of electricity.

The issue of preemption turned upon the *Atomic Energy Act of 1954.* Pursuant to this enactment, Congress created the Atomic Energy Commission (now the Nuclear Regulatory Commission) and gave it authority over the safety of nuclear power plant construction and operation. The Commission's charge included responsibility for licensing nuclear power plants and regulating the disposal of radioactive waste. Despite the argument that the moratorium violated the supremacy clause, the Court found no conflict between federal and state law. Justice Byron White, speaking for a majority, drew a distinction distinguished between the federal concern with the safety of nuclear power plants and their economic viability. In this regard, he noted that the federal enactment did not take away from states their traditional authority to regulate the economics of the power industry. If a state determined that nuclear power did not make economic sense, moreover, the federal government could not force a contrary decision. Absent competing or conflicting impositions, therefore, the Court found no basis for preemption. A different result would have been achieved if the state had acted upon safety grounds.

Justice Harry Blackmun, in a concurring opinion, contended that the moratorium was allowable even if it was grounded in concern with the safety of nuclear power. The *Atomic Energy Act,* as Justice Blackmun understood it, intended to diversify the nation's sources of electricity. From his perspective, there was no reason to deny states a parallel interest in accounting for safety. Justice Blackmun's position that the moratorium should be upheld regardless of the state's purpose reflects awareness that an effort to identify motive typically is a futile undertaking. The challenge of identifying a true motive is heightened in the legislative context, where outcomes typically reflect negotiation and trade-offs. The majority opinion indicates that a state regulation will not be preempted when the federal and state interests and objectives are distinct. This emphasis upon separate federal and state concerns actually might invite lawmakers, whose real concern is with safety, to adopt a false front.

Either way, the majority opinion effectively illuminates the key principles of preemption doctrine. Regardless of the case, review commences with a presumption that the state law is valid. Barring explicit congressional language announcing the intent to preempt state law, a court must assess whether there are indications to this effect. Within this context, three possibilities for preemption arise. First, an intent to preempt may be found when the "scheme of federal regulation [is] so pervasive as to make reasonable the inference that Congress left no room to supplement it." Because responsibility for electric power generation was shared by federal and state government, a pervasive national interest could not be identified. A second possibility for preemption arises when "the federal interest is so dominant that the federal system will be assumed to preclude enforcement of state laws on the same subject." Given the states' power and interest with respect to the generation of electricity, the federal interest was not dominant to the point of precluding state regulatory action. Preemption also is appropriate when state law imposes requirements that are at odds with federal law. This third basis for preemption also was inapplicable. The federal law was based upon safety concerns and did not mandate the use of nuclear power. The moratorium thus did not impose any demands that competed with federal law.

Regardless of whether the majority or Justice Blackmun provides the better model of analysis, the decision reflects the importance that the Court assigns to the imperatives of federalism. This principle of accommodation is key to balancing individual state interests and actions within the framework of a national union. Viewed in this light, the Court's decision connects closely with a premise that was central to the republic's founding and critical to the maintenance of a system governed by dual sovereigns.

Bibliography

S. Candice Hoke, *Preemption Pathologies and Civic Republican Virtues,* 71 *Boston University Law Review* 685 (1991). A general review of the nature and complexity of preemption doctrine is provided.

Ronald D. Rotunda, *The Doctrine of the Inner Political Check, The Dormant Commerce Clause, and Federal Preemption,* 53 *Transportation Practitioners Journal* 263 (1986). The relationship between federal preemption doctrine and the dormant commerce clause is examined.

CHAPTER 7

PRIVILEGES AND IMMUNITIES

The privileges and immunities clause of Article IV, Section 2, has a common history with the commerce clause. Both of these provisions reflect the framers' concern with state protectionism that undermines the viability of a national economic union. Cases under the privileges and immunities clause typically concern state efforts to manage public resources or opportunities (such as public employment). The Court's decision, in *Baldwin v. Fish and Game Commission of Montana* (1978), exemplifies the use of the privileges and immunities clause as a barrier to protectionist resource management.

Baldwin v. Fish and Game Commission of Montana

The privileges and immunities clause and commerce clause have a shared history. Both originated from concern with states using their police power to secure parochial advantage at the expense of a national economic union. Dormant commerce clause analysis requires the Supreme Court to measure a state law against the federal interest in efficient interstate commerce. The privileges and immunities clause also guards against state policies that would secure economic

Citation: 436 U.S. 371.

Issue: Whether higher license fees for out-of-state hunters violated the privileges and immunities clause.

Year of Decision: 1978.

Outcome: The fee differential did not abridge the privileges and immunities clause.

Author of Opinion: Justice Harry Blackmun.

Vote: 6-3.

advantage at the cost of interstate functionality. In these cases, the Court must determine whether a state law imposes economic burdens or disadvantages upon citizens of other states.

Inclusion of the commerce power in the Constitution established a mechanism to ensure that states did not pursue self-interested economic policies that undermined the interests of a viable economic union. Dormant commerce clause analysis, however, does not account for state actions that do not necessarily undermine federal interests but negatively impact other states' interests. This need is accounted for by Article IV, Section II, of the Constitution, which provides that "[t]he Citizens of each State shall be entitled to all Privileges and Immunities of Citizens in the several States." Put somewhat more simply, the privileges and immunities clause establishes a rule that states generally must not discriminate against citizens of other states merely because of their citizenship. Like other constitutional guarantees, the clause is not an absolute. Consequently, states can treat nonresidents differently under certain circumstances. Interpretation of the privileges and immunities clause thus has presented two primary challenges. The first is identifying interests that are protected under the clause. The second is determining the extent to which states may discriminate among persons on the basis of state citizenship.

There are two privileges and immunities clauses in the Constitution—one that is set forth in the Fourteenth Amendment and another that is enshrined by Article IV, Section II. The Fourteenth Amendment privileges and immunities clause secures the privileges and immunities of federal citizenship against state abridgment. As interpreted in *The Slaughter-House Cases* (1873), these privileges and immunities include:

> the right of the citizen ... to come to the seat of government to assert any claim he may have upon that government, to transact any business he may have with it, to seek its protection, to share its offices, to engage in administering its functions, ... [to] free access to [the nation's] seaports, ... to the subtreasuries, land offices, and courts of justices of the several States, ... to demand the care and protection of the Federal government over his life, liberty, and property when on the high seas or within the jurisdiction of a foreign government, ... [t]he right to peaceably assemble and petition for redress of grievances, the privilege of the writ of *habeas corpus,* ... [t]he right to use the navigable waters of the United States, ... all rights secured to our citizens by treaties with foreign nations, ...

The Article IV, Section II, privileges and immunities clause concerns itself with relationships and interactions among the states, particularly policies that favor local citizens over citizens of other states. In *Corfield v. Coryell* (1823), Justice Bushrod Washington characterized the privileges and immunities of state citizenship as including:

> those privileges and immunities which are *fundamental;* which belong of right to the citizens of all free governments, and which have at all times been enjoyed by the citizens of the several States which compose this Union.... What these fundamental principles are, it would be more tedious than difficult to enumerate. They may all, however, be comprehended under the following general heads: protection by the government, with the right to acquire and possess property of every kind, and to pursue and obtain happiness and safety, ... the right of a citizen to pass through, or to reside in any other state, for purposes of trade, agriculture, professional pursuits, or otherwise; to claim the benefit of the writ of habeas corpus; to institute and maintain actions of any kind in the courts of the state; to take, hold and dispose of property, either real or personal; and an exemption from higher taxes than are paid by other citizens of the state; [and] the elective franchise, as regulated and established by the law or constitution of the state in which it is to be exercised.

Although this itemization was set forth in a federal appeals court decision, the Supreme Court has cited it frequently and approvingly.

The privileges and immunities clause was central to the Court's review, in *Baldwin v. Fish and Game Commission of Montana,* of a state policy that imposed higher hunting license fees upon out-of-state residents. Under the fee system, Montana residents could hunt elk for $9 a year. Out-of-state hunters, however, were required to pay $225 for the same privilege. The state justified the differential on grounds it evenly distributed the cost of managing the state's elk herd.

Out-of-state hunters maintained that the license fee disparity violated the privileges and immunities clause. The Court, however, sided with the state. In so doing, it stated that the privileges and immunities clause does not prohibit all burdens or distinctions correlated to state citizenship or residency. In support of this proposition, the Court cited the right to vote. The Court pointed out that "[n]oone would suggest that the Privileges and Immunities Clause requires a state to open its polls to a 'nonresident.'" Appropriate distinctions between residents and nonresidents, as the

Court observed, "reflect the fact that this is a Nation composed of individual states." The privileges and immunities clause, from the Court's perspective, is offended only by those "distinctions" that "hinder the formation, the purpose or the development of a single Union of [all] States.... Only with respect to those 'privileges' and 'immunities' bearing upon the vitality of the Nation as a single entity must the State treat all citizens, resident and non-resident, equally."

Against this backdrop, the critical factor in support of the state's regulatory scheme was whether it burdened a basic right. Because elk hunting is a recreational pursuit that is the province of a small demographic, the Court found that it "did not rise to a level of national economic importance implicating the Privileges and Immunities Clause." A different outcome might have been reached if nonresidents had been denied their livelihood as a consequence of the policy. The bottom line in the Court's view was that elk hunting was not so significant to be "basic to the maintenance of well-being of the Union."

Justice William Brennan, in a dissenting opinion joined by Justices Byron White and Thurgood Marshall, criticized the Court's focus upon whether elk hunting was a "fundamental" interest. In this regard, he argued that the significance of the interest should not drive the inquiry. Rather, as Justice Brennan saw it, the concern should be with the state's reason for its discrimination. Differentiation on the basis of citizenship should be permissible, he maintained, only when a problem is attributable to nonresidents and the state's regulatory response "bears a substantial relation to the problem they present." Out-of-state hunters made up only 12 percent of Montana's hunting population. In light of these numbers, Justice Brennan argued that they posed no special danger to the elk population or the state's management of it. From his perspective, no "substantial relationship" existed between the discrimination against out-of-state hunters and the problem identified by the state. To the extent the state's discriminatory licensing system responded to this concern, it represented an overreaction.

The Court's inquiry into whether an interest is "fundamental" raises issues akin to those generated when the Court identifies and develops rights that are not enumerated by constitutional text. Judicial creation of fundamental rights, in interpreting the due process clause of the Fifth and Fourteenth Amendments, elicits objection on grounds the Court is overreaching its boundaries and performing a legislative function. A determination that a law violates the due process clause, however, restricts the legislative branch's ability to act. When the Court determines that an interest is fundamental for privileges and immunities clause analysis, however, it expands the ambit of opportunity for states to legislate. Either way, the focus upon relative degree of importance invites criticism that analysis is more subjective than it should be.

Bibliography

John E. Nowak and Ronald D. Rotunda, *Constitutional Law* (St. Paul, MN: West, 1995); and Laurence H. Tribe, *American Constitutional Law* (Mineola, NY: Foundation Press, 1988). A general review of the history and purpose of the privileges and immunities clause is provided.

William Wiecek, *The Sources of Antislavery Constitutionalism in America, 1760–1848* (Ithaca, NY: Cornell University Press, 1977). The privileges and immunities clause, as a basis for challenging slavery prior to the Civil War and Reconstruction, is discussed.

III

EQUALITY CONCEPTS

The guarantee of equal protection was not set forth in the Constitution as originally framed and ratified. Although the premise that "[a]ll men are created equal" was central to the Declaration of Independence, equal protection as a constitutional concept was an incident of Reconstruction following the Civil War. The equal protection clause of the Fourteenth Amendment responded primarily to the nation's experience with slavery and represented a fundamental statement with respect to each individual's common relationship to the law and the legal system. As written into the Fourteenth Amendment, the equal protection clause provides that no state shall "deny to any person within its jurisdiction the equal protection of the laws."

In its first significant interpretation of the equal protection clause, the Supreme Court in *Strauder v. West Virginia* (1879) announced that it was intended to secure for persons of African descent "all the civil rights that the superior race may enjoy." The Court further observed that the provision implied "a positive immunity, or right, most valuable to the colored race—the right to exemption from unfriendly legislation against them distinctively as colored, exemption from legal discrimination, implying inferiority in civil society ... and discriminations which are steps toward reducing them to the condition of a subject race." Despite this antidiscrimination interpretation, the equal protection guarantee for many decades was not a significant barrier to the official systems of segregation that managed much of racial reality. The separate but equal doctrine, which the Court announced in *Plessy v. Ferguson* (1896), was the dominant reference point for racially significant law and policy until it eventually was invalidated in *Brown v. Board of Education* (1954). The general significance of the equal protection guarantee until then was best captured by Justice Oliver Wendell Holmes, Jr., who, in *Buck v. Bell* (1927), described it as "the last resort of constitutional argument."

The determination in *Brown v. Board of Education,* that officially segregated schools were "inherently unequal," transformed the equal protection clause into a significant force against laws that discriminated on the basis of race. Over the next two decades, the Court expanded the guarantee's scope to account for discrimination on the basis of gender, alienage, and illegitimacy. The expanded reach of the equal protection clause contrasts with original interpretation reflected in the *Slaughter-House Cases* (1873), when the Court "doubt[ed] very much whether any action of a State not directed against the Negroes as a class, or on account of their race, will ever be held to come within the purview of this provision." Subsequent history disproved this prophesy. Although the slavery experience and its aftermath of racial inequality were primary sources of inspiration for the equal protection guarantee, the status and experience of other disadvantaged groups have been found to be sufficiently comparable to merit protected status. Equal protection also became a basis for striking down laws that selectively deny a right or liberty regardless of a person's group status. Decisions in this part of the book concern the desegregation experience, application of the equal protection guarantee to gender discrimination, principles that limit the provision's operation, and affirmative action.

CHAPTER 8

RACE

The equal protection guarantee emerged as a significant constitutional force when it was used to dismantle official segregation. Following the decision in *Brown v. Board of Education* (1954), the Court confronted widespread resistance to implementing its mandate to desegregate public schools. Over the course of nearly two decades following *Brown*, the Court consistently pressed for compliance. Despite an initially limited impact, passage of the *Civil Rights Act of 1964* enabled the federal government to use its power and litigation resources to advance the process of desegregation. As the case for desegregation expanded beyond the South, and into Northern and Western communities where racial separation often was a result of factors less traceable to government action, the Court pondered the equal protection guarantee's limits. In *Keyes v. School District No. 1* (1973), the Court narrowed desegregation obligations to circumstances where racial segregation had been compelled by the state. One year later, in *Milliken v. Bradley* (1974), the Court announced that interdistrict busing was impermissible when a district had not caused segregation in the other district. Taking this principle beyond just the desegregation process, the Court in *Washington v. Davis* (1976) determined that any equal protection claim was dependent upon proof of an actual intent to discriminate. This standard is readily satisfied in cases where a racial preference or disadvantage is manifest by the terms of the law itself. Racial preferences, aimed at accounting for past discrimination or to achieve the benefits of diversity, became a primary focal point of equal protection jurisprudence in the final quarter of the twentieth century and the first decade of the twenty-first century. They became the basis for significant decisions in *Regents of the University of California v. Bakke* (1978), *City of Richmond v. J.A. Croson Co.* (1989), *Adarand Constructors, Inc. v. Pena* (1995), and *Grutter v. Bollinger* (2003).

Keyes v. School District No. 1, Denver, Colorado

The Supreme Court's determination in *Brown v. Board of Education* (1954) that racially segregated schools were unconstitutional did not end segregation. The *Brown* Court's command for desegregation "with all deliberate speed" generally was met with resistance of and challenge to its authority. The Arkansas legislature enacted a law that purportedly freed its citizens from compliance and asserted its own authority to review "in every Constitutional manner the Unconstitutional desegregation decisions ... of the United States Supreme Court." In *Cooper v. Aaron* (1958), the Court reaffirmed that its word on the Constitution was final and binding. President Dwight Eisenhower backed the Court by dispatching federal troops to Arkansas to enforce implementation of desegregation.

Citation: 413 U.S. 189.

Issue: Whether segregation of public schools is unconstitutional only if required by law.

Year of Decision: 1973.

Outcome: De jure but not de facto segregation violates the Constitution.

Author of Opinion: Justice William Brennan.

Vote: 5-4.

Desegregation accomplishments overall in the decade after *Brown* were minimal. So limited was progress during this time that the Court eventually shifted from the "with all deliberate speed standard" to insistence upon remedies "that promise[ ] realistically to work now." Even as the Court held firm in its demand to abolish racially segregated schools, public attitude toward desegregation became an increasingly significant factor in the process. The busing of students to achieve desegregation became a major issue in the 1968 presidential election. It was a concern not just in the South but in the North and West where racially segregated schools also were a common phenomenon. Outside the South, segregated public schools were less a consequence of legal mandate than of residential demographics. In *Keyes v. School District No. 1,* the Court was called upon to decide whether this type of segregation also violated the Constitution.

At issue in this case were decisions by the Denver, Colorado, school board with respect to the location of public schools, drawing of district lines, and placement of students. The Court found that the school board had developed policies and made implementations in these areas for the purpose of maintaining racial segregation. Whether legislated or otherwise, the Court determined that officially prescribed segregation conflicted with the equal protection guarantee. More significantly, it decided that proof of government's intent to segregate was a prerequisite for establishing a constitutional violation. The other side of this premise was that if segregation was not the result of intentional state action, it was not constitutionally significant.

The *Keyes* Court thus drew a line between what it characterized as *de jure* segregation and *de facto* segregation. The key aspect of *de jure* segregation, and the basis for its unconstitutionality, is official segregative intent. As the Court put it, "the differentiating factor between *de jure* segregation and so-called *de facto* segregation … is *purpose* or *intent* to segregate." Pursuant to its determination that racial segregation in Denver public schools was purposeful, the Court ordered their desegregation. Absent the finding of segregative intent, racial segregation would have been characterized as *de facto* and thus constitutionally inconsequential.

Significant as the difference between *de jure* and *de facto* segregation may be, the line between these two conditions is not necessarily precise. Residential segregation outside the South typically has been viewed as the result of private choice in choosing where to live. Racially identifiable neighborhoods in the North and West, however, often were facilitated and maintained by official policy. Until they were found unconstitutional in *Shelley v. Kraemer* (1948), restrictive covenants were used to create and preserve segregated neighborhoods. Such agreements are negotiated and executed as a private transaction, but their viability is dependent upon judicial enforcement. Government involvement in this manner was the basis for the Court's eventual finding that restrictive covenants were unconstitutional. Their segregative consequences, however, lasted long beyond the determination that they were invalid.

Federal home loan policies contributed further to racially segregated neighborhoods and derivatively to racially segregated public schools. The Federal Housing Administration denied loans for home purchases that would undermine the racial identity of a neighborhood. Residential segregation was fortified further by government policies regarding the siting of public schools and public housing distribution of urban renewal funds. These linkages, as Justice William Douglas observed, established a clear line between government action and racial segregation. The Court, however, was not persuaded that these connections moved it from a *de facto* to a *de jure* condition.

Justice Lewis Powell, like Justice Douglas, was unable to differentiate segregation in the way that the Court did. He viewed it as unfair that desegregation obligations should be the work of only one region. The primary evil he perceived in racial segregation related less to official intent and more to its effect on educational opportunity. In an opinion that concurred in part with and dissented in part from the majority, Justice Powell thus advocated an outcome that would eliminate any distinction between *de jure* and *de facto* segregation.

The bottom line of *Keyes v. School District No. 1* was that the constitutional duty to desegregate hinged upon proof of official segregative intent. Making such a case was not difficult insofar as segregation was a clear and open mandate of the law, as it was during the separate but equal era. With segregation prohibited, a purpose to segregate typically did not manifest itself openly. Justice Powell noted the difficulty of identifying such a motive and that it could be disguised. Within the public school context, he mentioned how segregation could be achieved and maintained through a variety of methods that could hide the real purpose. Among these ways were the location and size of new schools, the configuration of attendance zones, faculty recruiting and assignment, curriculum, and tracking of students into academic or vocational programs.

In his dissenting opinion, Justice Thurgood Marshall expressed dissatisfaction with the distinction between *de jure* and *de facto* segregation. In Justice Marshall's view, racially segregated schools were a source of stigma regardless of causation or intent. He maintained that constitutional rights should not turn upon whether a child was "born into a *de facto* society." From his perspective, racially segregated schools under any circumstance created a sense of inferiority among students, impaired their educational opportunity, and undermined their development.

Despite the contrary views of Justices Douglas, Powell, and Marshall, the distinction between *de jure* and *de facto* segregation has become a settled boundary. The practical result has been a narrowed reach of the desegregation mandate and an impact primarily upon the South. Exceptions to this norm arose in the North and West to the extent school boards had established racially segregated schools and had not dismantled them consistent with the dictate of *Brown v. Board of Education*. In *Columbus Board of Education v. Penick* (1979), for example, the Court found segregation in Columbus, Ohio, schools attributable to knowing acts of omissions by the school board. As in *Keyes v. School District No. 1,* it thus also found a constitutional violation. The Court thus rejected arguments that segregated schooling was unconstitutional even if not commanded by state law as in the South. Noting that segregation was the direct result of cognitive acts or omissions by the school board that resulted in an enclave of separate, black schools, the Court found a constitutional violation.

By requiring proof of official segregative purpose, the Court established a significant limiting principle. Despite criticism that the distinction between *de jure* and *de facto* segregation is artificial, it is a dividing line between constitutional and unconstitutional. The result in *Keyes v. School District No. 1* did not break a two decade tradition of forceful application of the desegregation mandate. The segregative intent standard, however, made proof of a constitutional violation much more difficult. This consequence has become evident in the declining number of instances in which racially segregated schools, although still a widespread phenomenon, presented a constitutional issue.

Bibliography

Frank I. Goodman, *De Facto Segregation: A Constitutional and Empirical Analysis,* 60 *California Law Review* 275 (1972). The concept of *de facto* segregation is examined.

Kenneth L. Karst, *Not One Law at Rome and Another at Athens: The Fourteenth Amendment in Nationwide Application,* 1972 *Washington University Law Quarterly* (1972). The distinction between *de jure* and *de facto* segregation is criticized.

Private and sometimes violent action that deterred racial integration in the North is the subject of William Tuttle, Jr., *Race Riot: Chicago in the Red Summer of 1919* (New York: Atheneum, 1971).

Milliken v. Bradley

Citation: 418 U.S. 717.

Issue: Whether suburban schools could be included in a plan to desegregate schools in a major city.

Year of Decision: 1974.

Outcome: An interdistrict desegregation plan was permissible only if segregation in one district was the result of purposeful segregative action by officials in the other district.

Author of Opinion: Chief Justice Warren Burger.

Vote: 5-4.

Racial segregation outside the South is grounded in processes that were less formal and comprehensive but nonetheless effective in achieving separation of the races. During the early twentieth century, many African-Americans moved northward in search of economic opportunity and to escape the harsh racial realities of the South. This migration coincided with industrial expansion and demand for labor in the North's large cities. It was spurred further by World War II and its demands for increased factory productivity.

Although a source of economic opportunity, the North was not a haven from racial prejudice. Northern states did not have the comprehensive systems of racial management that typified the South. African-Americans who relocated there, however, were routed into separate neighborhoods by legal and extralegal processes. Segregated housing was established and maintained pursuant to restrictive covenants. These private agreements barred a homeowner from selling his or her dwelling to persons of a different race. Federal lending policies prohibited loans to home buyers whose purchase would undermine racially identifiable neighborhoods. Neighborhood schools in the North thus reflected residential demographics and thus became segregated on the basis of race. School district boundaries, pupil placement policies, and faculty recruiting and assignments further reflected these realities.

The duty to desegregate racially segregated public schools, set forth in *Brown v. Board of Education* (1954), arose in the context of other significant changes. The advent of the automobile and emergence of suburban communities reflected an increasingly mobile society. The movement of families to new middle class and upper class communities near but apart from traditional urban centers resulted in school systems that did not even exist when *Brown v. Board of Education* (1954) was decided. These communities, although composed of persons who might have supported or facilitated segregation in their previous environment, had no history of segregation themselves. Minus this legacy, there was no record of the segregative intent that the Court had identified as the key prerequisite for an equal protection violation. As Justice Lewis Powell put it, "[t]he type of state-enforced segregation that *Brown* condemned no longer exists in this country." Despite this change, public schools in major cities reflected the historical realities of racial discrimination. Coupled with the accelerated exodus of white families to suburban communities, urban schools increasingly became racially identifiable. In cities like Baltimore, Detroit, New York, and Washington, D.C., African-American students ranged from 70 percent to more than 90 percent of total enrollments. Even in the event of a constitutional violation in such circumstances, a desegregation order could not alter racial makeup of the system if it did not cross district lines.

In *Milliken v. Bradley* (1974), the Court considered the permissibility of interdistrict remedies as a means of achieving desegregation in function as well as in form. At issue was a federal district court order requiring desegregation of public schools in the Detroit metropolitan area. The order was based upon detailed findings that segregation was the result of purposeful action by the city and state. In particular, the lower court found that segregated schools were attributable in part to the school board's attendance, transportation, and school siting policies. The trial court found that the state also had caused segregated schools by nullifying a voluntary desegregation plan, using transportation to maintain segregation, and signing off on pupil assignment plans that created racially identifiable schools.

The Supreme Court, although conceding that segregation in Detroit was the result of purposeful government action, refused to uphold the interdistrict remedy. Chief Justice Warren Burger, writing for a 5-4 majority, found that responsibility for the segregated schools extended no further than the city itself. Unless the state or suburbs had engaged in actions that purposefully contributed to the segregated conditions, the Court determined that they had no obligation to participate in the desegregation process. The Court thus concluded that the scope of the district court's remedy exceeded that of the violation. This understanding left open the possibility of interdistrict relief in theory, but limited it to the rare instance in which purposeful action to cause segregation in another community could be demonstrated.

The basic principle of *Milliken v. Bradley,* that the relief must not exceed the scope of the constitutional violation, has been criticized on grounds that the Court understated the state's role in causing segregation. The result nonetheless was a significant barrier to desegregation plans that would achieve racial mixing. For practical purposes, it also demonstrated that desegregation did not necessarily require integration. Even if caused by intentional government action, segregation could be addressed only with the obvious constraint of demographic limitations. Desegregation under such circumstances thus meant ridding the system of factors that caused racially identifiable schools but did not require the elimination of racial segregation conditions themselves.

Justice Byron White, in a dissenting opinion, contended that the Court effectively had denied a needed and justifiable remedy. Justice White pointed out that the actions and policies of state public school officials over many years were a primary cause of segregated schools in Detroit, so remedial responsibility extended beyond the city limits. The state's role, although a basis for the district court's order, was minimized by the majority. Reversal of the district court represented a significant turnabout from the Supreme Court's interaction with lower courts during the first two decades of school desegregation. After years of dissatisfaction with the failure of lower courts to press the desegregation mandate, the Court in *Milliken v. Bradley* expressed displeasure with the district court pushing too hard. As Justice Thurgood Marshall saw it, the outcome provided "no remedy at all ... guaranteeing that Negro children ... will receive the same separately and inherently unequal education in the future as they have in the past."

The Court's ruling defined the outer limits of the desegregation principle with respect to geography and prefaced a similar restriction with respect to time. Two years later, in *Pasadena City Board of Education v. Spangler* (1976), the Court determined that school districts that had achieved desegregation were not obligated to maintain an integrated condition. To the extent that white flight or other factors may cause resegregation, and unless official action recreates a dual school system based upon race, no constitutional duty exists to preserve the fruits of desegregation. From Justice William Rehnquist's perspective, demographic change that unsettled the results of desegregation were attributable to the quite normal pattern of human migration. Dissenting as he did in *Milliken,* Justice Marshall argued that a state that created a system where whites and Negroes were intentionally kept apart so that they could not become accustomed to learning together is responsible for the fact that many whites will react to the dismantling of that segregated system by attempting to flee to the suburbs.

The curtailment of desegregation demands during the 1970s reflected a growing attitude that conditions addressed in 1954 either had been accounted for or had changed. As Justice Powell saw it, segregated schools had become a function of familiar segregated housing patterns ... caused by social, economic, and demographic forces for which no school board is responsible. Despite the Court's initial resolve to have its orders implemented, the marking of desegregation boundaries two decades after *Brown* indicated a growing sense of limits to the judiciary's own influence. Consistent with this perspective, Justice Rehnquist observed that even if the Constitution required it, and it were possible for federal courts to do it, no equitable decree can fashion an Emerald City where all races, ethnic groups, and persons of various income levels live side by side. By the century's final decade, the Court itself had downscaled not just the principle but the rhetoric of desegregation. No longer would school systems be required to eliminate all vestiges of racial discrimination root and branch. Rather, as pointed out in *Board of Education of Oklahoma City Public Schools v. Dowell* (1991), good faith compliance with desegregation requirements was to be measured by whether those vestiges had been eradicated to the extent practicable.

Bibliography

St. Clair Drake and Horace R. Clayton, *Black Metropolis* (New York: Harcourt, Brace and Co., 1945). The massive migration of African-Americans from the South to the North and West, and its sociological implications, is examined.

Paul Jacobs, *Prelude to Riot: A View of Urban America from the Bottom* (New York: Vintage Books, 1967). Official action that contributed to segregation of public schools in the North and West is discussed.

Washington v. Davis

The equal protection guarantee during the final half of the twentieth century established itself as the primary constitutional barrier against racial discrimination. Determining what constitutes discrimination, however, was not a simple task. Government action or policy may have a disproportionate impact upon individuals based, among other things, upon their group status. Placement of a solid waste disposal site near a poor neighborhood, for instance, may impose a disparate burden upon members of a historically disadvantaged racial minority. Whether this action constitutes racial discrimination, however, depends upon how the term is defined.

In the context of school desegregation, the Court differentiated between *de jure* and *de facto* segregation. *De jure* segregation, which reflects an official segregative purpose, is constitutionally prohibited. *De facto* segregation, which is a consequence of private choice, has no constitutional implications. This distinction, made in *Keyes v. School District No. 1* (1973), narrowed the reach of desegregation to circumstances where an actual purpose to segregate could be demonstrated. Put another way, the equal protection guarantee's concern was with segregative intent rather than segregative effect.

Citation: 426 U.S. 229.

Issue: Whether a test to screen police officer candidates was unconstitutional because a disproportionate number of African-Americans failed it.

Year of Decision: 1976.

Outcome: Proof of discriminatory motive is an essential prerequisite for an equal protection violation.

Author of Opinion: Justice Byron White.

Vote: 5-4.

Whether discrimination should be understood in terms of purpose or effect is a question that extended beyond segregated schools. In *Washington v. Davis* (1976), the issue arose with respect to an employment test administered by the Washington, D.C., police department to all officer candidates. The examination, which assessed verbal ability, vocabulary, and reading, yielded racially disparate results. The number of African-Americans failing the test was four times greater than for whites. Despite these disproportionate results, the trial court found that the examination was reasonably related to police training and performance. It also determined that the examination was not designed or utilized in a manner that discriminated on the basis of race. The trial court's ruling was reversed by the Court of Appeals, which concluded that the disproportionate impact by itself established an equal protection violation. As the Court of Appeals viewed it, the constitutional offense was not dependent upon a showing of discriminatory purpose.

The Supreme Court sided with the trial court and reversed the Court of Appeals ruling. It thus determined that the unconstitutionality of government action cannot rest solely on the basis of a racially disproportionate impact. Rather, there must be proof that it was motivated by a discriminatory purpose. In finding that disproportionate effect by itself did not establish a constitutional violation, the Court noted too that disparity was not entirely irrelevant. Discrimination is not always self-evident, particularly when potential violators know that it is illegal and thus are motivated to disguise the true nature of their actions. Laws that may be racially neutral on their face also may be applied in a discriminatory manner. In this regard, the Court referenced *Yick Wo v. Hopkins* (1886). This case concerned a city ordinance prohibiting the operation of laundries in wood frame buildings. Although racially neutral on its face, this law was struck down because it was applied only to persons of Chinese descent.

Identifying a discriminatory purpose is uncomplicated when the law speaks openly with respect to its intent. Discerning a discriminatory purpose was easy, for instance, when enactments typical of the separate but equal era were challenged. Once segregation and discrimination were declared unconstitutional, however, overt indications of purposeful wrongdoing became harder to pinpoint. Against this backdrop, the Court indicated that discriminatory purpose might be inferred from a variety of factors including disproportionate impact. It also might be identified in circumstances where disproportionality is difficult to explain on nonracial grounds.

When discriminatory purpose is identified, the Court intensifies its review to the level of "strict scrutiny." Pursuant to this standard, a state must demonstrate that its action is justified by compelling reasons and is narrowly tailored to achieve the result desired. Disproportionate effect alone does not trigger this high level of review. When present without a showing of discriminatory purpose, the question is whether the action or regulation reflects a legitimate state interest and is reasonably related to its goal. Viewing the police candidate test itself as a legitimate method for determining critical skills, the Court found that it was racially neutral and reasonably related to its objective.

The Court's refusal to give greater weight to disproportionate effect reflected concern with making any difference the basis for a constitutional controversy. Such an orientation, the Court feared, would "rais[e] serious questions about and possibly invalidat[e] a whole range of tax, welfare, public service, regulatory and licensing statutes." These laws by their nature have disparate consequences, but they generally are not motivated by a purpose to discriminate.

In narrowing the range of the equal protection guarantee's concern, the decision in *Washington v. Davis* set the scene for controversy over how purposeful discrimination is demonstrated. In *Arlington Heights v. Metropolitan Housing Development Corp.* (1977), one year later, the Court reviewed a local zoning ordinance that limited land use to single family dwellings. Because the village denied an application to construct racially integrated housing, the zoning decision was challenged on grounds it discriminated on the basis of race. The Court acknowledged that "[t]he impact of the Village's decision does arguably bear more heavily on racial minorities." It found no evidence of discriminatory purpose, however, and restated the proposition that disproportionate effect by itself does not establish a constitutional violation or basis for strict scrutiny.

The Court indicated its awareness that proof of discriminatory purpose may be more challenging when a racial motive is not stated or otherwise manifest. It thus suggested ways in which discriminatory purpose may be inferred from relevant circumstances. Toward this end, it noted relevant factors such as "the historical background of a decision including any indications of invidious purposes, departures from normal procedures, changes in standards for decision-making, and legislative or administrative history including contemporaneous remarks by officials."

Collectively, these factors signaled that history is particularly relevant as a means of drawing inferences of discriminatory purpose. A decade later, in *McCleskey v. Kemp* (1987), the Court heard arguments against the Georgia death penalty that referenced the history of a dual system of criminal justice. The Court also was presented with a report that showed major disparities in the administration of capital punishment. Evidence showed that prosecutors pursued the death penalty in 70 percent of the cases involving black defendants and white victims, 32 percent of the cases involving white defendants and black victims, 15 percent of the cases involving black defendants and black victims, and 19 percent of the cases involving white defendants and black victims. The death penalty was applied in 22 percent of the cases involving black defendants and white victims, 1 percent of the cases involving black defendants and black victims, and 3 percent of the cases involving white defendants and black victims. The Court, in reviewing this evidence, reaffirmed the premise that disproportionality by itself does not establish an equal protection violation or basis for strict scrutiny. It also described the disparate results as a "discrepancy that appears to correlate with race … [and] an inevitable part of our criminal justice system."

Justice William Brennan authored a dissenting opinion that was joined by three other justices. Justice Brennan maintained that the Court had ignored historical reality and thus the factor that it had declared relevant. On this point, he cited a long tradition in Georgia of operating a dual system of criminal justice system. Of particular consequence, given this history, was the practical consequence for counsel when having to advise defendants in capital cases on whether to accept a plea bargain. In his view, an attorney in this context could not ignore the potential for outcomes that differed on the basis of race. As Justice Brennan put it, "[a]t some point in this case, [the defendant] doubtless asked his lawyer whether a jury was likely to sentence him to die. A candid assessment by the attorney invariably would include the information that cases involving black defendants and white victims are more likely to result in a death sentence than cases featuring any other racial combination of defendant and victim."

Although a settled premise of the law, the discriminatory purpose standard still is a magnet for criticism. Among its detractors is the noted constitutional scholar Laurence Tribe, who contends that equal protection is not just about "stamp[ing] out impure thoughts." Rather, it should factor "government action which in the light of history, context, source, and effect are likely to perpetuate subordination of or reflect hostility, blindness or indifference toward a group that traditionally has been subjugated." Other critics, such as Charles Lawrence III, argue that motive-based inquiry is obsolete and unproductive because it overlooks or cannot detect subtle discrimination and unconscious racism.

The validity of these concerns actually has been acknowledged by the Court in other constitutional settings. The Court, in *United States v. O'Brien* (1968), refused to inquire into whether a federal law banning the destruction of draft cards was motivated by the intent to punish speech. In so doing, it cited "a familiar principle of constitutional law that this Court will not strike down an otherwise constitutional statute on the basis of an alleged illicit motive." The reason for this reticence, as the Court has noted, relates to the difficulty of identifying legislative motive. In the context of collective action, legislators may have different reasons for supporting a law. At least in *United States v. O'Brien,* the Court concluded that "the constitutional stakes are sufficiently high for us to eschew guesswork."

Chief Justice William Rehnquist, who joined the majority in *Village of Arlington Heights v. Metropolitan Housing Authority,* also has expressed concern with motive-based inquiry in other constitutional contexts. In a commerce clause case that raised the question of whether a state transportation regulation discriminated against out-of-state highway users, Chief Justice Rehnquist dissented from an inquiry into actual intent. His concern, in *Kassel v. Consolidated Freightways Corp.* (1981), was that legislative intent generally was indeterminable.

Justice Antonin Scalia, although signing on to discriminatory motive inquiry for equal protection purposes, also has described it as a usually impossible task. In *Edwards v. Aguillard* (1987), Justice Scalia identified a multiplicity of reasons why a legislator might vote for a particular outcome. As he put it, a legislator might vote in a particular manner based

> not only the merits of the legislation but whether it would provide jobs for his district, might enable him or her to make amends with a [previously alienated political] faction, was sponsored by a close friend, presented an opportunity to repay[ ] a favor to another politician, earned him appreciation from influential colleagues or wealthy contributors, represented the strong will of his or her constituency, was a way of getting even with a political nemesis or even a spouse that had made him or her mad, or whether it was voted on while he or she was intoxicated and [thus] utterly *un*motivated.

Consistent with his understanding that a legislated outcome may reflect any combination of these and other motivations, Justice Scalia maintained that "looking for *the sole purpose* of even a single legislator is probably to look for something that does not exist."

Consistent with the difficulty of establishing discriminatory motive, when this factor is not manifest, the success rate of equal protection claims over the past few decades has diminished. The most notable equal protection victories in contemporary times concern cases challenging racial preferences in employment and education. Like official segregation, and although differing with respect to utility and objective, these programs have a manifest racial orientation. Based upon these decisions, equal protection review responds primarily to formality and has yet to develop the capacity to factor more subtle or disguised variants of discrimination.

Bibliography

Paul Brest, *Palmer v. Thompson: An Approach to the Problem of Unconstitutional Legislative Motive,* 1971 *Supreme Court Review* 95 (1971). This is an influential article on discriminatory motive that preceded formulation of the Court's model.

Charles R. Lawrence III, *The Id, the Ego, and Equal Protection: Reckoning with Unconscious Racism,* 39 *Stanford Law Review* 317 (1987). This sets forth the argument that discriminatory motive inquiry fails to account for modern methods of discrimination and racism.

Daniel R. Ortiz, *The Myth of Intent in Equal Protection,* 41 *Stanford Law Review* 1105 (1989). This advances the sense of discriminatory purpose review as a largely futile enterprise.

David A. Straus, *Discriminatory Intent and the Taming of Brown,* 56 *University of Chicago Law Review* 935 (1989). A view of the discriminatory purpose requirement, as a means for diminishing the force of the equal protection guarantee, is presented.

Regents of the University of California v. Bakke

Citation: 438 U.S. 265.

Issue: Whether a public university medical school's admissions policy, which reserved some seats for designated minorities, violated the equal protection guarantee.

Year of Decision: 1978.

Outcome: Race cannot be an exclusive factor in the admissions process, but it may be used as one of several factors in achieving a diverse student body.

Author of Opinion: No majority opinion.

Vote: 4-4-1.

The vision of a color-blind society represents an ideal that society has struggled to achieve. An initial understanding of the Constitution as "color-blind" was advanced by Justice John Harlan. Dissenting from the majority's embrace of the separate but equal doctrine, in *Plessy v. Ferguson* (1896), he maintained that "the Constitution permits no caste system." Justice Harlan's observation was coupled with a sense that, although the Constitution was color-blind, the white race still would dominate because of its superiority. Several decades later in *Brown v. Board of Education* (1954), when it struck down official segregation in public schools, the Supreme Court made no specific mention of constitutional color-blindness. It is an underlying premise of modern equal protection understanding, however, which assumes that any official classification on the basis of race is "suspect."

Prohibition of racial segregation and other forms of discrimination did not erase a history of disadvantage based upon group status. During the final decades of the twentieth century, this legacy became the basis for government initiatives designed to account for and overcome it. These efforts typically consisted of programs or policies that tried to offset historical disadvantage by establishing preferences for designated minorities in employment and education. The use of racial classifications in this manner, commonly referred to as affirmative action, ultimately became the basis for a new chapter of equal protection controversy.

The use of race to remedy the effects of prejudice and discrimination was not a foreign concept. Desegregation of public schools, for instance, necessarily factored race in redistributing students from single race schools to mixed race schools. The term "affirmative action" first made its way into government policy when President John F. Kennedy issued an executive order that mandated the hiring of federal contractors without regard to race. His successor, President Lyndon Johnson, established the Office of Federal Contract Compliance and charged it with developing federal antidiscrimination guidelines in contracting. Guidelines announced by the Office in 1968 included goals and timetables for implementing equal employment opportunity. These incidents were followed in subsequent years by policies that focused upon achievement of specific results. Paralleling government's activity in this regard were private sector programs that aimed to increase minority participation in business and education.

As these race-conscious plans took root, they were challenged by persons who saw the opposite side of an advantage to minorities as a disadvantage to members of other racial groups. The first of these cases to reach the Supreme Court, *DeFunis v. Odegaard* (1974), concerned the racially preferential admissions policy of the University of Washington School of Law. The plaintiff, a white male, argued that the policy resulted in his being denied admission on the basis of his race. The Court did not reach the merits of the dispute. Because the plaintiff had enrolled pursuant to a lower court decision, the university had not dismissed him, and he would graduate soon, the Court dismissed the case as moot. Four dissenting justices objected to the dismissal and maintained that the Court was avoiding an important issue.

Four years later, in *Regents of the University of California v. Bakke* (1978), the Court revisited preferential admission policies in the context of university professional schools. At issue was a program at the University of California–Davis medical school that allocated a certain number of seats in each entering class to members of designated minority groups. The plaintiff claimed that, but for the preferential admissions policy, he would have been admitted. Agreeing with his argument, the California Supreme Court declared the program unconstitutional. The United States Supreme Court affirmed this ruling, but did so without establishing a majority position. Rather, the Court fragmented into two opposing groups and a single justice whose opinion in this context had particular significance. The first bloc of four justices viewed that admissions policy as a violation of Title VI of the *Civil Rights Act of 1964*. Given a statutory basis for resolving the controversy, this group refused to address the constitutional question. Four other justices found that the program violated neither the equal protection guarantee nor Title VI. Writing only for himself, Justice Lewis Powell maintained that the policy was inconsistent with the equal protection clause and federal statute. Justice Powell indicated, however, that race could be factored to a limited extent in the admissions process. Coupling his position with that of the four justices who found no constitutional violation, a majority of the Court expressed support at least for taking race into account as a means of achieving a diverse student body—provided that it was not an exclusive factor in the admissions policy or process.

Because of its critical role in defining the permissible use of race in the case, Justice Powell's opinion generally has been viewed as the most significant of those presented. The initial question confronting the Court in *Bakke* was what standard of review it should use. The traditional standard of review for racial classifications was established in *Korematsu v. United States* (1944). In that case, the Court determined that any racial classification should be the subject of searching judicial review. This model of review, also referred to as "strict scrutiny," became the basis for striking down laws that discriminated against racial minorities. Proponents of affirmative action maintained that, given their remedial aim, they should be evaluated pursuant to a more relaxed standard. Justice Powell rejected this proposed differentiation and concluded that any racial classification, regardless of whom it benefits or burdens, should be the subject of searching judicial review.

Having embraced the most rigorous model of judicial review, Justice Powell applied it to the four justifications that the medical school had offered in support of its preferential admissions policy. The school's first argument was that the setting aside of seats for minorities was an appropriate means to diversify the student body. Justice Powell found this methodology of racial quotas or goals to be invalid on its face. The school's second argument was that its preferential admissions policy was a means of eliminating the consequences of historic discrimination. Justice Powell determined that the prerequisite for such remedial action was findings of prior discrimination by the school itself. Evidence to this effect was not presented, and Justice Powell maintained that the school could not respond merely to the general reality of societal discrimination. The institution's third argument was that its admissions policy would increase minority graduates and thus result in improved health care in disadvantaged communities. Justice Powell determined that this premise assumed too much and that it did not necessarily follow that minority graduates would practice in disadvantaged communities. The school's final contention was that the interest in a diverse student body by itself was compelling. Justice Powell agreed with this premise, but stressed that diversification objectives could not be limited to race or ethnicity alone. As he put it, "students with a particular background whether it be ethnic, geographic, culturally advantaged, or disadvantaged may bring to a professional school of medicine experiences, outlooks and ideas that enrich the training of its student body and better equip its graduates to render with understanding their vital service to humanity."

In an opinion joined by three of his colleagues, Justice John Paul Stevens maintained that the Constitution was color-blind for all purposes. From this perspective, racial classifications were impermissible regardless of their purpose or whom they helped or hurt.

Justice William Brennan, joined by three other colleagues, contended that racial classifications designed to benefit members of traditionally disadvantaged groups should not be assessed in the same manner as those that burdened them. Because strict scrutiny tends to limit legislative initiative, Justice Brennan would not have applied it to policy making that creatively tries to account for the nation's legacy of racial discrimination. From his perspective, affirmative action plans should be assessed on the basis of whether they reflect or perpetuate harmful racial stereotypes. He did not view the school's set-aside plan as a function of such stereotyping. Justice Brennan also believed that the interest in overcoming the consequences of societal discrimination outweighed any burden imposed upon persons of the majority race.

Justices Thurgood Marshall and Harry Blackmun, in separate opinions, referred to the nation's history of racial discrimination as a justification for race-conscious remedial efforts. As Justice Blackmun put it, "[i]n order to get beyond racism, we must first take account of race."

Significant as the decision was, the divided nature of the Court's thinking left the future of affirmative action in an uncertain state. One year later, in *Fullilove v. Klutznick* (1980), the Court upheld a federal program setting aside 10 percent of public projects works for minority contractors. The Court again was badly divided, and it was impossible to identify a clear trend in its analysis. Movement toward a more unified position was evidenced in *Wygant v. Jackson Board of Education* (1986). In this case, the Court invalidated a preferential layoff program provided for by the collective bargaining agreement reached between public school teachers and the school board. In an opinion authored by Justice Powell, four justices found that an interest in "alleviat[ing] the effects of societal discrimination" was not sufficiently compelling to withstand strict scrutiny.

Despite indications of evolution toward a restrictive view of affirmative action, the Court still had not achieved a majority position. In a case concerning a well-documented history of discrimination in hiring and promotion, the Court in *United States v. Paradise* (1987) actually implemented a quota system to remedy a state agency's employment practices. Still eluding the Court, however, was a standard of review that a majority of the Court would embrace. Persisting division among the justices, a decade after the *Bakke* decision, confirmed the accuracy of observations made when the Court first confronted the issue of affirmative action. As Justice Brennan put it in *DeFunis v. Odegaard,* and history has demonstrated, "few constitutional questions in recent history have stirred as much debate." Nor have many generated as much discord within the Court itself.

Bibliography

John Hart Ely, *The Constitutionality of Reverse Discrimination,* 41 *University of Chicago Law Review* 723 (1974); Richard Posner, *The DeFunis case and the Constitutionality of Preferential Treatment of Racial Minorities,* 1974 *Supreme Court Review* 1 (1974). These include significant commentaries on affirmative action, prior but relevant to the *Bakke* decision.
Thomas Sowell, *Race and Culture* (New York: Basic Books, 1994). This sets forth the argument that affirmative action is less relevant to progress than cultural values and marketable skills.
Jared Taylor, *Paved with Good Intentions* (New York: Carroll & Graf, 1992). A view of affirmative action as well-intended but counterproductive is provided.

City of Richmond v. J.A. Croson Co.

Affirmative action was one of the most divisive issues that the Court confronted over the final decades of the twentieth century. When the matter first was reviewed in *Regents of the University of California v. Bakke* (1978), Justice Harry Blackmun expressed support for affirmative action as a means to get beyond racism. In his view, racially preferential programs would not be necessary on a permanent basis. Slightly more than a decade later, the need for affirmative action continued to be debated. Constitutional uncertainty persisted, moreover, as the Court had yet to establish a majority position on a standard of review.

Citation: 489 U.S. 469.

Issue: Whether a city's set-aside plan for minority contractors, designed to remedy societal discrimination, violated the equal protection guarantee.

Year of Decision: 1989.

Outcome: Racial preferences are subject to strict scrutiny regardless of their purpose.

Author of Opinion: Justice Sandra Day O'Connor.

Vote: 5-4.

A significant step toward clarity was taken, however, in *City of Richmond v. J.A. Croson Co.* (1989). At issue in this case was a set-aside program approved by the Richmond, Virginia, City Council. The program was modeled upon a federal set-aside program that the Supreme Court had upheld, albeit without any majority opinion, in *Fullilove v. Klutznick* (1980). Like the federal prototype, the city reserved at least

10 percent of municipal building contracts for minority business enterprises. Architects of the plan cited the same evidence used by Congress to demonstrate a history of racial discrimination in the construction. Offered too was a study showing that minority businesses received less than 1 percent of city building contracts, even though African-Americans constituted half of Richmond's population. Enactment of the set-aside plan thus represented an effort to address historical discrimination and create opportunity in a field where minorities traditionally had not been able to compete.

Even though the set-aside program paralleled the federal model and had a remedial purpose, the Court found that it was unconstitutional. This decision was significant not just with respect to the outcome, but because a majority embraced strict scrutiny of all racial classifications regardless of their purpose. Any racial classification, even if well-intended, thus must be justified by a compelling reason. It also must account for that purpose effectively and be demonstrated that racially neutral methods are inadequate. Justice Sandra Day O'Connor, joined by three of her colleagues, asserted that "searching judicial inquiry was an essential tool for purposes of determining what classifications are 'benign' or 'remedial' and what classifications are in fact motivated by illegitimate notions of racial inferiority or simple racial politics." The plurality of four justices thus viewed strict scrutiny as an essential tool for detecting illegitimate uses of race by assuring that government "is pursuing a goal important enough to warrant use of a highly suspect tool."

Adoption of a strict scrutiny standard of review reflected the plurality's sense that distinctions between benign and harmful classifications were difficult to make. As the plurality viewed them, racial classifications regardless of their purpose are stigmatizing. Although they may be well-intended, race-conscious programs designed to remedy the past may "promote notions of racial inferiority and lead to a politics of racial hostility." Given this risk, the plurality maintained that they should be reserved only as a remedy for proven instances of racial discrimination. Adding to its concern in this case, the plurality noted that African-Americans constituted half of Richmond's population and controlled the city council. In this context, the plurality expressed concern that set-asides may be nothing more than a political entitlement. From its perspective, searching judicial review would minimize this danger and the risk that "race will always be relevant in America."

The plurality acknowledged what it characterized as "the nation's sorry history of both private and public discrimination." This historical reality by itself, however, was not sufficient to support race-conscious policies as a means to overcome it. Such methods may be permissible when a specific instance of discrimination has been proved. Minus such a showing, the plurality was concerned that there would be no ending point for policies that redistributed opportunity on the basis of race. The use of race in any remedial context, except when a specific instance of discrimination was proven, thus was barred. This outcome reflected the plurality's sense of what was necessary to ensure "[t]he dream of a Nation of equal citizens in a society where race is irrelevant to personal opportunity." If race was to be the basis for managing opportunity, the plurality feared, "achievement would be lost in a mosaic of shifting preferences based on inherently unmeasurable claims of past wrongs."

By itself, the plurality opinion did not reflect a majority position. The concurring opinion of Justice Antonin Scalia established a majority, however, in support of the strict scrutiny standard of review. Justice Scalia advocated an even more rigorous version of strict scrutiny that would deny reference to race under most any circumstance. From his perspective, the challenge was not so much overcoming the effects of discrimination but eliminating "the tendency, fatal to a nation such as ours to classify and judge men on the basis of their country of origin or the color of their skin." Policies that accounted for racial discrimination in a race-conscious manner, at least for Justice Scalia, were "no solution at all." In his opinion, race could be a factor only when necessary to undo a segregated school system or "in a social emergency rising to the level of imminent danger of life and limb." Outside these contexts, Justice Scalia contended that "[w]here injustice is the game … turn-about is not fair play."

The emergence of a majority in favor of strict scrutiny for all racial classifications drew a long and pointed dissent by Justice Thurgood Marshall. He was joined by Justices William Brennan and Harry Blackmun in arguing that the Court had moved in the wrong direction. Justice Marshall thought it was ironic that the Court would "second-guess the judgment" (the city council's judgment). Richmond, he pointed out, is "the former capital of the Confederacy … [and] knows what racial discrimination is." In his view, the Court had taken "a deliberate and giant step backward." Justice Marshall would have upheld the program on grounds that it served a useful and important purpose. As he saw it, the set-aside policy not only addressed the consequences of racial discrimination but ensured that city spending did not reinforce and perpetuate that legacy. Justice Marshall also contested the notion that the city had not produced sufficient evidence of specific acts of discrimination. In this regard, he cited federal and local studies and the absence of any dispute with respect to Richmond's discriminatory history. The analysis and outcome, in his view, reflected an inability to grasp why the contracting industry had such limited minority participation.

Justice Marshall found the strict scrutiny standard objectionable too because of what he perceived to be "[a] profound difference separat[ing] governmental actions that themselves are racist, and governmental actions that seek to remedy the effects of prior racism or to prevent governmental activity from perpetuating the effects of such racism." He criticized the Court for ignoring "the tragic and indelible fact that [racial] discrimination … has pervaded our Nation's history and continues to scar our society." Justice Marshall thus expressed dismay with the "signals that [the Court] regards racial discrimination as largely a phenomenon of the past, and that government bodies need no longer preoccupy themselves with rectifying racial injustice."

Justice Marshall's sense that the Court had foreclosed remedial initiatives altogether proved to be somewhat premature. In *Metro Broadcasting, Inc. v. Federal Communications Commission*, 497 U.S. 547 (1990), the Court upheld a federal regulation that established a preference for designated minorities in the licensing of radio and television broadcasters. This turnabout was short-lived, as the Court overturned this ruling in *Adarand Contractors, Inc. v. Pena* (1995). The *Croson* decision established that any racial classification would be subject to searching judicial review, at least to the extent it was established by a state. Left to be resolved were two primary questions. The first was whether the same standard would operate with respect to federal policy. The second was the extent to which the Court would find reasons for racial classifications to be sufficiently compelling. These issues eventually would be addressed in the final decade of the twentieth century and first decade of the twenty-first century.

Bibliography

Stephen L. Carter, *Reflections of an Affirmative Action Baby* (New York: Basic Books, 1991). A critical perspective on affirmative action by a self-described beneficiary of it is provided.

Randall Kennedy, *Persuasion and Distrust: A Comment on the Affirmative Action Debate,* 99 *Harvard Law Review* 1327 (1986). This sets forth arguments that affirmative action has been effective and its risks and shortcomings have been overstated.

Shelby Steele, *The Content of Our Character* (New York: St. Martin's Press, 1990). The Court's perception that affirmative action harms its intended beneficiaries is echoed.

Adarand Constructors, Inc. v. Pena

Citation: 515 U.S. 200.

Issue: Whether a federal program incentivizing general contractors to hire minority subcontractors should be strictly scrutinized.

Year of Decision: 1995.

Outcome: Race-conscious policies, whether federal or state and regardless of their purpose, are subject to strict scrutiny.

Author of Opinion: Justice Sandra Day O'Connor.

Vote: 5-4.

The American political system is grounded in two independent sovereigns—the federal and state governments. These two powers have separate functions and responsibilities but sometimes overlapping interests. The federal government, for instance, regulates the national economy on the basis of its constitutional power to govern commerce. Through their police power, states often enact laws that also operate as economic policy. Civil rights is another area of dual responsibility. Both federal and state governments have enacted laws concerning discrimination. Through the mid-twentieth century, many states not only permitted racial discrimination but prescribed it. After segregation was declared unconstitutional, and Congress passed the *Civil Rights Act of 1964,* both the federal government and states developed affirmative action policies that aimed to remedy past discrimination.

In *City of Richmond v. J.A. Croson Co.* (1989), the Supreme Court announced that racial preferences of any kind could not survive strict constitutional review unless they were narrowly tailored to remedy a specific instance of discrimination. Notwithstanding this determination, the Court in the following year upheld a federal program establishing racial preferences in the licensing of broadcasters. The basis for differentiation, set forth in *Metro Broadcasting, Inc. v. Federal Communications Commission* (1990), was Congress's aggregation of powers including the authority to regulate the national economy and enforce the Fourteenth Amendment by appropriate legislation. Given the Constitution's specific charge of power to Congress, the Court concluded that federal preferences for minorities should be subject to a less rigorous standard of review than those created by the states.

The *Metro Broadcasting* decision drew upon prior case law that gives deference to Congress in its Fourteenth Amendment enforcement role. Despite initial indications, however, the Court did not create a lasting safe harbor for minority preferences under federal law. In *Adarand Constructors, Inc. v. Pena* (1995), the Court overruled the *Metro Broadcasting* decision and made federal and state preferences for minorities subject to the same standard of review. At issue in *Adarand Constructors* was a Department of Transportation program that, through financial incentives, encouraged government contractors to hire subcontractors owned by persons with "socially and economically disadvantaged" backgrounds. This program was established pursuant to a federal law that established a minimum goal of five percent minority participation on all primary contracting and subcontracting awards. It also created a presumption that members of certain minority groups were disadvantaged for purposes of the law. The law was challenged by a nonminority subcontractor which, although it submitted the lowest bid, lost the contract to a minority owned business.

By a 5-4 margin, and in an opinion authored by Justice Sandra Day O'Connor, the Court held that federal affirmative action programs should be subject to strict scrutiny. In so doing, it identified three reasons why the use of racial or ethnic preferences should be subject to a rigorous level of review. First, the Court referenced the importance of "skepticism" in evaluating any racial classification. Attention to this factor reflected not only historical experience with racial discrimination, but also emphasis upon skepticism was grounded in an understanding that discrimination sometimes may be subtle rather than overt. Thus, it is essential to take a hard look at any racially preferential program or policy. Minus strict scrutiny, the Court concluded, there was no way to sort out benign or beneficial classifications from wrongly motivated ones. Strict scrutiny, as the Court put it, enables the judiciary to "smoke out " illegitimate uses and ensure that the classification was not a reflection of racial prejudice or stereotype.

The Court identified "consistency" as its second consideration in support of strict scrutiny. In this regard, the Court stressed that the standard of review for equal protection does not vary according to the race that is burdened or benefited. The third factor was the interest of "congruence." Whether an equal protection claim arises against the federal government under the Fifth Amendment or state government under the Fourteenth Amendment, the Court's position was that the same standard of review applies. As the Court observed, these propositions "derive from the basic proposition that the Fifth and Fourteenth Amendments to the Constitution protect persons, not groups." Taken collectively, they supported "the conclusion that any person, of whatever race, has the right to demand that any governmental actor subject to the Constitution justify any racial classification subjecting that person to unequal treatment under the strictest scrutiny." Consistent with this premise, the Court held that "all racial classifications, imposed by whatever federal, state, or local governmental actor, must be analyzed by a reviewing court under strict scrutiny. In other words, such classifications are constitutional only if they are narrowly tailored measures that further compelling governmental interests."

In a part of the opinion that did not command majority support, Justice O'Connor challenged any understanding that "strict scrutiny is 'strict in theory, but fatal in fact.'" Noting that the practice and effects of racial discrimination against minorities were a persisting reality, Justice O'Connor asserted that government was not disabled from responding to it. Although acknowledging that persons wronged by racial discrimination should have a remedy, Justice Antonin Scalia in a concurring opinion countered that "under our Constitution there can be no such thing as either a creditor or debtor race." For Justice Scalia, even well-intended "concept[s] of racial entitlement" reinforced and preserved for future mischief the ways of thinking that generated racially based slavery, privilege, and hatred. From his perspective, he considered "unlikely, if not impossible, that the challenged program would survive this understanding of strict scrutiny." This sentiment was echoed by Justice Clarence Thomas, who perceived the preferential program as an exercise in "paternalism" that was "at war with the principle of inherent equality that underlies and infuses our Constitution."

Justice John Paul Stevens, in a dissenting opinion joined by Justice Ruth Bader Ginsburg, challenged the majority's use of the terms "skepticism," "consistency," and "congruence." With respect to skepticism, Justice Stevens agreed that courts should be wary of racial classifications because race seldom provides a relevant basis for treating persons differently. On the point of consistency, Justice Stevens maintained that there are differences between a majority's decision to burden a racial minority and one to benefit it despite the incidental impact upon the majority itself.

From his perspective, there was neither a moral nor a constitutional equivalence between a policy that supports a caste system and enactments designed to eliminate racial subordination. Put simply, in Justice Stevens' view, the majority ignored the difference "between oppression and assistance." With respect to congruence, Justice Stevens also found untenable the premise that there is no meaningful difference between a congressional and state decision to adopt an affirmative action program. He referenced prior case law that had identified Congress's "special 'institutional competence'" and the need for deference toward the national legislature when it was acting under specific powers to provide for the "'general Welfare of the United States' and 'enforce ... the equal protection guarantee of the Fourteenth Amendment.'"

Justice David Souter, joined by Justices Ruth Bader Ginsburg and Stephen Breyer, authored a separate dissent. So did Justice Ginsburg, who was joined by Justice Souter. These opinions attempted to soften the impact of the majority opinion. Together, they stressed that the Court had not foreclosed the possibility that some racial classifications might survive strict scrutiny. In her opinion, Justice O'Connor had noted the permissibility of race-conscious methods remedies the effects of discrimination. The extent to which other interests might be found compelling, however, was reserved for future review.

Bibliography

Drew Days, *Fullilove*, 96 *Yale Law Journal* 453 (1987). The argument that government should have more than "good motives" when it allocates resources pursuant to racial criteria is presented.

"*Successful*, Affluent but Still 'Disadvantaged,'" *Wall Street Journal*, June 13, 1995, at B1, cols. 3–6. The aftermath of the *Croson* decision, including a dramatic drop in the city's minority construction contracts and the termination of similar programs nationwide, is the focus of this article.

Grutter v. Bollinger

Citation: 539 U.S. 306.

Issue: Whether a public university law school's admissions policy that factored race as a nonexclusive consideration in creating a diverse student body violated the equal protection clause.

Year of Decision: 2003.

Outcome: The use of race as a nonexclusive factor to achieve a diverse law school student body does not offend the equal protection guarantee.

Author of Opinion: Justice Sandra Day O'Connor.

Vote: 5-4.

Case law by the end of the twentieth century had curbed substantially the potential operation of affirmative action. Although acknowledging that racial discrimination and its consequences were not mere historical relics, the Court embraced an exacting standard of review for any policy or program designed to remedy racial discrimination. Whether any government initiative other than narrowly tailored remediation might be sufficient to satisfy the demands of strict scrutiny, however, was a question that spilled over into the twenty-first century. In its first reckoning with affirmative action, in *Regents of the University of California v. Bakke* (1978), the Court wrestled with the issue of whether diversity in the academic world was sufficiently important to justify a preferential admissions policy. Although the Court was closely divided and no majority opinion was rendered, five justices agreed that race or ethnicity could be a factor in the admissions process. Justice Lewis Powell, in an influential concurring opinion, stressed that race could not be an exclusive factor in the decision to admit students. He noted, however, that the university had a compelling interest in a diverse student body.

A quarter of a century later, *Grutter v. Bollinger* (2003) revisited this issue. It did so against the backdrop of *Hopwood v. Texas* (5th Cir. 1996), a court of appeals decision which held that diversity could not be a compelling interest. The *Hopwood* ruling invalidated a University of Texas policy that factored diversity into the law school admissions process. At issue in *Grutter* was the University of Michigan Law School admissions policy that too was grounded in the interest of a diverse student body. Under this policy, each applicant's file was reviewed individually by an admissions officer. An assessment was made not only of traditional academic quality indicators but also personal statements, letters of recommendation, and "an essay describing ways in which the applicant will contribute to the life and diversity of the Law School." Although the policy did not define diversity exclusively in terms of race or ethnicity, or restrict the scope of eligible diversity contributions, it reaffirmed the institution's particular interest in "groups which have been historically discriminated against, like African-Americans." The policy also provided that no applicant should be admitted without the school's expectation that he or she would be academically successful.

The policy was challenged by an applicant, who claimed that her rejection owed to the school's use of race as a "'predominant' factor" in the admissions process. Her argument was that, for practical purposes, the policy improved the admission prospects of certain minorities and thus created favored and disfavored racial groups. Drawing upon case law that requires strict scrutiny of any racial classification, she maintained that the program was unsupported by any compelling interest. The Supreme Court, in a majority opinion authored by Justice Sandra Day O'Connor, disagreed and held that "student body diversity is a compelling state interest that can justify the use of race in university admissions."

As a starting point for its analysis, the Court reaffirmed the proposition that all racial classifications are subject to strict scrutiny. The purpose of such rigorous review is to "'smoke out' illegitimate uses of race by assuring that [government] is pursuing a goal important enough to warrant use of a highly suspect tool." The Court made it clear that strict scrutiny is not necessarily fatal, however, and race-based action may be permissible provided it is narrowly tailored to achieve a compelling governmental interest. The strict scrutiny framework thus represents "a framework for carefully examining the importance and the sincerity of the reasons advanced by the governmental decisionmaker for the use of race" in a specific context.

Until *Grutter*, the Court had found no compelling interest in affirmative action beyond the remedying of past discrimination. It deferred to the school's judgment, however, that "diversity [was] essential to its educational mission." A basic premise of the policy was that, to achieve an "exceptionally academically qualified and broadly diverse" class, "a 'critical mass' of minority students" was essential. Such an aim, as the Court saw it, was different for constitutional purposes than seeking a specified percentage of a racial or ethnic group. Among the specific educational benefits that the Court attributed to a diverse student body were "cross-racial understanding," the breaking down of racial stereotypes, and enhanced classroom discussion. The Court noted that the learning experience helps incubate skills that are demanded "in today's increasingly global marketplace." Because law schools are a primary source of the nation's future leaders, the Court thought it particularly important that they "be inclusive of talented and qualified individuals of every race and ethnicity."

Having identified diversity as a compelling governmental interest, the Court turned its attention to whether the admissions policy was narrowly tailored. Stressing first that a racial quota system is impermissible, the Court observed that it must be flexible enough "to consider all pertinent elements of diversity in light of the particular qualifications of each applicant, and to place them on the same footing for consideration, although not necessarily according them the same weight." For race or ethnicity to be taken into account as a factor, therefore, the key element of an admissions process was "individualized consideration." Evaluating the program in these terms, the Court found that the goal of achieving a "critical mass" did not create a quota. This conclusion by itself did not satisfy the "individualized consideration" requirement. The Court, however, found that the school's "highly individualized, holistic review of each applicant's file" met the standard. It also determined that there were no viable race neutral alternatives for achieving the school's goals and the policy did not impose undue burdens on persons outside the favored group.

In closing, the Court stressed that any race-conscious admissions policy "must be limited in time." This premise aims to ensure that temporary methods for getting beyond discrimination do not become perpetual preserves or entitlements. Although the law school had no sunset provision, the Court accepted its promise to terminate the program as soon as possible. The Court noted, however, that "[w]e expect that 25 years from now, the use of racial preferences will no longer be necessary to further the interest approved today." Justice Ruth Bader Ginsburg, joined by Justice Stephen Breyer, authored a concurring opinion endorsing the proposition "that race-conscious programs 'must have a logical end point.'" Justice Ginsburg intimated, however, that the challenge of overcoming racial discrimination may require more time.

Chief Justice William Rehnquist, in a dissenting opinion joined by Justices Antonin Scalia, Anthony Kennedy, and Clarence Thomas, disputed the Court's finding that the admissions policy was narrowly tailored. Chief Justice Rehnquist saw the "critical mass" premise as a "veil ... [for] a naked effort to achieve racial balancing." Because African-American admissions were dramatically higher than for other minority groups, his view was that the extreme disproportionality among underrepresented groups undermined achievement of a real "critical mass." Chief Justice Rehnquist also pointed to evidence that virtually every applicant from the targeted minority groups was admitted. From his perspective, this correlation "must result from careful race based planning by the Law School." In addition to finding such "racial balancing ... 'patently unconstitutional,'" Chief Justice Rehnquist also faulted the program for having no precise time limit on its duration.

Justice Kennedy, in a separate dissent, maintained that the school failed to prove its compliance with the individualized consideration requirement. He noted that up to 85 percent of the seats in an entering class were awarded on the basis of grade point averages and standardized admission tests. Race and ethnicity, Justice Kennedy observed, became a factor only with respect to the remaining seats that were filled late in the process. Given the school's interest in a diverse student body and tightness of competition for a small number of spots, he saw "the real potential to compromise individual review." Consistency of minority enrollment percentages over the years also led Justice Kennedy to infer "that the Law School subverted individual determination."

Justice Scalia, joined by Justice Thomas, also added a separate dissent. He described the school's "'critical mass' justification" as a challenge even for "the most gullible mind." Justice Scalia also challenged the "educational benefits" that the institution attributed to a diverse student body. As he described it, factors like "cross-racial understanding" and preparing students "for an increasingly diverse workforce and society" represented "lessons in life" that were not unique to a law school or necessarily teachable. Based upon the Court's ruling, Justice Scalia predicted an increased volume of litigation that would need to sort out issues of whether educational institutions had provided individualized consideration, created actual or *de facto* quotas, realized tangible educational benefits, or were committed to diversity in a *bona fide* sense. His proposed solution was a reading of the Constitution that "proscribes government discrimination on the basis of race, and [makes] state-provided education … no exception."

In his separate opinion concurring in part and dissenting in part, and joined for the most part by Justice Scalia, Justice Thomas maintained that the success of all students regardless of their color would be facilitated best "without the meddling of university administrators." Insofar as a law school such as the University of Michigan maintains an "elitist admissions policy," Justice Thomas observed, "racially disproportionate results" knowingly will follow. He added, however, that "[r]acial discrimination is not a permissible solution to the[se] self-inflicted wounds."

Asserting that a public university law school is not a pressing public necessity, Justice Thomas challenged the Court's finding of a compelling interest. Even if a diversified student body provided educational benefits, Justice Thomas could find no basis for a race-conscious admissions policy absent a compelling interest in the school's existence. He also contended that the school's interest in maintaining its elite status was not compelling, and that this concern with academic ranking was the only barrier to the racially neutral alternative of relaxed admission standards. As Justice Thomas saw it, "the Law School should be forced to choose between its classroom aesthetic and its exclusionary admissions system." By accepting all students who met a minimum qualifications standard, the school could achieve a racially diverse "student body without the use of racial discrimination."

Justice Thomas contested the Court's deference to the law school's judgment, noting that the interest in "educational autonomy" does not confer a license to ignore the equal protection clause. He also questioned the premise that educational benefits will flow from diversity. In this regard, Justice Thomas referenced social science data indicating that "heterogeneity actually impairs learning among black students." It thus was conceivable, from Justice Thomas's perspective, that a historically black college or university could justify a racially exclusionary admissions policy. Against this backdrop, he characterized the Court's opinion as "the seed of a new constitutional justification for … racial segregation."

In his dissent, Justice Thomas also criticized the school for ignoring the diversity successes of other elite state law schools that did not factor race into their admissions process. He also chastised it for relying heavily upon flawed standardized admission tests that then create the need for the race-conscious policy. Further, Justice Thomas faulted the school for building a "façade" that "looks right" but essentially admitting "overmatched students" who are unable to succeed in the competitive environment of an elite institution. Asserting that most "blacks are admitted to Law School because of discrimination," Justice Thomas complained that "all are tarred as undeserving" and thus "stigmatized."

Despite the strong urging of the dissenting justices, *Grutter* rejected the proposition that racial classifications are impermissible under any circumstance. Key to the viability of any race-conscious admissions policy is whether it is perceived as operating on the basis of quotas or more flexible and individualized review. The importance of this factor is highlighted not only by the *Grutter* decision but by the outcome of the companion case of *Gratz v. Bollinger* (2003). In *Gratz*, the Court held that a

University of Michigan undergraduate admissions policy violated the equal protection clause. The program was structured on a basis that enabled an applicant to received a total of 150 points. Admission was guaranteed with 100 points, and 20 points were awarded automatically to any applicant who was the member of an underrepresented minority. Because "virtually any minimally qualified minority applicant" was admitted under this program, the Court saw it as a "practical quota." A critical missing link differentiating the undergraduate model from the law school system, from the Court's perspective, was the absence of individualized consideration.

Bibliography

Patricia J. Williams, *Metro Broadcasting, Inc. v. Federal Communications Commission*, 104 *Harvard Law Review* 525 (1990). The value of racial diversity as an end in its own right is discussed.

CHAPTER 9

GENDER

As originally framed and ratified, the Constitution reflected the input and interests of white males. The Reconstruction Amendments factored racial reality into the constitutional framework. Gender remained beyond the pale of constitutional concern, however, until the twentieth century. Until then, constitutional challenges to laws restricting freedom of or opportunities for women were unsuccessful. Typifying the Supreme Court's early thinking was its decision in *Bradwell v. Illinois* (1873), upholding a state law that barred women from practicing law. In support of this result, the Court observed that "[t]he paramount destiny of and mission of woman are to fulfill the noble and benign offices of wife and other. This is the law of the Creator. And the rules of civil society must be adapted to the general constitution of things."

In 1920, the Nineteenth Amendment established that the right "to vote shall not be denied or abridged ... on account of sex." For another half century, however, the Court resisted interpreting the equal protection guarantee as a means of accounting for gender inequality. In the early 1970s, the Court gave indications that laws discriminating on the basis of gender might implicate the equal protection clause. This possibility became a reality in *Craig v. Boren* (1976), when the Court announced that it would take a harder look at gender classifications. This decision, and case law that followed it, established the equal protection clause as a barrier to traditional distinctions on the basis of gender. Representative of these decisions was *United States v. Virginia* (1996), which emphasized the importance of basing public policy on the basis of dated stereotypes.

Craig v. Boren

Original pronouncements on the meaning of the equal protection clause made it clear, at least at the time, that it had nothing to do with gender. This understanding was evident in the Supreme Court's first decision concerning the equal protection guarantee. In *The Slaughter-House Cases* (1873), the Court "doubt[ed] very much whether any action of a State not directed by way of discrimination against the Negroes as a class, or on account of their race, will ever be held to come within the purview of this provision." This point was made even more directly with respect to gender during the same term the Court upheld a state law denying women the opportunity to practice law. This determination, in *Bradwell v. Illinois* (1873), was coupled with the observation that "[i]n the nature of things it is not every citizen of every age, sex and condition that is qualified for every calling and position."

Citation: 429 U.S. 190.

Issue: Whether a law prohibiting the sale and consumption of beer to males between the ages of 18 and 21, but not to females in the same age category, violated the equal protection clause.

Year of Decision: 1976.

Outcome: The gender-based discrimination violated the equal protection guarantee.

Author of Opinion: Justice William Brennan.

Vote: 6-2.

The Court's rulings through the middle of the twentieth century reflected a sense that the legislature could account for traditional differences associated with men and women. Underlying this orientation was an understanding, referenced in *Bradwell v. Illinois,* that "the family institution is repugnant to the idea of a woman adopting a distinct and independent career from that of her husband." Even as the social and legal standing of women changed over the decades, the Court was slow to change its thinking with respect to the equal protection clause. In *Goesart v. Cleary* (1949), it thus upheld a state law barring women from working as bartenders unless related to the owner. As the Court put it, "[t]he fact that women may now have achieved the virtues that men have long practiced, does not preclude the States from drawing a sharp line between the sexes."

Over the course of the twentieth century, significant changes took place with respect to the status of women. The Twenty-first Amendment prohibited gender-based abridgment of the right to vote. The *Civil Rights Act of 1964* barred discrimination in employment not merely on the basis of race but also on the basis of gender. This progress represented the work of the political process, rather than any changed understanding of the Constitution. Evolution in this regard began to manifest itself, however, in the early 1970s.

An early indication of impending change was the Court's decision in *Reed v. Reed* (1971). In this case, the Court invalidated an Idaho law that favored the use of men to administer estates in probate. Although it announced no new standard of review in *Reed v. Reed,* the Court drove a result that indicated a change in orientation. Two years later, in *Frontiero v. Richardson* (1973), the Court reviewed a federal benefits law presuming that a military serviceman's spouse was dependent upon him. The regulation required a servicewoman, however, to prove the dependency of her spouse. Although no majority opinion was announced, Justice William Brennan and three other justices maintained that gender classifications were no different than racial classifications under the equal protection clause. Accordingly, they concluded that such classifications are suspect and should be subject to searching judicial review. In a concurring opinion, Justice Lewis Powell agreed with the outcome but refused to adopt strict scrutiny as the appropriate model of review. He also noted that an equal rights amendment to the Constitution was pending possible ratification. Justice Powell thus favored withholding a determination with respect to a standard of review so as not to preempt the political process.

Although the equal rights amendment eventually failed the ratification process, the Court announced a standard of review that would subject gender classifications to heightened scrutiny. The key decision in this regard was *Craig v. Boren* (1976), when the Court indicated that it no longer would defer to legislative judgment on matters of gender. The issue in this case was an Oklahoma law that banned the sale of 3.2 percent beer to and by males under the age of 21. Sale to females between the ages of 18 and 21 was not similarly prohibited. In support of this gender-based classification, the state argued that males in the relevant age group presented a higher risk of driving while intoxicated and to highway safety. Actual data evidenced that men between the ages of 18 and 21 accounted for 2 percent of the state's driving while intoxicated arrests. Females in the age group made up .18 percent of the state's arrests.

If the law had been evaluated on the basis of traditional standards of review, it would have survived. Barring a classification such as race that merits searching judicial review, the Court typically asks only whether the state has a rational basis for its action and its regulatory means are reasonably related to the regulatory objective. The Court announced, however, that classifications on the basis of gender are subject to a higher level of scrutiny under the equal protection clause. It thus implemented a standard of review requiring the state to demonstrate that a gender classification serves an important governmental objective and is substantially related to achieving this goal.

Judged by this standard, the Oklahoma law was found wanting. The Court accepted that the state's interest in safe highways was important. It determined that this interest was not substantially advanced, however, by gender-specific regulation. The major deficiency of the male-only prohibition was its failure to account for the state's regulatory interest. In this regard, the Court noted that the relationship between the gender-based restriction and traffic safety was minimal. Undermining the enactment's efficacy too was the fact that the measure did not prohibit consumption of beer purchased by a third party. The state also failed to demonstrate that the sale of 3.2 percent beer presented a greater risk to highway safety than other forms of liquor. Statistical evidence was seen as weak in documenting risk differentials on the basis of age and gender. Despite acknowledging the legitimacy and importance of the state's interest, the Court determined that the state's use of a gender classification conflicted with the equal protection clause.

Justice William Rehnquist opposed the equal protection guarantee's extension to gender. In a dissenting opinion, he argued for an interpretation consistent with original understanding that confines the equal protection clause to matters of racial discrimination. Justice Rehnquist also was mystified why the Court had decided to use a heightened standard of review when men were the target of gender-based regulation. As he saw it, the status of men was unlike that associated with the condition of historically disadvantaged groups. For Justice Rehnquist, they were the last group needing protection from the political process.

The Court's ruling represented a significant expansion of the equal protection guarantee's boundaries. Despite a century of resistance to this extension, the result is consistent with the history of any principle that operates to equalize some condition or status. Various constitutional authorities have noted that, when an equality principle is introduced on behalf of one group, it invariably is pushed to account for the interests of other groups. Charles Fairman, who wrote extensively on the Fourteenth Amendment, observed that "equal protection as it spreads out tends to lift all to the level of the most favored." Consistent with this phenomenon, the determination that racial classifications warranted heightened judicial review represented a starting point rather than an ending point for the evolution of equal protection doctrine. Its application to gender reflects an acquired sense of commonality in racial and gender experiences based upon exclusion from the political process, historical disadvantage based upon group status, and immutable characteristics.

Because women have full access to the political process, some critics maintain that gender should not be an object of special judicial attention. The Court largely has rejected this argument. Although its standards for reviewing gender classifications are not as intense as those used for assessing racial classifications, the Court nonetheless continues to be alert to classifications that reflect outdated stereotypes with respect to the role of women.

Bibliography

Ruth Colker, *Anti-Subordination Above All: Sex, Race and Equal Protection*, 61 *New York University Law Review* 1003 (1986). The argument that review of gender-based classifications should focus upon their subordinating potential, rather than on just discrimination or difference, is advanced.

Sylvia Law, *Rethinking Sex and the Constitution*, 132 *University of Pennsylvania Law Review* 955 (1984). The alleged failure of equal protection doctrine to acknowledge certain biological differences is criticized.

Catharine A. MacKinnon, *Toward a Feminist Theory of the State* (Cambridge, MA: Harvard University Press, 1991). A critical assessment of gender-based equal protection theory, and competing perspectives, is provided.

United States v. Virginia

Citation: 518 U.S. 515.

Issue: Whether a state military college's male-only admission policy violated the equal protection clause.

Year of Decision: 1996.

Outcome: The gender exclusive policy violated the equal protection guarantee.

Author of Opinion: Justice Ruth Bader Ginsburg.

Vote: 7-1.

Race is a factor that the law cannot take into account unless the state has a compelling reason and cannot achieve its purpose in a racially neutral manner. Regardless of whether racial classifications are intended to burden or benefit historically disadvantaged groups, as the Court put it in *Adarand Constructors, Inc. v. Pena* (1995), they are subject to the same "searching review." Although gender classifications are subject to a heightened standard of review, scrutiny of them is not as intense as it is for race. The operative standard, as described by the Court in *Craig v. Boren* (1976), is whether they "serve important [rather than compelling] government interests and are substantially [rather than necessarily] related to achievement of those objectives."

Also, unlike distinctions on the basis of race, some gender classifications are considered altogether unworrisome. The state thus may treat men and women separately in instances where there are legitimate differences between them. When gender classifications are assessed, therefore, a preliminary question is whether men and women are "similarly situated." The underlying premise is that there are characteristics or interests unique to men and women that require or deserve a gender-based accounting. In *Rostker v. Goldberg* (1981), for instance, the Court determined that Congress could authorize registration of men only for the military draft. The reason for this result was that, because women were restricted from combat, they were not similarly situated with men.

In determining whether men and women are similarly situated, the central question is whether a gender-based distinction reflects an outdated stereotype or speaks to a real concern. An easy case for gender differentiation would arise in the context of separate public restrooms. Segregation on the basis of race, at least since the mid-twentieth century, is constitutionally unthinkable. Given well-established and uncontested conventions with respect to propriety, it is hard to imagine separate restrooms for men and women becoming a constitutional issue. Cases and controversies are more likely to arise when perspectives on gender are in competition rather than the basis for consensus.

This reality, and an associated standard of review that probes for outdated stereotypes, was evidenced in *Mississippi University for Women v. Hogan* (1982). In this case, the Court determined that a state university's single-sex admission policy violated the equal protection clause. The state argued that the policy aimed to compensate women for discrimination. Because women were not underrepresented in the field of nursing, the Court found that exclusion of males from the school "perpetuated the stereotyped view of nursing as an exclusively women's job."

The question of same-sex education arose in *United States v. Virginia* (1996), when the Court reviewed the male-only admission policy of Virginia Military Institute (VMI). Writing for the majority, Justice Ruth Bader Ginsburg determined that the policy failed the traditional standard of review for gender classifications. The state identified two justifications for the exclusionary policy. These rationales were that single-sex education at VMI (1) facilitated "diversity in educational approaches," and (2) enabled a unique "adversative" model of "character development and leadership training" that would have to be modified if women were admitted. Although acknowledging that diverse models of education may be laudable, the Court was not convinced that the state's interest in this regard was real. It noted, for instance, the absence of any single-sex educational program for women. The Court also disagreed that VMI would have to alter its "adversative" methods if women were admitted. In this regard, it noted that "many men would not want to be educated in such an environment."

The Court thus saw the issue as being "not whether women or men should be forced to attend VMI," but whether the state can deny women who have "the will and capacity, the training and opportunity that VMI uniquely affords." On this matter, the Court determined that the state had failed to prove the admission of women "downgrade[s] VMI's stature, destroy[s] the adversative system, and, with it, even the school." It equated these concerns to "other 'self-fulfilling prophecies' once routinely used to deny rights or opportunities" to enter fields such as law and medicine. Consistent with its sensitivity to gender-based stereotypes, the Court stressed that "[s]tate actors controlling gates to opportunity cannot exclude qualified individuals based on 'fixed notions' concerning the roles and abilities of males and females." It also found that a proposed remedy, which would have created a parallel women's institute, also reflected inappropriate stereotypes.

The single-sex policy failed because it lacked a substantial relationship to an important government interest. Compared with prior decisions on gender, however, the Court's analysis suggested a more rigorous standard of review. Typically, as noted previously, the inquiry is into whether the state has shown that a challenged classification "serves important governmental objectives and that the discriminatory means employed are substantially related to those objectives." In *United States v. Virginia*, the Court described its role further as having to "determine whether the proffered justification is exceedingly persuasive." It further noted that the state's "justification must be genuine, not hypothesized or invented *post hoc* in response to litigation. And it must not rely on overbroad generalizations about the different talents, capabilities, or preferences of males and females."

In a concurring opinion, Chief Justice William Rehnquist agreed that the single-sex policy was at odds with the equal protection guarantee. He advocated, however, a more forthright application of traditional standards of review relating to gender. In this regard, Chief Justice Rehnquist expressed his sense that the "exceedingly persuasive justification" criterion had heightened the standard for reviewing gender classifications.

Justice Antonin Scalia perceived in the Court's terminology and orientation a new standard of review for gender classifications. As Justice Scalia put it in his dissenting opinion, the Court had "drastically revise[d] our established standards for reviewing sex-based classifications." His understanding is shared by other observers who view the "exceedingly persuasive justification" terminology as being more akin to the strict scrutiny hallmark of a "compelling justification." Justice Scalia also maintained that the Court improvidently had removed a matter of education and social policy from the political process where it properly belonged. In his view, the Court merely had substituted its own debatable policy preferences as a basis for "displac[ing] longstanding national traditions as the primary determinant of what the Constitution means." He thus saw the Court "bemoaning ... 'fixed notions'" and making "smug assurances" regarding women and substituting its own "notions so fixedly that it is willing to write them into the" Constitution. From Justice Scalia's perspective, "[t]his is not the interpretation of a Constitution, but the creation of one."

The decision in *United States v. Virginia* marks a significant evolution from the original understanding of the equal protection doctrine as it relates to gender. Over the course of its first century, the Fourteenth Amendment provided no recourse for arguments that it was a proper basis for addressing gender-based discrimination. Modern case law indicates that review of gender classification is not as intense as the strict scrutiny that applies to race but more rigorous than the assessment of garden-variety social and economic classifications. This "intermediate" standard of review has enabled the Court to strike down laws that it perceives to be the function of dated stereotypes. At the same time, as the Court explained in *United States v. Virginia,* the standard respects "inherent differences between men and women [that] are enduring." Although "inherent differences" are unacceptable grounds for differentiation in the context of race, "the two sexes are not fungible." Consistent with this premise, the Court's focus upon gender classifications has become increasingly sharpened. Notwithstanding legitimate differences that may be identified, review of gender-based classifications aims to ensure that they are not used "for denigration of the members of either sex or for artificial constraints on an individual's opportunity."

Bibliography

Carol Gilligan, *In a Different Voice: Psychological Theory and Women's Development* (Cambridge, MA: Harvard University Press, 1982). The development paths of male and female children and the implications of these differences are explored.

Richard Posner, *Sex and Reason* (Cambridge, MA: Harvard University Press, 1992). Differences between men and women and their consequent relation to the law are examined.

Robert Wright, *The Moral Animal: Why We Are the Way We Are* (New York: Pantheon Books, 1994). A psychological perspective on gender-based differences is provided.

CHAPTER 10

FUNDAMENTAL RIGHTS

The primary concern of the equal protection clause over the course of its history has been with racial classifications. Grounds for an equal protection claim expanded during the final decades of the twentieth century, as the Supreme Court recognized gender, alienage, and illegitimacy as classifications that merited heightened judicial review. In cases concerning persons in these categories, group status by itself is sufficient to establish an equal protection interest.

Group status, although the dominant basis for equal protection concern, is not an exclusive prerequisite. Since the 1960s, the Court has evolved another dimension of equal protection doctrine that is implicated whenever a fundamental right is denied selectively. If a state allowed Democrats but not Republicans to use a public park for political rallies, for instance, the Republicans would have a claim that their freedom of speech was abridged. They also would have an equal protection claim based not on their group status but on the fact that a fundamental right had been denied in a selective manner.

EDUCATION

The federal constitution by its specific terms provides no right to an education. When the Court determined that racially segregated public schools were unconstitutional in *Brown v. Board of Education* (1954), however, it described public education as "perhaps the most important function of state and local governments." This observation reflected the Court's "recognition of the importance of education to our democratic society." Two decades later, in *San Antonio Independent School District v. Rodriguez* (1973), the Court reviewed a public school financing plan that resulted in significant funding disparities among school districts. Notwithstanding the close relationship between education and constitutionally protected interests such as voting and expression, the Court rejected the notion that the Constitution implied a right to education.

San Antonio Independent School District v. Rodriguez

Public education over the course of the twentieth century came to be recognized as one of the most significant functions of state and local government. This role contrasted with conditions after the Civil War when the Fourteenth Amendment was framed and ratified. At that time, taxpayer supported education had not taken hold in the South and was unevenly developed in the North. Given these circumstances,

Citation: 411 U.S. 1.

Issue: Whether a state funding plan for public education, resulting in financial disparities among school districts violated the equal protection clause.

Year of Decision: 1973.

Outcome: The funding plan did not violate the equal protection clause, because it neither created a suspect classification nor burdened a fundamental right.

Author of Opinion: Justice Lewis Powell.

Vote: 5-4.

as the Supreme Court noted in *Brown v. Board of Education* (1954), it was not surprising that debates over the Fourteenth Amendment made slight reference to public education.

The evolution of public education by 1954 had reached a point that the Court in *Brown* was constrained to assess it "in the light of its full development and its present place in American life throughout the nation." By then, public education was universally provided, and mandatory attendance through high school was the norm. In *Brown*, the Court described "education [a]s perhaps the most significant function of state and local governments and noted its importance … to our democratic society." The Court further characterized it as "the very foundation of good citizenship, a principal instrument in awakening the child to cultural values, in preparing for later professional training, and in helping him to adjust normally to his environment." So central had education become to personal development that the Court was "doubtful that any child may reasonably be expected to succeed in life if he is denied the opportunity of an education." It thus observed that "where the state has undertaken to provide it, it is a right that must be made available to all on equal terms."

The notion of public education as a right that had special significance was restated in *Bolling v. Sharpe* (1954). This decision reached the same result with respect to the federal government that the *Brown* ruling obtained with respect to the states. The *Brown* decision rested on the equal protection clause of the Fourteenth Amendment, which operates against the states. No comparable provision applies to the federal government so, in *Bolling v. Sharpe,* the Court inferred an equal protection guarantee from the due process clause of the Fifth Amendment. In thus striking down segregation of public schools in Washington, D.C., the Court determined that segregation was not reasonably related to any legitimate purpose. It thus imposed "a burden that constitutes an artificial deprivation of liberty in violation of the Due Process Clause."

For nearly two decades after the *Brown* and *Bolling* decisions, the Court persisted in its demand for desegregation at first "with all deliberate speed" and eventually with remedies "that promise realistically to work now." By the early 1970s, however, it had limited the reach of the desegregation mandate. This result was achieved by rulings that conditioned the duty to desegregate upon proof of segregative intent, *Keyes v. School District No. 1* (1973); limited the use of interdistrict remedies even when they were the only practical means for achieving racially mixed schools, *Milliken v. Bradley* (1974); and permitted resegregation of public schools to the extent this condition was not intentionally induced by the state, *Pasadena City Board of Education v. Spangler* (1976).

Taken together, these decisions indicated that desegregation would be limited to circumstances where purposeful segregation was provable and would reach no farther or extend no longer than the scope of the violation itself. Desegregation's primary concern was with the impact of officially separated schools upon educational opportunity. It did not address broader issues of equality in education. Inequality of funding, for instance, was a widespread phenomenon during the separate but equal era. Public spending on education in segregated states typically reflected extreme disparities based on race. In declaring segregated public schools unconstitutional, the *Brown* Court relied upon desegregation as the means to address inequality. Unlike its rulings in the two decades preceding *Brown,* the Court made no demand for equalization of spending.

Notwithstanding the desegregation process, issues with respect to public school funding disparities eventually resurfaced. In *San Antonio Independent School District v. Rodriguez* (1974), the Court reviewed a Texas plan for financing public education on the basis of state funding allocations and local property taxes. Given variations among communities with respect to their wealth, funding disparities statewide and even in a particular municipality were significant. Expenditures in San Antonio's wealthiest district were $594 per student. In the poorest district, spending was $356 per student. These funding disparities became the basis for arguments that the Texas plan violated the equal protection clause of the Fourteenth Amendment.

Justice Lewis Powell, writing the majority opinion for the Court, commenced his analysis by whether the funding system discriminated against poor persons and, if so, whether indigence was a suspect classification. On this matter, the Court determined that wealth discrimination was a constitutional concern only if a person was unable to pay for a particular benefit and thus was precluded altogether from accessing it. For an example of when wealth discrimination counts, the Court cited *Griffin v. Illinois* (1956). In this case, the Court invalidated a state law that denied indigent defendants access to trial transcripts necessary for appeal. Absent a showing that the Texas system presented a unique disadvantage to the poor, and because education was not deprived altogether, the Court found no basis for finding that the economic disadvantage was suspect in the same manner as race.

Reminded of the significance that the *Brown* Court placed on education, the Court acknowledged its value both for the individual and for society. It noted, however, that "the importance of a service performed by the State does not determine whether it must be regarded as fundamental for purposes of examination under the Equal Protection Clause." This determination reflected an unease on the part of the Court that manifests itself periodically when it is asked to identify a right as fundamental. It thus echoed the sentiments expressed of Justice John Harlan, Jr., in *Shapiro v. Thompson* (1969). Dissenting from the Court's recognition of a right to travel, which became the basis for striking down a state's waiting period for collecting welfare payment, Justice Harlan observed that "[v]irtually every state statute affects important rights." Consistent with this perspective, Justice Powell warned that the Court would become a "super-legislature" if it were to render decisions based upon its own sense of importance.

With these concerns in mind, the Court determined that it had no authority or basis for declaring education a fundamental right. As the Court put it, "the key to discovering whether education is 'fundamental'" did not lie in comparing its relative importance to other interests. Rather, "the answer lies in assessing whether there is a right to education explicitly or implicitly guaranteed by the Constitution. Education is not among the rights explicitly protected by the Constitution."

The argument that education is a fundamental right draws upon the close relationship that the *Brown* Court perceived between it and "other rights and liberties accorded protection under the Constitution." The majority acknowledged this connection between education and freedom of expression and voting. Although these interests are constitutionally protected, the Court observed that it had no authority to guarantee "the most *effective* speech or the most *informed* choice" (emphasis in original). Insofar as the quality of speech or electoral decision making was to be improved, the Court maintained that the responsibility belonged to the legislature rather than the judiciary.

The Court thus rejected the proposition that education was a fundamental right implied by the Constitution. Having reached this conclusion, it reserved the possibility "that some identifiable quantum of education is a constitutionally protected prerequisite to the meaningful exercise of either right." Such a case, at least from the majority's perspective, was not presented by the Texas funding plan. Without a suspect classification (such as race) or a fundamental right, the Court would not engage in searching review. Although the plan might be imperfect, the Court found it rationally related to a legitimate state purpose of facilitating local control of education.

Less than a decade after its decision in *San Antonio Independent School District v. Rodriguez* (1974), the Court reviewed another Texas funding plan that denied state funds to educate children of illegal aliens. At issue, in *Plyler v. Doe* (1982), was whether the state had denied a "quantum of education" sufficient to trigger constitutional concern. The Court reaffirmed the premise that education is not a right secured by the Constitution. It also observed that education was not a garden variety benefit. Emphasizing education's importance to the individual and "our basic institutions," the Court reasoned that it could not "ignore the significant social costs borne by our Nation when select groups are denied the means to absorb the values and skills upon which our social order rests." Unlike a case of disparate funding, the total and categorical denial of education, as the Court saw it, was an irrational and unconstitutional deprivation. Having previously reserved the possibility that some identifiable quantum of education might be constitutionally significant, the Court determined that a state could not deny basic public education on a categorical basis.

Since the Court's ruling in *San Antonio Independent School District v. Rodriguez*, numerous challenges of public school funding disparities have been made under state constitutions. Included among these was a state court case brought under the Texas Constitution, which establishes a state duty to establish, support, and maintain "an efficient system of public free schools." The state also is required to facilitate a "general diffusion of knowledge" that is "essential to the preservation of the liberties and rights of the people." The Texas Supreme Court, in *Edgewood Independent School District v. Kirby* (1989), found that spending on a student's schooling "has a real and substantial impact on the educational opportunity offered that student." Measuring the plan against this standard, the Texas Supreme Court determined that the funding system was efficient neither on financial grounds nor in promoting the general diffusion of knowledge.

The Texas high court ruling paralleled outcomes in several other states that had reached the same outcome in reviewing similar plans. As the ultimate authority on the law of its state, the Texas Supreme Court was not subject to review by the United States Supreme Court. Based upon the Texas Supreme Court ruling, students in Texas have educational rights that are broader than what the Court has recognized under the federal Constitution. This outcome reflects the nature of a system of dual sovereigns and the capacity for differentiation in the availability and scope of rights within the union.

Bibliography

William Brennan, Jr., *State Constitutions and the Protection of Individual Rights,* 90 *Harvard Law Review* 489 (1977). The importance of state constitutions as a means of securing rights that are not protected by the United States Constitution is noted.

John Coons, William Clune, and Stephen Sugarman, *Private Wealth and Public Education* (1970). Funding of education and issues of wealth and disparities among districts are examined.

Philip Kurland, *Equal Educational Opportunity: The Limits of Constitutional Jurisprudence,* 35 *University of Chicago Law Review* 583 (1968). This is a critical inquiry into the role of the judiciary in accounting for educational opportunity.

VOTING

The right to vote is not enumerated by the Constitution. Given its centrality to a system of representative governance, however, the Court has had no difficulty inferring its existence. In *Reynolds v. Sims* (1964), the Court established the principle that the apportionment of state legislatures must reflect the principle of "one person–one vote." The Court thus secured the right to vote against processes that would dilute its weight for some. The relationship between equal protection and voting rights resurfaced as an issue in *Bush v. Gore* (2000), when the Court extended the antidilution principle to vote recounts.

Bush v. Gore

The right to vote is not enumerated specifically by the Constitution. It is a guarantee that has been inferred, however, from the political system that the Constitution has established. As the Court put it in *Reynolds v. Sims* (1964), "[t]he right to vote freely for the candidate of one's choice is of the essence of a democratic society, and any restrictions on that right strike at the heart of representative governance." Supreme Court decisions concerning suffrage generally are grounded in the equal protection

Citation: 531 U.S. 98.

Issue: Did a selective recount of ballots cast in Florida in a presidential election violate the equal protection clause.

Year of Decision: 2000.

Outcome: The selective recount of ballots diluted the right to vote and thus violated the equal protection clause.

Author of Opinion: Per Curiam.

Vote: 5–4.

clause and mostly have concerned efforts to deny the right to vote on the basis of race or dilute it through processes of apportionment. In either circumstance, the issue typically has related to a policy or strategy consciously designed to advantage one group or interest at the expense of another.

The process of allocating the franchise, however, is not the only means by which the right to vote can be debased or diluted. Voting integrity also can be compromised by methods of counting or recounting. In *Bush v. Gore* (2000), the Supreme Court confronted this issue in the context of a closely contested presidential election. Based upon the initial machine count of approximately six million ballots in Florida, George W. Bush had a 1,700 vote edge over his rival Al Gore. This narrow margin automatically triggered a machine recount which, when completed, reduced Bush's margin to several hundred votes. Gore, who actually won the national popular vote, then demanded manual recounts in four counties. When the Florida Secretary of State refused to extend the deadline for canvassing boards to submit their returns, Gore succeeded in having the Florida Supreme Court overturn her decision. The Court later ordered a statewide manual recount of ballots for purposes of identifying votes that the machines had not been able to detect. These "undervotes" typically were the result of punch cards that had not been completely perforated and thus bore only an indent or a hanging "chad." Pursuant to its understanding that the Florida legislature intended the state's electors to be determined by December 12, so that it would be in accord with federal law requiring any electoral controversy to be resolved by then, the United States Supreme Court stayed the state supreme court's judgment on December 9 and reversed it on December 11. The Court's decision effectively resolved the outcome of the election.

The Court's ruling was supported by a *per curiam* opinion representing the views of Chief Justice William Rehnquist and Justices Sandra Day O'Connor, Antonin Scalia, Anthony Kennedy, and Clarence Thomas. It led with the observation that no citizen has the right to vote for President, unless the state chooses an election as the means for implementing its constitutional power to appoint members of the Electoral College. To the extent that a state gives the people this right to vote, however, it is fundamental. A critical incident of its fundamental nature, the Court observed, "lies in the equal weight accorded to each vote and the equal dignity owed to each voter."

The Court noted that equal protection applies to both the allocation of the franchise and its exercise, and the state may not "value one person's vote over that of another." Pursuant to this premise, the Court had no objection "as an abstract proposition and starting principle" with the Florida Supreme Court's order to discern voter intent from the undercounted ballots. Its concern, however, was with "an absence of specific standards to ensure its equal application." From the Court's perspective, it was problematic that "standards for accepting or rejecting contested ballots might vary from county to county [and even] within a single county from one recount team to another." Citing instances in which standards for defining a legal vote varied and even changed in midstream, the Court concluded that "[t]his is not a process with sufficient guarantees of equal treatment."

Several other factors contributed to the Court's conclusion that the manual recount process was standardless and constitutionally flawed. Concerns included the State Court's exclusion of "overvotes" from the recount process. Overvotes consist of ballots that contained more than one punched hole. Also troublesome to the Court was its readiness to accept partial recounts when the certification deadline was reached and lack of direction with respect to whom should count ballots. Against this backdrop of perceived procedural shortcomings, the Court concluded that "[t]he recount process ... is inconsistent with the minimum procedures necessary to protect the fundamental right of each voter in the special instance of a statewide recount under the authority of a single state judicial officer."

Having put an end to the manual recount process on constitutional grounds, the Court then limited the scope of its decision. It stressed that the issue was not one of whether local entities can implement different election systems. Rather the point was that, when ordering a statewide remedy, a court must provide "at least some assurance that the rudimentary requirements of equal treatment and fundamental fairness are satisfied." Chief Justice William Rehnquist, in a concurring opinion joined by Justices Antonin Scalia and Clarence Thomas, identified further grounds for reversing the Florida Court. As Chief Justice Rehnquist saw it, the Florida Court had deviated so far from state law concerning the appointment of electors that it violated Article II, Section 1, of the Constitution. This section relates to the qualifications of electors in each state.

Justice John Paul Stevens authored a dissenting opinion that was joined by Justices Ruth Bader Ginsburg and Stephen Breyer. Justice Stevens maintained that the lack of specific detail for discerning voter intent did not "rise to the level of a constitutional violation." Although recognizing that different standards from county to county might raise serious concerns, these problems could be alleviated by the use of a single judge to adjudicate all objections that might arise. Justice Stevens also argued for a remand of the case for development of more specific procedures. His sense was that time existed for more processes, because the December 12 deadline was relevant only in the event there were conflicting slates of electors. Justice Stevens saw no barrier to "counting what the majority concedes to be legal votes until a *bona fide* winner is determined."

Justice David Souter, in a dissent joined by Justices Stephen Breyer, John Paul Stevens, and Ruth Bader Ginsburg, objected on grounds that the Court effectively usurped the state's ability to proceed under the opinions of its own court. He would have remanded the case with instructions to implement uniform standards. Justice Souter also regarded the December 12 deadline as artificial. In her dissent, joined by Justice Stevens, Justice Ginsburg maintained that even a flawed recount would be no less fair than the count that had been certified. Justice Breyer, joined by Justices Stevens, Souter, and Ginsburg, contended that the Court should not have taken the case, should not have entered the stay, and "should now vacate that stay and permit the Florida Supreme Court to decide whether the recount should resume."

The Court's decision was as highly controversial as the presidential election had been hotly contested. Critics maintain that the majority, for result-oriented reasons, departed from its usual aversion to intruding into state matters. They also note that the political process eventually would have resolved the outcome of the election (most likely in Bush's favor given the makeup of the House of Representatives). Allies of the majority maintain that the Court was right to intervene, because the Florida Court had strayed so far from constitutional markings. Although many detractors predicted a one-term presidency and Democratic Party resurgence, the 2004 election yielded President Bush's reelection coupled with even stronger Republican majorities in the House and Senate.

Bibliography

Richard Posner, *Breaking the Deadlock: The 2000 Election, the Constitution, and the Courts* (Princeton, NJ: Princeton University Press, 2001).

Cass Sunstein and Richard Epstein, eds., *The Vote: Bush, Gore, and the Supreme Court* (Chicago: University of Chicago Press, 2001).

IV

INDIVIDUAL RIGHTS AND LIBERTIES

The motivation for framing the United States Constitution was to establish a structure of governance. As the original states debated whether to ratify the Constitution, a key concern was with the dangers perceived in a centralized national government. Fear that concentrated power would imperil individual rights and freedoms generated a movement for a specification of rights and liberties that the federal government could not abridge. Although many of the framers and supporters of the Constitution believed that such an itemization was unnecessary, and that the political process itself would safeguard personal liberty, support for a Bill of Rights grew pursuant either to a sense of necessary or as a concession to secure ratification.

Although initially conceived as a check against federal power, the Bill of Rights in many instances has been made applicable to the states. This result has been achieved by the judiciary's determination that most provisions of the Bill of Rights are incorporated into the Fourteenth Amendment. In addition to being a vehicle for extending the reach of constitutionally enumerated rights and liberties, the Fourteenth Amendment has emerged as an independent source of fundamental rights. Constitutional review in the early twentieth century thus established economic liberty as a basic freedom that often defeated governmental efforts to regulate conditions in the workplace. Over the past few decades, the right of privacy has emerged as the basis for several protected interests including the freedom to procreate, elect an abortion, live as an extended family, marry, and decline medical treatment. It also has become a source of protection for sexual orientation.

Part IV commences with an examination of decisions concerning what many regard as the most fundamental liberty. Freedom of speech and freedom of the press traditionally have been regarded as the foundation of self-government. Without it, citizens would be impaired in their ability to make informed judgments and thus performance of their function as the ultimate power in a representative democracy. The First Amendment operates not only to guarantee expressive liberty but also to secure associational and religious freedom. The First Amendment cases are followed by a series of decisions related to the criminal justice system. These rulings implicate, respectively, the Fourth, Fifth, and Sixth Amendments. The final category of cases concerns fundamental rights that, although not specifically enumerated by the Constitution, nonetheless have been established as an incident of due process and judicial review.

CHAPTER 11

FIRST AMENDMENT: FREEDOM OF SPEECH (CONTENT REGULATION)

Freedom of speech has been referred to as the most essential liberty. As the Court put it *Palko v. Connecticut* (1937), expressive liberty is "the matrix, the indispensable condition of nearly every other form of freedom." This observation is consistent with a jurisprudential tradition that views freedom of speech as essential to informed self-government. The nation's first century included some significant abridgments of expressive freedom. Congress and the Adams administration in the late eighteenth century, for instance, enacted the Sedition Act, which essentially criminalized criticism of the president and legislature. This law was targeted at Jeffersonian critics who, upon being elected to power, turned the law against its architects. Antislavery literature generally was banned from the South prior to the Civil War. Despite this suppression, it was not until the twentieth century that the freedom of speech clause was reviewed by the Supreme Court.

The meaning of freedom of speech, like other constitutional guarantees, has evolved from debate over theory, values, and applications. Among the most eloquent statements with respect to the value of expressive freedom, and the need to tolerate and protect speech challenging the very foundations of the political system, is the concurring opinion of Justices Louis Brandeis and Oliver Wendell Holmes, Jr., in *Whitney v. California* (1927). As they put it, the framers "believed that freedom to think as you will and to speak as you think are means indispensable to the discovery and spread of political truth.... If there be time to expose through discussion the falsehood and fallacies, to avert the evil by the processes of education, the remedy to be applied is more speech, not enforced silence." In trumpeting the virtues of the marketplace of ideas, and the need for government to allow free competition among political views, ideologies, and programs, their views shaped a long-term meaning of expressive freedom in favor of individual rather than authoritative selection.

Perhaps the most straightforward theory was propounded by Justice Hugo Black, who described freedom of speech as an "absolute." Justice Black's understanding of the First Amendment was never embraced by the Court. Rather, it has adopted a more complex model of review that conditions freedom upon content, context, or regulatory purpose. Within the resulting hierarchy of expressive freedom, speech essential to informed self-government is the most protected. Less protected are commercial expression and certain types of defamatory speech. Some expression, such as obscenity and fighting words, is categorically excluded from the First Amendment's protective ambit.

TORTS

State law historically has established grounds for civil liability activity that constitutes a tort. Although most tort law does not implicate the Constitution, actions for defamation, invasion of privacy, and intentional infliction of emotional distress may operate at cross-purposes with freedom of speech. Libelous or slanderous expression, referred to collectively as defamation, traditionally has been viewed as valueless and thus unworthy of First Amendment protection. Early English law actually made criticism of the king or queen a capital offense. Even in colonial America, truth was an aggravating rather than mitigating factor. A key influence upon the eventual nature of defamation law was the civil rights movement during the middle of the twentieth century. In *New York Times Co. v. Sullivan* (1964), the Supreme Court reviewed an Alabama jury's award of damages to state officials who had been criticized in an editorial advertisement published in the *New York Times*. Realizing that politically motivated defamation actions could chill speech essential to informed self-government, the Court carved out a category of defamation for First Amendment protection. It thus adopted an "actual malice" standard that requires public officials to prove that an allegedly defamatory statement about them was made with knowledge of the falsehood or reckless disregard of the truth. The Court, in *Curtis Publishing Co. v. Butts* (1968), extended the actual malice standard to public figures. In *Gertz v. Robert Welch, Inc.* (1974), the Court determined that this criterion should be extended to private persons. It also adopted the actual malice standard, in *Hustler Magazine v. Falwell* (1988), to a public figure's claim of intentional infliction of emotional distress.

Gertz v. Robert Welch, Inc.

Citation: 418 U.S. 323.

Issue: Whether the actual malice standard in a defamation action extends beyond public officials and public figures to private persons.

Year of Decision: 1974.

Outcome: Private persons, unlike public officials and public figures, are not required to establish that a defamatory statement was made with actual malice.

Author of Opinion: Justice Lewis Powell.

Vote: 5-4.

Defamation is a form of expression that provides the basis for a claim on grounds it causes harm to reputation. Historically, it has been viewed as speech with slight social value and thus beyond the protective range of the First Amendment. Even libelous or slanderous speech, however, may add value to political discourse that advances informed self-governance. This understanding was embraced in *New York Times Co. v. Sullivan* (1964), when the Supreme Court established a higher standard of proof for public officials who brought defamation actions. The Court reached this outcome "against the background of a profound national commitment to the principle that debate on public issues should be uninhibited, robust, and wide-open and that it may well include vehement, caustic, and sometimes unpleasantly sharp attacks on government and public officials."

The actual malice standard, which requires public officials to prove that a defamatory statement was made with knowledge of the falsehood or reckless disregard of the truth, provides breathing space for freedom of speech that previously did not exist. The higher standard of proof for public officials was supported by a logic that had the potential to expand with respect to other persons or contexts. Soon after its decision in *New York Times Co. v. Sullivan*, the Court extended the actual malice standard to public figures. It characterized public figures, in *Curtis Publishing Co. v. Butts* (1968), as persons who are "intimately involved in the resolution of important public questions or [who], by reason of their fame, shape events in areas of concern to society at large." The rationale for equating public figures with public officials was that each had special relevance to the information marketplace and processes of informed self-governance.

The focus upon public officials and public figures established protection on the basis of an individual's status. To the extent the aim is to protect speech essential to informed self-government, there is a logical argument that expression should be protected on the basis of subject matter rather than personal function. In *Rosenbloom v. Metromedia, Inc.* (1971), four justices embraced this premise and extended the actual malice standard to "statements concerning matter[s] of general or public interest." Justice Hugo Black advocated an even stronger principle that freedom of speech was absolute, and thus defamation laws were barred entirely by the First Amendment. This position effectively prevented the public interest standard from becoming established as a governing principle. It did not end the process, however, of determining the outer boundaries of the actual malice standard. In *Gertz v. Robert Welch, Inc.* (1974), the Court revisited the scope of the actual malice standard and reverted to a focus upon the status of the person rather than the nature of the speech.

At issue was a defamation claim by an attorney (Elmer Gertz), who had brought a wrongful death action on behalf of a family whose son had been shot by a Chicago policeman. A periodical described Gertz as the "architect [of a] Communist frame-up" who also had an extensive police file. Key to the outcome of the case was whether Gertz was a public figure or whether the actual malice standard extended to public issues or private persons. Justice Lewis Powell, in a majority opinion, determined that the actual malice standard governed only public officials and public figures. Noting an inevitable tension between the interest of "vigorous and uninhibited" expression and the need to remedy reputational harm, the Court reaffirmed the importance of some "strategic protection" for defamatory speech. It could identify no basis, however, for correlating the actual malice standard to public interest or extending it to private persons. Its limits thus reached no further than public officials and those persons "who by reason of the notoriety of their achievements or the vigor and success with which they seek the public's attention are properly classified as public figures."

Requiring persons to prove that a statement was made with knowledge that it was false, or with reckless disregard of the truth, represented what the Court described as a "powerful antidote" to self-censorship. It also, as the Court put it, imposed "a correspondingly high price from the victims of defamatory falsehood." This increased burden was warranted, however, on grounds that public and nonpublic defamation plaintiffs are not similarly situated for First Amendment purposes. A key difference, for instance, is the relatively greater power of public persons to command the media's attention and tell his or her side of the story. Because public persons have greater access to the media than nonpublic persons, the Court believed that they "have a more realistic opportunity to counteract false statements than private individuals normally enjoy."

Significant too, in the Court's view, was the sense that public officials and figures by seeking government office or high profile positions assume the risk of public scrutiny. Whether as a political candidate or having achieved "especial prominence in the affairs of society," public persons "invite attention and comment." Although exceptions to these norms may exist, the Court reasoned that the "media are entitled to act on the assumption that public officials and public figures have voluntarily exposed themselves to increased risk of injury from defamatory falsehood concerning them." The same determination could not be made, at least from the Court's perspective, with respect to private individuals. Because they did not aspire to be in the public eye, by seeking public office or stature, they ceded no interest in their "good name." Being more vulnerable to reputational harm, as the Court saw it, private persons were more deserving of protection.

Separating public figures and private persons is not always an easy task. As the Court observed, public figures break down into three categories. The first is what the Court characterized as "involuntary public figures." Persons in this group are public figures through no intentional effort of their own. The involuntary public figure, as the Court described it, is an "exceedingly rare" category. The second category of public figures are persons who "occupy positions of such pervasive power and influence that they are deemed public figures for all purposes." The third category comprises those who "have thrust themselves to the forefront of particular public controversies in order to influence the resolution of the issues involved." The Court noted that this group represents the most common type of public figure. With these three possibilities for public figure status, the key question for the Court was whether Gertz fit into any of the categories.

Although Gertz had served on various government commissions and as an attorney was an officer of the Court, the Court found that he did not qualify as a public official for purposes of the action. Despite the official nature of Gertz' positions, the defamatory statements did not pertain to his government service. The Court also was reluctant to subject attorneys as a class to the actual malice standard. Nor did it view him as a public figure. In this regard, the Court specifically determined that he had not attained public figure status involuntarily, on the basis of pervasive power or influence, or by thrusting himself into a public controversy. Rather, the Court saw him as a private person whose claim accordingly was not governed by the actual malice standard. The bottom line was a rule that limits the actual malice standard to public official and public figures, but allows states the latitude to establish liability for defamation of private persons—so long as it is not imposed "without fault."

Justice Byron White, in a concurring opinion, criticized the Court for having struck what he viewed as an improvident balance. From his perspective, the media were powerful enough to assume liability for reputational harm to a private person whether or not a showing of fault had been made. Justice William Brennan dissented on grounds that the decision underserved First Amendment interests. Justice Brennan voiced concern with the risk of self-censorship when issues of public importance did not implicate public persons.

Case law in the aftermath of *Gertz* has construed the public figure concept narrowly. The Court, in *Time, Inc. v. Firestone* (1976), determined that a high profile Palm Beach socialite was not a public figure in the context of a divorce proceeding. At issue in this case was an article stating that her divorce had been granted on grounds of extreme cruelty and adultery. Despite the public process and the plaintiff's regular news conference, the Court determined that she was not an all-purpose public figure and had not voluntarily injected herself into "the forefront of any particular public controversy in order to influence the resolution of the issues involved in it." In *Wolston v. Reader's Digest Association* (1979), the Court determined that a public figure had become a private person over the course of time. In *Dun and Bradstreet, Inc. v. Greenmoss Builders, Inc.* (1985), the Court determined that the type of damages recoverable may turn upon whether the defamation touches upon a matter of public concern. In a concurring opinion, Justice White urged reconsideration of the actual malice standard. Central to his argument was a sense that constitutional protection of falsehood actually undermined First Amendment interests by distorting the information marketplace. At least in the context of public officials and public figures, the Court has continued to favor a free flow of information even if this stream carries some pollutants.

Bibliography

Richard Epstein, *Was New York Times v. Sullivan Wrong?* 53 *University of Chicago Law Review* 782 (1986). A critical perspective on the decision is provided.

Harry Kalven, *The New York Times Case: A Report on "The Central Meaning of the First Amendment,"* 1964 *Supreme Court Review* 191 (1964). This is a primary resource for understanding *New York Times Co. v. Sullivan.*

Hustler Magazine v. Falwell

Political satire has been a part of American political dialogue since the nation's founding. However, satire can sometimes be brutal and can inflict emotional distress on the subject. In such cases, there is a natural tension between the tort interest in providing compensation for mental and emotional distress and the constitutional right to freedom of speech.

Hustler Magazine v. Falwell presents this tension in dramatic relief. The Reverend Jerry Falwell was a nationally prominent minister who was "active as a commentator on politics and public affairs." He was the host of a nationally syndicated television show and the founder and president of a political group known as the "Moral Majority." He was also the founder of Liberty University in Lynchburg, Virginia, and he authored a number of books and publications. *Hustler Magazine,* Falwell's antagonist, was a pornographic magazine that frequently published relatively base material.

Citation: 485 U.S. 46.

Issue: Whether a "public figure" can recover damages for intentional infliction of mental and emotional distress when he suffers an outrageous parody (suggesting that he engaged in an incestuous relationship with his mother) in a pornographically oriented magazine.

Year of Decision: 1988.

Outcome: Parodies and satire are speech, within the meaning of the First Amendment, and no recovery is permitted unless the parody involves a false assertion of fact that the parodist knew was untrue or acted in reckless disregard for whether it was true or false.

Author of Opinion: Chief Justice William Rehnquist.

Vote: 9-0.

In 1983, *Hustler Magazine* decided to parody Falwell using a Campari Liqueur advertisement. The actual Campari ads portrayed interviews with various celebrities about their "first times." Although the advertisements actually focused on the first time that the celebrities had sampled Campari, the ads played on the double entendre of the first time that the interviewees had engaged in sex. *Hustler Magazine* mimicked the Campari format and created a fictional interview with Falwell in which he stated that his "first time" was during a drunken incestuous rendezvous with his mother in an outhouse. The Hustler parody was written in such a way as to suggest that Falwell is "a hypocrite who preaches only when he is drunk."

Falwell could not sue Hustler for defamation because that cause of action requires a false assertion of fact, and the magazine had not represented the ad parody as "fact." Indeed, at the bottom of the page, in small print, the ad contained the following disclaimed: "ad parody—not to be taken seriously." In addition, the magazine's table of contents flatly stated: "Fiction; Ad and Personality Parody." Because of the disclaimer and the table of contents, it was clear that the parody was false and therefore that there was no false assertion of fact.

Unable to bring a defamation suit, Falwell sued Hustler for intentional infliction of mental distress. A jury awarded Falwell compensatory damages of $100,000 and punitive damages of $50,000. The case eventually made its way to the United States Supreme Court where, in an opinion written by Chief Justice William Rehnquist, the Court reversed.

The Court phrased the issue as whether "a public figure may recover damages for emotional harm caused by the publication of an ad parody offensive to him, and doubtless gross and repugnant in the eyes of most." In answering that question in the negative, the Court emphasized that the First Amendment emphasizes the "fundamental importance" of allowing people to express themselves "on matters of public interest and concern." The Court also recognized that "robust political debate" is likely to result in speech that is critical of public officials and public figures who are "intimately involved in the resolution of important public questions or, by reason of their fame, shape events in areas of concern to society at large." Moreover, those who comment on public affairs are generally protected against liability. For example, when defamation is involved, the Court's landmark decision in *New York Times Co. v. Sullivan,* 376 U.S. 254 (1964), provided that public officials and public figures may not recover unless they can satisfy the actual malice standard. In other words, they must show that the statement was made "with knowledge that it was false or with reckless disregard of whether it was false or not."

Falwell argued that, in emotional distress cases, the courts should impose liability when speech subjects an individual to "severe emotional distress," and the "utterance was intended to inflict emotional distress, was outrageous, and did in fact inflict serious emotional distress." In such circumstances, in Falwell's view, courts should impose liability without regard to "whether the statement was a fact or an opinion, or whether it was true or false." In other words, the defendant's intent to cause injury is critical, and "the State's interest in preventing emotional harm simply outweighs whatever interest a speaker may have in speech of this type."

While the Court agreed that utterances designed to inflict emotional distress should not "receive much solicitude," the Court disagreed with Falwell. The Court noted that "many things done with motives that are less than admirable are protected by the First Amendment." Relying on its prior decision in *Garrison v. Louisiana,* 379 U.S. 64 (1964), the Court noted that, even when a speaker or writer is motivated by hatred or ill-will, his expression may be protected by the First Amendment. Otherwise, there might be a chilling effect on speech. The Court held that these principles apply with particular force to political cartoonists and satirists, recognizing that cartoons and satires have consistently played a significant role in political discussion since the very beginning of the country, and such cartoons were rarely fair and reasoned. For example, early cartoonists had portrayed George Washington as an ass. Moreover, cartoons are "often based on exploitation of unfortunate physical traits or politically embarrassing events—an exploitation often calculated to injure the feelings of the subject of the portrayal and attempt to bring "scorn and ridicule and satire" on the recipient. In the Court's view, such representations are "usually as welcome as a bee sting." But the Court emphasized the political importance of such satire noting Thomas Nast's sustained "graphic vendetta against William M. 'Boss' Tweed and his corrupt associates in New York City's 'Tweed Ring.'"

Falwell also argued that, even if political satire were generally acceptable, *Hustler's* caricature of him was so "outrageous" as to "distinguish it from more traditional political cartoons" and should be subject to liability. While the Court expressed distaste for *Hustler's* parody of Falwell, the Court doubted that it was possible to clearly differentiate between traditional political cartoons and more outrageous endeavors. In the Court's view, "outrageousness" in "the area of political and social discourse has an inherent subjectiveness about it which would allow a jury to impose liability on the basis of the jurors' tastes or views, or perhaps on the basis of their dislike of a particular expression." The Court expressed concern that damages would, therefore, be awarded simply "because the speech in question may have an adverse emotional impact on the audience."

As a result, the Court concluded that Falwell (and other public figures and public officials) may not recover for intentional infliction of emotional distress unless they can show that the publication contains a false statement of fact which was made with "actual malice," i.e., with knowledge that the statement was false or with reckless disregard as to whether or not it was true. However, since satire and cartoons almost always suggest that they are portraying fiction, this standard can almost never be met. The Court expressed concern that a lesser standard would not provide adequate "breathing space" for "the freedoms protected by the First Amendment." Since the ad parody did not involve assertions of actual facts, Falwell could not, consistently with the First Amendment, recover damages for Hustler's ad parody.

Falwell is an important decision for free speech in this country. It continues the Court's well-established tradition of providing a high level of protection for those who comment on public affairs, and makes it extremely difficult for politicians and public figures to recover against those who comment on their actions. It also provides protection for the long-established practice of political satire.

Bibliography

Robert C. Post, *The Constitutional Concept of Public Discourse: Outrageous Opinion, Democratic Deliberation, and Hustler Magazine v. Falwell,* 103 *Harvard Law Review* 603 (1990).

Jerome K. Skolnick, *The Sociological Tort of Defamation,* 74 *California Law Review* 677 (1986).

Rodney A. Smolla, *Jerry Falwell v. Larry Flynt: The First Amendment on Trial* (Urbana: University of Illinois Press, 1990).

Russell L. Weaver and Donald E. Lively, *Understanding the First Amendment* (Newark, NJ: LexisNexis, 2003), 64–69.

OBSCENITY

Obscene expression, like defamation, traditionally has been categorically unprotected by the First Amendment. At the time of the nation's founding, state laws prohibiting vulgar, profane, and obscene expression were commonplace. Federal regulation of obscenity traces back to the *Comstock Act of 1875,* which criminalized dissemination of obscenity through the mail. In its seminal decision on obscenity, *Roth v. United States* (1957), the Supreme Court held that the social value of obscenity was too slight to deserve First Amendment protection. Despite its consistency on this point, the Court has found itself challenged in trying to define obscenity. Reflecting the exasperation experienced by the Court in trying to capture obscenity in an objectifiable manner was Justice Potter Stewart's observation, in *Jacobellis v. Ohio* (1964) that, even if he could not describe obscenity, "I know it when I see it." After years of frustration, the Court in *Miller v. California* (1973) set forth a framework for defining and determining obscenity. In *New York v. Ferber* (1982), the Court determined that child pornography, even if not obscene under *Miller,* could be categorically prohibited without offense to the First Amendment.

Miller v. California

Citation: 413 U.S. 15.

Issue: Whether expression must be utterly lacking in redeeming social value to be found obscene.

Year of Decision: 1973.

Outcome: The state is not obligated to demonstrate that allegedly obscene material is "utterly without redeeming social value."

Author of Opinion: Chief Justice Earl Warren.

Vote: 5-4.

Obscene expression is entirely without First Amendment protection. This outcast status was established by the Supreme Court's decision, in *Roth v. United States* (1957), when it determined that obscenity had "slight, if any, value." The Court's decision to place obscenity outside the boundaries of constitutionally protected expression has eliminated virtually any barrier to regulating it. It has not, however, foreclosed continuing controversy and litigation. Even though obscenity is not sheltered by the First Amendment, constitutionally significant problems arise in relationship to it. Foremost among these difficulties is the challenge of defining obscenity.

The vexing nature of this problem quickly manifested itself in the aftermath of the *Roth* decision. For more than a decade, the Court struggled to develop a consensus for determining whether expression was obscene. Justice Potter Stewart effectively captured the nature of the task when he suggested that efforts to capture the meaning of obscenity required "trying to define what may be undefinable." Expressing his sense of futility with attempts to define obscenity, Justice Stewart operated on the premise that "I know it when I see it."

In *Memoirs v. Massachusetts* (1966), three justices advocated a test that would require the government to establish:

> that (a) the dominant theme of the material taken as a whole appeals to a prurient interest in sex; (b) the material is patently offensive because it affronts contemporary community standards relating to the description of representation of sexual matters; and (c) the material is utterly without redeeming social value.

As the Court continued to decide obscenity cases without a precise and settled definition, it increasingly was subject to criticism that it was operating without a standard. Chief Justice Warren Burger described the Court's function essentially as "an unreviewable board of censorship for the 50 states, subjectively judging each piece of material brought before us." Against this backdrop, and to reduce the "strain" of a steady flow of obscenity cases into the judicial system, the Court attempted to resolve the definitional problem. The case that led to a majority rule in this regard was *Miller v. California* (1973). In this case, the Court reviewed a criminal conviction based upon mailing advertisements "very explicitly depicting men and women in groups of two or more engaging in a variety of sexual activities, with genitals often prominently displayed." Charges were based upon a California law prohibiting the knowing distribution of obscene materials.

Chief Justice Warren Burger commenced his opinion for a majority of the Court with the premise that state regulation of obscenity "must be carefully limited" and confined "to works which depict or describe sexual conduct." Consistent with this premise, Chief Justice Burger noted that the proscribed conduct must be defined specifically. He then proceeded to announce a definition of obscenity covering "works which, taken as a whole, appeal to the prurient interest in sex, which portray sexual conduct in a patently offensive way, and which, taken as a whole, do not have serious literary, artistic, political, or scientific value." This definition was coupled with guidelines that would aid juries in applying it. The definition of "prurient interest," for example, should be developed from the perspective of "the average person, applying contemporary community standards." Whether a work was patently offensive should be assessed in conjunction with legislation that "specifically defined" the relevant sexual conduct. It also abandoned an inquiry into whether a work was "utterly without redeeming social value" into a determination of whether taken as a whole it "lacked serious literary, artistic, political, or scientific value."

Disclaiming any "function to propose regulatory schemes for the States," the Court stated that the states themselves have the responsibility for specifically defining the type of sexual expression that could be prohibited. Even so, it offered a model regulation that states could use to satisfy the specificity requirement. Pursuant to the Court's formula, portrayal of sexual conduct could be prohibited by specific language barring "[p]atently offensive representations or descriptions of ultimate sexual acts, normal or perverted, actual or simulated" and "[p]atently offensive representation of descriptions of masturbation, excretory functions, and lewd exhibition of the genitals." A critical aspect of the majority's opinion was that "[s]ex and nudity may not be exploited without limit by films and pictures." At a minimum, therefore, prurient and patently offensive depictions of sexual conduct must have serious literary, artistic, political, or scientific value to receive First Amendment protection. An easy example of protected expression in this context would be "medical books for the education of physicians." Despite their "graphic illustrations and descriptions of human anatomy," these publications have obvious scientific value. Arguably, they also do not appeal to the prurient interest and do not contain patently offensive representations of sexual acts or other specifically described sexual conduct.

Use of contemporary community standards, for purposes of assessing prurient interest and patent offensiveness, represented an effort by the Court to move the question of obscenity from a national to a local forum. It also reflected a sense that a universal standard for determining obscenity is difficult in a society that is "too big and too diverse." The Court accordingly concluded that it could not establish a constitutional standard requiring "that the people of Maine or Mississippi accept public depiction of conduct found tolerable in Las Vegas, or New York City." The Court's new model thus was informed by an understanding that "[p]eople in different States vary in their tastes and attitudes, and this diversity is not to be strangled by the absolutism of imposed uniformity." Responding to concern that it was embracing a standard of "repression," the Court maintained that prohibition of obscenity historically had not burdened serious literary, artistic, political, or scientific expression. Given what it saw as the First Amendment's concern with speech critical to informed self-governance, the Court saw no risk that political liberty would be compromised by state efforts to regulate "commercial exploitation of human interest in sex." Rather, the Court concluded that assigning value to obscenity would cheapen "the grand conception of the First Amendment and its high purposes in the historic struggle for freedom."

Despite describing the majority's opinion as "earnest and well intentioned," Justice William O. Douglas reiterated his sense that the First Amendment was an absolute barrier against content-based regulation. From his perspective, the First Amendment unconditionally protected speech and precluded the Court's removal of some speech from its protective reach. Given the operation of the First Amendment as he viewed it, Justice Douglas argued that no "regime of censorship" could be implemented except "by constitutional amendment after full debate by the people." He also found it "astounding" that a judge or jury could punish ideas on grounds they are offensive. This capacity, as Justice Douglas saw it, was "a sharp and radical break with the traditions of a free society" which keep debate open to "offensive" as well as "staid" people. Even if the expression might be described as "garbage," Justice Douglas observed that "so is much of what is said in political campaigns, in the daily press, on TV, or over the radio." In this regard, Justice Douglas's main concern was with the potential for expanding power to regulate speech based upon its capacity to offend. Justice Douglas concluded that judges are without constitutional power to define obscenity, and despite its definitional efforts, still had no guidelines "except our own predilections."

Justice William Brennan, who authored the majority opinion in *Roth* finding that obscenity was constitutionally unprotected, concluded that the Court's case law had become demonstrably misconceived. As he viewed it, the problem of defining obscenity was too great and the constitutional costs of applying vague standards too high. Justice Brennan, in repudiating his original position and the majority's current thinking, suggested that obscenity concerns should be restricted to instances when the interests of children and nonconsenting adults were present.

Despite the dissenting views, the *Miller* decision is a cornerstone of modern obscenity law. Despite the *Miller* Court's objective, the problem of constructing a precise definition of obscenity remains. Justice Antonin Scalia has suggested that "[j]ust as there is no use arguing about taste, there is no use litigating about it." Despite persisting concern that the Court has foreclosed constitutional inquiry in the context of obscenity, some theorists have advocated restrictive regime based not upon obscenity's lack of value but upon the harm that it causes to women. In the 1980s, several communities adopted ordinances pursuant to the premise that pornography facilitates the subordination of women by characterizing them as sex objects and reinforcing harmful ways of viewing women. In striking down an Indianapolis ordinance structured on this premise, a federal appeals court in *American Booksellers, Inc. v. Hudnut* (1985) determined that freedom of speech assumes the risk that insidious expression may "influence the culture and shape our socialization." It further noted that "if a process of [cultural] conditioning were enough to permit governmental regulation, that would be the end of freedom of speech." Despite dissatisfaction from both proponents and opponents of obscenity regulation, the Court's decision in *Miller* has survived the challenges and appears to have evolved doctrine from a very uncertain to a settled status.

Bibliography

Literature exploring the possible relationship between pornography and violence or harm to women includes Susan Brownmiller, *Against Our Will: Men, Women and Rape* (New York: Bantam Books, 1976); Richard Posner, *Sex and Reason* (Cambridge, MA: Harvard University Press, 1992); Frederick Schauer, "Causation Theory and the Cases of Sexual Violence," *American Bar Foundation Research Journal* 737 (1987). The notion that women's interests may be accounted more effectively by allowing rather than prohibiting pornography is advanced in Nadine Strossen, *Defending Pornography* (New York: Scribner, 1995).

A few years before the *Miller* case, a federal panel concluded that there was no connection between obscenity and antisocial behavior. "Report of the Commission on Obscenity and Pornography" (1970). This finding was challenged by a subsequent federal study that identified a linkage between pornography and aggression toward women. "Report of the Attorney General's Commission on Pornography" (1986).

New York v. Ferber

Although the First Amendment provides broad protection for freedom of speech, there has been much dispute about whether its protections are "absolute" or "qualified." Justice Black, the leading proponent of the absolutist position, argued in *Konigsberg v. State Bar of California,* 366 U.S. 36 (1961), that the "unequivocal command that there shall be no abridgement of the rights of free speech and assembly shows that [those] who drafted our Bill of Rights did all the 'balancing' that was to be done in this field. [The] very object of adopting the First Amendment [was] to put the freedoms protected there completely out of the area of any congressional control that may be attempted through the exercise of precisely those powers that are now being used to 'balance' the Bill of Rights out of existence." Justice Oliver Wendell Holmes disagreed and offered his now famous statement that "[t]he most stringent protection of free speech would not protect a man in falsely shouting fire in a theater and causing a panic." *See Schenck v. United States,* 249 U.S. 47 (1919). Justice Holmes's position ultimately prevailed in the United States Supreme Court.

Citation: 458 U.S. 747.

Issue: Whether child pornography (e.g., depictions of children engaged in sexual conduct) that is not necessarily obscene can be prohibited consistently with the First Amendment to the United States Constitution.

Year of Decision: 1982.

Outcome: Child pornography fits in a category of speech that derives no protection under the First Amendment because of the harm to, and exploitation of, children in its production.

Author of Opinion: Justice Byron White.

Vote: 9-0.

Once the Court recognized that First Amendment protections were not absolute, the Court then focused on whether particular categories of speech fall outside the parameters of constitutional protection. In *Chaplinsky v. New Hampshire,* 315 U.S. 568 (1942), the Court held that there are "certain well-defined and narrowly limited *classes* of speech, the prevention and punishment of which have never been thought to raise any Constitutional problem. These include the lewd and obscene, the profane, the libelous, and the insulting or 'fighting' words...." While the Court no longer treats all of the *Chaplinsky* classifications as beyond constitutional protection (e.g., defamatory speech is now protected), the Court continues to hold that certain categories of speech receive no constitutional protection.

New York v. Ferber concerns one category of unprotected speech: child pornography. *Ferber* involved a New York criminal statute that prohibited persons from knowingly promoting sexual performances by children under the age of 16 through the distribution of such performances. The law was passed in an effort to combat the exploitive use of children in the production of pornography, and applied to both obscene and nonobscene depictions of child pornography. Violations could be prosecuted as class D felonies.

The case arose when Paul Ferber, the proprietor of a Manhattan bookstore specializing in sexually oriented products, sold two films to an undercover police officer that depicted young boys masturbating. Although Ferber was acquitted of possessing obscene materials, he was convicted for possession of nonobscene child pornography. In upholding Ferber's conviction, the United States Supreme Court emphasized that the states have a "compelling" interest in "safeguarding the physical and psychological well-being" of minors, and that the New York law was based on concerns about such exploitation and the proliferation of sexual performances that exploit children. The Court refused to "second-guess this legislative judgment."

In reaching its decision, the Court found that the "distribution of photographs and films depicting sexual activity by juveniles is intrinsically related to the sexual abuse of children in at least two ways." First, the materials themselves constitute a "permanent record of the children's participation, and the harm to the child is exacerbated by their circulation." Second, the "distribution network for child pornography must be closed if the production of material which requires the sexual exploitation of children is to be effectively controlled." The Court found that the "most expeditious if not the only practical method of law enforcement may be to dry up the market for this material by imposing severe criminal penalties on persons selling, advertising, or otherwise promoting the product."

The Court concluded that the state could not be limited to simply prosecuting those who distribute materials that are legally obscene, because children could be harmed physically or psychologically even by the production of nonobscene works. Moreover, the Court concluded that there was an economic motive for the production.

The Court also concluded that, in the hierarchy of free speech values, the value of child pornography (which the Court defined as "lewd sexual conduct") was "*de minimis.*" While the Court conceded that there might be instances in which depictions of children "performing sexual acts or lewdly exhibiting their genitals" might form an "important and necessary part of a literary performance or scientific or educational work," the Court doubted whether this would often be so. Moreover, the Court noted that, if such representation were an "important and necessary" part of a performance, an older person (who appeared younger) could be used in place of a child.

The Court did not hold child pornography was entitled to no protection under the First Amendment. On the contrary, the Court flatly stated that, in order to have a valid prohibition, the "conduct to be prohibited must be adequately defined by the applicable state law, as written or authoritatively construed," that a valid statute must be limited to visual depictions of sexual conduct of children below a specified age, and that the definition of sexual conduct must be "suitably limited and described." Finally, a valid statute must contain an element of scienter. Finally, Court reaffirmed the proposition that other depictions of sexual conduct retain First Amendment protection.

Ferber produced a couple of major concurrences. Justice Sandra Day O'Connor argued that the state has a compelling interest in prohibiting child pornography that might allow it to ban child pornography regardless of its social value. However, she would have exempted "depictions that do not actually threaten the harms identified by the Court including clinical pictures of sexuality, such as those that might appear in medical textbooks, if they do not involve sexual exploitation and abuse." She also argued that "pictures of children engaged in rites widely approved by their cultures, such as those that might appear in issues of the National Geographic, might not trigger the compelling interests identified by the Court." Justice Brennan, joined by Justice Thurgood Marshall, also concurred arguing that the "State has a special interest in protecting the well-being of its youth" and states should have leeway in their regulation unless a depiction has "serious literary, artistic, scientific, or medical value." He viewed child pornography as one of those "limited classes of speech, the suppression of which does not raise serious First Amendment concerns" since it has "slight social value" and since the State has a compelling interest in regulation. However, he distinguished child pornography from "serious contributions" to art, literature, and science."

Ferber is a significant contribution to First Amendment jurisprudence. *Ferber* reaffirms *Chaplinsky's* conclusion that certain categories of speech deserve no constitutional protection, and *Ferber* creates a new category of unprotected speech, child pornography.

Bibliography

Susan G. Caughlan, *Private Possession of Child Pornography: The Tensions Between Stanley v. Georgia and New York v. Ferber*, 29 *William and Mary Law Review* 187 (1987).

William Green, *Children and Pornography: An Interest Analysis in System Perspective,* 19 *Valparaiso University Law Review* 441 (1985).

Frederick Schauer, *Codifying the First Amendment: New York v. Ferber,* 1982 *Supreme Court Review* 285 (1982).

Russell L. Weaver and Donald E. Lively, *Understanding the First Amendment* (Newark, NJ: LexisNexis, 2003), 64–70.

FIGHTING WORDS

First Amendment jurisprudence reflects an understanding that freedom of speech is not an absolute guarantee. Expressive liberty can be abridged on a case-by-case basis when the reasons for regulating it outweigh the freedom interest or categorically when the speech itself possesses inadequate societal value. Obscenity is a primary example of speech that, because it is perceived as mostly valueless, categorically implicates little if any constitutional concern. Another form of expression that is denied First Amendment protection on a categorical basis is "fighting words." The Court, in *Chaplinsky v. New Hampshire* (1942), described fighting words as expression "which by [its] very utterance inflict[s] injury or tend[s] to incite an immediate breach of peace." Like obscenity, fighting words are regarded as inessential to "the exposition of ideas" and having "such slight social value as a step to truth that any benefit which may be derived from them is clearly outweighed by the social interest in order and morality." Also like obscenity, fighting words are difficult to define. Consistent with this reality, the Court has tended to resolve cases on grounds that the pertinent regulation is vague or overbroad. It also has resisted efforts to convert fighting words doctrine into a means of regulating speech that is merely offensive. In *Cohen v. California* (1971), the Court determined that the wearing of a jacket that had "Fuck the Draft" emblazoned may have been offensive. Minus the tendency to induce violent reaction, however, the speech could not be characterized as fighting words. The notion that fighting words are constitutionally unprotected has become subject to at least one significant qualification. In *R.A.V. v. City of St. Paul* (1992), the Court held that the state could not regulate fighting words on a selective basis. Prohibition based upon whether government agreed or disagreed with an underlying political or social view thus represented an unconstitutional exercise in viewpoint discrimination. In *Virginia v. Black* (2002), the Court upheld a state law that criminalized cross burning. Although cross burning is a form of expressive activity, the Court found that it could be singled out for regulatory purposes because it represented a "true threat" of violence.

R.A.V. v. City of St. Paul

A primary driver of expanded First Amendment freedom has been the civil rights movement. As protests and demonstrations spread throughout the South during the 1950s and 1960s, states responded with a variety of measures designed to curb expressive activity. These methods included arrests for disturbing the peace,

Citation: 505 U.S. 337.

Issue: Whether an ordinance prohibiting symbols that "arouse anger, alarm or resentment in others on the basis of race, color creed, religion, or gender" violates the First Amendment.

Year of Decision: 1992.

Outcome: The ordinance discriminates on the basis of content and viewpoint and thus violates the First Amendment.

Vote: 9-0.

censorship, arbitrary processes that denied permits for public demonstrations, mandatory disclosure of membership lists of civil rights organizations, and aggressive use of defamation laws. In each of these contexts, First Amendment case law was developed in ways that provided space and opportunity for the civil rights agenda to be heard. So close was the linkage between the civil rights movement and expanded First Amendment freedom that a noted constitutional scholar, Harry Kalven, Jr., credited "the Negro with reclaiming the First Amendment freedom of all Americans."

Notwithstanding the historic relationship between freedom of speech and civil rights, some advocates by the 1980s began to assert that expressive liberty was not always compatible with or facilitative of equality interests. To the contrary, they maintained that speech which disparages persons on the basis of their group status actually is inimical to and undermines those concerns. Consistent with the sense that hate speech represents a verbal assault that harms its victims, many institutions and communities adopted codes that prohibited and punished such expression. Those who favor regulation of hate speech describe it as an "instantaneous slap in the face" that causes immediate and significant injury. Traditional First Amendment principles favor reliance on the marketplace of ideas to put any single viewpoint into perspective. Advocates of hate speech control, however, maintain that hate speech is not motivated by an interest in dialogue or searching for the truth, and the harm it causes is not ameliorated by discussion. They thus view it as an "implement" of racism that "reinforc[es] conditions of domination."

In response to arguments that hate speech diminishes and marginalizes its victims, critics maintain that its regulation chills some important expression and fails to account effectively for equality interests. These competing perspectives eventually came before the Supreme Court in a case concerning a St. Paul, Minnesota, hate speech ordinance. The measure provided that "anyone placing a symbol or object such as a swastika or burning cross on public or private property, with reason to know it would cause anger, alarm or resentment on grounds of race, religion, color, creed or gender, is guilty of disorderly conduct." At issue specifically was its use as the basis for convicting several teenagers who had burned a cross in the yard of an African-American family. The Minnesota Supreme Court upheld the ordinance on grounds it targeted fighting words only and thus regulated a category of expression that was not constitutionally protected.

Justice Antonin Scalia, writing for the majority in *R.A.V. v. City of St. Paul* (1992), reversed the state supreme court's decision. Although acknowledging that the expression constituted fighting words, he noted unacceptable risks in allowing government to single out certain types of offending or objection speech for regulation—even if the expression fit into an unprotected category. A key aspect of the decision, therefore, was the Court's determination that traditionally unprotected speech is not "entirely invisible to the Constitution." Even if fighting words may be categorically prohibited for content reasons, the Court concluded that government may not regulate within the category on a selective basis. As the Court put it, government "may not regulate use based on hostility C or favoritism C toward the underlying message expressed."

This determination thus established a constitutional interest in speech that historically has been denied any constitutional protection.

The Court's gloss on categorically unprotected speech evidenced concern with the consequences of excluding some thoughts and views from the marketplace of ideas. Minus indications that government is favoring a particular view or burdening one that it dislikes, the Court indicated that some selective regulation of offensive expression may be permissible. For purposes of the St. Paul case, however, the majority was concerned that the city was favoring a particular viewpoint. This perception was supported by the law's concern with a narrow range of speech that had the potential to insult or provoke violence. Left untouched by the regulation were other forms of expression "containing abusive invective, no matter how vicious or severe." Referencing the ordinance's selective focus, the Court determined that the city unconstitutionally had "impose[d] special prohibitions on those speakers who express views on disfavored subjects." The Court also viewed the law as an unconstitutional means for advancing the city's preferred viewpoint. An interest in tolerance and equality accordingly may not be the basis for denying expressive freedom to those with a contrary agenda. Allowing members of one group to trade in fighting words, while prohibiting their usage by another, is impermissible. The Court thus found that the city could not "license one side of a debate to fight freestyle, while requiring the other to follow Marquis of Queensbury rules."

Although striking down the ordinance, the Court recognized a community's interest in reckoning with racist behavior and beliefs. The St. Paul ordinance failed, however, because it disregarded the First Amendment's hostility toward regulation constituting a "selective limitation upon speech." The Court stressed that fighting words are categorically excluded from the First Amendment's protection, not because they communicate a particular idea, but because they represent "a particularly intolerable (and socially unnecessary) mode of expressing whatever idea the speaker wishes to convey." Because the city had not identified a "particularly intolerable" mode of fighting words, and regulated on a selective basis, the Court concluded that the enactment aimed "to handicap the expression of particular ideas."

The city had hoped for a different result on grounds the law accounted for some compelling interests, including an effective accounting for "the basic human rights of members of groups that have historically been subjected to discrimination, including the right of such group members to live in peace where they wish." The Court did not reject the proposition that the city's interest was compelling. Rather, it determined that the city could not discriminate on the basis of speech content to achieve the desired objective. Singling out a specific subset of bias or prejudice, from the Court's perspective, "is precisely what the First Amendment forbids." The city thus was left in a position where it could account for its interest but not by regulation that was selective in its application.

In a concurring opinion joined by three others, Justice Byron White, maintained that the Court had complicated an otherwise simple case and proposition. He would have invalidated the ordinance on grounds "it criminalized not only unprotected expression but expression protected by the First Amendment." Justice White also found it risky to deny First Amendment status to speech that caused generalized reactions such as "anger, alarm or resentment." As he put it, the capacity of speech to cause "hurt feelings, offense, or resentment" does not render it unprotected.

Justice Harry Blackmun, in a separate concurring opinion, expressed "fear that the Court has been distracted from its proper mission by the temptation to decide the issue over 'politically correct speech' and 'cultural diversity.'" From his perspective, neither of these factors was relevant to the case. Rather, Justice Blackmun viewed the Court's opinion as a manipulative exercise that enabled it to avoid the reality that some fighting words are more harmful than others. He would have permitted lawmakers to single out fighting words reflecting racial prejudice for special regulatory attention. As he put it, First Amendment interests would not be undermined by a law that prohibited "hoodlums from driving minorities out of their homes by burning crosses on their lawns." Justice Blackmun agreed with Justice White, however, that the St. Paul law was constitutionally overbroad because its reach extended beyond fighting words.

The Court's decision invalidated the city's regulation of speech motivated by racial prejudice. In *Wisconsin v. Mitchell* (1993), however, the Court upheld a state law that increased the punishment for certain crimes driven by racial animus. The *Mitchell* ruling thus limited the *R.A.V.* principle to viewpoint selective regulation of unprotected expression. Whether a differentiation between racist speech and racist conduct is sensible remains a subject of debate. Both sides, and the Court itself, would agree that racist expression is a source of harm to persons who are members of groups that historically have been disadvantaged. The consensus breaks down, however, when the issue is how to remedy such injury. Advocates of speech control maintain that racist speech undermines equality, while opponents contend that regulation underestimates the utility of expressive freedom in accounting for this interest.

Bibliography

Henry Louis Gates, Jr., Anthony P. Griffin, Donald E. Lively, Robert C. Post, William R. Rubinstein, and Nadine Strossen, *Speaking of Race, Speaking of Sex* (New York: New York University Press, 1994). A collection of essays arguing against hate speech regulation is provided.

Mari Matsuda, Charles R. Lawrence III, Richard Delgado, and Kimberle Crenshaw, *Words That Wound* (Boulder, CO: Westview Press, 1993). This sets forth support for hate speech regulation as a means of actualizing equality interests.

Martin Redish, *Freedom of Thought as Freedom of Expression: Hate Crime Sentencing Enhancement and First Amendment Theory,* 1992 *Criminal Justice Ethics* 29 (1992). The logic of differentiating punishment on the basis of whether a crime was motivated by race is examined.

Virginia v. Black

Citation: 538 U.S. 343.

Issue: Whether cross burning can be criminalized.

Year of Decision: 2003.

Outcome: Cross burning can be prohibited when it reflects an intent to intimidate.

Author of Opinion: Justice Sandra Day O'Connor.

Vote: 9-0.

So-called "hate speech" has generated considerable litigation and controversy in recent years. In general, legislation regulating or proscribing hate speech has the salutary objective of protecting minorities and others who are the targets of such speech. At the same time, whenever government attempts to regulate the content of public discourse, legitimate fears arise regarding the wisdom and propriety of governmental intervention. Historically, when government has been able to regulate speech, it has used that power to prohibit unpopular or objectionable viewpoints.

The Court's prior decision in *R.A.V. v. City of St. Paul,* 505 U.S. 377 (1992), involved a St. Paul, Minnesota, ordinance that prohibited the placement of symbols "which one knows or has reasonable grounds to know arouses anger, alarm or resentment in others on the basis of race, color, creed, religion or gender." When the ordinance was used to prosecute teenagers who assembled a crudely made cross and burned it in the front yard of a black family that lived across the street, the Court struck the ordinance down on the basis that the government was discriminating against the teenager's speech based on its content. The Court held that the "First Amendment does not permit St. Paul to impose special prohibitions on those speakers who express views on disfavored subjects." The Court also held that the St. Paul ordinance involved "viewpoint discrimination." In other words, in addressing the topics prohibited by the ordinance, "fighting words" could be used "*in favor* of racial, color, etc., tolerance and equality, but could not be used by those speakers' opponents." The Court offered the following example of how the ordinance applied: one could hold up a sign saying, for example, that all "anti-Catholic bigots" are misbegotten, but not that all "papists" are, for that would insult and provoke violence "on the basis of religion." The Court concluded that "St. Paul has no such authority to license one side of a debate to fight freestyle, while requiring the other to follow Marquis of Queensberry rules."

One argument offered by the City of St. Paul was that the ordinance could be justified by compelling state interests in helping "to ensure the basic human rights of members of groups that have historically been subjected to discrimination, including the right of such group members to live in peace where they wish." While the Court agreed that these interests were compelling, it concluded that the City must achieve its objective without censorship except as "*necessary* to serve the asserted [compelling] interest." The Court concluded that the City of St. Paul could respond to cross burning with content-neutral alternatives. For example, it could punish cross burners under content-neutral arson and trespass statutes. In addition, the City could respond with speech encouraging tolerance.

The question of cross burning came back to the Court in the *Black* case. That case involved a Virginia statute that made it illegal to burn a cross "with the intent of intimidating any person or group of persons." The statute also provided that "Any such burning of a cross shall be prima facie evidence of an intent to intimidate a person or group of persons."

Black involved two separate and distinct convictions for violating the cross-burning statute. In the first, Barry Black led a Ku Klux Klan (KKK) rally in Virginia at which a cross was burned on private property. Onlookers testified that speakers talked "real bad about the blacks and the Mexicans," and one speaker stated that "he would love to take a .30/.30 and just random[ly] shoot the blacks." An onlooker testified that the cross burning made her feel "awful" and "terrible." The second incident involved three individuals (Elliott, O'Mara, and a third person) who tried to burn a cross in the yard of James Jubilee, an African-American who lived next door to Elliott. Prior to the cross burning, Jubilee had spoken to Elliott's mother inquiring about some gunfire behind Elliott's home, and it appears that the cross was burned to "get back" at Jubilee for complaining about the shooting. After seeing the cross, Jubilee was "very nervous" because he "didn't know what would be the next phase," and because "a cross burned in your yard ... tells you that it's just the first round."

In reviewing the convictions, the Court noted that burning crosses had been used for various purposes throughout history (e.g., Scottish tribes that used them to signal a call to arms in the fourteenth century). However, in the United States, burning crosses have long been associated with the KKK, which viewed itself as a group of heroes "saving" the South from blacks and the "horrors" of Reconstruction. During the twentieth century, the KKK used violence as an elemental part of its strategy, including murders, floggings, and tar-and-featherings. When cross burnings were directed at particular persons not affiliated with the Klan, the burning cross often involved a "message of intimidation," designed to place the victim in fear of bodily harm. Moreover, because of the KKK's past, "the possibility of injury or death was not just hypothetical." On the contrary, the burning cross conveyed a "serious threat, meant to coerce the victim to comply with the Klan's wishes unless the victim was willing to risk the wrath of the Klan."

In upholding Virginia's cross burning statute, the Court began by recognizing that cross burning can constitute symbolic or expressive speech. However, the Court concluded that the Commonwealth of Virginia could regulate some categories of speech notwithstanding their expressive conduct including "fighting words." The Court concluded that cross burning fit within a category of speech referred to as "true threats"—statements where the speaker communicates an intent to "commit an act of unlawful violence to a particular individual or group of individuals." The Court held that it did not matter whether the speaker actually intended to carry out the threat because the prohibition on true threats protects people from the "fear of violence" and "from the disruption that fear engenders," in addition to protecting them against "the possibility that the threatened violence will occur." The Court viewed cross burning as fitting within the scope of a true threat because "cross burning is often intimidating, intended to create a pervasive fear in victims that they are a target of violence."

The Court rejected the argument that *R.A.V.* required invalidation of the Virginia statute as a content-based restriction on speech. In this regard, it noted that *R.A.V.* did not preclude regulation of "*all* forms of content-based discrimination within a proscribable area of speech." On the contrary, when the basis for the "content discrimination consists entirely of the very reason the entire class of speech at issue is proscribable, no significant danger of idea or viewpoint discrimination exists." Consequently, while *R.A.V.* held that a state may not ban only obscenity based on "offensive *political* messages," or "only those threats against the President that mention his policy on aid to inner cities," the First Amendment permits content discrimination "based on the very reasons why the particular class of speech at issue is prohibitable." The Court viewed cross burning as outside First Amendment protections "because burning a cross is a particularly virulent form of intimidation" given its "long and pernicious history as a signal of impending violence." As a result, "just as a State may regulate only that obscenity which is the most obscene due to its prurient content, so too may a State choose to prohibit only those forms of intimidation that are most likely to inspire fear of bodily harm." The Court went on to emphasize that Virginia's statute did not single out speech directed toward "one of the specified disfavored topics." Moreover, it did not matter whether an individual burns a cross with intent to intimidate because of the victim's race, gender, or religion or because of the victim's "political affiliation, union membership, or homosexuality."

The Court did hold that the "prima facie" evidence portion of Virginia's statute was unconstitutional because it provided that "[a]ny such burning of a cross shall be prima facie evidence of an intent to intimidate a person or group of persons." Va. Code Ann. § 18.2-423 (1996). The Court concluded that the provision permits the Commonwealth to arrest, prosecute, and convict a person based solely on the fact of cross burning itself. The Court concluded that "the provision as so interpreted would create an unacceptable risk of the suppression of ideas." The Court noted that, while a cross burning might involve an attempt to intimidate, it might also involve core political speech. As a result, the Court found that the "provision chills constitutionally protected political speech" by creating a presumption of conviction.

Justice David Souter concurred in part and dissented in part. He agreed with the Court that the Virginia law created a content-based distinction, but he would have applied *R.A.V.* and struck down the law. He feared that the government may have singled out cross burning because "of disapproval of its message of white supremacy, either because a legislature thought white supremacy was a pernicious doctrine or because it found that dramatic, public espousal of it was a civic embarrassment."

Justice Clarence Thomas also dissented. He agreed that it is constitutionally permissible to "ban cross burning carried out with intent to intimidate," but he would even have upheld the prima facie evidence provision noting that "Virginia law still requires the jury to find the existence of each element, including intent to intimidate, beyond a reasonable doubt." He went on to note that cross burning subjects its targets, and, sometimes, an unintended audience, to extreme emotional distress and is virtually never viewed merely as "unwanted communication."

In evaluating *Black,* it is important to realize that the decision did not (as some media accounts suggested) allow states to summarily prohibit all cross burnings. The Court held that Virginia could prohibit only those cross burnings that conveyed a message of violence and intimidation. Consistent with this holding, the Court reversed Black's conviction and dismissed the case against him. Although he burnt a cross in a field, there was no evidence of a direct and imminent threat against any specific person. In this respect, *Black* was consistent with the Court's prior decision in *Brandenburg v. Ohio,* which suggested that cross burners at KKK rallies could not be prosecuted for illegal advocacy unless it could be shown that they intended to produce imminent lawless conduct and that their message was likely to produce such imminent lawless conduct.

Whether *Black* will have much precedential impact outside the cross-burning area is debatable. The decision contains an extensive analysis of cross burning and links that history to violence and intimidation. However, in rendering its decision, the Court did not suggest that any other symbol might convey such a virulent message of hate and violence. In addition, *Black* did not reverse *R.A.V.,* but instead created an exception for situations in which cross burning is used to convey a message of violence and intimidation. In future cases, the Court would still apply its prohibition against content-based and viewpoint-based restriction on speech to other governmental attempts to repress speech and to other less virulent symbols.

Bibliography

Jeannine Bell, *O Say Can You See: Free Expression by the Light of Fiery Crosses,* 39 *Harvard Civil Rights–Civil Liberties Law Review* 335 (2004).

Roger C. Hartley, *Cross Burning–Hate Speech as Free Speech: A Comment on Virginia v. Black,* 54 *Catholic University Law Review* 1 (2004).

Russell L. Weaver and Donald E. Lively, *Understanding the First Amendment* (Newark, NJ: LexisNexis, 2004), 130–33.

COMMERCIAL SPEECH

Commercial speech until the late twentieth century categorically was beyond the First Amendment's range of protection. This exclusion was based upon an understanding that expression relating to the speaker's economic interests had no constitutional value. Modern First Amendment jurisprudence reflects a different perspective. Beginning in the 1970s, the Supreme Court began to acknowledge that commercial speech may have significant value for the public. Consistent with this premise, the Court in *Bigelow v. Virginia* (1975) determined that restrictions on abortion advertising violated the First Amendment. In *Virginia State Board of Pharmacy v. Virginia Citizens Consumer Council, Inc.* (1976), the Court placed commercial expression squarely within the zone of constitutionally protected speech.

Virginia State Board of Pharmacy v. Virginia Citizens Consumer Council, Inc.

Citation: 425 U.S. 748.

Issue: Whether commercial expression is protected by the First Amendment.

Year of Decision: 1976.

Outcome: Speech does not lose First Amendment protection because of its commercial nature.

Author of Opinion: Justice Harry Blackmun.

Vote: 7-1.

As the obscenity and fighting words cases evidence, not all expression is protected by the First Amendment. Even among categories of constitutionally safeguarded speech, there are variations with respect to the extent of protection provided. A key premise of modern First Amendment jurisprudence is that speech facilitating informed self-governance has the highest value. Consistent with this proposition, the Supreme Court has been especially protective of political expression. The more distance that is perceived between speech and informed self-governance, however, the more disposed it has been to uphold regulation. As initially regarded by the Court, commercial speech had no significant constitutional currency. During the second half of the twentieth century, as the Court expanded the range of constitutionally protected expression, commercial speech became a primary beneficiary of this evolution.

The process of expanding the spectrum of constitutionally protected expression commenced in the 1960s, as the Court began to recognize that speech beyond the purely political had significant value. The first stage of expansion conferred First Amendment status upon defamatory speech. This development reflected the Court's understanding, expressed in *New York Times Co. v. Sullivan* (1964), "of a profound national commitment to the principle that debate on public issues should be uninhibited, robust, and wide-open, and that it may well include vehement, caustic, and sometimes unpleasantly sharp attacks on government and public officials." Defamation of public officials and public figures thus was afforded constitutional shelter in *Sullivan* and *Curtis Publishing Co. v. Butts* (1968), respectively. Sexually explicit expression, provided it does not rise to the level of obscenity, also is constitutionally protected. Decisions in this context, such as *Federal Communications Commission v. Pacifica Foundation* (1978), have suggested that sexually explicit expression has a lower value and thus may be more susceptible to regulation. Although central to a free market economy, commercial speech had no First Amendment currency until the 1970s. This condition reflected the Supreme Court's decision, in *Valentine v. Chrestensen* (1942), that the First Amendment was not a barrier to regulating "purely commercial advertising."

Three decades after *Valentine v. Chrestensen*, the Court began to rethink its commercial speech doctrine. In *Pittsburgh Press Co. v. Pittsburgh Commission on Human Relations* (1973), it upheld a city ordinance prohibiting newspapers from running gender-based help-wanted advertisements. The *Pittsburgh Press* decision established a first line of protection for commercial speech to the extent states could prohibit advertising only when the underlying activity was illegal. Subsequently, in *Bigelow v. Virginia* (1975), the Court determined that the advertising of legal activities could not be barred. This ruling reversed the conviction of a person who had been prosecuted for violating a state ban on advertisements for abortion. The *Pittsburgh Press* and *Bigelow* decisions prefaced a more comprehensive overhaul of commercial speech doctrine in *Virginia State Board of Pharmacy v. Virginia Consumer Citizens Council, Inc.* (1976). At issue in this case was a state law prohibiting pharmacies from advertising the cost of prescription drugs. In defense of this regulation, the state maintained that it was essential for maintenance of professional standards, safeguarded against competitive pressures that might cause pharmacists to cut corners and thus endanger public health, enabling small pharmacies to remain competitive with drug store chains.

Justice Harry Blackmun wrote the majority's opinion. At the outset, he conceded that the advertisement of prescription drug prices had no political significance and merely provided information as the basis for a commercial transaction. From his perspective, the issue was whether speech that "does 'no more than propose a commercial transaction' is so removed from any 'exposition of ideas' and from 'truth, science, morality, and arts in general'" that it lacks all protection. The Court not only concluded that commercial speech merited First Amendment protection but that the consumer interest in such expression was "as keen, if not keener by far, than his interest in the day's most urgent political debate." It further found a ban on advertising to be at odds with the interests of a free market economy and of consumers wanting to make informed decisions in exercising their purchasing power. The Court accordingly observed that the allocation of resources in a free market economy responds to cumulative private decisions that must be "intelligent and well informed." Within this context, "the free flow of commercial information is indispensable." The Court observed that laws blocking this flow represent a "highly paternalistic" model of regulation. Given a choice, the Court favored a system grounded in the assumption that "people will perceive their own best interests only if they are well enough informed, and that the best means to that end is to open the channels of communication rather than to close them."

Despite finding that commercial speech had significant value and utility, the Court indicated that it could be more prone to regulation. Consistent with earlier case law, the Court reaffirmed that states could prohibit advertising of illegal services or activities. The right to trade in commercial speech also might be conditioned upon disclosures that are state mandated to avoid fraud, injury, or unfair dealing. The lower threshold for regulating commercial speech was grounded in a sense that commercial speech presents risks that can be differentiated from those associated with political expression. The Court thus identified "commonsense differences" that justify a lesser "degree of protection." The key differentiating factors, as the Court perceived it, are the "hardier" and "more easily verifiable" nature of commercial speech. Neither of these premises is beyond dispute. Arguments that commercial expression is "hardier" may discount the resilience of political speech. Although used in a different context, political speech like commercial speech typically is driven by the powerful force of self-interest. The drive to win an election or promote a particular agenda (which like commercial speech may serve an economic interest) may be as potent a factor as the interest in material enrichment. Debatable too is the premise that the truth of commercial speech is uniquely easier to verify. Whether in the political or commercial context, misleading or false information can be a source of significant public or private harm. Misrepresentation in either context, moreover, may be a function of conscious or calculated thinking. Ease of verification thus depends less upon the category of speech than the speaker's state of mind.

Modern commercial speech doctrine, although expanding the boundaries of the First Amendment, generates concern with the process of classifying speech for constitutional purposes. As defined by the Court, commercial speech is expression that "invites a commercial transaction." The most common form of commercial expression is advertising. The line between commercial speech and more protected forms of expression blurs when it comes to classifying speech in the context of political, social, or charitable fundraising. This difficulty was evidenced in *Schaumburg v. Citizens for a Better Environment* (1980). The majority determined that charitable fundraising "does more than inform private economic decisions and is not primarily concerned with providing information about the characteristics and costs of goods and services." Justice Rehnquist disagreed with the majority and, in a dissenting opinion, described the expression as purely commercial.

By striking down the regulation of prescription advertising, the Court set a new standard that facilitated regulatory reform in other contexts where commercial speech had been tightly controlled. Restrictions on lawyer advertising and solicitation were among the regulatory barriers that fell soon after the *Virginia Board of Pharmacy* decision. The primary achievement of this ruling was to establish clearly that commercial speech is protected by the First Amendment. Further case law was necessary, however, to establish specific standards for reviewing commercial speech regulation. This need was met several years later, in *Central Gas and Electric Co. v. Public Service Commission* (1984), when the Court introduced a four-part test for assessing the constitutionality of such regulation. The threshold qualification for First Amendment protection is that the speech neither misleads nor promotes an unlawful activity. If the expression satisfies this first criterion, the analysis turns to whether the regulation is supported by an important governmental interest, whether it directly advances that interest, and whether it is no more extensive than necessary to account for that interest. Subsequent case law has varied the intensity of this review, from more relaxed to more intense. The basic premise that commercial speech merits First Amendment protection, however, appears to be well-settled.

Bibliography

C. Edwin Baker, *Advertising and a Democratic Press* (Princeton, NJ: Princeton University Press, 1994). The societal risks incident to advertising are discussed.

Rodney Smolla, *Information, Imagery, and the First Amendment: A Case for Expansive Protection of Commercial Speech,* 71 *Texas Law Review* 777 (1993). This sets forth the proposition that commercial speech should have the fullest measure of constitutional protection.

SYMBOLIC SPEECH

Pure speech commonly is understood as the rendering of words through processes of speaking or writing. These methods of expression, however, may be augmented, paralleled, or even superseded by other communicative factors. Message content thus may be influenced by body language, sound amplification, or visual symbols. Political agendas often rely not just upon strength of logic or force of rhetoric but upon conduct that draws attention to or makes a point with heightened emphasis or efficacy. The success of the civil rights movement during the 1960s, for instance, was facilitated by highly visible public protests and demonstrations that depended as much upon symbols as content. Consistent with the utility of symbolic speech in the marketplace of ideas, the Court has acknowledged its First Amendment status. It also has determined that, when government attempts to regulate conduct that is mixed with speech, First Amendment interests diminish somewhat. This premise was established in *United States v. O'Brien* (1968), when the Court upheld the conviction of a protestor who burned his draft card in violation of federal law. The Court determined that the enactment was aimed at protecting the integrity of the selective service system rather than suppressing legitimate expression. It upheld the law on grounds the regulation was supported by a substantial government interest and the incidental burden on expression was no greater than necessary. Had it found Congress's target to be speech itself, the Court would have demanded a compelling government interest and proof that the regulation was the least burdensome means of accounting for that concern. In *Texas v. Johnson* (1989), the Court was called upon to determine whether a law prohibiting flag desecration punished speech or conduct and thus should be reviewed pursuant to an exacting or more relaxed standard.

Texas v. Johnson

Symbolic speech is a form of expression that enhances substitutes for the spoken word. It often represents the speaker's effort to make a point more effectively and increase attention to his or her agenda. Cases concerning symbolic expression tend to arise from contexts that include significant controversy or divisions in public thought. Against this backdrop, it is not surprising that symbolic speech cases provide some of the First Amendment's most dramatic and controversial scenarios.

Citation: 491 U.S. 397.

Issue: Whether a conviction for burning the American flag as a political protest abridges the First Amendment.

Year of Decision: 1989.

Outcome: Burning an American flag to make a political statement is protected by the First Amendment.

Author of Opinion: Justice William Brennan.

Vote: 5-4.

Squarely within this context are cases concerning desecration of the American flag. For many, the flag is a unique symbol of unity and national definition. It is precisely this symbolism, however, that has made it a favored target for desecration by persons who are alienated or dissatisfied by government policy. Consistent with the notion that the flag is a special symbol that needs to be preserved and protected, numerous stages have enacted laws that prohibit and punish its desecration. Early challenges to these enactments resulted in decisions that struck them down, but with the Court usually not addressing the First Amendment issues. It thus reversed the flag-burning conviction, in *Street v. New York* (1969), of a demonstrator who simultaneously yelled "[w]e don't need no damned flag." Avoidance of the constitutional issue, as related to the flag burning itself, reflected the Court's sense that the conviction may have rested upon the defendant's contemporaneous statement rather than action. In *Spence v. Washington* (1974), the Court reversed a conviction based upon a law prohibiting "improper use" of the flag. This case concerned the taping of a black peace symbol onto a flag for purposes of protesting the Vietnam War. A key turning point for the decision was the fact that the tape did not disfigure the flag permanently. In *Smith v. Goguen* (1974), the Court reversed the conviction of a person whose trousers had a flag sewn into the bottom of them. The prosecution had been based upon a statute that made it a crime to "publicly mutilate, trample upon, deface, or treat contemptuously the flag of the United States." The Court found the law overbroad and vague.

Speech coupled with conduct constitutes symbolic expression. Government's ability to regulate symbolic speech is dependent upon three factors. First, the state must demonstrate that regulation furthers an important or substantial government interest. Second, the government regulatory interest must be unrelated to suppression of expression. Third, the regulatory impact upon expressive freedom must be no greater than is necessary to account for the government interest. In *United States v. O'Brien*, the Supreme Court applied these principles in reviewing the conviction of an individual who burned his draft card to protest the Vietnam War. In this case, the Court accepted the government's argument that destruction of draft cards undermined the Selective Service System's operational efficiency. It thus found the regulatory interest substantial, unrelated to the content of the message, and no more burdensome than necessary upon First Amendment freedom.

In symbolic speech cases, as the *O'Brien* case illustrates, a primary challenge for lawyers and courts is determining whether the regulation reflects concern with the content of the message or an unrelated interest. The distinction in *O'Brien* was a close call, as evidenced by a 5-4 decision in favor of the government. So, too, was the result when the Court, in *Texas v. Johnson*, determined that a state law prohibiting desecration of the American flag could not be the basis for convicting a protestor who burned it to make a political statement. The flag burning occurred in the context of a political demonstration against the presidential renomination of Ronald Reagan at the 1984 Republican National Convention. As the flag burned, protesters chanted, "American, the red, white, and blue, we sit on you." Johnson was prosecuted under a Texas law that prohibited intentional or knowing desecration of "state or national flag." As defined by the law, desecration "mean[t] deface, damage, or otherwise physically mistreat in a way that the actor knows will seriously offend one or more persons likely to observe or discover his action." Several witnesses testified that the flag burning had "seriously offended" them. Both the state and the defendant agreed that the flag burning was expressive conduct. As the defendant himself testified, "a more powerful statement of symbolic speech, whether you agree with it or not, couldn't have been made at that time."

In justifying the flag desecration law, the state argued that it had two legitimate and significant interests. The first concern related to preventing breaches of peace. The second interest was with regard to maintaining the flag as a symbol of national unity. The Court, in an opinion by Justice Anthony Kennedy, determined that each of these concerns was generated by the content of the message rather than by some factor unrelated to speech. This determination was the key to differentiating the case from *O'Brien* and for applying a stricter standard of review. Because prosecution of the demonstrator was content-based rather than content-neutral, the Court asked not whether the government's interest was merely "substantial" but whether it was "compelling." This chosen terminology is the hallmark of a particularly rigorous standard of review.

With respect to the breach of peace argument, the Court noted that the flag burning generated no disturbance. It accordingly was unmoved by the state's concern with "disorderly action." The Court was unwilling to leap from the premise that an audience offended by the symbolic expression would engage in activity that disturbed the peace. To the contrary, it embraced the proposition that expressive liberty anticipates dispute and disagreement. Freedom of speech actually serves society best, the Court noted, "when it induces a condition of unrest, creates dissatisfaction with conditions as they are, or even stirs people to anger."

Regarding the state's "interest in preserving the flag as a symbol of nationhood and national unity," the Court referenced the "bedrock principle underlying the First Amendment" that government may not curb expression of ideas merely because society finds them "offensive or disagreeable." It also indicated concern with government restricting the use of a symbol to one purpose. Ascertaining which images deserve such special attention would force the Court "to consult our very own political preferences, and impose them on the citizenry, in the very way that the First Amendment forbids us to do." Freedom of speech, as the Court saw it, does not guarantee that "sacred" concepts "will go unquestioned in the marketplace of ideas." Noting that those who authored the First Amendment "were not known for their reverence for the Union Jack," the Court refused "to create for the flag an exception to the joust of principles protected by the First Amendment."

The Court also determined that the state had overstated the likelihood of harm associated with flag burning. Assumptions that a breach of peace would be an incident of flag burning were disproved by the incident at issue. It further noted that the flag's "cherished place" in the national community was fortified by a decision that reaffirmed principles of freedom, inclusiveness, and "the conviction that our toleration of criticism such as Johnson's is a sign and source of our strength." Instead of punishment for flag burning, the Court suggested that the best remedy is speech from a competing perspective—like waving a flag or saluting the flag being destroyed.

In a dissenting opinion joined by two other justices, Chief Justice William Rehnquist argued that the statute and conviction should be upheld. From his perspective, the American flag was not "just another symbol." Chief Justice Rehnquist described it as "the visible symbol embodying our Nation" that transcends the views of any political party or philosophy. Viewing the flag as a symbol that rose above other ideas or views, and noting that 48 of 50 states prohibited burning it in public, he rejected the notion that the First Amendment was a barrier to its protection. In response to the argument that flag burning represented a significant political statement, Chief Justice Rehnquist countered that it "was no essential part of any exposition of ideas." As he saw it, the defendant could have made his point effectively by verbally denouncing the flag, burning it in private, or desecrating other official symbols or effigies of political leaders. Chief Justice Rehnquist thus concluded that flag burning merited no protection under the First Amendment, because (like obscenity and fighting words) it has "such slight social value as a step to truth that any benefit that may be derived from ⌊it⌋ is clearly outweighed" by the public's interest in avoiding a probable breach of the peace.

Justice John Paul Stevens also dissented on grounds the flag is "an important national asset." Given this status, he maintained that it could be protected for the same reason that political graffiti could be banned from national monuments. Justice Stevens viewed the interest in maintaining the flag's unique symbolic value as a legitimate and significant interest. Insofar as "ideas of liberty and equality" are worth fighting for, Justice Stevens concluded that it must be "true that the flag that uniquely symbolized their power is ... itself worthy of protection from unnecessary desecration."

The Court's decision generated a firestorm among critics who quickly mobilized Congress to enact a federal law prohibiting flag desecration. The statute aimed to protect the flag against action that undermined its symbolic value. The Court found, in *United States v. Eichman* (1990), that this regulatory concern arose only in response to expression which conflicted with the flag's symbolic value. By the same 5-4 vote that yielded the outcome in *Texas v. Johnson*, therefore, the Court struck down the federal law. In so doing, it reinforced the understanding that government's ability to prohibit expressive conduct because of the message is limited. In such instances, regulation is permissible only to the extent the state can demonstrate a compelling interest and employs a method that imposes the least burden on expressive freedom.

The Court's flag-burning decisions have not deterred periodic efforts to enact flag desecration statutes. They also have inspired unsuccessful efforts toward a constitutional amendment. The potential for legislative success is dependent upon the ability to identify a content neutral justification for regulation or the ability to demonstrate a concern that the Court accepts as compelling and minimally invasive of expressive freedom. Given the strong sentiments that drive interest in protecting the flag from desecration, and the narrow margin by which such laws have been invalidated, further legislative initiative would not be unexpected. It is an area where a shift in outcome could be no further away than one resignation from and one new appointment to the Court.

Bibliography

Lee Bollinger, *The Tolerant Society* (New York: Oxford University Press, 1986). The value of tolerance as a basis for defining First Amendment principles is examined.
George Fletcher, *Loyalty* (New York: Oxford University Press, 1993). The nature of patriotism and loyalty toward a society is explored.

CAMPAIGN FINANCING

Speech that facilitates informed self-governments is the highest priority of the First Amendment. Consistent with this premise, standards of review are most exacting when government attempts to regulate political speech. Experience has demonstrated that money can be a corrupting influence upon the political process. Political expenditures and contributions, however, also are a means of expression. Efforts to regulate them, even for well-intended reasons, thus implicate the freedom of speech clause. In *Buckley v. Valeo* (1976), the Court acknowledged that the reality and perception of corruption may be valid grounds for regulating campaign contributions. Limitations on expenditures by individuals, candidates, and associations would not survive constitutional review, however, because they represented substantial and direct abridgments of political speech. In *McConnell v. Federal Election Commission* (2004), the Court upheld a federal law that imposed new limitations upon political fundraising and contributions.

McConnell v. Federal Election Commission

Citation: 124 S.Ct. 619.

Issue: Whether the Bipartisan Campaign Reform Act of 2002 (BCRA), which regulates political campaign financing, is constitutional.

Year of Decision: 2003.

Outcome: In most respects, BCRA is upheld because the Court is concerned about potential circumventions of campaign finance laws.

Author of Opinion: Justices John Paul Stevens and Sandra Day O'Connor and Chief Justice William Rehnquist.

Vote: 5-4.

Campaign finance laws have generated much controversy and much litigation in recent decades. In its 1976 decision in *Buckley v. Valeo*, 424 U.S. 1 (1976), the United States Supreme Court recognized that expenditures on political campaigns constitute protected speech within the meaning of the First Amendment because "[d]iscussion of public issues and debate on the qualifications of candidates are integral to the operation of the system of government established by our Constitution." Since the presence or absence of money affects a candidate's ability to speak, the government does not have a free and unfettered right to regulate campaign finance expenditures. Nevertheless, many have argued that campaign finance expenditures are "out of control" and have corruptly and improperly influenced the political process.

In *Buckley,* despite its pro-free-speech rhetoric, the Court held that campaign finance activity is not entitled to absolute constitutional protection. The Court drew a distinction between "expenditure" limitations ("expenditures" are amounts spent by candidates, individuals, and political parties) and "contribution" limitations ("contributions" are amounts donated to candidates or political parties). In the Court's view, expenditure limitations are more objectionable because they directly limit communication about or by candidates and elected officials. By contrast, contribution limitations entail "only a marginal restriction upon the contributor's ability to engage in free communication" because, while contributions serve as "a general expression of support for the candidate and his views," they do not "communicate the underlying basis for the support." The nature of the communication does not change significantly because of the size of the contribution. Moreover, the Court expressed concern that campaign contributions might be given in expectation of a *quid-quo-pro* vote or action by the candidate, or could create an appearance of corruption. Nevertheless, even restrictions on campaign contributions were subject to review.

Relying on the distinction between contributions and expenditures, the Court struck down *Federal Election Campaign Act of 1971* expenditure limitations, which prohibited individuals from making expenditures "relative to a clearly identified candidate" in excess of $1,000. The Court found that the governmental interest in preventing corruption and the appearance of corruption was inadequate to justify the limitation given the absence of prearrangement and coordination of expenditures with candidates or their agents. The Court rejected the argument that the government has a sufficient interest "in equalizing the relative ability of individuals and groups to influence the outcome of elections." The Court also struck down limitations on expenditures by a candidate "from his personal funds, or the personal funds of his immediate family, in connection with his campaigns during any calendar year." The candidate, no less than any other person, has a First Amendment right to "engage in the discussion of public issues and vigorously and tirelessly to advocate his own election and the election of other candidates. Indeed, the use of personal funds reduces the candidate's dependence on outside contributions and thereby counteracts the coercive pressures and attendant risks of abuse." The Court also struck down limitations on overall campaign expenditures by candidates seeking nomination for election and election to federal office.

In *Buckley,* the Court upheld various disclosure requirements. The Court concluded that there must be a "relevant correlation" or "substantial relation" between the governmental interest and the information required to be disclosed. The Court concluded that disclosure requirements provide the electorate with information regarding the source of contributions. In addition, disclosure requirements "deter actual corruption and avoid the appearance of corruption by exposing large contributions and expenditures to the light of publicity." Finally, disclosure requirements help the government detect contribution violations.

In *McConnell,* the Court was confronted by a challenge to the *Bipartisan Campaign Reform Act of 2002* (BCRA), which amended various campaign finance laws including the *Federal Election Campaign Act of 1971* (FECA). Following *Buckley,* Congress became concerned about a number of problems in the campaign finance area. First, federal law permitted corporations and unions, as well as individuals who had already made the maximum permissible contributions to federal candidates, to contribute "nonfederal money"—also known as "soft money"—to political parties for activities intended to influence state or local elections. While hard money was limited in various ways, soft money was not. Second, *Buckley* held that FECA's disclosure and reporting requirements, as well as its expenditure limitations, applied only "to funds used for communications that expressly advocate the election or defeat of a clearly identified candidate." As a result, so-called "issue ads" could be financed with soft money even though little difference existed between "an ad that urged viewers to 'vote against Jane Doe' and one that condemned Jane Doe's record on a particular issue before exhorting viewers to 'call Jane Doe and tell her what you think.'" Finally, the Senate Committee on Governmental Affairs issued [a] report which found that the "soft money loophole" had led to a "meltdown" of the campaign finance system. "[B]oth parties promised and provided special access to candidates and senior Government officials in exchange for large soft-money contributions [and] both parties began to use large amounts of soft money to pay for issue advertising designed to influence federal elections." In addition, national parties frequently transferred soft money to state and local parties for "generic voter activities" that benefitted federal candidates and were effectively controlled by national committees.

In an effort to remedy these problems, BCRA amended federal election laws in a number of ways. First, BCRA prohibited national party committees and their agents from soliciting, receiving, directing, or spending any soft money. In upholding these provisions, the Court in the first majority opinion (the case produced *three* majority opinions) relied on *Buckley* and held that such activities have only a marginal impact on political speech and can "corrupt [or] create the appearance of corruption of federal candidates and officeholders" because "candidates would feel grateful for such donations and that donors would seek to exploit that gratitude." The Court noted that national party committees "peddle access to federal candidates and officeholders in exchange for large soft-money donations and actually furnish their own menus of opportunities for access to would-be soft-money donors."

The Court noted that this rationale applied even to restrictions on the source and amount limits that applied to purely state and local elections in which no federal office is at stake. The Court emphasized "the close relationship between federal officeholders and the national parties, as well as the means by which parties have traded on that relationship, that have made all large soft-money contributions to national parties suspect."

BCRA also prohibited national, state, and local party committees, and their agents or subsidiaries, from "solicit[ing] any funds for, or mak[ing] or direct[ing] any donations" to any organization established under § 501(c) of the Internal Revenue Code that makes expenditures in connection with an election for federal office, and any political organizations established under § 527 (basically, organizations created solely to engage in protected political activity) "other than a political committee, a State, district, or local committee of a political party, or the authorized campaign committee of a candidate for State or local office." Absent the solicitation provision, national, state, and local party committees "had significant incentives to mobilize their formidable fundraising apparatuses, including the peddling of access to federal officeholders, into the service of like-minded tax-exempt organizations that conduct activities benefiting their candidates. The Court used like analysis to extend the ban to § 527 organizations."

BCRA also prohibited federal candidates and officeholders from "solicit[ing], receiv[ing], direct[ing], transfer[ring], or spend[ing]" any soft money in connection with federal elections. It also limited the ability of federal candidates and officeholders to solicit, receive, direct, transfer, or spend soft money in connection with state and local elections. The Court found that large "soft-money donations at a candidate's or officeholder's behest give rise to all of the same corruption concerns."

BCRA also prohibited candidates for state or local office, or state or local office-holders, from spending soft money to fund "public communications"—i.e., a communication that "refers to a clearly identified candidate for Federal office [and] that promotes or supports a candidate for that office, or attacks or opposes a candidate for that office." The Court upheld the provision, noting that it focused "narrowly on those soft-money donations with the greatest potential to corrupt or give rise to the appearance of corruption of federal candidates and officeholders."

The Court also upheld Section II of BCRA, which required political committees to file detailed financial reports with the Federal Election Commission, and a provision that precluded corporations and unions from financing electioneering communications out of their general treasuries within 60 days of an election. In order to engage in such communications, corporations were essentially forced to create new corporations who solicit segregated funds solely for political purposes. The Court concluded that the state interest in this provision was compelling given that "the special characteristics of the corporate structure require particularly careful regulation."

BCRA also contained a provision that excluded from the definition of electioneering communications any "communication appearing in a news story, commentary, or editorial distributed through the facilities of any broadcasting station, unless such facilities are owned or controlled by any political party, political committee, or candidate." The Court noted that this provision applied to news items and commentary only and did not afford *carte blanche* to media companies generally to ignore FECA's provisions.

In the second majority opinion, this one by Chief Justice Rehnquist, the Court BCRA provisions requiring that "certain communications 'authorized' by a candidate or his political committee clearly identify the candidate or committee or, if not so authorized, identify the payor and announce the lack of authorization." The Court held that the provision "bears a sufficient relationship to the important governmental interest of 'shed[ding] the light of publicity' on campaign financing." However, the Court struck down a prohibition that precluded individuals "17 years old or younger" from making contributions to candidates and contributions or donations to political parties. The Court noted that even minors enjoy the protection of the First Amendment and that the asserted governmental interests (protection against corruption by conduit, that is, donations by parents through their minor children to circumvent contribution limits applicable to the parents) were insufficient to sustain the provision. In addition, that interest could be served in other ways (e.g., a restriction on the total amount that could be contributed by a single family).

In the third majority opinion, this one written by Justice Stephen Breyer, the Court upheld BCRA's candidate request requirements [which required broadcast licensees to "keep" a publicly available file "of all requests for broadcast time made by or on behalf of a candidate for public office," along with a notation showing whether the request was granted, and (if granted) a history that includes "classes of time," "rates charged," and when the "spots actually aired"]. The Court held that such requirements were justifiable as part of the government's effort to ensure that broadcasters were satisfying their broadcast obligations under federal law.

Justice Scalia, concurring and dissenting, questioned the Court's decision to uphold BCRA's campaign finance restrictions while previously striking down restrictions on child pornography and sexually explicit cable programming. He argued that campaign finance laws cut "to the heart of what the First Amendment is meant to protect: the right to criticize the government." He also noted that BCRA "*targets* for prohibition" certain categories of campaign speech that are particularly harmful to incumbents and questioned whether it was purely "accidental" that such speech was targeted. He also questioned the decision to ban attack ads. "The premise of the First Amendment is that the American people are neither sheep nor fools, and hence fully capable of considering both the substance of the speech presented to them and its proximate and ultimate source. If that premise is wrong, our democracy has a much greater problem to overcome than merely the influence of amassed wealth." While the Government's briefs [focused] on the horrible "appearance of corruption," the most passionate floor statements [on] this legislation pertained to so-called attack ads.

Justice Thomas also concurred in part and dissented in part, arguing that because "the First Amendment 'has its fullest and most urgent application' to speech uttered during a campaign for political office," the Court is obligated to subject those restrictions to the "strictest scrutiny." He noted that the majority had abandoned the "fundamental principle" that "the best test of truth is the power of the thought to get itself accepted in the competition of the market" in favor of its purported objective of preventing "corruption," or the mere "appearance of corruption." He went on to note that the evidence suggested only that "federal officeholders have commonly asked donors to make soft-money donations to national and state committees solely in order to assist federal campaigns, including the officeholder's own." He concluded that bribery laws could have been used to deal with such abuses.

Justice Kennedy concurred and dissented arguing that only one interest justifies campaign finance laws: "eliminating, or preventing, actual corruption or the appearance of corruption stemming from contributions to candidates." He viewed BCRA as extending far beyond that rationale to "any conduct that wins goodwill from or influences a Member of Congress." He particularly objected to provisions prohibiting corporate communications referring to a candidate for federal office in the weeks immediately before an election. "[To] say [that corporations and unions] cannot alert the public to pending political issues that may threaten the country's economic interests is unprecedented."

In *McConnell's* wake, some have questioned whether there is a meaningful distinction to be made, in terms of campaign finance laws, between media and nonmedia corporations. With regard to advertisements run by nonmedia corporations, the Court upheld restrictions on the basis that candidates and officeholders might look with favor on corporations that run such advertisements. But, in dissent, Chief Justice Rehnquist notes that: "Newspaper editorials and political talk shows *benefit* federal candidates and officeholders every bit as much as a generic voter registration drive conducted by a state party. [T]here is little doubt that the endorsement of a major newspaper *affects* federal elections, and federal candidates and officeholders are surely 'grateful' for positive media coverage." As a result, he asks whether *McConnell* might permit Congress to regulate editorials and political talk shows.

McConnell is an important decision because it affirms broad congressional authority to regulate campaign finance contributions. However, the breadth of the prohibition is staggering and seems to impose significant restrictions on the ability of individuals to communicate with each other and to participate in the political process.

Bibliography

John M. De Figueiredo and Elizabeth Garrett, *Paying for Politics*, 78 *Southern California Law Review* 591 (2005).

Edward B. Foley, *"Smith for Congress" and its Equivalents: An Endorsement Test under Buckley and MCFL*, 2 *Election Law Journal* 3 (2003).

Spencer Overton, *Restraint and Responsibility*, 61 *Washington and Lee Law Review* 663 (2004).
Russell L. Weaver and Donald E. Lively, *Understanding the First Amendment* (Newark, NJ: LexisNexis, 2003), 137–158.

STUDENT SPEECH

Freedom of expression extends to all persons regardless of age, but maturity may be a factor in determining the degree of the liberty. Government power to restrict access by minors to sexually explicit broadcasting, as discussed later in *Federal Communications Commission v. Pacifica Foundation* (1978), manifests this premise. Public schools are a primary incubator of case law concerning the speech liberties of minors. In *Tinker v. Des Moines Independent School District* (1969), the Court upheld the right of high school students to wear black armbands in protest of the Vietnam War. This ruling hinged in part upon the passive nature of the protest and finding that there was no disruption of school operations. The Court's decision in *Hazelwood School District v. Kuhlmeier* (1988) reaffirmed the proposition that students do not lose "their constitutional rights to freedom of speech or expression at the schoolhouse gate." It also determined, however, that student expression need not be tolerated if it was inconsistent with the school's educational mission. This finding expanded the power of school authorities to determine appropriate speech in the public school setting.

Hazelwood School District v. Kuhlmeier

In First Amendment jurisprudence, there has been continuing debate about whether students should be accorded free speech rights comparable to those granted to adults. In *Tinker v. Des Moines Independent School District*, 393 U.S. 503 (1969), students wore black arms bands to protest United States involvement in the Vietnam War. The Court overturned school official's suspension of the students noting that students have First Amendment rights, but

Citation: 484 U.S. 260.

Issue: Whether a high school principal can censor a school newspaper for inappropriate content.

Year: 1988.

Outcome: While high school students are protected by the First Amendment, they are not protected against such censorship.

Author of Opinion: Justice Byron White.

Vote: 6-3.

that those rights are tempered by the "special characteristics of the school environment." However, in the Court's subsequent decision in *Bethel School District No. 403 v. Fraser*, 478 U.S. 675 (1986), it held that a student could be disciplined for statements made as part of a school campaign speech.

Student rights issues returned to the Court in the *Hazelwood School District* case, a case involving a student newspaper. In that case, a high school principal withheld from a student newspaper two pages containing student-authored stories about pregnancy and divorce. The decision was based on the principal's concern that the identity of pregnant students might be identifiable from the text, that references to sexual activity and birth control were inappropriate for some of the younger students, and that the parents of a student in the divorce story should be asked for consent to the publication of their daughter's comments about their divorce.

In considering the case, the Court began by recognizing that students do not "shed their constitutional rights [at] the schoolhouse gate." At the same time, the First

Amendment rights of students in the public schools "are not automatically coextensive with the rights of adults in other settings." Reaffirming *Tinker,* the Court held that protections for student First Amendment rights must be considered "in light of the special characteristics of the school environment." The Court concluded that a school need not tolerate student speech that is inconsistent with its "basic educational mission," even if the government may not censor comparable speech outside the school environment.

Ultimately, in upholding the principal's actions, the Court held that "educators [may exercise] editorial control over the style and content of student speech in school-sponsored expressive activities so long as their actions are reasonably related to legitimate pedagogical concerns." The Court explained as follows: "[Activities such as] school-sponsored publications, theatrical productions, and other expressive activities that students, parents, and members of the public might reasonably perceive to bear the imprimatur of the school [may] fairly be characterized as part of the school curriculum, whether or not they occur in a traditional classroom setting, so long as they are supervised by faculty members and designed to impart particular knowledge or skills to student participants and audiences." The Court also noted that "A school may in its capacity as publisher of a school newspaper or producer of a school play 'disassociate itself,' not only from speech that would 'substantially interfere with [its] work [or] impinge on the rights of other students,' but also from speech that is, for example, ungrammatical, poorly written, inadequately researched, biased or prejudiced, vulgar or profane, or unsuitable for immature audiences. A school must be able to set high standards for the student speech that is disseminated under its [auspices]."

In evaluating the principal's actions, the Court found that the principal had legitimate pedagogical concerns in rejecting the articles. In regard to the pregnant students, he legitimately worried that student anonymity was not sufficiently ensured. "In addition, he could reasonably have been concerned that the article was not sufficiently sensitive to the privacy interests of the students' boyfriends and parents, who were discussed in the article but who were given no opportunity to consent to its publication or to offer a response." In addition, since some of the articles contained frank talk about sexual activity, the principal was legitimately concerned "that such frank talk was inappropriate in a school-sponsored publication distributed to 14-year-old freshmen and presumably taken home to be read by students' even younger brothers and sisters." Finally, the Court concluded that the principal was legitimately concerned about the fact that a divorce was "sharply critical" of a child's father and that the father had not been given the chance to defend himself.

Justice Brennan, joined by Justices Marshall and Blackmun, dissented on grounds a school has no right to censor unless the speech "materially disrupts classwork or involves substantial disorder or invasion of the rights of others." Finding that this standard was not met, he concluded that the principal had engaged in impermissible "censorship authority." He rejected the notion that the school has a right to exercise control over "school-sponsored speech." In addition, he concluded that the school did not have the right to shield impressionable students from the speech: "*Tinker* teaches us that the state educator's undeniable, and undeniably vital, mandate to inculcate moral and political values is not a general warrant to act as 'thought police' stifling discussion of all but state-approved topics and advocacy of all but the official position."

Hazelwood School District is an important decision because it recognizes that, even though high school students retain free speech rights, those rights are more limited than the rights of adults. In the context of school-sponsored activities, such as a school newspaper operated as a part of a class activity, school officials retain some power of censorship.

Bibliography

Erwin Chemerinsky, *The Deconstitutionalization of Education*, 36 *Loyola University Chicago Law Journal* 111 (2004).

Mark D. Rosen, *The Surprisingly Strong Case for Tailoring Constitutional Principles*, 153 *University of Pennsylvania Law Review* 1513 (2005).

Russell L. Weaver and Donald E. Lively, *Understanding the First Amendment* (Newark, NJ: LexisNexis, 2003), 204–207.

CHAPTER 12

FIRST AMENDMENT: FREEDOM OF SPEECH (CONTENT NEUTRAL REGULATION)

The concept of content neutrality, during the final decades of the twentieth century, has evolved as a particularly significant limiting principle. Insofar as a regulation is understood to regulate a concern unrelated to or secondary to speech, standards of review are more relaxed than they would be if content itself was regulated. The earliest content neutrality cases arose in the context of accounting for interests such as traffic flow and competing uses in public forums. In the late 1960s, as evidenced in *United States v. O'Brien* (discussed in the subsection on symbolic speech), content neutrality principles expanded beyond the public forum context. The content neutrality concept represents a particularly profound development insofar as it increases space and opportunity for regulation and diminishes the range of constitutional concern.

PUBLIC FORUMS

The quality of expressive freedom turns in significant part upon opportunity to access a place to speak, communicate, or interact. Consistent with this premise, Justice Owen Roberts in *Hague v. C.I.O.* (1939) observed that "streets and parks ... have immemorially been held in trust for the use of the public and, time out of mind, have been used for purposes of assembly, communicating thoughts between citizens, and discussing public questions. Such use of the streets and public places has, from ancient time, been a part of the privileges, immunities, rights, and liberties of citizens." Justice Roberts's characterization of the availability of streets and parks for expressive purposes exaggerated the First Amendment tradition associated with them. Less than half a century earlier, the Court in *Davis v. Massachusetts* (1897) rejected the premise that parks or highways "from time immemorial" had been open to speech. It thus found government denial of public access to be no different than a decision by a private property owner.

Although the "time immemorial" understanding may be overstated, it nonetheless has shaped modern understanding of public forums. Two primary First Amendment interests arise in the public forum context. The first is whether a forum actually is accessible to the public. The second concerns the extent to which government may regulate it. With respect to the first issue, access depends upon how the forum is characterized. On the second matter, the constitutionality of regulation hinges upon whether it is content-based or content-neutral. If government aims to control content, its reasons and means will be strictly scrutinized. A diminished standard of review may operate if the speech is perceived as having a low value. Content-neutral regulation typically manifests itself in the form of time, place, or manner restrictions. Typical concerns in this context include management of competing uses, protection of property, maintaining traffic flow, and public safety.

Public forum doctrine has become an increasingly significant and complex aspect of First Amendment jurisprudence. The Court, in *Perry Education Association v. Perry Local Educators' Association* (1983), identified different types of public forums and set forth the basic rules governing each of them. In *Rosenberger v. University of Virginia* (1995), the Court demonstrated the elastic and sometimes abstract nature of a public forum.

Perry Education Association v. Perry Local Educators' Association

Freedom of speech standards of review are at their peak when government attempts to regulate on the basis of content. Even when regulation is not directed at content, it may have an impact on speech. Under such circumstances, First Amendment interests may abate but they do not disappear. A classic example of this phenomenon arose in *United States v. O'Brien* (1968) when the Court upheld the conviction of an antiwar protester who burned his draft card. Although the demonstrator's symbolic expression became the basis for the prosecution, the Court found that the government was acting primarily upon the content-neutral concern of ensuring the operational efficiency of the selective service system.

Citation: 460 U.S. 37.

Issue: Whether an interschool mail system and teacher mailboxes were public forums and thus accessible to parties other than those provided for by a collective bargaining agreement.

Year of Decision: 1983.

Outcome: The mail system and mailboxes were not public forums, so the collective bargaining agreement limiting access to them did not violate the First Amendment.

Author of Opinion: Justice Byron White.

Vote: 5-4.

Regulation is content-neutral, even if it affects speech, when the law accounts for an interest unrelated to expression. Content neutrality is evidenced, for instance, in symbolic speech regulation that targets conduct rather than expression. It also is manifested when the law attempts to manage those effects of speech that are secondary rather than primary. An example of secondary affects regulation arises when, as in *Young v. American Minitheatres, Inc.* (1976), a city zoning ordinance restricted the location of adult movie theatres pursuant to an interest in neighborhood quality. The richest source of content-neutral regulation, however, pertains to governance of public forums on the basis of time, place, or manner.

In public forum cases, the threshold issue is one of definition. Private property implicates no state action and thus is beyond the scope of First Amendment concern. Public property may be available for expressive purposes, however, depending upon its use. Certain types of forums must be accessible. In any event, legitimate public forum management must account for interests unrelated to speech content. Typical concerns include protection of property, scheduling competing uses, efficient traffic flow, and public safety. These types of interests provide the basis not for regulation of content but of the time, place, and manner of expression.

Public forum doctrine was introduced in the late 1930s, when the Supreme Court in *Hague v. CIO* (1938) determined that streets and parks "immemorially have been held in trust for the use of the public and, time out of mind, have been used for purposes of assembly, communicating thoughts between citizens, and discussing public questions." The characterization of streets and parks as forums that "immemorially" have been reserved for speech may have overstated reality. Four decades previously, in *Davis v. Massachusetts* (1897), the Court specifically had rejected the premise that "from time immemorial," parks had been accessible for public speaking. Notwithstanding the historical glitch, the *Hague* decision recognized what modern case law refers to as the traditional public forum.

The civil rights era was a time of significant growth for public forum doctrine. Official efforts to deter protests in public places during the 1960s affirmed the freedom to speak and assemble on state capitol grounds, *Edwards v. South Carolina* (1963), and on public sidewalks, *Cox v. Louisiana* (1965). Decisions like these accounted effectively for speech interests in traditional public forums. In *Brown v. Louisiana* (1966), however, the Court reversed breach of peace convictions of persons who protested silently in a public library. The Court in the same term, in *Adderley v. Florida* (1966), upheld the trespass convictions of demonstrators who protested on jailhouse grounds. These cases indicated uncertainty with respect to the boundaries of traditional public forums. Insofar as a forum's compatibility with speech may be a legitimate state concern, a library might be viewed as an inappropriate venue for any activity (including speech) that is a distraction. The grounds of a jailhouse like those of "an executive mansion, a legislative chamber, a courthouse, or the statehouse," as Justice William Douglas noted, is a "seat[ ] of government."

Given the need for better definition and clarity, the Court eventually responded with a framework that categorizes public forums and establishes constitutional rules for their governance. This evolution took place in *Perry Educational Association v. Perry Local Educators' Association* (1983). The *Perry* case concerned a rival union's claim that it was entitled to access public school teacher mailboxes. Under a collective bargaining agreement, access was provided exclusively to the union that had been elected to represent the teachers. Access also was permitted for community, civic, and religious groups. Selective access to a public forum entails the risk of abridging not only freedom of speech but equal protection. As the Court concluded in *Police Department of Chicago v. Mosley* (1972), "[o]nce a forum is opened to assembly or speaking by some groups, government may not prohibit others from assembling or speaking on the basis of what they intend to say."

The *Mosley* decision responded to a municipal ordinance that prohibited all picketing near schools except during specified hours and in the context of labor disputes. This regulation, although styled as a time, place, and manner regulation, manifestly discriminated on the basis of content. Minus a compelling reason for differentiating one type of picketing from another, the ordinance was contrary to the First Amendment. Despite arguments that the public schools likewise discriminated on the basis of content, when access to its internal mail system was provided on a selective basis, the Court refused to equate teacher mailboxes with public sidewalks. Finding that teacher mailboxes were not public forums, it concluded that the school system could limit access to organizations engaged in official school business.

The long-term value of the *Perry* decision owes less to its specific result, which critics have questioned, than to its effort to establish an orderly framework for public forum analysis. Toward this end, the Court established three forum categories and the constitutional rules that govern each. The first model is the "quintessential" public forum consisting of those "places which by long tradition or by government fiat have been devoted to assembly and debate." Primary examples of the traditional public forum are parks, streets, and sidewalks. Content-based regulation in this context must be supported by a compelling state interest and must be narrowly drawn in accounting for it.

The second category is the designated public forum. Such a venue is one that government has opened "for use by the public as a place for expressive activity." The designated public forum may consist of a public school auditorium, fairground, or any other property that government has opened to expressive activity. The basis for differentiating it from a traditional forum is that government has no obligation to open it to speech activity and reserves the right to close it. So long as the state opens the forum, however, content-based regulation is subject to the same strict review associated with traditional forums. To the extent that government closes the forum, it must do so on a wholesale rather than selective basis.

The third category is the nonpublic forum, "which is not by tradition or designation for public communication." In this context, government is not bound by prohibitions against content-based regulation or restrictive access. The standard of review for such regulation is not strict scrutiny but whether it is reasonable. For each type of forum, however, government is precluded from conditioning access or punishing expression on the basis of disagreement with the speaker's opinion. This rule against viewpoint discrimination would deny government the ability to control access on the basis of political philosophy or position.

Time, place, and manner regulation, even in the context of a traditional or designated public forum, is subject to a lesser standard of review than for content-based regulation. The general rule is that such content-neutral regulation is consistent with the First Amendment, provided it promotes a substantial government interest and provides speakers an adequate alternative means for communicating their message. Common models of time, place, and manner controls include park and parade permits, limitations on door-to-door solicitation, and restrictions on sidewalk or street use. Since *Perry,* the Court has upheld time controls on the broadcast of indecent programming, place limitations that prohibit picketing in front of a home, and manner restrictions that regulate the volume of amplified music in a public park.

Despite the Court's framing of a more orderly structure for public forum analysis, loose ends and concerns remain. As times and conventions evolve, it is not always easy to determine the boundaries of tradition. Not surprisingly, therefore, the Court, in *International Society for Krishna Consciousness, Inc. v. Lee* (1992), fragmented over whether an airport terminal was a traditional public forum. Since *Perry,* moreover, the Court has reduced analysis of public forum regulation primarily to the question of whether government has a rule because of disagreement with a particular message. So long as government can demonstrate that its objective is unrelated to the content of expression, as the Court observed in *Ward v. Rock Against Racism* (1989), its officially stated purpose "is controlling." Given this relaxed standard of review, critics maintain that the state can accomplish indirectly through public forum regulation what it cannot achieve through direct content control. An ordinance prohibiting residential picketing altogether, which the Court upheld in *Frisby v. Schultz* (1988), can be viewed as a form of prior restraint. As the Court observed in *United States v. New York Times Co.* (1971), "any system of prior restraint carries a heavy burden of justification against its constitutional validity." Diminished standards for reviewing time, place, and manner regulation, so long as government can articulate a credible rationale that is content-neutral, create a potential bypass to this central First Amendment principle.

Bibliography

Harry Kalven, Jr., *The Concept of the Public Forum*, 1965 *Supreme Court Review* 1 (1965). The nature of public forums is discussed.

Robert Post, *Between Governance and Management: The History and Theory of the Public Forum*, 34 *UCLA Law Review* 1713 (1987). General principles governing public forums, and underlying rationales, are examined.

Rosenberger v. University of Virginia

Citation: 515 U.S. 819.

Issue: Whether a state university's exclusion of a campus religious publication, from a program that funded student organization publications, denied access to a public forum and thus abridged freedom of speech.

Year of Decision: 1995.

Outcome: The selective exclusion of a student religious publication from the general funding program denied access to a public forum and abridged freedom of speech.

Author of Opinion: Justice Anthony Kennedy.

Vote: 5-4.

The First Amendment comprises a set of freedoms that often are bundled together in the same breath. The guarantees of freedom of speech and of the press often merge into the concept of expressive freedom. Religious freedom represents the convergence of the establishment clause and free exercise clause. Although these provisions typically are viewed as mutually enhancing, they sometimes are in conflict with each other. The establishment clause and free exercise clause point in different directions, for instance, when issues such as state aid to parochial schools or public prayer must be reviewed. Prayer or religious displays in public settings may be viewed as official support for religion in derogation of the establishment clause. Exponents and sometimes the Court, however, maintain that these activities should be permitted to accommodate the free exercise of religion.

The establishment clause and free exercise clause are not the only tension in the First Amendment. Conflict also arises between the establishment clause and the freedom of speech clause. The Court initially confronted this clash of constitutional interests in *Widmar v. Vincent* (1981) when it reviewed a state university policy that denied campus facilities access to student religious organizations. Insofar as the university had opened its facilities to some student organizations, the Court determined a designated public forum had been created. Because exclusion of religious groups was driven by content concerns, rather than considerations of time, place, or manner, the Court strictly scrutinized the policy. Although acknowledging that compliance with the establishment clause would constitute a compelling interest, under appropriate circumstances, it determined that restrictive access was not necessary in this instance. Rather, the Court determined that an equal access policy would not have a secular purpose, would not have the primary effect of promoting religion, and would not excessively entangle government and religion. Consistent with modern understanding of the establishment clause, therefore, the Court concluded that the university could accommodate the freedom of speech clause without crossing the establishment clause.

The *Widmar* decision became the basis for invalidating restrictions on church access to school facilities that were open to other groups, *Lamb's Chapel v. Center Moriches Union Free School District* (1993), and allowing the Ku Klux Klan to erect religious symbols on a statehouse plaza, *Capitol Square Review Board v. Pinette* (1995). These cases, arising in designated public forums and traditional public forums, respectively, reaffirmed the principle that equal access to a public forum for speech purposes does not abridge the establishment clause. These decisions were unsatisfactory to critics, such as Justice Ruth Bader Ginsburg, who argued that official disclaimers were necessary to avoid any public perception that government was endorsing religion.

Despite these concerns, the balance between freedom of speech and the establishment clause moved even more decisively toward the accommodation of religious expression. In *Rosenberger v. Rector and Visitors of the University of Virginia* (1995), the Court reviewed a university program for funding student publications. Although providing financial support for "student news, information, opinion, entertainment and academic communications media groups," the program specifically excluded religious publications. This exclusion was based upon the university's concern that funding religious messages would violate the establishment clause.

In an opinion authored by Justice Anthony Kennedy, the Court held that the establishment clause constituted no barrier to public funding of religious publications. From its perspective, the object of university funding was "to open a forum for speech and to support various student enterprises ... in recognition of the diversity and creativity of student life." The Court thus characterized the funding program as a designated public forum. Consistent with public forum doctrine, and because the denial of funding was content-based, the university was obligated to demonstrate that exclusion of student religious groups was supported by a compelling interest and represented a narrowly tailored means of accounting for it. Noting as it did in *Widmar* that compliance with the establishment clause may represent a compelling interest, the Court nonetheless concluded that a restrictive access policy was not necessary to meet this need. As the Court saw it, "[a]ny benefit to religion is incidental to the government's provision of secular services for secular purposes on a non-religious basis." In other words, it was not necessary to deny funding on the basis of religious views to obey the establishment clause.

For Justice Sandra Day O'Connor, who authored a concurring opinion, the key consideration was whether university funding of the religious publication would constitute an endorsement of religion. Insofar as it received the same assistance provided to other publications, Justice O'Connor was satisfied that its funding would not represent an endorsement of the magazine's religious perspective. Critical to her opinion were requirements that student organizations be independent of the university and provide disclaimers of any association with the university and its responsibility for content. Given the university's objective of a free and diverse market of ideas, and consequent improbability that anyone would perceive its endorsement of a religious message, Justice O'Connor saw exclusion on the grounds of religious viewpoint as a free speech violation.

Justice David Souter, in a dissenting opinion joined by Justices John Paul Stevens, Ruth Bader Ginsburg, and Stephen Breyer, found a clear-cut establishment clause violation. His reading of the majority opinion was that the Court "for the first time, approves direct funding of core religious activities by an arm of the state." From the dissenters' viewpoint, the university's policy against funding religious publications was not only justified but compelled by the establishment clause. Further strengthening the university's position, at least in the dissenters' eyes, was the publication's content, which did not merely discuss religious doctrine but espoused a particular religious view. The use of public money to subsidize religious messages, as Justice Souter saw it, "strikes at what we have repeatedly held to be the heart of the prohibition on establishment."

The *Rosenberger* decision represents a significant expansion of free speech doctrine, insofar as it emphasizes the importance of religious speech and extends the concept of a public forum into a somewhat abstract realm. What the Court characterizes as equal access to funding, however, may be viewed less as a public forum issue than as an economic benefit. If so, the decision is at odds with a long line of cases supporting the proposition that the state cannot abridge basic freedom but is not constitutionally obligated to subsidize them. The trimming of the establishment clause is the inevitable result of a choice between constitutional provisions perceived to be in conflict with each other. Whether the case presented an either-or proposition was debated before and has been debated since the Court's ruling. By making it a choice between constitutional principles, the Court in one decision achieved the dual result of enhancing freedom of speech and subtracting from antiestablishment interests.

Bibliography

Martin Redish and Daryl Kessler, *Government Subsidies and Free Expression,* 80 *Minnesota Law Review* 543 (1996). Government funding that impacts speech is discussed.
Keith Werhan, *The Liberalization of Freedom of Speech on a Conservative Court,* 80 *Iowa Law Review* 51 (1994). The challenges of categorizing different types of forums is examined.

SECONDARY EFFECTS

Regulation may have an impact upon expression that is direct or indirect. When government controls expression because of its content, and the speech is in a constitutionally protected category, standards of review tend to be rigorous. A lesser standard of review operates, however, when government's regulatory interest is unrelated to expression itself. Rules governing access and use of public forums, when properly devised, represent the most established model of content-neutral regulation. Laws targeting the secondary effects of a particular communication mode are a more recently recognized form of content-neutral regulation. In *City of Renton v. Playtime Theatres, Inc.,* the Court reviewed a zoning ordinance restricting the location of adult entertainment businesses. Secondary effects doctrine was the basis for upholding this law.

City of Renton v. Playtime Theatres, Inc.

Obscene expression historically and consistently has been placed beyond the protective range of the First Amendment. Although sexually oriented expression that is not obscene is afforded constitutional protection, much case law views it in a devalued or disfavored manner. The primary challenge to the law of obscenity was defining the term. With respect to sexually explicit expression that falls short of obscenity, the Court has struggled not only with definition but identifying a basis for justifying its regulation.

Renton involved a zoning ordinance that prohibited adult movie theatres from locating within 1,000 feet of any residential zone, single- or multiple-family dwelling, church, park, or school. The ordinance was aimed, not at the content of the films shown in the theatres, but rather at the "secondary effects"—such as crime and deteriorating property values—that these theaters fostered: "It is th[e] secondary effect which these zoning ordinances attempt to avoid, not the dissemination of 'offensive' speech."

In deciding the case, the Court treated the Renton ordinance as a "content-neutral" time, place, and manner regulation. This treatment was important because, in a number of prior decisions, the Court has held that content-based speech restrictions should be subjected to strict scrutiny. As a "content-neutral" restriction, the Renton ordinance would be subjected to a lower standard of scrutiny and would be upheld if it was "designed to serve a substantial governmental interest" and did "not unreasonably limit alternative avenues of

Citation: 475 U.S. 41.

Issue: Whether a city may prohibit adult movie theatres from locating in residential neighborhoods.

Year: 1986.

Outcome: Because of the "secondary effects" of adult movie theatres, specifically their connection with crime and deteriorating property values, their location may be restricted.

Author of Opinion: Justice William Rehnquist.

Vote: 7-2.

communication." The Court justified treating the ordinance as content-neutral because it was "aimed not at the *content* of the films shown at 'adult motion picture theatres,' but rather at the *secondary effects* of such theaters on the surrounding community." The Court accepted the secondary effects as Renton's "*predominate* concerns" and concluded that the "ordinance does not contravene the fundamental principle that underlies our concern about 'content-based' speech regulations: that government may not grant the use of a forum to people whose views it finds acceptable, but deny use to those wishing to express less favored or more controversial views."

The Court readily concluded that the Renton ordinance was designed "to serve a substantial governmental interest and allows for reasonable alternative avenues of communication." The Court concluded that a city's strong "interest in attempting to preserve the quality of urban life is one that must be accorded high respect." The Court noted that Renton had properly relied on the experiences of other cities who had suffered such secondary effects, as well as on expert testimony regarding the effects of adult theatres.

The Court found that Renton's zoning provision was a constitutionally permissible method of dealing with the secondary effects. "Cities may regulate adult theaters by dispersing them, as in Detroit, or by effectively concentrating them, as in Renton." In addition, the Court concluded that the ordinance was "narrowly tailored" to regulate only theatres producing the unwanted secondary effects.

The Court also rejected the argument that the ordinance was "under-inclusive" because it failed to regulate other adult business that might involve similar secondary effects. The Court noted that there were no other adult businesses in the city at the time, and none were trying to locate there. "That Renton chose first to address the potential problems created by one particular kind of adult business in no way suggests that the city has 'singled out' adult theaters for discriminatory treatment." The Court assumed that Renton would deal with other problems as they arose.

Finally, the Court concluded that the ordinance left open "reasonable alternative avenues of communication" because the ordinance left 520 acres of the city, slightly more than five percent of the entire city, available for use by adult theatres. The Court rejected the argument that none of the possible sites were "commercially viable" adult theatre sites.

Justice William Brennan, joined by Justice Thurgood Marshall, dissented. He argued that, since the ordinance imposed limitations based "exclusively on the content of the films shown there," it could not be treated as a content-neutral time, place, and manner restriction. He rejected the argument that, rather than being content-based, the ordinance was based solely on the secondary effects of theaters. As a result, he would have required the government to show that the ordinance served a compelling governmental interest and could be served by less intrusive alternatives. He concluded that the City failed to show that its objectives could not be served by "less intrusive restrictions."

City of Renton is an important decision because it gives cities broad authority to "zone" adult movie theaters to places separated from churches and residences.

Bibliography

Amy Adler, *Girls! Girls! Girls! The Supreme Court Confronts the G-String*, 80 *New York University Law Review* 1108 (2005).
John Fee, *Speech Discrimination*, 85 *Boston University Law Review* 1103 (2005).
Eugene Volokh, *Speech as Conduct: Generally Applicable Laws, Illegal Courses of Conduct, "Situation-Altering Utterances," and the Uncharted Zones*, 90 *Cornell Law Review* 1277 (2005).
Russell L. Weaver and Donald E. Lively, *Understanding the First Amendment* (Newark, NJ: LexisNexis 2003), 10, 111–112.

PROCEDURAL REGULATION

The content neutrality cases illustrate how speech may be burdened for reasons unrelated to substantive message. In accounting for its interests within their purview, states also employ processes that impose a burden on expression. A system of licensing or permits, for example, may be established to manage competing uses in public forums. Such methods have been upheld to the extent that administrative discretion is minimized and fidelity to content-neutral decision making is maintained. Injunctions are a form of relief that, when entered by a court, prohibit or mandate a specific action. This procedure, when applied to speech, typically constitutes a prior restraint. As discussed in *Nebraska Press Association v. Stuart* (1976), prior restraints are highly disfavored under the First Amendment. The Court distinguishes, however, between injunctions that directly and indirectly burden expression. In *Madsen v. Women's Health Center* (1994), the Court determined that an injunction limiting the place and manner of antiabortion picketing was entered without reference to content. The injunction thus was not subject to the presumption against its constitutionality and strict scrutiny that would apply to a prior restraint.

Madsen v. Women's Health Center, Inc.

Recent United States Supreme Court First Amendment jurisprudence has drawn a distinction between "content-based" and "content-neutral" speech restrictions, as well as between "viewpoint-based" and "viewpoint-neutral" speech restrictions. In a representative democracy, where citizens are expected to vote on candidates and have the right to influence the democratic process, freedom of speech is the engine by which citizens communicate with each other. Content-based restrictions (and, for that matter, viewpoint-based restrictions) are antithetical to democracy because they involve governmental attempts to restrict speech—rather than allowing the people to set the speech agenda.

In *Madsen*, abortion protestors sought to challenge a court order that limited their ability to protest outside an abortion clinic. The court entered an initial order enjoining petitioners from blocking or interfering with public access to the clinic and from physically abusing persons entering or leaving the clinic. When the protestors violated that injunction, the clinic sought to broaden the injunction because the protestors were impeding access, discouraging potential patients from entering the clinic, and having deleterious physical effects on others. The trial court agreed and issued a broader injunction.

The *Madsen* Court was called upon to determine whether the lower-court's injunction should be subjected to heightened review because it was content-based or viewpoint-based. *See R.A.V. v. City of St. Paul*, 505 U.S. 377 (1992). The Court began by rejecting the argument that, because the injunction restricts only the speech of antiabortion protesters, it is necessarily content-based or viewpoint-based. The Court noted that an injunc-

Citation: 512 U.S. 753.

Issue: Whether an injunction against abortion protestors involves "viewpoint-based" discrimination against speech and therefore should be subjected to strict scrutiny.

Year of Decision: 1994.

Outcome: Injunctions against abortion protestors are not necessarily "viewpoint-based" and therefore may be subjected to intermediate scrutiny.

Author of Opinion: Chief Justice William Rehnquist.

Vote: 5-4.

tion, by definition, applies only to an individual, or group of individuals, and regulates the activities of that individual or group. However, the decision to issue the injunction was based on the protestor's past actions, in the context of a specific dispute, and the trial court was simply trying to fashion a remedy to deal with those past actions. As a result, one could not, and would not, expect the injunction to prohibit demonstrations by those who favor abortion. The protestors were enjoined here not because of their message but because "they repeatedly violated the court's original order."

Because the *Madsen* Court concluded that the injunction was not viewpoint-based or content-based, the Court decided not to apply strict scrutiny. Strict scrutiny is the highest standard of review and requires the government to show that its action is supported by a "compelling" or "overriding" governmental interest that is pursued by the least restrictive means possible. At the same time, the Court was unwilling to apply the lower standard of review applicable to statutes imposing so-called time, place, and manner restrictions. This standard inquires whether the injunction is narrowly tailored to serve a significant government interest. The Court concluded that there were "obvious differences" between injunctions and statutes or ordinances. Unlike ordinances, which involve legislative choices and decisions to promote particular societal interests, injunctions "are remedies imposed for violations (or threatened violations) of a legislative or judicial decree." In any event, injunctions "carry greater risks of censorship and discriminatory application than do general ordinances." As a result, the Court formulated a new standard that demanded a "close attention to the fit between the objectives of an injunction and the restrictions it imposes on speech." In particular, the Court required that "the challenged provisions of the injunction burden no more speech than necessary to serve a significant government interest."

Applying this standard, the Court upheld some aspects of the trial court's injunction, but struck down others. For example, the Court upheld a prohibition on chanting and singing outside the clinic, on the basis that the protest could upset women undergoing abortion procedures, but struck down a ban on carrying signs and posters. The Court concluded that the latter restriction burdened more speech than necessary because the clinic could deal with the problem by closing its curtains. In general, the Court upheld a 36 foot no-demonstration zone around the clinic, but struck the ban down as applied to private property that abutted the clinic. The Court also struck down a ban on approaching individuals entering the clinic. The Court concluded that the restriction burdened more speech than necessary by prohibiting all approaches and was not appropriately limited to independently proscribable speech (i.e., "fighting words" or threats). Finally, the Court struck down a prohibition against demonstrations within 300 feet of the residences of clinic staff. In prior cases, the Court had held that it was permissible to prohibit picketing focused on an abortion provider's house. However, the 300 foot limitation burdened more speech than necessary because it was broad enough to prohibit general picketing in the neighborhood.

Justice Stevens, concurring in part and dissenting in part, argued that judicial review of injunctions should be less stringent than judicial review of legislation. In his view, the propriety of an injunction depends on the "character of the violation and the likelihood of its recurrence." As a result, "repeated violations may justify sanctions that might be invalid if applied to a first offender or if enacted by the legislature." Concluding that the protestors in this case had committed repeated violations, Justice Stevens would have deferred to the trial court judge's conclusions.

Justice Antonin Scalia, joined by two other justices, concurred in the judgment in part but dissented in part. He argued that injunctive decrees should be subjected to strict scrutiny because there is a significant risk of discrimination against unpopular groups. He noted that "the injunction in this case was sought against a single-issue advocacy group by persons and organizations with a business or social interest in suppressing that group's point of view." In addition, injunctions against speech "are the product of individual judges rather than of legislatures—and often of judges who have been chagrined by prior disobedience of their orders." As a result, Justice Scalia was uncomfortable with the idea of placing such a "powerful weapon" as injunctive relief in the hands of a single person. "Persons subject to a speech-restricting injunction who have not the money or not the time to lodge an immediate appeal face a Hobson's choice: they must remain silent, since if they speak their First Amendment rights are no defense in subsequent contempt proceedings."

Madsen is an important decision because it establishes the standard of review applicable to speech-restricting injunctions. The Court rejects strict scrutiny, and also rejects the more limited standard of review applicable to time, place, and manner regulations, and instead imposes an intermediate standard of review: whether "the challenged provisions of the injunction burden no more speech than necessary to serve a significant government interest."

Bibliography

Tracy S. Craig, *Abortion Protest: Lawless Conspiracy or Protected Free Speech?*, 72 *Denver University Law Review* 445 (1995).

Charles Hersch, *Five Tellings of an Abortion Clinic Protest: Madsen v. Women's Health Center and the Limits of Legal Narrative*, 19 *Legal Studies Forum* 395 (1995).

Tracy S. Thomas, *The Prophylatic Remedy: Normative Principles and Definitional Parameters of Injunctive Relief*, 52 *Buffalo Law Review* 301 (2004).

Russell L. Weaver and Donald E. Lively, *Understanding the First Amendment* (Newark, NJ: LexisNexis 2004), 95–105.

GOVERNMENT SUBSIDIES AND CONDITIONS

So long as it is acting pursuant to a valid power, and not precluded by a constitutional guarantee, government may exercise discretion with respect to the objectives it targets and how it distributes resources. The First Amendment does not preclude government from communicating a particular message directly or through proxies. In funding expression, however, it may not discriminate on the basis of viewpoint.

In *National Endowment for the Arts v. Finley* (1998), the Court determined that Congress could require the National Endowment for the Arts to factor standards of decency into its processes for distributing grants to artists. The Court also rejected the notion of an unconstitutional condition in *United States v. American Library Association, Inc.* (2004). This case concerned the denial of federal Internet funding to libraries that did not use software that blocked access to obscenity and child pornography.

National Endowment for the Arts v. Finley

The United States Supreme Court has repeatedly held that the First Amendment's speech clause protects not only traditional speech, but also art and artistic activity. Indeed, art can sometimes convey ideas more effectively or with greater emotional and intellectual impact than traditional speech.

National Endowment for the Arts v. Finley involved the *National Foundation on the Arts and Humanities Act of 1965* (Act) which provided government financial support for art and artistic activity, but which placed restrictions on projects entitled to receive governmental funding. Under the Act, Congress established the National Endowment for the Arts

Citation: 524 U.S. 569.

Issue: Whether Congress can require the National Endowment for the Arts to consider "general standards of decency and respect for the diverse beliefs and values of the American public" in awarding arts grants.

Year of Opinion: 1998.

Outcome: Congress has the power to compel the National Endowment for the Arts to consider "general standards of decency and respect for the diverse beliefs and values of the American public" in awarding grants.

Author of Opinion: Justice Sandra Day O'Connor.

Vote: 8-1.

(NEA) and authorized it to provide grants to support artistic activity. The Act specifically articulated the objective of helping to "create and sustain not only a climate encouraging freedom of thought, imagination, and inquiry but also the material conditions facilitating the release of ... creative talent," and the Act gave the NEA discretion to award grants and identified only broad funding priorities ("artistic and cultural significance, giving emphasis to American creativity and cultural diversity," "professional excellence," and the encouragement of "public knowledge, education, understanding, and appreciation of the arts"). Under the Act, the NEA distributed several billion dollars in grants to individuals and organizations. Grants were made by the NEA's chairperson based on recommendations made by advisory panels.

Although most of the NEA grants were relatively uncontroversial, a few grants produced much controversy. One of the controversial grants was a $15,000 grant that financed "Piss Christ," a photograph that depicted a religious crucifix immersed in urine. A second controversial grant involved a $30,000 grant that was used to finance a retrospective on photographer Robert Mapplethorpe's work composed of homoerotic (allegedly pornographic) photographs.

In response to the "Piss Christ" and Mapplethorpe exhibits, Congress initially considered whether to cut the NEA's budget by the amount spent on those two exhibits ($45,000). However, Congress ultimately decided to amend the governing statute to provide that no NEA funds may be used to promote, disseminate, or produce materials that "may be considered obscene, including but not limited to, depictions of sadomasochism, homoeroticism, the sexual exploitation of children, or individuals engaged in sex acts and which, when taken as a whole, do not have serious literary, artistic, political, or scientific value." The NEA responded by requiring grantees to certify that federal funds would not be used inconsistently with the criteria. However, this restriction was subsequently struck down by a federal district court.

Following the invalidation, Congress considered and rejected a proposal to abolish the NEA. Congress chose, instead, to amend the Act to require the NEA to ensure that "artistic excellence and artistic merit are the criteria by which [grant] applications are judged, taking into consideration general standards of decency and respect for the diverse beliefs and values of the American public." The amendments were challenged by four artists who had applied for grants before the amendments were enacted and had been recommended for funding. However, after the Amendments took effect, the Chairperson's requested reconsideration and all four grants were ultimately denied. The four artists claimed that the NEA had violated their First Amendment rights by rejecting the applications and sought restoration of the recommended grants.

Before the United States Supreme Court, the artists argued that the Amendments constituted "a paradigmatic example of viewpoint discrimination because it rejects any artistic speech that either fails to respect mainstream values or offends standards of decency." The United States Supreme Court disagreed, emphasizing that the amendments merely admonished the NEA to take "decency and respect" into consideration and were aimed at "reforming procedures rather than precluding speech." As a result, the Court rejected the artists' argument that the amendments required the NEA to discriminate against their viewpoints, and expressed uncertainty about how concepts like "decency" and "respect" would be applied in the grant application process.

The Court also rejected the argument that the criteria are so "subjective that the agency could utilize them to engage in viewpoint discrimination." The Court felt that the NEA's general criteria, involving "artistic excellence," already introduced subjectivity into the process, and noted that concepts like "decency" are appropriate criteria, especially in reference to some types of grants (i.e., for schools). Moreover, the Court concluded that the NEA has limited resources, and it must deny the majority of the grant applications that it receives, including many that propose "artistically excellent" projects. As a result, the NEA may fund projects for a wide variety of reasons, "such as the technical proficiency of the artist, the creativity of the work, the anticipated public interest in or appreciation of the work, the work's contemporary relevance, its educational value, its suitability for or appeal to special audiences (such as children or the disabled), its service to a rural or isolated community, or even simply that the work could increase public knowledge of an art form." The "very assumption" of the NEA is that grants will be awarded according to the "artistic worth of competing applicants," and absolute neutrality is simply "inconceivable."

The Court noted that plaintiffs did not allege or show discrimination in regard to any of their funding decisions, and, in fact, two of them later received grants. Nevertheless, the Court suggested that it might be inclined to step in if the NEA transformed the subjective criteria into a penalty on disfavored viewpoints. The Government may not "ai[m] at the suppression of dangerous ideas." Unless § 954(d)(1) is applied in a manner that raises concern about the suppression of disfavored viewpoints, however, we uphold the constitutionality of the provision. Nevertheless, the Court indicated that it might be willing to permit greater governmental discretion for grant funding than it would be inclined to permit if government were regulating speech. "So long as legislation does not infringe on other constitutionally protected rights, Congress has wide latitude to set spending priorities" and may "selectively fund a program to encourage certain activities it believes to be in the public interest, without at the same time funding an alternative program which seeks to deal with the problem in another way." In doing so, "the Government has not discriminated on the basis of viewpoint; it has merely chosen to fund one activity to the exclusion of the other."

Justice Scalia, joined by Justice Clarence Thomas, concurred. He disagreed with the majority's conclusion that the Act did not impose content-based restrictions. "It is entirely, 100% clear that decency and respect are to be taken into account in evaluating applications. To the extent a particular applicant exhibits disrespect for the diverse beliefs and values of the American public or fails to comport with general standards of decency, the likelihood that he will receive a grant diminishes. This unquestionably constitutes viewpoint discrimination." But he concluded that government was free to "selectively fund a program to encourage certain activities it believes to be in the public interest, without at the same time funding an alternative program."

Justice Souter dissented, arguing that, if "there is a bedrock principle underlying the First Amendment, it is that the government may not prohibit the expression of an idea simply because society finds the idea itself offensive or disagreeable." He would have applied this nondiscrimination principle even to governmental funding decisions: "[A] statute disfavoring speech that fails to respect America's 'diverse beliefs and values' is the very model of viewpoint discrimination; it penalizes any view disrespectful to any belief or value espoused by someone in the American populace."

Finley is important because it grants the government greater power to impose restrictions on government financing of artistic speech. Congress may require the National Endowment for the Arts to take into consideration "general standards of decency and respect for the diverse beliefs and values of the American public."

Bibliography

Albert J. Rosenthal, *Conditional Federal Spending and the Constitution*, 39 *Stanford Law Review* 1103 (1987).

Kathleen M. Sullivan, *Unconstitutional Conditions*, 102 *Harvard Law Review* 1413 (1989).

Cass R. Sunstein, *Why the Unconstitutional Conditions Doctrine is an Anachronism (with Particular Reference to Religion, Speech and Abortion)*, 70 *Boston University Law Review* 593 (1990).

Russell L. Weaver and Donald E. Lively, *Understanding the First Amendment* (Newark, NJ: LexisNexis, 2003), 211–13.

Mark G. Yudof, *Politics, Law, and Government Expression in America* (Berkeley: University of California Press, 1983).

United States v. American Library Association, Inc.

The Internet has enormous potential and capacity for spreading information and knowledge because it enables persons to communicate directly and inexpensively. However, those very characteristics also suggest that the Internet has a great potential for harm. Included on the Internet is a significant amount of potentially objectionable material (e.g., child pornography and sexually explicit material that can be harmful to children).

United States v. American Library Association, Inc., involved a challenge to congressional attempts to control Internet access. In the *Telecommunications Act of 1966* and the *Library Services and Technology Act,* Congress provided financial assistance to help libraries offer Internet access to their patrons. After passing the acts,

Citation: 539 U.S. 194.

Issue: Whether libraries can be denied federal funding for Internet access unless they install software that blocks obscenity and child pornography and prevents access to such material by minors.

Year of Decision: 2003.

Outcome: Libraries can be denied federal Internet funding unless they comply with the stated congressionally imposed requirements.

Author of Opinion: Chief Justice William Rehnquist.

Vote: 6-3.

Congress became concerned that federal funds might be used to facilitate patron access to pornography. To prevent this from happening, Congress passed the *Children's Internet Protection Act* (CIPA), which prohibited public libraries from receiving federal assistance for offering Internet access unless they installed software designed to block images containing obscenity or child pornography and prevented minors from obtaining access to material that is harmful to them. In *American Library Association,* in an opinion by Chief Justice William Rehnquist, the Court upheld the law on the basis that "Congress has wide latitude to attach conditions to the receipt of federal assistance in order to further its policy objectives."

A major issue in the case involved the question of whether Internet access at public libraries should be treated as either a "traditional" or a "designated" public forum. Historically, the Court has treated public streets, parks, and roads as "public fora" on the basis that such venues have been used since "'time immemorial' for purposes of assembly, communication of thoughts between citizens, and discussing public questions." Under the Court's "public forum" doctrine, the Court has held that government has limited authority to restrict the content of speech in such fora. In *American Library Association,* the plurality held that Internet access at public libraries should not be regarded as either a "traditional" or a "designated" public forum. The plurality noted that libraries had not historically been treated as public fora, and it held that the mere addition of Internet terminals did not "create a public forum for Web publishers to express themselves, any more than it collects books in order to provide a public forum for the authors of books to speak." The plurality concluded that libraries provide Internet access, not to "encourage a diversity of views from private speakers," but "to facilitate research, learning, and recreational pursuits by furnishing materials of requisite and appropriate quality."

In rendering its decision, the plurality recognized that libraries have historically exercised broad authority to make qualitative judgments regarding the materials that they choose to include in their collections. For example, since most libraries exclude pornography from their print materials, the plurality concluded that they must also retain the authority to block such material from their Internet sites. However, the Court recognized that it was not possible for libraries to "segregate" materials on the Internet in the way that they segregate or remove unsuitable print materials. If libraries tried to limit Internet access only to sites reviewed and found acceptable by their staff, they would necessarily exclude an enormous amount of material that staff librarians were unable to review. Therefore, the plurality concluded that libraries could use filters to exclude categories of content and thereby avoid the need for making individualized judgments regarding the universe of available Web sites.

Of course, using Internet filtering software ran the risk of blocking "constitutionally protected speech that falls outside the categories that software users intend to block." The reason for this problem is that filters are not precise and sometimes overblock or overfilter. Nonetheless, the plurality upheld the law, noting that it authorizes library officials to disable filters to allow individuals to conduct legitimate research or pursue other permissible research objectives.

The plurality rejected the argument that CIPA imposed an "unconstitutional condition" on the federal Internet grants. The "unconstitutional conditions" doctrine provides that the government may not attach impermissible limitations on a governmental program or subsidy. The plurality held that the Internet subsidy programs were "intended to help public libraries fulfill their traditional role of obtaining material of requisite and appropriate quality for educational and informational purposes," and that Congress had the right to insist that the funds be spent for the purposes for which they were authorized. Moreover, the plurality noted that libraries had already excluded pornographic material from their print collections, and that "Congress could reasonably impose a parallel limitation on its Internet assistance programs." As a result, the plurality concluded that the filtering software restriction imposed a permissible condition.

Because the Court was able to muster only a plurality opinion, the case produced much disagreement among the justices. Justice Kennedy concurred in the judgment because he concluded that the interest in protecting children from inappropriate material is legitimate, if not compelling. He did not believe that CIPA imposed an impermissible burden on the ability of adult library users to access material. Justice Breyer also concurred in the decision. He argued that the Court should have applied "heightened scrutiny," rather than "strict scrutiny," because the higher standard would "unreasonably interfere with the discretion necessary to create, maintain, or select a library's 'collection.'" Under "heightened scrutiny," he would have asked "whether the harm to speech-related interests is disproportionate in light of both the justifications and the potential alternatives," and he would have upheld CIPA because he found that it serves a legitimate, if not compelling, interest in preventing minors from seeing harmful material. Even though software filters tend to "overblock" Internet material, and thereby screen out some "perfectly legitimate material," Justice Breyer noted that an adult patron could request that the filter be disabled or that a particular Web site be unlocked.

American Library also produced a number of dissents. Justice Stevens dissented, arguing that CIPA violated the "unconstitutional conditions" doctrine because it "impermissibly conditions the receipt of Government funding on the restriction of significant First Amendment rights." Even though Justice Stevens agreed that libraries could choose to use filtering software, he doubted that Congress could force libraries to install them. He worried that filters tend to "overblock," thereby excluding large quantities of Internet information, as well as "underblock," thereby giving parents a false sense of security regarding the safety of their children. Justice Stevens argued that there were less restrictive alternatives to blocking and filtering, including the imposition of Internet policies that prohibit patrons from accessing illegal speech. In addition, he argued that libraries could use recessed monitors, and place unfiltered Internet terminals outside of sight-lines "to prevent patrons from being unwillingly exposed to sexually explicit content on the Internet."

Justice Souter, who also dissented, agreed with Justice Stevens that the "unconstitutional conditions" doctrine applied. Justice Stevens would have voted to uphold the statute had adult patrons been able to readily obtain unblocked terminals. However, he expressed concern that libraries had discretion about whether to unblock terminals, thereby making adult access dependent on the discretion of library staffs. As a result, adults may be denied access to "nonobscene material harmful to children but lawful for adult examination, and a substantial quantity of text and pictures harmful to no one [because of the] indiscriminate behavior of current filtering mechanisms...." Moreover, he argued that CIPA could have limited children to blocked terminals while providing unblocked terminals for adults. Justice Souter also rejected the plurality's suggestion that CIPA is comparable to a library making acquisition decisions. He noted that, historically, scarce resources had forced libraries to make choices about which books to require, and the acquisition of some materials precluded the choice of others. Internet access, he argued, was different. Once a library spends money for Internet access, it costs nothing to allow patrons to access that material. As a result, he concluded that the "proper analogy" is not "to passing up a book that might have been bought; it is either to buying a book and then keeping it from adults lacking an acceptable 'purpose,' or to buying an encyclopedia and then cutting out pages with anything thought to be unsuitable for all adults." He concluded that filtering amounts to censorship and that a filtering requirement is constitutionally impermissible.

The *American Library* case is important because it allows the government to place restrictions on the use of federal grant money and requires that grantees adhere to those grant requirements. The decision does not provide broad support for government censorship of speech in this limited context. However, the decision probably has limited impact. Outside the context of government-financed Internet connections, the Court has held that the government may not prohibit adults from accessing indecent material. See *Reno v. ACLU*, 521 U.S. 844 (1997).

Bibliography

F. Jones, *Defusing Censorship: The Librarian's Guide to Handling Censorship Conflicts* (Phoenix, AZ: Oryx Press, 1983), 92–99.

M. Fiske Lowenthal, *Book Selection and Censorship: A Study of School and Public Libraries in California* (Berkeley: University of California Press, 1959), 69–73.

E. Moon, "'Problem' Fiction," in *Book Selection and Censorship in the Sixties,* ed. E. Moon (New York: Bowker, 1969), 56–58.

Russell L. Weaver and Donald E. Lively, *Understanding the First Amendment* (Newark, NJ: LexisNexis, 2003), 208–16.

CHAPTER 13

FIRST AMENDMENT: FREEDOM OF ASSOCIATION

Freedom of association is not specifically enumerated by the First Amendment. The Supreme Court, however, has established this liberty as a fundamental incident of freedom of speech. It is a guarantee that is crucial to the ability of individuals to organize, mobilize, or affiliate on the basis of shared views. Freedom to associate thus derives its constitutional stature from an understanding that it is essential to full enjoyment of those guarantees actually specified by the First Amendment. Restrictions on associational freedom, as the Court recognized in *NAACP v. Alabama* (1958), have the potential to undermine the freedom of speech that the First Amendment contemplates and secures. Over the years, as evidenced by *Roberts v. United States Jaycees* (1984), the concept of freedom of association has expanded.

Roberts v. United States Jaycees

Since the nation's founding, citizens have "associated" for expressive and intimate purposes. Even though the United States Constitution does not explicitly mention or provide for a right of association, the United States Supreme Court has affirmed this right in numerous decisions. In an early decision, *NAACP v. Alabama*, 357 U.S. 449 (1958), the Court upheld the NAACP's refusal to turn over its membership lists. The NAACP feared that those lists would be used to harass and intimidate its members, thereby impinging their right to freely associate. The Court upheld the NACCP's right to refuse to turn over the lists.

Citation: 468 U.S. 609.

Issue: Whether the constitutional right to freely associate gives the United States Jaycees the right to exclude women from regular membership.

Year of Decision: 1984.

Outcome: The Jaycees do not have a constitutional right to exclude women.

Author of Opinion: Justice William Brennan.

Vote: 9-0.

Roberts is important because it helps define the outer limits of the right of association. That case involved the United States Jaycees (Jaycees), a nonprofit membership corporation, whose objective was to promote young men and young men's organizations. While the Jaycees had various membership levels, "regular" membership was limited to men between the ages of 18 and 35. Women and older men could apply only for "associate" membership, which meant (among other things) that they could not vote. The Jaycees had approximately 295,000 members in 7,400 local chapters affiliated with 51 state organizations. Of those, only two percent were female associate members. The case arose when the Minneapolis and St. Paul Jaycees chapters began admitting women to regular membership. When the national Jaycees moved to revoke the chapter's charters, the chapters responded by filing a complaint with the Minnesota Department of Human Rights charging a violation of the *Minnesota Human Rights Act* ("Act"). The Act made it illegal to deny "the full and equal enjoyment of the goods, services, facilities, privileges, advantages, and accommodations of a place of public accommodation because of race, color, creed, religion, disability, national origin or sex." The Minnesota Department of Human Rights concluded that the Jaycees provided a place of public accommodation and found a violation of the Act. The Jaycees challenged the determination in federal court as a violation of their constitutional rights of free speech and association.

In rejecting the Jaycees' associational claim, the United States Supreme Court engaged in an extended discussion of the right. The Court noted that "freedom of association" cases contain two separate and distinct strands. The first strand is based on the concept of "personal liberty." This strand gives individuals the freedom to choose their intimate human relationships and guarantees those relationships against state control or intrusion. The second strand derives from the First Amendment's guarantee of the right to engage in speech and assembly, to petition for the redress of grievances, and to freely exercise religion. This strand of association is guaranteed "as an indispensable means of preserving other individual liberties."

The Court recognized that the strand of association that covers intimate relationships guarantees citizens "a substantial measure of sanctuary from unjustified interference by the State." However, the Court held that a limited number of relationships fit the definition of "intimate" or "highly personal," and these include relationships "that attend the creation and sustenance of a family—marriage, childbirth, the raising and education of children, and cohabitation with one's relatives." The Court characterized family relationships as being unique because they "involve deep attachments and commitments to the necessarily few other individuals with whom one shares not only a special community of thoughts, experiences, and beliefs but also distinctively personal aspects of one's life." Family relationships are "distinguished by such attributes as relative smallness, a high degree of selectivity in decisions to begin and maintain the affiliation, and seclusion from others in critical aspects of the relationship." The Court held that only relationships with the quality of families qualify as "personal liberty" associational interests and would not include large business enterprises. However, as the Court recognized, "a broad range of human relationships" lie between family relationships and business enterprises, and the Court concluded that analysis of these other relationships necessarily "entails a careful assessment of where that relationship's objective characteristics locate it on a spectrum from the most intimate to the most attenuated of personal attachments" including "size, purpose, policies, selectivity, congeniality, and other characteristics that in a particular case may be pertinent." The Court concluded that businesses, especially large businesses, do not fit within the definition of intimate relationships.

Applying these criteria, the Court quickly concluded that the Jaycees did not fit within the category of "intimate" association. The Court noted that local Jaycees chapters are large (the Minneapolis chapter had 400+ members) and relatively unselective groups. The only criteria for membership are age and sex, and new members are admitted without background checks. Even though they were not eligible to be "members," women could attend various meetings, participate in projects, and attend many social functions.

As for the second strand of freedom of association, the strand designed to protect association for speech or religious purposes, the Court recognized "a corresponding right to associate with others in pursuit of a wide variety of political, social, economic, educational, religious, and cultural ends." The Court found that the Minnesota law implicated this right because the right of association includes governmental attempts to interfere with the internal organization or affairs of a protected group, and includes the right not to associate. In other words, freedom of association is implicated by a law requiring an advocacy group to accept members that it does not want.

Even though the Court recognized that the Jaycees are protected by the right of expressive association, the Court held that the Jaycees' rights can be infringed by "regulations adopted to serve compelling state interests, unrelated to the suppression of ideas, that cannot be achieved through means significantly less restrictive of associational freedoms." The Court found that Minnesota had a compelling interest in eradicating discrimination against women and held that this interest was sufficient to justify the law's impact on the associational rights of the Jaycees' male members. The Court noted that government was legitimately concerned about discrimination based on "archaic and overbroad assumptions about the relative needs and capacities of the sexes" that "forces individuals to labor under stereotypical notions that often bear no relationship to their actual abilities." The Court found that such discrimination "deprives persons of their individual dignity and denies society the benefits of wide participation in political, economic, and cultural life." The Court also found "compelling" the state's interest in ensuring access to the provision of purely tangible goods and services.

In addition to holding that the Minnesota law was supported by a compelling governmental interest, the Court also found that Minnesota had advanced its compelling interests by the least restrictive means. The Court found that the Jaycees remained able to engage in protected activities and to disseminate its preferred views, including its creed of promoting the interests of young men. In addition, the Court concluded that, notwithstanding the Minnesota nondiscrimination law, the Jaycees remained free to exclude women who disagree with that goal. However, the Court rejected the notion that women would inevitably have different views than men on these issues. As a result, the Court concluded that: "[E]ven if enforcement of the Act causes some incidental abridgment of the Jaycees' protected speech, that effect is no greater than is necessary to accomplish the State's legitimate purposes. Like violence or other types of potentially expressive activities that produce special harms distinct from their communicative impact, such practices are entitled to no constitutional protection."

Justice Sandra Day O'Connor, concurring in the judgment, argued that the Jaycees is essentially a commercial organization, and therefore should be treated as a "commercial" association rather than an organization devoted to "protected expressive activity." She went on to note that the "Jaycees itself refers to its members as customers and membership as a product it is selling."

Roberts is an extremely important decision because it distinguishes between different types of association and suggests that different standards of review should be applied to different categories. The decision is also important because it holds that the Jaycees, being a large and unselective group, does not fit within the protections for so-called "intimate" activities or "highly personal" relationships. The Jaycees do associate for expressive purposes, but the Court concluded that the government had a "compelling" interest in prohibiting the Jaycees from discriminating against women.

Bibliography

C. Edwin Baker, *Scope of the First Amendment Freedom of Speech*, 25 *UCLA Law Review* 964 (1978).

Kenneth Karst, *Freedom of Intimate Association*, 89 *Yale Law Journal* 624 (1980).

Douglas Linder, *Freedom of Association After Roberts v. United States Jaycees*, 82 *Michigan Law Review* 1878 (1984)

Reena Raggi, *An Independent Right to Freedom of Association*, 12 *Harvard Civil Rights-Civil Liberties Law Review* 1 (1977).

CHAPTER 14

FIRST AMENDMENT: FREEDOM OF THE PRESS

Freedom of the press in the United States emerged against a centuries old backdrop of official suppression. Introduction of the printing press in the fifteenth century presented a threat to established political and religious orders accustomed to controlling the stream of information. Responding to the perils they perceived in mass disseminated information, authorities strictly controlled access to print technology and imposed harsh sanctions for criticism of church or state. Although intolerance of speech challenged established centers of power carried over to the American colonies, resentment of royal policies and privileges fueled and facilitated interest in a system of press liberty. Prior to and during the American Revolution, the press played a critical role in defining and mobilizing anti-British sentiment. Widespread mob violence against pro-British publishers, however, demonstrated that appreciation of a free press was often selective rather than universal. This tension between freedom of the press and suppressive instincts outlived the colonial experience. Abolitionists were largely unheard from in the South, for instance, where they were subject to punishment if they distributed antislavery literature. Publications criticizing American participation in World War I triggered prosecutions and resulted in harsh sentences under federal espionage laws. During the 1950s, anticommunist fervor similarly daunted mass dissemination of expression advocating radical political change. Although the terms of the press clause have remained unchanged since the republic's founding, the press itself has redefined itself dramatically. Communications technologies, such as broadcasting, cable, satellite, and networked computers, did not exist when the First Amendment was framed and ratified. A constitutional response to their emergence, however, has become a primary preoccupation of modern First Amendment review.

PRIOR RESTRAINT

Central to a system of freedom of expression is the notion that prior restraints are generally impermissible. Concern with the chilling consequences of official censorship relates back to the late seventeenth century England. Pursuant to the English Licensing Act, printing was tightly controlled by the Crown. This enactment empowered the Crown to determine who could publish. The Act was repealed in 1694, but the legacy of prior restraint extended into the American colonies and beyond the founding of the republic. Systems of prior restraint, ranging from prohibition of antislavery literature in southern states to movie censorship boards, have operated with limited or no constitutional constraint. The notion that prior restraints generally are inconsistent with the First Amendment, however, was affirmed in *Near v. Minnesota*

(1931). In *New York Times Co. v. United States* (1971), the Court established two key propositions. The first is that prior restraints have a strong presumption of unconstitutionality. The second is that government has a heavy burden of justifying any system of prior restraint. Against this backdrop, the Court in *Nebraska Press Association v. Stuart* (1976) examined prior restraint in the context of the judicial process. At issue specifically was the constitutionality of gag orders designed to control pretrial publicity and limit risks to a defendant's right to a fair trial.

Nebraska Press Association v. Stuart

Citation: 427 U.S. 539.

Issue: Whether a trial judge may prohibit reporting on a criminal trial in an effort to protect the defendant against excessive and prejudicial publicity.

Year of Decision: 1976.

Outcome: The national commitment to free speech, and the aversion against prior restraints, precludes a trial court judge from imposing restraints on publication provided that adequate alternatives exist for protecting a defendant's right to a fair trial.

Author of Opinion: Chief Justice Warren Burger.

Vote: 9–0.

Press coverage of criminal trials can result in tension between the Fifth and Fourteenth Amendments to the United States Constitution, which guarantee criminal defendants the right to due process of law including the right to a fair trial, and the First Amendment right to free speech and a free press. In some instances, media publicity regarding criminal cases can be so intrusive that it creates the potential for an unfair and prejudicial impact on a criminal trial.

Illustrating the tension between the defendant's right to a fair trial and the media's right to report is the United States Supreme Court's landmark decision in *Sheppard v. Maxwell,* 384 U.S. 333 (1966). In *Sheppard,* the defendant was convicted of murdering his wife and children in a trial at which "bedlam reigned at the courthouse." Much of the material printed or broadcast was never presented at the trial, including charges that Sheppard had purposely impeded the murder investigation, that he must be guilty since he hired a prominent criminal lawyer, that he was a perjurer, that he had sexual relations with numerous women, that his slain wife had characterized him as a "Jekyll-Hyde," that he was "a bare-faced liar," and that a woman convict claimed Sheppard to be the father of her illegitimate child. The Court assumed that some of this material must have reached members of the jury because the trial judge did not protect Sheppard from "inherently prejudicial publicity" and did not control disruptive influences in the courtroom. In granting Sheppard's habeas petition, the Court concluded that no one may be convicted without "a charge fairly made and fairly tried in a public tribunal free of prejudice, passion, excitement, and tyrannical power."

After *Sheppard,* trial courts were obligated to protect a defendant's right to due process, but there were questions about how this goal was to be achieved. In *Nebraska Press Association,* the trial court confronted its obligation in the context of a sensational multiple murder trial (six victims) that attracted widespread media publicity. In an effort to ensure that the defendant received a fair trial, the trial judge entered an order restraining the media from publishing or broadcasting accounts of confessions or admissions made by the defendant to either law enforcement officers or third parties, except members of the press. It also prohibited them from publishing other facts "strongly implicative" of the defendant.

Petitioners—several press and broadcast associations, publishers, and individual reporters—challenged the order. The trial judge rejected the challenge, noting that, "because of the nature of the crimes charged in the complaint that there is a clear and present danger that pre-trial publicity could impinge upon the defendant's right to a fair trial." The judge continued the order, which specifically prohibited petitioners from reporting on five topics: (1) the existence or contents of a confession Simants had made to law enforcement officers, which had been introduced in open court at arraignment; (2) the fact or nature of statements Simants had made to other persons; (3) the contents of a note he had written the night of the crime; (4) certain aspects of the medical testimony at the preliminary hearing; and (5) the identity of the victims of the alleged sexual assault and the nature of the assault. It also prohibited reporting the exact nature of the restrictive order itself. Like the County Court's order, this order incorporated the Nebraska Bar-Press Guidelines. Finally, the order set out a plan for attendance, seating, and courthouse traffic control during the trial.

In striking down the gag order, the United States Supreme Court began by noting that "prior restraints on speech and publication are the most serious and the least tolerable infringement on First Amendment rights," especially when they involve the "communication of news and commentary on current events." The Court emphasized that truthful reporting about judicial proceedings has been accorded special protection, especially reports on criminal proceedings, because the press is regarded as "the handmaiden of effective judicial administration, especially in the criminal" justice context. "The press does not simply publish information about trials but guards against the miscarriage of justice by subjecting the police, prosecutors, and judicial processes to extensive public scrutiny and criticism."

Although the trial court order only postponed the publication of relevant information, the Court questioned whether the delay was constitutionally permissible. The Court concluded that the element of time is important if "press coverage is to fulfill its traditional function of bringing news to the public promptly," and the Court doubted whether it was permissible for government "to insinuate itself into the editorial rooms of this Nation's press."

Despite the important public interest in prompt reporting, the Court recognized that a prior restraint might be justifiable if the "gravity of the evil" were high enough. As a result, in evaluating the *Nebraska Press* restrictions, the Court inquired "whether the record supports the entry of a prior restraint on publication, one of the most extraordinary remedies known to our jurisprudence." Even though the Court expressed concern regarding the impact of "intense and pervasive pretrial publicity" on the case, the Court concluded that the trial court had other means at its disposal for protecting the defendant's right to a fair trial. The trial court judge could have taken any of the following actions: (1) ordered a change of venue to "a place less exposed to the intense publicity"; (2) it could postpone the trial until public attention subsided; (3) it could ask searching questions of jurors designed to ensure that they are capable of fairly and impartially assessing the evidence; (4) it could clearly and emphatically instruct jurors regarding their sworn duty to decide the issues only on evidence presented in open court; and (5) the judge could sequester the jury to insulate them from the impact of pretrial publicity.

The Court also raised other questions regarding the trial court's order. For example, the Court questioned the trial court's ability to enforce its order, especially against media interests outside its jurisdiction. Moreover, the Court doubted that press reports would necessarily be more damaging than the alternatives. Even without media reports, rumors regarding the defendant's guilt were likely to circulate in the community: "One can only speculate on the accuracy of such reports, given the generative propensities of rumors; they could well be more damaging than reasonably accurate news accounts. But plainly a whole community cannot be restrained from discussing a subject intimately affecting life within it."

Nebraska Press is an important decision because it reaffirms the nation's commitment to free speech, and the general impermissibility of prior restraints. While the Court was sensitive to the important governmental interest in ensuring that criminal defendants receive fair trials, untainted by the threat of excessive and prejudicial publicity, the Court concluded that a trial court has other means, besides prior restraints, for ensuring the right to a free trial.

Bibliography

Alberto Bernabe-Riefkohl, *Another Attempt to Solve the Prior Restraint Mystery: Applying the Nebraska Press Standard to Media Disclosure Attorney-Client Communications,* 18 *Cardozo Arts & Entertainment Law Journal* 307 (2000).

Warren Freedman, *Press and Media Access to the Criminal Courtroom* (New York: Quorum, 1988).

Russell L. Weaver, Leslie W. Abramson, John M. Burkoff, and Catherine Hancock, *Principles of Criminal Procedure* (St. Paul, MN: Thomson/West, 2004), 359–69.

Russell L. Weaver and Donald E. Lively, *Understanding the First Amendment* (Newark, NJ: LexisNexis 2004), 225–29.

THE NEWSGATHERING FUNCTION

Although protecting freedom of the press, the First Amendment provides nothing in the way of a definition for "the press." The modern press consists of much more than the print media that existed at the time of the First Amendment's framing. An understanding of its boundaries is important, therefore, for purposes of determining the scope of the press clause. The Supreme Court, despite the definitional void, has made no concerted effort to fill it. During the 1970s, some members of the Court engaged in a debate over the nature of the press. Justice Potter Stewart, for instance, argued that the press consists largely of organized media that provide the public with access to information necessary for informed self-government. Given this important proxy function, he would have protected the press not just in its publishing but in its newsgathering role. Over the years, the Supreme Court largely has rejected this premise. In *Branzburg v. Hayes* (1972), for instance, it rejected the notion of a First Amendment privilege that would protect journalists from revealing confidential sources or testifying to a grand jury. Likewise, in *Zurcher v. Stanford Daily* (1979), the Court spurned arguments that the press's unique role immunizes it from otherwise legitimate police searches and seizures. The notion that the press has no special standing under the First Amendment was reaffirmed in *Globe Newspaper Co. v. Superior Court* (1982). Although acknowledging that court proceedings typically are open and the press may cover them, the Court in *Globe* emphasized that the press had no greater right of access than the public.

Zurcher v. Stanford Daily

Freedom of speech and freedom of the press are set forth explicitly and separately in the First Amendment. For some constitutional experts, separation of the speech and press clauses means that the provisions have independent significance. Whether this differentiation was intended or real has been a continuing topic of debate. Although not officially resolved, case law largely has been consistent with the notion that the press clause adds no further meaning to the speech clause.

Freedom of expression sometimes has been referred to as occupying a "pre-ferred position" in relationship to other constitutional provisions. Exponents of this proposition have maintained that lib-erty of expression is more important than any constitutional interest that may be in competition with it. Some, such as Jus-tices William Douglas and Hugo Black, maintained that freedom of expression is of such significance that it cannot be abridged for any reason. The Supreme Court has resisted an understanding of the First Amendment in absolute terms, either in its rela-tionship with other constitutional provisions or other policy interests that the Court may view as overriding.

Citation: 436 U.S. 547.

Issue: Whether the search of a newsroom for criminal evidence violated the Fourth Amendment.

Year of Decision: 1978.

Outcome: The First Amendment is no barrier to an otherwise valid search for criminal evidence.

Author of Opinion: Justice Byron White.

Vote: 5-3.

The Court's interpretation of the press clause has reflected a similar reluctance to give it special force. Arguments that the press clause has relevance above and beyond the speech clause are based upon the media's special role in informing the public. A leading advocate of this position was Justice Potter Stewart. He maintained that the speech clause protected individuals, but the press clause gives "protection to an insti-tution." As Justice Stewart saw it, the gathering of news was essential to the public's interest in being well-informed. Given the close relationship between the role of the press and the imperative of informed self-government, he urged protection not only for the process of publishing but newsgathering itself. When the Court held that the First Amendment did not shield reporters from having to reveal confidential sources to a grand jury, in *Branzburg v. Hayes* (1972), Justice Stewart predictably dissented.

Although his rationale has not been officially repudiated, the Court generally has been guided by the competing reasoning of Chief Justice Warren Burger in *First National Bank of Boston v. Bellotti* (1978). In this decision, Chief Justice Burger could find no difference "between the right of those who seek to disseminate ideas by way of a newspaper and those who give lectures or speeches." This understanding, that the media do not have special status through the press clause, was the basis for the Court's ruling on the claim that a police search of a newsroom violated the First Amendment. The search aimed to locate and seize photographs taken by a campus newspaper photographer, who had shot pictures of a demonstration at Stanford Uni-versity. The newspaper had run a story detailing a clash between protesters and police. Following normal procedures, law enforcement officials obtained a warrant to search for photographs that would enable them to identify demonstrators. Justice Byron White, writing for a majority, found that the case implicated both the First Amend-ment and Fourth Amendment (which guarantees against "unreasonable searches and seizures"). The key question was whether First Amendment interests outweighed Fourth Amendment concerns.

The Court's answer was that the search of a newsroom was governed exclusively by the Fourth Amendment. Although indicating that the First Amendment was not a factor in this context, the Court noted that procedures for an otherwise constitutional search and seizure must be adhered to "with 'scrupulous exactitude'" in a newsroom search. As in any search context, a warrant allowing police to rummage through records, documents, and papers would violate the Fourth Amendment. The Court restated the well-established principle that search warrants should "leave as little as possible to the discretion or whim of the officer in the field." It also referenced the historical struggle between "Crown and press," and what it regarded as the framers' consequent awareness of the need to safeguard against official intrusion with the editorial process. In particular, the Court noted that the framers did not preclude the use of search warrants in the context of newsgathering. Even in a newsroom, the Fourth Amendment standards for a search warrant—"probable cause, specificity with respect to the place to be searched and the things to be seized, and overall reasonableness"—provided sufficient protection. The risk of official overreaching could be managed, moreover, by the Fourth Amendment requirement that the objects of a search be specifically defined in the warrant. By insisting upon satisfaction of this specificity requirement, the Court was convinced that no additional constitutional protection was necessary.

Justice Lewis Powell concurred with the majority. He was similarly influenced by the lack of historical evidence that the "Framers had believed that the press was entitled to a special procedure." Justice Powell suggested, however, that a judicial officer issuing a warrant to search a newsroom should be mindful "of the independent values protected by the First Amendment." In a dissenting opinion, Justice Stewart was more specific with respect to what those factors should be. As he saw it, police searches of newspapers manifestly burdened freedom of the press. Among the burdens was the interference with editorial processes (newsgathering, writing, and publishing) during the search itself. More significant, from Justice Stewart's perspective, was the possibility that confidential information or sources might be revealed. A search provides the opportunity for police to read "each and every documental until they have found the one named in the warrant." Without more than the standard Fourth Amendment protection, however, the end result was "a diminishing flow of potentially important information to the public." Such an outcome, as Justice Stewart viewed it, was inimical to First Amendment interests.

Justice Stewart also thought it relevant that there were no emergency circumstances requiring immediate investigative action or evidence of criminal activity by the newspaper. Minus such exigencies, he believed that the evidence should have been obtained by less intrusive means. Specifically, Justice Stewart maintained that the appropriate methodology would have been a *subpoena duces tecum* that required the newspaper to produce the photographs by a specific date. This procedure would not have disrupted editorial operations or entailed the risk of chilling information sources.

Justice Stewart's reasoning did not carry the day for constitutional purposes. It nonetheless was reflected in a legislative response to the decision. Two years after the ruling, Congress passed the *Privacy Protection Act of 1980*. This enactment bars newsroom searches except when there is probable cause that the evidence sought is in the possession of a person who committed a crime or it is necessary to prevent death or serious bodily harm. Minus such conditions, law enforcement officers must obtain evidence by means of a *subpoena duces tecum*. Among the grounds for challenging such a process is that it is unconstitutional or the evidence sought is confidential. The aftermath of *Zurcher* is a classic illustration of how the political process sometimes accounts for constitutional values that the Court itself has denied.

Bibliography

Wayne R. LaFave, Jerold H. Israel, and Nancy J. King, *Criminal Procedure* (St. Paul, MN: Thomson/West, 2004). A survey of the law governing search and seizure is provided.

Leonard W. Levy, *Emergence of a Free Press* (New York: Oxford University Press, 1985). A primary study of freedom of the press that includes a discussion of whether the free press clause is independent of the free speech clause.

Globe Newspaper Co. v. Superior Court

Speech essential for informed self-government historically has been given the highest value under the First Amendment. Consistent with this premise, the Supreme Court has been particularly protective of political speech. State and federal legislation, in the form of freedom of information and open meeting laws, reflects this imperative. Central also to a free flow of politically relevant speech is access to government proceedings and information. Like other First Amendment interests, such access is not absolutely guaranteed. Even when having a constitutional basis, it may be outweighed by competing interests that are

Citation: 457 U.S. 596.

Issue: Whether closure of trial under state law, when testimony is provided by the victim of an alleged sex offense, violates the First Amendment.

Year of Decision: 1982.

Outcome: A mandatory closure rule abridges the First Amendment; denial of public access is permissible only when supported by a compelling government interest and when the law is narrowly tailored to account for that concern.

Author of Opinion: Justice William Brennan.

Vote: 6-3.

found to be more compelling under the circumstances. Norms of open proceedings or access to information thus may give way, for instance, in light of national security concerns, law enforcement interests, privacy considerations, or other countervailing factors.

Generally speaking, the judiciary historically has been the least accessible branch of government. Through most of the twentieth century, strict limits were placed upon media coverage of judicial proceedings. Even today, cameras are barred from federal courts except for designated ceremonial events. Gag orders were commonly used to manage the risk of prejudicial publicity, until the Court restricted their use in *Nebraska Press Association v. Stuart* (1976). Equally strong as a remedy is the closure of proceedings to press and public. Controlling the flow of information through these strict measures typically aims to preserve the right of a fair trial, and thus requires a balancing of competing constitutional concerns. Specifically at odds with the First Amendment in these contexts is the guarantee of a fair trial incident to due process and the right to a public trial.

In *Gannett, Inc. v. DePasquale* (1979), the Court referenced the Sixth Amendment guarantee of a public trial in support of a trial court's order to close a pretrial hearing. This decision reflected an understanding that the right was personal to the defendant and could not be claimed by the press or public. Noting that the Court provided transcripts of the proceeding after the risk of prejudicial publicity had abated, the Court determined that the impact upon any First Amendment interest was inconsequential. The *Gannett* decision was written in rather imprecise terms and thus raised concern that the rule for closing pretrial proceedings might extend to actual trials. Many critics urged a narrow reading of it and hoped the Court would find an opportunity to limit and clarify its reach.

The Court responded to this concern the following term. In *Richmond Newspapers, Inc. v. Virginia* (1980), it determined that a right for the public and press to attend and cover trials was grounded in the First Amendment. By doing so, it extended the

First Amendment beyond the protection of expression itself to the securing of access to a critical government process. Noting that trials had a tradition of being open, and that closed proceedings carried inherent risks of abuse, the Court limited the power of judges to operate beyond public view. Although the result was supported by a strong majority, the Court split on a supporting rationale. Two years later, in *Globe Newspaper Co. v. Superior Court,* the Court settled on a premise that has provided a long-term guide for review.

At issue in the *Globe Newspaper* case was a state law authorizing closed proceedings when a minor was called to testify as a sex offense victim. As the Court saw it, the enactment's goal of protecting sex offense victims from embarrassment or injury was laudable. So too was the objective of encouraging them to testify in criminal proceedings. The statute's mandatory nature, however, made it constitutionally problematic. In particular, it excessively discounted the public's and press's interest in attendance. The Court was sensitive to the possibility that victims of child sex abuse may be harmed further if called upon to testify in open court. It also was alert to the reality, however, that factors such as age, maturity, family preferences, and the nature of the crime may cut against closure. The Court thus concluded that decisions on closure in such circumstances should be made not on a wholesale basis but pursuant to standards that drove resolution on a case-by-case basis.

Justice William Brennan, Jr., who wrote the majority opinion, announced the premise that the First Amendment protects not only expressive freedom but interests that facilitate this liberty. As he observed, "[t]he First Amendment is ... broad enough to encompass those rights that, while not unambiguously enumerated in the very terms of the Amendment, are nonetheless necessary to the enjoyment of other First Amendment rights." Pursuant to this understanding, the right to attend a criminal trial was crucial to the "free discussion of public affairs." The Court's recognition of a First Amendment right of access was grounded in two key premises. First, criminal trials historically (and even before the Constitution) have been open to the press and public. In support of this observation, the Court noted its inability "to find a single instance of a criminal trial conducted *in camera* in any federal, state, or municipal court during the history of this country." Beyond the historical significance of this reality was what the Court identified as "the favorable judgment of experience." The Court's second point was that open trials represented an important safeguard of quality and integrity. The ability of the press and public to access trials, in the Court's view, "fosters an appearance of fairness, thereby heightening public respect for the judicial process." Open proceedings also constitute an important "check upon the judicial process."

The Court, although invalidating the state law, did not altogether preclude the possibility of closed trials. It limited closure, however, to instances when the government presented such a remedy that was a "narrowly tailored" means of accounting for "a compelling governmental interest." Press and public might be excluded from a trial, therefore, when the state can show that the child would experience real injury if required to testify in open court.

Although setting a clear standard for the closure of trials, the *Globe Newspaper* decision gave no clear indication of whether it applied to other types of judicial proceedings. The scope of the ruling was particularly important, in light of the high volume of criminal cases that are resolved prior to trial. In *Press Enterprise Co. v. Superior Court* (1986), the Court expanded First Amendment access rights to preliminary hearings. Consistent with the *Globe Newspaper* premise, it noted the historical and unbroken preference for open proceedings. It also characterized the *Gannett* decision as a departure from this norm and emphasized that access to criminal proceedings was not restricted to any particular phase or event. Connecting its decision with overarching First Amendment values, the Court embraced the proposition that open proceedings ensure that the "constitutionally protected discussion of governmental affairs is an informed one."

Unlike simpler times, modern life imposes demands that limit the opportunity for citizens to attend judicial or other proceedings in person. Information that leads to understanding of and perspective on important government processes thus depends upon intermediaries that can access and disseminate relevant information. Media largely perform this function and, although the Court protects their ability to do so, the right of access extends equally to the public. The constitutional parity of press and public, with respect to accessing information, is consistent with the Court's sense that the press has no preferred or privileged constitutional status. Whatever the media's right of access, as noted in *Branzburg v. Hayes* (1972), it does not extend beyond information "available to the public generally." The media, as the Court observed in *Pell v. Procunier* (1974), may be "free to seek out sources of information not available to members of the general public." The Court's interpretation of the First Amendment, however, does not "impose upon government the affirmative duty to make available to journalists sources of information not available to members of the public generally." Even if the media play a critical role in facilitating the citizenry's ability to make informed judgments about government, therefore, case law consistently has made the point that they are to have no constitutional advantage beyond the people that they inform.

Bibliography

Wayne R. LaFave and Jerold H. Israel, *Criminal Procedure* (St. Paul, MN: Thomson/West, 2004). The constitutional balance that must be struck when free press and fair trial interests are at stake is examined.

Donald E. Lively, Allen S. Hammond IV, Blake D. Morant, and Russell L. Weaver, *Communications Law* (Cincinnati, OH: Anderson Publishing Co., 1997). This sets forth an overview of the law governing public and media access to government proceedings and information.

MEDIUM SPECIFIC STANDARDS

The First Amendment was framed at a time when mass communication consisted of the published word. Since then, numerous new technologies have evolved and presented challenges to how the First Amendment should be understood. For any new medium, the threshold question has been whether it falls within the purview of the First Amendment. When initially confronted with this question in *Mutual Film Co. v. Burstyn* (1915), the Supreme Court determined that motion pictures were more in the nature of "spectacle" and "entertainment" and thus did not fit within the boundaries of freedom of press.

By the middle of the twentieth century, when broadcasting had emerged as a significant medium, the Court's thinking had evolved and its view of the First Amendment had become more expansive. Although the new media that grew and developed over the course of the twentieth century achieved First Amendment status, the Court established different standards of review and thus varying levels of protection for each of them. This resulting model of medium specific analysis begins with the premise that each medium presents unique problems that require a customized definition and application of the First Amendment. As Justice Robert Jackson put it, in *Kovacs v. Cooper* (1949), "[t]he moving picture screen, the radio, the newspaper, the handbill, the sound truck and the street orator have differing natures, abuses, and dangers. Each … is a law unto itself."

Consistent with this analytical method, the Court in *Miami Herald Publishing Co. v. Tornillo* (1974) established that print media have the highest level of First Amendment protection. Broadcasting, as the Court found in *Federal Communications Commission v. Pacifica Foundation* (1978), has the least First Amendment protection despite being the nation's dominant medium. Within these constitutional extremes, and often with analogies to print or broadcasting, the Court has attempted to fix the appropriate level of security for other media. During the final decades of the twentieth century, cable television emerged as a significant medium. The Court has recognized that cablecasters are protected by the First Amendment. In *Turner Broadcasting System, Inc. v. Federal Communications Commission* (1994), it determined that federal rules requiring them to carry the signals of local broadcasters were content-neutral rather than content-based (and thus subject to a less rigorous standard of review). Efforts to extend the *Pacifica* ruling to other media have been unsuccessful, as evidenced by the Court's decision in *Sable Communications of California, Inc. v. Federal Communications Commission* (1989). This decision struck down a federal law that would have prohibited access to pornography through telephone dial-up services. A similar outcome was achieved in *Reno v. American Civil Liberties Union* (1995), when the Court determined that a federal law prohibiting indecent and patently offensive material on the Internet violated the First Amendment. The Court in *New York v. Ferber* (1982), as discussed previously, determined that child pornography could be criminalized even though it did not rise to the level of obscenity. In *Ashcroft v. Free Speech Coalition* (2002), however, the Court determined that Congress could not ban virtual child pornography.

Miami Herald Publishing Co. v. Tornillo

Citation: 418 U.S. 421.

Issue: Whether a state law giving political candidates a right to reply to an editorial violates the First Amendment.

Year of Decision: 1974.

Outcome: The right of access provision abridged the publisher's editorial freedom.

Author of Opinion: Chief Justice Warren Burger.

Vote: 9-0.

The First Amendment was framed and ratified in an environment of intense debate between political factions that had sharply different views over the nation they were founding. A key medium for this debate was the press. Publishers in the late eighteenth century typically reflected and were motivated by strong partisan sentiments. Consistent with this reality, they traded in pointed criticism over government officials and policy. In addition to their partisanship, early newspapers tended to have limited circulation with respect to readership and geography. This limited reach reflected underdeveloped distribution methods and literacy. As the national economy evolved and modernized, and mass production and dissemination became possible, the newspaper business grew into a major industry. The introduction of photojournalism in the late nineteenth century expanded the dimensions and influence of newspapers and heightened the impact of a medium that traditionally had relied upon print and drawings.

So disturbing were some changes in the newspaper industry that critics suggested the need for a legal response to its impact. Louis Brandeis, two decades before being appointed to the United States Supreme Court, coauthored an influential law review article that expressed concern with increasingly aggressive and intrusive news reporting. From Brandeis's perspective, media that a century ago had been facilitators of partisan debate had become instrumentalities of intrusion and gossip that appealed to people's lower instincts. Media emphasis upon sensationalism and entertainment, as Brandeis saw it, diverted space from "matters of genuine community concern" to the interests of "the indolent." With the press "overstepping in every direction the obvious bounds of propriety and decency," through "[i]nstantaneous photographs" and "newspapers enterprise," Brandeis believed the law must shore up the individual's "right 'to be let alone.'"

Change was not limited to the media's interests, the tone of its coverage, and its means of reporting. A primary trend of the newspaper industry, especially over the course of the twentieth century, has been the emergence of chains that have resulted in many publications being operated by group ownership. Another phenomenon has been the decline of the total number of daily newspapers. In 1910, a total of 2,600 daily newspapers were published in American metropolitan areas. By the final decade of the century, that number had diminished to fewer than 1,750. Cities with more than one newspaper, which had been a common feature at the beginning of the century, were a rarity by its end. As the Supreme Court observed in the early 1970s, one-newspaper towns "have become the rule, with effective competition operating in only four percent of our large cities." With increasingly concentrated ownership of newspapers, and a shrinking market for them, concern has been expressed that power to inform the American people and influence public opinion rests in the hands of a relative few. Whether this circumstance affects the meaning of freedom of the press, however, has been a question that the Court has answered in the negative.

The issue with respect to whether concentrated ownership necessitates constitutional doctrine that ensures not just a free but balanced flow of information arose in connection with a Florida "right to respond law." Under the terms of the statute, political candidates had "a right to equal space to reply to criticism and attacks on [their] record by a newspaper." In determining whether this provision undermined press freedom, the Court acknowledged how the newspaper industry increasingly had become characterized by concentrated ownership and diminished competition. Because editorial output was a function of centralized and homogenized opinion, commentary, and analysis, the argument for a right of response was that "the public has lost any ability to respond to or contribute in a meaningful way to the debate on issues." A public right of access to the media, to ensure broad and balanced coverage of important public concerns, thus was advocated as a constitutional check against "the vast accumulations of unreviewable power in the modern media empires."

The Court noted that economic facts had altered the right of free public expression as initially experienced in the society. Editorial competition, which had been common at the nation's outset, was difficult if not impossible to achieve because entry into the publishing business had become prohibitively expensive. Despite these profound changes, and their impact on First Amendment circumstances, the Court rejected the notion that the state might attempt to secure a publisher's fairness, accuracy, or accountability. Writing for the majority, Chief Justice Warren Burger indicated that "a responsible press" might be a "desirable goal," but it could not be achieved by constitutional interpretation without offending the First Amendment. The core issue presented by Florida's right to response law was whether government can force "editors to publish that which 'reason tells them should not be published.'" To the extent that news coverage is officially mandated or directed, the impact upon the editorial process is notable. As the Court observed, a public right of access requires a setting aside of "space that could be devoted to other material the newspaper may have preferred to print." Viewing the law not only as impermissible because it compromised editorial autonomy, which is the essence of press freedom, the Court noted that it might encourage editors to shy away from controversy so that they do not trigger a right to reply. Such a result would be detrimental not only to editorial freedom but to the needs of the information marketplace.

The constitutional bottom line for the Court was the state law was unacceptable "because of its intrusion into the function of editors." Because it compelled printing of a reply, the statute was viewed as extracting a penalty on the basis of content. The costs included "printing and composing time and materials and … space" that might be used for other stories. Even if it did not impose additional costs, a right of reply was unacceptable because it intruded into the function of editors. As the Court described them, newspapers are "more than a passive receptacle or conduit for news, comment, and advertising." The content of a newspaper and decisions concerning size and attitude toward persons and policy "constitute the exercise of editorial control and function." Whether editorial judgment is "fair or unfair," it is a central aspect of press freedom. Recognizing the importance of editorial autonomy, the Court stressed that it has not yet been "demonstrated how governmental regulation of this crucial process can be exercised consistent with First Amendment guarantees as they have evolved to this time."

The Court's decision reflects an appreciation of the role that the press plays as a check on government and how that function might be undermined if the state were to assume responsibility for fairness and balance. It reflects a philosophy faithful to founding sentiments expressed by John Adams, who drafted the free press clause of the Massachusetts Constitution. Adams penned the observation that "liberty of the press is essential to the security of the state, … [and] the relevant metaphor … is the metaphor of the Fourth Estate." The "Fourth Estate" is a term coined in pre-Revolutionary England in reference to the "Reporters' Gallery" that observed the "Three Estates in Parliament." Justice Byron White in a concurring opinion reinforced the value of this role in referring to "the unhappy experiences of other nations where government has been allowed to meddle in the internal editorial affairs of newspapers." No matter how well-intentioned the regulation might be, Justice White stressed the need to "remain intensely skeptical about those measures that would allow government to insinuate itself into the editorial rooms of this Nation's press." For him, a right of reply law advanced an important interest but ignored how "[w]oven into the fabric of the First Amendment is the unexceptional, but nonetheless timeless, sentiment that 'liberty of the press is in peril as soon as the government tries to compel what is to go into a newspaper.'" Modern circumstances of concentrated ownership and declining numbers of newspapers have challenged the ability of press freedom to achieve fairness and balance. By striking down Florida's right to reply law, the Court conclusively repudiated the notion that the First Amendment either permits or requires government to promote fairness and evenhandedness through official regulation.

Bibliography

Louis D. Brandeis and Samuel D. Warren, *The Right to Privacy,* 4 *Harvard Law Review* 193 (1890). Critical reaction to the increasingly intrusive methods of newspaper reporters and sensationalized stories in the late nineteenth century is provided.

Zechariah Chafee, *Government and Mass Communications* (Chicago: University of Chicago Press, 1947). This is a seminal work on the constitutional relationship between government and the media.

Edward Emery, *The Press and America* (Englewood Cliffs, NJ: Prentice-Hall, 1962). The history of American newspapers is examined.

Cass Sunstein, *Democracy and the Problem of Free Speech* (New York: The Free Press, 1993). This sets forth a critical view of the *Tornillo* decision and its rationale.

Federal Communications Commission v. Pacifica Foundation

Broadcasting is the primary source of information for Americans. Despite its dominance, the Supreme Court has given it the least protection under the First Amendment. This diminished status reflects in part the sense that broadcasting is a "scarce medium." Pursuant to an understanding that there are more persons wanting to broadcast than available frequencies, the Court has upheld regulations requiring broadcasters to balance their coverage of controversial issues or make time available for a specific use in the public interest.

Citation: 438 U.S. 726.

Issue: Whether the First Amendment bars the Federal Communications Commission from prohibiting sexually indecent but not obscene expression on radio and television.

Year of Decision: 1978.

Outcome: The First Amendment does not preclude regulation of sexually indecent expression.

Author of Opinion: Justice John Paul Stevens.

Vote: 5-4.

Regulation of broadcasting flows from the general premise that, as the Court observed in *Metromedia, Inc. v. San Diego* (1981), "[e]ach method of communicating is a 'law unto itself,' reflecting the 'differing natures, values, abuses, and dangers' of each method." Beyond the concerns that drove efforts to promote fairness and balance in the coverage of controversial public issues, regulatory authorities have been particularly concerned with radio and television's impact upon children. Government power to regulate on these grounds was tested, in *Federal Communications Commission v. Pacifica Foundation* (1978), when the Supreme Court reviewed the use of profane and sexually explicit language over the airwaves. At issue specifically was a comedian's (George Carlin's) monologue concerning "words you couldn't say on the public ... airwaves." The presentation, entitled "Filthy Words" had been recorded before a live audience. It was broadcast during the middle of a weekday by a New York radio station that specialized in "alternative" programming. It was preceded by warnings that the language might offend some listeners. The program generated a complaint to the Federal Communications Commission (FCC) by a listener who heard it while riding in a car with his 15-year-old son. The complainant was an official in an organization called "Morality in Media." Despite the radio station's argument that the humorist was a "significant social satirist," and no other complaints were received, the FCC determined that federal indecency standards had been violated.

Although vested with regulatory authority over broadcasting, the FCC under federal law is prohibited from "interfer[ing] with the right of free speech by means of radio communication." Congress, however, also has prohibited broadcasters from airing "any obscene, indecent, or profane language." Obscene speech is constitutionally unprotected regardless of the medium that propagates it. Indecent or profane language, however, typically is within the scope of First Amendment protection. Because the monologue was not obscene, the radio station argued that the FCC could not prohibit it without violating the First Amendment. The question, therefore, was "whether the First Amendment denies government any power to restrict the public broadcast of indecent language in any circumstances." In an opinion by Justice John Paul Stevens, the Court acknowledged that the speech was protected by the First Amendment. Nonetheless, it considered whether there were important reasons for prohibiting such programming on radio or television.

The Court began by restating the general proposition that speech cannot be regulated merely because it is "offensive." It further noted that the First Amendment was a bar to any regulation based upon political content. Having stated these premises, however, the Court determined that First Amendment interests were not significant. From the Court's perspective, the monologue was offensive "for the same reasons that obscenity offends." Although the First Amendment interest was found to be minimal, the Court noted that this reading could change depending upon context. It thus contrasted "a two-way radio conversation between a cab driver and a dispatcher, or a telecast of an Elizabethan comedy." Describing the programming as "vulgar," "offensive," and "shocking," the Court focused upon the actual setting in which it was broadcast. As a starting point, the Court observed that "of all forms of communication, it is broadcasting that has received the most limited First Amendment protection." The starting point for analysis thus reflected a dual sense that the monologue had slight social value and the medium that broadcast it had limited First Amendment standing.

Broadcasting's devalued constitutional status was explained on two grounds. First, as the Court put it, the medium has "a uniquely pervasive presence in the lives of all Americans." In this regard, a central concern was with the listener's privacy—particularly in the home where "the right to be left alone plainly outweighs the First Amendment rights of an intruder." A well-established line of cases holds that, when confronted with offensive expression in public contexts, a person can simply ignore what he or she finds offensive. With respect to broadcasting, however, the Court found it insufficient that viewers or listeners can change a station or turn off the offending medium. Placing total responsibility upon the viewer or listener, the Court observed, is "like saying that the remedy for an assault is to run away after the first blow." Even if the broadcaster provided warnings, the Court thought them insufficient for a broadcast audience that is "constantly tuning in and out."

The Court also identified the medium's "unique[ ] accessib[ility] to children" as a reason for downgrading its First Amendment status. Differentiating broadcasting from print media, it noted that "even [for] those too young to read" the monologue would "have enlarged a child's vocabulary in an instant." Although the content might be prohibited in broadcasting, it could be disseminated without constraint in other media and, in fact, was set forth in an appendix to the Court's opinion. Nonetheless, the easy access children have to radio and television led the Court to conclude that regulation advanced the state's interest in "the well-being of its youth."

The Court closed its opinion by comparing indecent broadcasting to a nuisance. Building upon this premise, it noted that regulation depended upon several factors, including the time of day, the makeup of the audience, and whether indecent content was disseminated over the air or by closed circuit. The Court described a nuisance as "merely a right thing in the wrong place—like a pig in the parlor instead of the barnyard." Consistent with this observation, it held "that when the [FCC] finds that a pig has entered the parlor, the exercise of its regulatory power does not depend on proof that the pig is obscene."

Justice William Brennan authored a pointed dissenting opinion alleging that the Court misconceived the privacy interests at stake and undervalued the interests of expressive diversity, particularly as this interest relates to consenting viewers and listeners. As Justice Brennan saw it, the Court actually undercut the authority of parents to make decisions pursuant to their sense of what is in the best interests of their children. He described the Court's opinion as an effort "to unstitch the warp and woof of First Amendment law in an effort to reshape its fabric to cover [a] patently wrong result." In this regard, he perceived a "depressing inability to appreciate that in our land of cultural pluralism, there are many who think, act, and talk differently from the Members of this Court, and who do not share their fragile sensibilities." The opinion thus represented, at least for Justice Brennan, "an acute ethnocentric myopia that enables the Court to approve the censorship of communications solely because of the words they contain." Reality from Justice Brennan's perspective was that the words at issue were "the stuff of everyday conversations" in many of the nation's subcultures. Banning them would burden those who dispute or challenge the "dominant culture." For Justice Brennan, the ruling established a preferred "way of thinking, acting and speaking" that was inconsistent with the First Amendment.

The aftermath of *Pacifica* consisted of nearly two decades of interplay between the FCC and the courts with respect to indecency regulation. After several failed efforts, the FCC adopted rules that provide a safe harbor for indecent programming between the hours of 10 PM and 6 AM. A federal appeals court, in *Action for Children's Television v. Federal Communications Commission* (1995), upheld this time channeling provision. In so doing, it recognized a compelling interest in protecting children under the age of 18. The court also was satisfied that the adult audience was not denied access altogether to a constitutionally protected form of expression.

Efforts to extend indecency regulation to other contexts largely have failed on grounds that media, like cable, provide better means for viewers and listeners to block unwanted programming. Technology's utility in other settings highlights how relevant differences among media may drive different First Amendment results. At a time when most broadcast signals are carried to the audience by cable, however, the different outcomes also evidence how technology ultimately may break down the logic of medium specific analysis.

Bibliography

Nat Hentoff, *The First Freedom* (New York: Delacorte Press, 1980). A detailed history of the *Pacifica* case is provided.

Alexander Meiklejohn, *Free Speech and Its Relation to Self-Government* (New York: Harper, 1948). A mid-twentieth century assessment that broadcasting merits no First Amendment protection, because it does not facilitate taste, reasoned judgment, integrity, and other qualities, is offered.

Lucas A. Powe, Jr., *American Broadcasting and the First Amendment* (Berkeley: University of California Press, 1987). Official efforts to regulate indecency in broadcasting are examined.

Matthew Spitzer, *Seven Dirty Words and Six Other Stories* (New Haven, CT: Yale University Press, 1986). A critical perspective upon the *Pacifica* decision is provided.

Sable Communications of California, Inc. v. Federal Communications Commission

First Amendment case law establishes that expression which may be fit for one medium is not necessarily acceptable in another medium. Sexually explicit content that may be published in a book or magazine, therefore, may not be permissible on radio or television. This result reflects a basic premise, as the Supreme Court noted in *Federal Communications Commission v. Pacifica Foundation* (1978), that "each

144 Individual Rights and Liberties

Citation: 492 U.S. 115.

Issue: Whether a congressional ban on indecent commercial telephone messages violated freedom of speech.

Year of Decision: 1989.

Outcome: The federal ban was not narrowly tailored in its effort to protect minors and thus abridged freedom of speech.

Author of Opinion: Justice Byron White.

Vote: 8-1.

medium of expression presents specific First Amendment problems." The starting point for reviewing the constitutionality of a content-based regulation, therefore, is to determine whether it responds to a unique or identifiable problem that the medium presents.

Finding that radio and television had a "uniquely pervasive presence" and were "uniquely accessible to children," the *Pacifica* Court upheld federal regulation of indecent programming. With this precedent established, it was only a matter of time before the Court would confront the same issue in the context of other electronic media. Barely a decade after its *Pacifica* ruling, the Court reviewed a federal law banning both indecent and obscene commercial telephone messages. At issue, in *Sable Communications of California, Inc. v. Federal Communications Commission,* were the sexually oriented telephone recordings of a dial-a-porn service. To access this service, users were required to dial a particular number and pay a fee. Drawing upon the rationale for regulating indecent expression in broadcasting, the government maintained that the regulation was necessary to protect against access by children.

In a majority opinion authored by Justice Byron White, the Court found that the *Pacifica* decision was easily distinguished because it did not demand a total prohibition of indecent programming. Rather, it required a channeling of such content to times of the day when children were less likely to be exposed to it. Even if the ban was not absolute, the Court observed that the characteristics of broadcasting that provided a basis for concern in *Pacifica* were not present in telephone communications. The uniquely pervasive presence problem that affects broadcasting, as the Court explained, is that a viewer or listener may not receive a warning with respect to program content that enables him or her to avoid it. This issue does not arise in connection with the use of telephones, insofar as the user must take affirmative steps to access the service. The decision to use the service, moreover, indicates a state of mind that is "manifestly different from a situation in which a listener does not want to receive the message."

With respect to concern with access by children, the government maintained that nothing could account for this interest short of a total ban of the expression. The Court found this argument to be "quite unpersuasive." It noted that the Federal Communications Commission, in its own rule making proceedings, had found credit card, access codes, and scrambling rules to be sufficient barriers to access by minors. In response to the government's contention that enterprising youngsters could bypass these safeguards, the Court found no evidence to justify the concern. To the contrary, the record as the Court read it could support the inference that technology was an "extremely effective" means for balancing the interests of consenting adults and the state's concern with protecting children.

In a concurring opinion, Justice Antonin Scalia agreed that the First Amendment prohibits Congress from banning the type of indecent telephone communications at issue. At the same time, he noted that telephone companies were not obligated to provide or contract for such services. Justice Scalia's observation restates two important principles. First, the First Amendment like other constitutional rights governs only action by the government. Second, telephone companies typically are public utilities and typically have no First Amendment interests. To the contrary, they are common carriers and thus are obligated to provide access on a nondiscriminatory basis to any user willing to pay the designated tariff. This rule does not apply insofar as telephone companies develop other lines of business, such as video programming that competes with cable. When functioning in such a capacity, the company is a content provider and protected by the First Amendment.

Justice William Brennan, in a concurring opinion joined by Justices Thurgood Marshall and John Paul Stevens, maintained that the prohibition of indecent telephone communication was "patently unconstitutional." He departed from the Court's determination, however, that the law as applied to obscene expression should stand. This conclusion was consistent with Justice Brennan's evolution since authoring the majority opinion in *Roth v. United States* (1958) that defined obscenity as unprotected speech. In *Paris Adult Theatre I v. Slaton* (1973), as a dissenting justice, he expressed his sense that obscenity should be protected to the extent that the interests of children and unconsenting adults were not implicated. The circumstances of *Sable*, in which dial-a-porn services were restricted to consenting adults and generally inaccessible to children, represented a logical opportunity for reaffirming this principle. It is a premise, however, that has not commanded a majority of the Court, which continues to regard obscenity as unprotected speech.

The *Sable* decision represents an important boundary of government's ability to regulate indecent expression. The *Pacifica* Court itself emphasized that its holding was narrow. Despite this express limitation, the ruling became a basis for regulatory initiative that attempted to impose similar restrictions upon other electronic media. In *Denver Area Educational Telecommunications Consortium v. Federal Communications Commission* (1996), the Court examined a federal law regulating the availability of "patently offensive" programming on cable television. Among the provisions of the law that the Court struck down was one that required cable operators to route all sexually explicit programming to a single channel and block access to it minus written consent by the subscriber. Borrowing heavily from its decision in *Sable*, the Court noted that technology can provide viewers with the ability to block or code access to unwanted programming.

The *Sable* ruling is notable also because of the rigorous standard of review it employed. Specifically, the Court insisted upon a compelling government interest to support the regulation and evidence that the rule was a narrowly tailored means of achieving its end. Although acknowledging that the interest in protecting children was compelling, the Court referenced technology as a solution that was effective and did not compromise First Amendment freedom. To decide otherwise, as the Court put it, would "reduce the adult population ... to only what was fit for children."

Bibliography

Daniel A. Farber, *Civilizing Public Discourse: An Essay on Professor Bickel, Justice Harlan, and the Enduring Significance of Cohen v. California*, 1980 *Duke Law Journal* 283 (1980). The general issue of civil discourse, arising in diverse First Amendment contexts, is discussed.

Donald E. Lively, William D. Araiza, Phoebe A. Haddon, John C. Knechtle, and Dorothy E. Roberts, *First Amendment Law* (Cincinnati, OH: Anderson Publishing Co., 2003). A review and assessment of cases concerning regulation of indecent expression, including the *Sable* decision, are provided.

Turner Broadcasting System, Inc. v. Federal Communications Commission

Citation: 512 U.S. 622.

Issue: Whether federal rules requiring cable television operators to carry broadcast signals were content-based or content-neutral.

Year of Decision: 1994.

Outcome: The must-carry rules were content-neutral and subject to less exacting constitutional review than if they were content-based.

Author of Opinion: Justice Anthony Kennedy.

Vote: 5-4.

The cable television industry originated as a means for distributing broadcast signals into regions that, because of topography or distance, had difficulty accessing television. By the late twentieth century, cable television had become a dominant medium in its own right. Instead of merely enhancing broadcast television, modern cable systems provide multiple channels of programming from other sources. With cable penetrating approximately three-quarters of the nation's households by the beginning of the twenty-first century, it is a medium that no longer is ancillary to but in competition with traditional broadcasting.

As cable became a more powerful presence, the Federal Communications Commission (FCC) grew concerned with the medium's potential for causing economic harm to broadcasters. Television's revenue stream flows from advertisers whose interest in purchasing time for commercials depends upon the ability to reach an audience. With cable having become the primary gateway for delivering broadcast programming, the FCC became increasingly worried by the possibility that cable operators might drop local television stations from their systems.

To avoid the possibility that cable might use its market power to displace broadcasters, and thus destroy an industry that provides service with no direct charge to users, Congress included provisions in the *Cable Television Consumer Protection and Competition Act of 1992* that required operators to carry most if not all local broadcast signals. Twice during the 1980s, the FCC had proposed must-carry regulations only to have them invalidated by lower courts. Congressional action reflected a growing sense, however, that economic power was becoming concentrated in the cable industry to a point that broadcasting's ability to compete was becoming endangered. Must-carry regulation thus rested upon findings that, without them, there was a "substantial likelihood" that cable would erode the advertising revenue base that sustains free local television and its economic viability.

The cable industry, in *Turner Broadcasting System, Inc. v. Federal Communications Commission* (1994), challenged the must-carry provisions on grounds that they abridged the freedom of speech and freedom of the press secured by the First Amendment. Its primary arguments were that must carriage invaded the editorial discretion of cable operators and burdened the ability of other programming sources to obtain channel access. From the cable industry's standpoint, the must-carry requirement constituted content-based regulation and thus should be subject to a high standard of review. Pursuant to this strict scrutiny model, which applies when a fundamental right has been burdened, the Court would be required to ask whether the regulation was narrowly tailored toward achieving a compelling interest. The government, however, maintained that must carriage was nothing more than antitrust legislation. It thus pushed for a relaxed standard of review consistent with precedent that governs constitutional analysis of economic regulation. Further supporting its argument for judicial deference, the government maintained that cable regulation should be reviewed under the less rigorous standards that apply to broadcast regulation.

Justice Anthony Kennedy commenced the majority's analysis with the proposition that cable programmers and operators are safeguarded by the First Amendment. Their constitutional protection responds to two primary communicative interests—the origination of programming and exercise of editorial discretion in selecting the content that is carried on their systems. In factoring these concerns, the Court rejected the notion that the less rigorous standard of review governing broadcasting should apply to cable. Radio and television are more vulnerable to regulation because, as noted in *Red Lion Broadcasting Co. v. Federal Communications Commission* (1969), there is a scarcity of broadcast signals. Cable, by way of contrast, is characterized by a multiplicity of channels and the potential for unlimited access and use. Having explained why it would not use the relaxed standard of review governing broadcasting, the Court then turned its attention to the cable industry's argument for strict scrutiny. Insofar as the must carriage requirement singled out cable for special treatment, by imposing unique burdens upon it, the Court determined that some degree of heightened First Amendment scrutiny was necessary. To the extent that the regulation burdened expression on account of its content, it would have found a basis for particularly rigorous review. The Court concluded, however, that the regulation was unrelated to the content of speech. As the Court saw it, Congress's purpose was not to favor a particular type or source of programming but to preserve access to free television for those persons without cable. Finding the must-carry requirement to be content-neutral, the Court opted for a level of review that was more intense than the deferential model advocated by the government but more relaxed than the strict scrutiny urged by the cable industry.

The intermediate standard of review that the Court applied was the same criterion introduced in *United States v. O'Brien* (1968), a case that concerned the conviction of an individual who burned his draft card to protest the Vietnam War. Consistent with *O'Brien,* the Court inquired into whether the regulation advanced "a substantial government interest" and "burden[ed] substantially more speech than is necessary to further [its] legitimate interests." Having announced the appropriate standard of review, the Court declined to apply it pending further development of the record. Based upon the evidence presented by the government, the Court found a lack of evidence indicating that cable would deny carriage to broadcasters and that such denial would endanger the television industry. Missing too were findings regarding the actual impact of must carriage on the speech of cable operators and programmers. Without such information, the Court concluded that it could not determine whether the regulation suppressed "'substantially more speech than … necessary' to ensure the viability of broadcast television." Given these unresolved factual questions, the Court remanded the case for further proceedings at the district court level.

Justice Sandra Day O'Connor, joined by three other justices, authored an opinion that concurred in part with and dissented in part from the majority. Although concurring with the Court that content-neutral regulations need not be strictly scrutinized, she disagreed with its determination that the must carriage provisions were not content-based. In support of the proposition that the regulation was referenced to content, Justice O'Connor cited congressional findings that favored diversity of views through multiple media, educational programming, and locally originated programming, particularly with respect to news and public affairs. She maintained that these preferences, which Congress had cited in support of protecting broadcasting from the risk that cable operators might exclude them from their systems, represented content considerations. Insofar as must carriage was justified with reference to content,

Justice O'Connor argued that it could not be justified unless "narrowly tailored to a compelling state interest." Although recognizing diversity, educational programming, and local service and educational programming as "important" interests, she maintained that they fell short of being "compelling." From her perspective, these concerns should be managed not by government but by market shaped by the interaction of private speakers and listeners. In a separate concurrence and dissent, Justice Ruth Bader Ginsburg criticized the must-carry requirement as "an unwarranted content-based preference [that] hypothesizes a risk to local stations that remains imaginary."

Three years later, after further review by the district court, the Court revisited the case. In *Turner Broadcasting System, Inc. v. Federal Communications Commission II* (1997), it found that a more fully developed factual record supported the must-carry provisions. The Court thus accepted Congress's judgment that cable systems would drop broadcasters in many instances without must carriage and, as a consequence, local broadcasting would become financially imperiled. It also identified important regulatory interests in the form of preserving free broadcasting, multiple sources of information, and fair competition. Applying the intermediate standard of review that it referenced in the preceding case, it found that must-carry regulation was content-neutral, directly advanced important government interests, was unrelated to the suppression of expression, and burdened substantially no more speech than necessary to account for the government interests.

Although not prevailing in the context of the must carriage controversy, cable operators actually scored significant First Amendment points. The *Turner Broadcasting* decision not only reaffirmed that cable has First Amendment interests but that the standard for reviewing content-based or content-neutral regulation is not the deferential model that governs broadcasting. Although a victory for broadcasters with respect to must carriage, therefore, the *Turner Broadcasting* decision is significant for placing cable operators in a more favorable position under the First Amendment. It is a position that is likely to endure pending a rethinking of underlying rationales or the long-standing preference for developing each medium's constitutional status in isolation from other media.

Bibliography

Daniel Brenner, *Cable Television and the Freedom of Expression*, 1988 *Duke Law Journal* 329 (1988). The relationship between cablecasting and the First Amendment is explored.

Lucas A. Powe, Jr., *American Broadcasting and the First Amendment* (Berkeley: University of California Press, 1987). An overview and assessment of regulation designed to promote diversity in the media is provided.

Reno v. American Civil Liberties Union

The First Amendment has developed in the context of technological change that has evolved media beyond print formats into a variety of electronic methods for disseminating information. In response to these changes that have occurred since the First Amendment was framed and ratified, the Supreme Court has developed different models of review. The utility of this medium specific basis of analysis depends upon the existence of real differences among media. It is for this reason that the emergence of the Internet poses significant challenges to traditional constitutional thinking.

Instead of being characterized by differences from other media, the Internet represents the convergence of various media. It is an international network of computers

connected by telephone lines that provides access to and interaction with information sources and on-line services. A
primary Internet feature is the World
Wide Web, which enables users to search,
read, view, research, publish, communicate, and purchase. Unlike mass media
such as publishing, broadcasting, and
cablecasting, the Internet is characterized
by its decentralization. Any person connected to the Internet, therefore, can be
a publisher.

Citation: 521 U.S. 844.

Issue: Whether a congressional prohibition of
indecent and patently offensive material on the
Internet abridged freedom of speech.

Year of Decision: 1997.

Outcome: The restrictions on indecent and
patently offensive material abridged freedom of
speech.

Author of Opinion: Justice John Paul Stevens.

Vote: 7-2.

Studies of Internet utilization indicate
that sites providing access to sexually explicit material are among its most popular
attractions. With Internet use growing rapidly, along with concern that children
might be exposed to obscene and indecent content, Congress enacted the *Communications Decency Act of 1996* (CDA). This enactment prohibited anyone from knowingly using a telecommunications device to make, create, or solicit and transmit any
"obscene or indecent" communication to persons under the age of 18. It also barred
the use of interactive computer services for knowingly sending any "patently offensive" communication to persons under the age of 18 or displaying it in a manner making it available to them. Exempted from the prohibitions were those who took "good
faith, reasonable, effective, and appropriate actions" to restrict access by minors.

In support of the enactment, Congress cited the need to protect children from
obscene and indecent communications. Although acknowledging the legitimacy and
importance of this objective, a federal district court found that the law violated the
First Amendment. In *Reno v. American Civil Liberties Union,* the Supreme Court
considered the government's appeal for reversal of the lower court. The government's
case consisted of three primary arguments. First, it maintained that Congress had the
power to define obscenity for children differently than for adults. Second, the government argued that the same principles governing indecency in broadcasting should
apply to the Internet. Third, it contended that the CDA merely operated as a zoning
ordinance like regulations that govern the placement and availability of adult movie
theaters.

The Court found each of the government's arguments unpersuasive and struck
down the law. With respect to the first point, it acknowledged a state's power to differentiate materials that were obscene to minors even if not obscene for adults. For
this proposition, it cited the nearly three decades old case of *Ginsberg v. New York*
(1968). The Court distinguished the statute upheld in *Ginsberg* from the CDA on
grounds the former did not deny availability of the material to adults. Because the
law swept so broadly as to impact protected speech, the Court determined that it
was fatally overbroad on its face. Absent a meaningful definition of the term "indecent," it also was unconstitutionally vague.

The Court also found significant differences between indecency controls upheld in
broadcasting and the CDA. Contrary to the government's argument that the Court's
decision in *Federal Communications Commission v. Pacifica Foundation* supported a
like outcome with respect to the Internet, the Court found significant differences in
the circumstances. First, unlike the CDA, regulation of broadcast indecency pertained
not to whether but to when indecent programming could be aired. Second, and also
different from the CDA, the regulatory order reviewed in *Pacifica* was an exercise in
agency action rather than criminal prosecution. Third, indecency regulation in the

context of broadcasting operates against a medium that has "received the most limited First Amendment protection."

With respect to the government's contention that the CDA was akin to a zoning ordinance that kept adult-themed enterprises out of residential neighborhoods, the Court found that the law swept more broadly. Rather than "cyberzoning" the Internet, the law was found to apply to the entire cyberspace universe. Because the CDA aimed to protect children from "indecent" and "patently offensive" speech, moreover, it was clear to the Court that content was a primary rather than secondary legislative concern.

In structuring an appropriate standard of review for the Internet, the Court reaffirmed as its starting point the premise that "each medium of expression ... may present its own problems" that justify a customized regulatory response. It thus referenced case law that justified broadcasting controls on grounds the medium had a "tradition of extensive government regulation," frequencies were scarce, and its nature was "invasive." None of these factors, from the Court's perspective, applied to the Internet. Contrary to being grounded in tradition, the CDA represented the first regulatory initiative relating to the Internet. Unlike the scarcity phenomenon in broadcasting, the Internet provides "relatively unlimited, low-cost capacity for communication of all kinds." Finally, because access to the Internet requires affirmative steps by the user, it does not carry the risk of intrusion that inheres in "turning on a radio and being taken by surprise by an indecent message." Based upon these differentiating considerations, the Court concluded that the CDA should not be evaluated pursuant to the relaxed standard of review urged by the government.

Using a strict scrutiny standard of review instead, the Court agreed with the district court that protecting children from indecent material was a compelling interest. Because the CDA could not be enforced against foreign sites and age is difficult to verify, it determined that the legislation would not achieve its purpose. The law also denied large amounts of speech to adults, who have a First Amendment right to receive or disseminate indecent expression. Against this backdrop, and if there were less constitutionally burdensome means of achieving Congress's objectives, the Court determined that the CDA was wanting. In this regard, it cited favorably the district court's finding that user-based filtering software would "soon be widely available."

Justice Sandra Day O'Connor, joined by Chief Justice William Rehnquist, concurred in part and dissented in part. Her primary objection was that the majority based its decision upon the hope rather than the reality of technology. She thus agreed with the Court that the "display" provision of the CDA was unconstitutional, insofar as a speaker could avoid liability only by refraining from indecent speech altogether. Because such expression is protected in relationship to adults, the law unconstitutionally would "reduce[ ] the adult population [on the Internet] to reading only what is fit for children." With respect to the provision prohibiting knowing transmission of indecent material to minors, Justice O'Connor would have reached a different result. She would have upheld the law as it related to e-mails knowingly addressed to minors and on-line chats between an adult and minor, but not in connection with interaction with other adults even when there is a risk that minors may be present.

In response to the Court's decision, Congress enacted the *Child On Line Pornography Act* (COPA). This legislation, like the CDA, was designed to protect children from indecent materials on the World Wide Web. The COPA prohibits knowing communication for commercial purposes of any material that appeals to the "prurient interest" of or is "patently offensive" to minors. It also establishes "community standards" as the basis for determining whether these factors are present. In *Ashcroft v. American Civil Liberties Union* (2002), the Court found that this provision was not unconstitutionally overbroad. It did not rule on other constitutional issues, however, and remanded the case to the federal district court for further development. The lower court entered a preliminary injunction against the COPA on grounds it was likely that the statute was unconstitutional. In *Ashcroft v. American Civil Liberties Union II,* the Court affirmed on grounds there appeared to be less restrictive means for achieving the regulatory objectives.

Even if the COPA were to be enjoined permanently, it is unlikely that such a ruling would deter further legislative efforts to regulate indecency on the Internet. The Court itself has acknowledged that limiting access to children is a compelling interest. The challenge for legislators, however, is to regulate in a manner that restricts access to minors but not adults. Given the Internet's nature and easy accessibility, such selective control may be more attainable through technology than by regulation. Pending widespread availability and real efficacy of filtering software, however, indecency on the Internet is likely to be of continuing interest to regulators.

Bibliography

Ethan M. Katsh, *The Electronic Media and the Transformation of Law* (New York: Oxford University Press, 1989). This sets forth an examination of how new information technology and the convergence of electronic media will impact established social and economic institutions.
Ithiel de Sola Pool, *Technologies of Freedom* (Cambridge, MA: Belknap Press, 1983). The challenges of evolving media technology are identified and assessed.

Ashcroft v. Free Speech Coalition

As technology has advanced, it has become possible for pornographers to simulate real sexual conduct on the computer. So-called "virtual pornography" has been controversial to the extent that it has been used to create virtual child pornography. In *United States v. Ferber,* 458 U.S. 747 (1982), the United States Supreme Court held that child pornography (pornography depicting children involved in lewd sexual conduct) was not protected under the First Amendment. In *Ashcroft v. Free Speech Coalition,* 535 U.S. 564 (2002), the Court was

Citation: 535 U.S. 564.

Issue: Whether Congress may prohibit "virtual" child pornography (pornography produced by computer without the participation of any real children).

Year of Decision: 2002.

Outcome: Virtual child pornography cannot be prohibited consistently with the First Amendment.

Author of Opinion: Justice Anthony Kennedy.

Vote: 7-2.

forced to decide whether virtual child pornography could be included within the ban.

Ashcroft involved the constitutionality of the *Child Pornography Prevention Act of 1996* (CPPA). CPPA extended the federal prohibition against child pornography to sexually explicit images that appear to depict minors but are produced without using any real children (also known as "virtual child pornography). Section 2256(8)(B) prohibited "any visual depiction, including any photograph, film, video, picture, or computer or computer-generated image or picture" that "is, or appears to be, of a minor engaging in sexually explicit conduct." The literal terms of the statute were broadly defined to include not only classical paintings but also movies (including older actors who appeared to be minors engaged in sexual intercourse). The CPPA applied not only to obscene depictions of virtual child pornography but also to nonobscene depictions.

The Court was not asked to decide whether Section 2256(8)(C), dealing with morphed images (images of real children that have been altered), was constitutional. However, the Court indicated that it would have upheld the antimorphing provision because such images "implicate the interests of real children and are in that sense closer to the images in *Ferber*."

As for the remainder of the Act, in an opinion by Justice Kennedy, the Court struck down most of the CPPA. The Court invalidated Section 2256(8)(D), which defined child pornography to include any sexually explicit image that was "advertised, promoted, presented, described, or distributed in such a manner that conveys the impression" it depicts "a minor engaging in sexually explicit conduct." The Court expressed concern that the provision applied not only to those who pander child pornography, but also "those possessors who took no part in pandering. Once a work has been described as child pornography, the taint remains on the speech in the hands of subsequent possessors, making possession unlawful even though the content otherwise would not be objectionable." The Court was especially concerned about the fact that the law imposed serious criminal penalties (15 years in prison for the first offense and 30 years in prison for second or later offenses).

In striking down Section 2256(8)(D), the Court reaffirmed *Ferber* in noting that "sexual abuse of a child is a most serious crime and an act repugnant to the moral instincts of a decent people," and the Court recognized that there "are subcultures of persons who harbor illicit desires for children and ... trade pictures and written accounts of sexual activity with young children." However, the Court noted that Congress is free to enact laws protecting children against sexual abuse. Moreover, the Court distinguished *Ferber*, which was based on the Court's recognition of the State's compelling interest in stamping out child sexual abuse. Since virtual child pornography does not involve a "record of sexual abuse," and does not record a crime or create victims by its production, *Ferber* did not necessarily permit its prohibition.

In striking down the ban on virtual child pornography, the Court rejected the government's argument that "child pornography rarely can be valuable speech." The Court noted that *Ferber* did not hold that child pornography lacked value, but instead focused on the manner in which it was created. On the contrary, the Court concluded that, when child pornography is not obscene and does not result from sexual abuse, it can have value. Indeed, in *Ferber*, itself, the Court recognized that some examples of child pornography may have value, but concluded that virtual images could be used to create that speech without using actual children. Of course, the CPPA would have prohibited those images as well.

The Court also rejected the government's claim that virtual pornography imposes specific harms on society, specifically that it can be used to seduce children or to whet the appetites of pedophiles. The Court noted that there are many things that can be used to seduce children (e.g., candy and video games), but concluded that "we would not expect those to be prohibited because they can be misused." The Court concluded that any restriction must be narrowly drawn, and the Court noted that the "mere tendency of speech to encourage unlawful acts is not a sufficient reason for banning it." The Court concluded that the State had "shown no more than a remote connection between speech that might encourage thoughts or impulses and any resulting child abuse."

The Court also rejected the argument that virtual images are part of the same market, as the market for actual images, and are often exchanged for actual images, therefore promoting the trafficking in works produced through the exploitation of real children. The Court found that, if virtual images were identical to illegal child pornography, the illegal images "would be driven from the market by the indistinguishable substitutes." Indeed, the Court noted that "few pornographers would risk prosecution by abusing real children if fictional, computerized images would suffice."

In the final analysis, the Court focused on the values underlying the First Amendment and concluded that "the First Amendment bars the government from dictating what we see or read or speak or hear." The Court was also concerned that the CPPA applies without regard to whether the work has serious literary, artistic, political, or scientific value. In addition, the CPPA prohibits the "visual depiction of an idea—that of teenagers engaging in sexual activity—that is a fact of modern society and has been a theme in art and literature throughout the ages." The Court noted that both themes (teenage sexual activity and child sex abuse) "have inspired countless literary works." The Court specifically referenced Shakespeare's famous play, *Romeo and Juliet* (which involved a thirteen-year-old girl), and the movie *Traffic* (nominated for best picture). The Court noted that, if such films "contain a single graphic depiction of sexual activity within the statutory definition, the possessor of the film would be subject to severe punishment without inquiry into the work's redeeming value." In the Court's view, this result would be inconsistent with an essential First Amendment rule: The artistic merit of a work does not depend on the presence of a single explicit scene. Under *Miller*, the First Amendment requires that redeeming value be judged by considering the work as a whole."

Finally, the Government argued that the possibility of producing images by using computer imaging makes it very difficult for it to prosecute those who produce pornography by using real children. In other words, experts might have difficulty determining whether a given set of pictures was made using real children or by using computer imaging. The Court rejected this argument noting that the government may not suppress lawful speech as a means of suppressing unlawful speech.

Justice O'Connor, joined by Chief Justice Rehnquist and Justice Scalia, concurred in part and dissented in part. She emphasized the "compelling interest" in protecting children and noted that even virtual images "whet the appetites of child molesters who may use the images to seduce young children." In addition, she feared that possessors of "actual child pornography may evade liability by claiming that the images attributed to them are in fact computer-generated," and she feared that this problem would only grow worse as technology improved.

Chief Justice Rehnquist, joined by Justice Scalia, dissented. He argued that the government has a "compelling interest" in prohibiting actual child pornography, and he expressed concern that "rapidly advancing technology soon will make it all but impossible" to distinguish between actual pornography and child pornography. Nevertheless, he concluded that he would have serious "First Amendment concerns" if someone were prosecuted for possession or distribution of a film with serious literary or artistic value. He avoided that problem by construing the CPPA to apply only to hard core pornography.

Ashcroft is an important contribution to First Amendment jurisprudence. It distinguishes *Ferber* in holding that "virtual child pornography," which does not depict any real children, still qualifies for constitutional protection provided that it is not obscene.

Bibliography

Susan G. Caughlan, *Private Possession of Child Pornography: The Tensions Between Stanley v. Georgia and New York v. Ferber*, 29 *William and Mary Law Review* 187 (1987).

William Green, *Children and Pornography: An Interest Analysis in System Perspective*, 19 *Valparaiso University Law Review* 441 (1985).

Frederick Schauer, *Codifying the First Amendment: New York v. Ferber*, 1982 *Supreme Court Review* 285.

Russell L. Weaver and Donald E. Lively, *Understanding the First Amendment* (Newark, NJ: LexisNexis, 2003), 64–70.

CHAPTER 15

FIRST AMENDMENT: FREEDOM OF RELIGION

Many provisions of the Bill of Rights respond to colonial experience with abuses of power under British authority. Attention to religious freedom reflects an appreciation of the historical reality that colonization in large part was driven by persons seeking to escape religious persecution. The constitutional guarantee of religious freedom is twofold. Under the establishment clause, government may not enact laws "respecting an establishment of religion." Pursuant to the free exercise clause, it may not prohibit "the free exercise" of religion. Taken together, these provisions prevent government from imposing a particular creed by law and from interfering with an individual's chosen set of religious beliefs. The establishment clause and free exercise clause, however, are not always easy to reconcile with each other. State aid to religious schools, for instance, may be viewed as an unconstitutional support of religion. At the same time, denial of such assistance might be regarded as interference with the free exercise of religion. Such conflicting perceptions illuminate a tension between the clauses that is reflected throughout the relevant case law.

ESTABLISHMENT CLAUSE

Establishment clause review has been a source of striking metaphors but uncertain doctrine and results. Central to many of the Supreme Court's decisions in the field is a notion that the establishment clause erects "a wall of separation between church and State." This understanding, drawn from the writings of Thomas Jefferson and James Madison in support of religious freedom in Virginia, suggests more clarity than relevant case law actually has generated. The concept of a wall dividing church and state suggests a clear dividing line between politics and religion. It is a barrier, however, that has many holes and leaks in it. Previewing and perhaps preordaining this reality was the Court's ruling in *Everson v. Board of Education* (1947). Although stressing the existence of a wall between church and state, the Court determined that state reimbursement of transportation costs for students (including those attending parochial schools) did not violate the establishment clause. Since the *Everson* decision, the Court has grappled with the task of developing standards of review that are perceived as principled and effective. This effort has been complicated, especially to the extent that many critics including some justices do not subscribe to the wall metaphor. In *Lemon v. Kurtzman* (1971), the Court nonetheless settled on establishment clause standards that generally govern the field even as they continue to be sources of debate. The *Lemon* test provides the basis for invalidating laws that are driven by a religious purpose, have a principal or primary effect of advancing or inhibiting religion, or foster excessive government entanglement with religion. A religious purpose also was the basis for the Court's finding, in *McCreary v. American Civil Liberties Union of Kentucky* (2005), that the posting of the Ten Commandments on courthouse walls violated the establishment clause. The Court's decision in *Wallace v. Jaffree* (1984), concerning a state law authorizing a moment of silence at the beginning of the school day, exemplifies legislation action that violated the purpose element of the *Lemon* test. In *Lynch v. Donnelly* (1984), the Court deemphasized the *Lemon* formulation. It nonetheless found that a nativity scene reflected a secular purpose of holiday celebration, provided no significant benefit to religion, and constituted no meaningful entanglement of government and religion. In *Lee v. Weisman* (1992), the Court determined that school-sponsored prayer at a high school graduation ceremony violated the establishment clause. This conclusion hinged upon what the Court perceived as the "subtle coercive pressure" that official supervision and control created. Establishment clause case law consists of numerous decisions concerning the permissibility of government financial aid to religious schools. In *Agostini v. Felton* (1997), the Court determined that state-provided remedial education in parochial schools did not violate the purpose, effect, or entanglement prongs of the *Lemon* test. It also upheld, in *Zelman v. Simmons-Williams* (2002), a state voucher plan that enabled parents to choose between public and private schools (including parochial schools) for their children's education.

Wallace v. Jaffree

Citation: 472 U.S. 38.

Issue: Whether the State of Alabama's statute, authorizing a period of silence "for meditation or voluntary prayer," violates the establishment clause of the United States Constitution.

Year of Decision: 1985.

Outcome: Because the state law represented a purposeful effort to reintroduce prayer into public schools, it violated the establishment clause.

Author of Opinion: Justice John Paul Stevens.

Vote: 8-1.

During the 1960s, the Supreme Court announced a series of rulings that eliminated religious practices or references in public schools. Among these decisions was *Engel v. Vitale* (1961), which struck down a state statute requiring prayer in public schools. The Court concluded that it is no business of government to compose or mandate prayer. *Engel* produced much controversy, as some members of Congress pushed for adoption of a constitutional amendment authorizing school prayer. The amendment never came close to passage.

Following *Engel,* many states experimented with programs of "meditation" or meditation coupled with voluntary prayer. *Wallace v. Jaffree* concerned an Alabama statute that provided for a period of meditation or prayer. This statute was the third passed by the state. The first statute, § 16-1-20, authorized a one-minute period of silence in all public schools "for meditation." The second statute, § 16-1-20.1, passed three years later, authorized a period of silence "for meditation or voluntary prayer." The final statute, § 16-1-20.2, enacted a year later, authorized teachers to lead "willing students" in a prescribed prayer to "Almighty God [the] Creator and Supreme Judge of the world."

In *Wallace,* the Court was called upon to determine whether the final Alabama statutes violated the establishment clause of the First Amendment of the United States Constitution (as applied to the states via the Fourteenth Amendment due process clause). In deciding the case, the Court applied the three part test articulated in

Lemon v. Kurtzman, 403 U.S. 602 (1971). That test, the so-called *Lemon* test, provides that courts should evaluate three factors in deciding whether governmental action violates the establishment clause: "First, the statute must have a secular legislative purpose; second, its principal or primary effect must be one that neither advances nor inhibits religion; finally, the statute must not foster 'an excessive government entanglement with religion.'"

In applying the *Lemon* test to the Alabama statutes, the Court concluded that all three statutes violated the first prong of the test because there was no secular purpose. On the contrary, the Court found that all three statutes were religiously motivated. In reaching that conclusion, the Court relied on statements by the bill's sponsor who affirmed that the purpose of legislation was "to return voluntary prayer" to the public schools. In testimony before the trial court, when asked whether the law had any purpose "other than returning voluntary prayer to public schools," the primary sponsor stated: "No." The Court also emphasized the nature of the successive statutes. The only difference between the final statute and the earlier ones was the addition of the words "or voluntary prayer." The Court noted that the earlier statute already gave students the right to meditate and did not preclude them from engaging in voluntary prayer. As a result, the Court concluded that by adding the words "or voluntary prayer" to the word "meditation," the legislature did so for "the sole purpose of expressing the State's endorsement of prayer activities for one minute at the beginning of each schoolday."

It was unclear whether *Wallace* doomed all moment of silence statutes. Justice Sandra Day O'Connor, who concurred in the judgment, pointed out that a moment of silence should be treated differently than school-sponsored prayer or Bible readings because it "is not inherently religious." As a result, she suggested that moment of silence statutes might be valid because a student could participate without compromising his religious beliefs. "[A] student who objects to prayer is left to his or her own thoughts, and is not compelled to listen to the prayers or thoughts of others." She argued that, even if a statute provides that students may pray, the state has not necessarily encouraged prayer over other alternatives. On the contrary, the state has simply indicated that voluntary prayer is a permissible alternative. Nevertheless, Justice O'Connor agreed that the Alabama statute should be invalidated because it was motivated by a religious purpose. However, she argued that judicial "inquiry into the purpose of the legislature in enacting a moment of silence law should be deferential and limited. [If] a legislature expresses a plausible secular purpose for a moment of silence statute in either the text or the legislative history, or if the statute disclaims an intent to encourage prayer over alternatives during a moment of silence, then courts should generally defer to that stated intent...."

The *Wallace* dissents reveal much disagreement about what the establishment clause means and how it should be applied. Chief Justice Warren Burger, dissenting, argued that it "makes no sense to say that Alabama has 'endorsed prayer' by merely enacting a new statute 'to specify expressly that voluntary prayer is *one* of the authorized activities during a moment of silence.'" In addition, he found irony in the fact that the Court opens its sessions with a plea for Divine protection and that both the United States Senate and the House of Representatives open each day with a prayer, but that school prayer is prohibited. This irony led him to quip that: "[S]ome wag is bound to say that the Court's holding today reflects a belief [that] members of the Judiciary and Congress are more in need of Divine guidance than are schoolchildren." In addition, he doubted that the Court should have placed such reliance on the sponsor's statements, all of which were made after the statute was passed, especially since the sponsor testified that "one of his purposes in drafting and sponsoring the moment-of-silence bill was to clear up a widespread misunderstanding that a school-child is legally prohibited from engaging in silent, individual prayer once he steps inside a public school building." He concluded that "[The] statute does not remotely threaten religious liberty; it affirmatively furthers the values of religious freedom and tolerance that the Establishment Clause was designed to protect."

Justice Byron White, dissenting, argued that a majority of the Court would approve a statute that provided for a moment of silence without mentioning prayer, and he doubted that the Alabama statute should be struck down merely because it did. In his view, the final statute simply cleared up the question of whether students could engage in voluntary prayer during the moment of silence. Justice William Rehnquist, who also dissented, argued that the framers of the Bill of Rights did not intend to prohibit the states from "endorsing" prayer. He noted that "George Washington himself, at the request of the very Congress which passed the Bill of Rights, proclaimed a day of public thanksgiving and prayer, to be observed by acknowledging with grateful hearts the many and signal favors of Almighty God."

Wallace is important because it strikes down a moment of silence (for meditation or prayer) statute as unconstitutional. *Wallace* does not foreclose the possibility of a valid moment of silence statute. However, if such statutes are to be upheld, they must be true "moment of silence" provisions and must be motivated by a secular purpose.

Bibliography

Jesse H. Choper, *The Religion Clauses of the First Amendment: Reconciling the Conflict*, 41 *University of Pittsburgh Law Review* 673 (1980).

Philip B. Kurland, *Of Church and State and the Supreme Court*, 29 *University of Chicago Law Review* 1 (1961).

Norman Redlich, *Separation of Church and State: The Burger Court's Tortuous Journey*, 60 *Notre Dame Law Review* 1094 (1985).

Alan Schwarz, *No Imposition of Religion: The Establishment Clause Value*, 77 *Yale Law Journal* 692 (1998).

Russell L. Weaver and Donald E. Lively, *Understanding the First Amendment* (Newark, NJ: LexisNexis, 2003), 256–57.

McCreary County v. American Civil Liberties Union of Kentucky

Citation: 125 S. Ct. 2722.

Issue: Whether posting of the Ten Commandments on a courthouse wall abridged the establishment clause.

Year of Decision: 2005.

Outcome: The posting of the Ten Commandments violated the establishment clause because it was motivated by a religious purpose.

Author of Opinion: Justice David Souter.

Vote: 5–4.

Many early immigrants to the American colonies came fleeing religious persecution in Europe. Because of this history, the United States Constitution provided protections against the establishment of an official religion, as well as a guarantee for the free exercise of their religion. In construing the establishment clause, the courts are rarely confronted by situations in which government (state, local, or federal) actually decree that some religion is the "official" religion and that all citizens must adhere to and support that religion. Most alleged establishments involve something less dramatic. A number of cases have involved allegations that financial assistance to religious schools or mandates that public school students must recite an official prayer at the beginning of each school day constitute "establishments" of religion. In recent years, there has been considerable litigation regarding the extent to which government may "acknowledge" religion in the public square. While a number of these cases have focused on whether the government can erect Christmas displays, with cases focusing on whether the government may erect a crèche on public property, many recent cases have involved whether the government may post the Ten Commandments in public places.

The Court first addressed the Ten Commandments issue in *Stone v. Graham* (1980). In *Stone,* the Court struck down a Kentucky statute that required the posting of the Ten Commandments in public schools. Applying a test derived from *Lemon v. Kurtzman* (1971), the so-called *Lemon* test, the Court indicated that a three-factor test should be used to evaluate alleged establishments: "First, the statute must have a secular legislative purpose; second, its principal or primary effect must be one that neither advances nor inhibits religion ...; finally the statute must not foster 'an excessive government entanglement with religion.'" A statute that violates any of the three prongs of the *Lemon* test—because it has the purpose or effect of advancing religion or causes an excessive entanglement—"must be struck down under the Establishment Clause." In *Stone,* the Court concluded that the legislature was motivated by a religious purpose and struck down the law.

Following *Stone,* there remained doubt about whether the establishment clause prohibited all public displays of the Ten Commandments. The issue was particularly poignant because the United States Supreme Court building contains a depiction of Moses holding a copy of the Commandments, and other public buildings contain similar displays. As a result, if all depictions of the Commandments are invalid, the Supreme Court frieze (and the other depictions) might have to be removed.

In *McCreary County,* and its companion case, *Van Orden v. Perry* (2005), Ten Commandments issues returned to the Court. In *McCreary County,* a county posted a gold-framed copy of the King James version of the Ten Commandments along with a citation to the Book of Exodus. The county subsequently expanded the display to include eight additional documents, each with a religious theme (e.g., the "endowed by their Creator" passage from the Declaration of Independence; the Preamble to the Constitution of Kentucky; the national motto, "In God We Trust"; a page from the Congressional Record of February 2, 1983, proclaiming the Year of the Bible and including a statement of the Ten Commandments; a proclamation by President Abraham Lincoln designating April 30, 1863, a National Day of Prayer and Humiliation; an excerpt from President Lincoln's "Reply to Loyal Colored People of Baltimore upon Presentation of a Bible," reading that "[t]he Bible is the best gift God has ever given to man"; a proclamation by President Reagan marking 1983 the Year of the Bible; and the Mayflower Compact). As litigation over the display proceeded, the county attempted to "secularize" the display by adding nonreligious documents including "framed copies of the Magna Carta, the Declaration of Independence, the Bill of Rights, the lyrics of the Star Spangled Banner, the Mayflower Compact, the National Motto, the Preamble to the Kentucky Constitution, and a picture of Lady Justice." The display was labeled "The Foundations of American Law and Government Display," and each framed document included a statement of its "historical and legal significance." The County argued that, by displaying the Commandments alongside secular documents, the entire display was permissible under the establishment clause.

Relying on its prior holding in *Stone,* and that decision's *Lemon*-based purpose analysis, the Court invalidated "The Foundations of American Law" display. The

Court suggested that the manner in which the Commandments are displayed is critical to the outcome. Whereas symbolic representations of the Ten Commandments —like the frieze at the United States Supreme Court building that depicts Moses holding the Ten Commandments—might be permissible, displays of the actual text are more likely to be invalidated. The Court found that displays of the text are more objectionable because they declare a monotheistic god (prohibiting acknowledgment of other gods), they regulate the details of religious observance (prohibiting graven images, sabbath breaking, vain oath swearing), and they impose divinely imposed prohibitions (prohibiting murder, theft, and the like). Accordingly, the Court concluded that, when the text of the Ten Commandments is set out, "the insistence of the religious message is hard to avoid in the absence of a context plausibly suggesting a message going beyond an excuse to promote the religious point of view."

In addition, the Court analyzed the entire display, recognizing that "the notion of the religious message can be undermined by inclusion of the Ten Commandments in a secular display." In *McCreary County,* despite the County's addition of the secular documents, the Court found a religious purpose. The Court noted that "the ceremony at which the Commandments was displayed conveyed an unmistakable religious message" because the county executive, accompanied by a pastor, affirmed his belief in the certainty of God. As a result, the Court concluded that "the original text viewed in its entirety is an unmistakably religious statement dealing with religious obligations and with morality subject to religious sanction."

McCreary County involved considerable debate between the majority and the dissent regarding the permissibility of governmental acknowledgments of religion. Justice Antonin Scalia, dissenting, would have upheld the Ten Commandments display noting that "the United States was founded based on an acknowledgment of God." He claimed that "the Framer's practices reflected that acknowledgment," and he pointed to the fact that the first Congress invited the President to proclaim a day of "thanksgiving and prayer." President Washington honored the invitation by issuing the first Thanksgiving Proclamation "to the service of that great and glorious Being who is the beneficent author of all the good that is, that was, or that will be." The Court rejected Justice Scalia's historical analysis noting that "[h]istorical evidence ... supports no solid argument for changing course[,] whereas public discourse at the present time certainly raises no doubt about the value of the interpretative approach invoked for 60 years now."

The Court decided *Van Orden* on the same day that it decided *McCreary County. Van Orden* involved a textual display of the Ten Commandments on the grounds of the Texas capitol. Although the display was mounted on a six-foot by three-foot slab, and contained the actual text of the Commandments, the display was located on the 22 acre capitol grounds that contained 16 other monuments and 21 historical markers. The other displays were entitled Heroes of the Alamo, Hood's Brigade, Confederate Soldiers, Volunteer Fireman, Terry's Texas Rangers, Texas Cowboy, Spanish-American War, Texas National Guard, Ten Commandments, Tribute to Texas School Children, Texas Pioneer Woman, The Boy Scouts' Statue of Liberty Replica, Pearl Harbor Veterans, Korean War Veterans, Soldiers of World War I, Disabled Veterans, and Texas Peace Officers.

In a plurality opinion by Chief Justice Rehnquist, joined by Justice Scalia who dissented in *McCreary County,* the Court upheld the display. The plurality argued that the Court's decisions on religion permit some governmental acknowledgment of religion noting that those decisions point "Januslike ... in two directions in applying the Establishment Clause. One face looks toward the strong role played by religion and religious traditions throughout our Nation's history.... The other face looks toward the principle that governmental intervention in religious matters can itself endanger religious freedom." In upholding the Texas capitol display, the Court noted that the United States Supreme Court building and that both the Executive and Legislative branches had acknowledged "the historical role of the Ten Commandments." The Court indicated that it was less inclined to uphold Commandments displays in public school classrooms because the Court has "been particularly vigilant in monitoring compliance with the Establishment Clause in elementary and secondary schools." But the Court viewed the Capitol grounds or legislative chamber as different, and it viewed the Texas display as a "far more passive" use of the texts than in *Stone,* "where the text confronted elementary school students every day." Since Texas treated its Capitol grounds as "representing the several strands in the State's political and legal history," the Court viewed the Ten Commandments monument as a permissible addition because it "has a dual significance, partaking of both religion and government."

McCreary County is important because it represents the Court's latest pronouncement regarding the permissibility of governmental acknowledgment of the Ten Commandments. Reaffirming *Stone,* the Court struck down the *McCreary County* display because it was motivated by the purpose of advancing religion. However, as both *McCreary County* and *Van Orden* suggest, Ten Commandments displays are not necessarily or inherently violative of the establishment clause. Much depends on the purpose behind the displays and the way the displays are structured and displayed.

Bibliography

Jesse H. Choper, *The Religion Clauses of the First Amendment: Reconciling the Conflict,* 41 *University of Pittsburgh Law Review* 673 (1980).

Philip Kurland, *Of Church and State and the Supreme Court,* 29 *University of Chicago Law Review* 1 (1961).

Philip Kurland, *The Religion Clauses and the Burger Court,* 34 *Catholic University Law Review* 1 (1984).

Alan Schwartz, *No Imposition of Religion: The Establishment Clause Value,* 77 *Yale Law Journal* 692 (1968).

Russell L. Weaver and Donald E. Lively, *Understanding the First Amendment* (Newark, NJ: LexisNexis, 2003), 296–97.

Lynch v. Donnelly

The tension between the religion clauses of the First Amendment have been an ongoing source of doctrinal uncertainty. The establishment clause historically has been a barrier to state action that promotes religion. The free exercise clause operates as a counterforce, however, to the extent that government may be required to provide space of recognition for religious tradition. State assistance to parochial schools thus may implicate the establishment clause if it is perceived as having a religious purpose, has a primary effect that is religious, or

Citation: 465 U.S. 668.

Issue: Whether a city-funded nativity scene, integrated with secular holiday displays in a park owned by a nonprofit organization, violated the establishment clause.

Year of Decision: 1984.

Outcome: The nativity scene accommodated rather than endorsed religion and thus did not abridge the establishment clause.

Author of Opinion: Chief Justice Warren Burger.

Vote: 5-4.

excessively entangles church and state. Exclusion of parochial schools from a program of general educational aid, however, may be viewed as burdensome to the free exercise of religion. The sometimes competing orientations of the religion clauses have required the Court to develop standards of review that reconcile the conflict they otherwise present.

Central to this process of reducing their tension have been concepts of neutrality and accommodation. From these premises, the Court has developed an understanding of the establishment clause that is not an absolute barrier to religion in public life and actually provides room for religion in this context. The accommodation principle has been exemplified in the allowance of prayer in certain public proceedings. The Court in *Marsh v. Chambers* (1983), for instance, upheld religious invocations at the beginning of state legislative sessions. Even though the state paid for and provided for the chaplain who performed the invocation, the Court determined that such prayer was "simply a tolerable acknowledgment of beliefs widely held among the people of this country." Similar analysis has governed the reference to God on currency and coins and in various ceremonial contexts. These results contrast with outcomes in the context of public schools, where the Court is more concerned with the potential for indoctrination or divisiveness. Prayer in public schools, as the Court's decisions in *Santa Fe Independent School District v. Doe* (2000) and *Lee v. Weisman* (1992) evidence, is less likely to be regarded in terms of "tolerable acknowledgment" or mere "ceremony."

Accommodation has been a primary factor in resolving controversies arising from public holiday displays that include a religious symbol or message. The seminal case on this point is *Lynch v. Donnelly* (1984). At issue in this case was an inexpensive nativity scene that the city paid for and that was displayed in a park owned by a nonprofit organization. Elements of the display included secular symbols and images associated with Christmas, including Santa Claus, reindeer, a Christmas tree, and a banner with the message "Season's Greetings." Also present was a crèche displaying "the Infant Jesus, Mary and Joseph, angels, shepherds, kings, and animals." Cost and maintenance of the nativity scene was relatively insubstantial.

Writing for the majority in a 5-4 decision, Chief Justice Warren Burger commenced his analysis with an accommodation premise. The challenge of "every Establishment Clause case," from his perspective, was to "reconcile the inescapable tension between the objective of preventing unnecessary intrusion of either the church or the state upon the other, and the reality that ... total separation of the two is impossible." The Court also took issue with the oft-referenced "wall between church and state." Although having relied upon this metaphor in the past, and regarding it as a useful "figure of speech," the Court indicated that its utility was overrated in many establishment clause contexts. For the Court, the metaphor was "not a wholly accurate description of the practical aspects of the relationship that in fact exists between church and state." Viewing matters from a realistic perspective, the Court noted that institutions cannot function in total isolation from the society to which they belong. Given this dynamic, the Court determined that the establishment clause does not "require complete separation of church and state." To avoid what it characterized as a "callous indifference" to free exercise interests, the Court concluded that these concerns must be accommodated.

Accommodation, from the Court's perspective, reflected a historical acknowledgment by each branch "of government of the role of religion in American life from at least 1789." In this regard, the Court cited numerous examples of national traditions that incorporate a religious heritage. Included among these are the observance of Thanksgiving which, like Christmas, originated as a religious holiday but evolved also as a national holiday. The Court noted the imprint of "In God We Trust" on coinage and the reference to "one nation under God" in the Pledge of Allegiance. It also referenced federal support for art exhibits that include religious paintings and an annual "National Day of Prayer" proclaimed by the President.

Given these traditional references to religion, the Court maintained that the establishment clause could not be viewed as a barrier to any government action that may benefit or recognize religion. The appropriate inquiry thus was whether official conduct or policy "in reality … establishes a religion or religious faith, or tends to do so." Relevant considerations, as in other establishment clause cases, were whether government action had a secular purpose, had a principal or primary effect of advancing religion, or excessively entangled church and state. The Court stressed, however, that establishment clause analysis should not be confined exclusively to these considerations in all circumstances.

The Court viewed the display as having a secular purpose, insofar as it was designed to celebrate the holiday and showcase its origins. Although the crèche had a religious meaning, its incorporation into the overall exhibit diluted its significance. From the Court's perspective, therefore, the primary effect of the display did not aid religion. Nor did the Court discern excessive entanglement of government and religion. It found no evidence of government consulting church officials with respect to the content, design, or presentation of the crèche.

The Court noted that the crèche might have "special meaning" in a religious sense but nonetheless viewed it as a source of "a friendly community spirit of goodwill in keeping with the season." Given the centuries old tradition of the holiday celebration, the Court believed that it could not view the crèche as such a "taint … as to render [the display] violative of the Establishment Clause." Such a determination, in the Court's words, would be "a stilted overreaction contrary to our history and to our holdings." It accordingly dismissed "[a]ny notion that these symbols pose a real danger of establishment of a state church [a]s far-fetched indeed."

Justice Sandra Day O'Connor agreed with the outcome, but wrote a concurring opinion offering "a clarification of our Establishment Clause doctrine." Justice O'Connor contended that an establishment clause violation should depend upon whether church and state were excessively entangled with each other or on when government acts to approve or endorse religion. The key issue from her perspective was whether display of the crèche constituted an official endorsement of Christianity. As she described the display, it represented an acknowledgment of religion as one of any number of historical and ubiquitous practices that government may reference without being seen as approving or endorsing it.

Justice William Brennan, in a dissenting opinion joined by three of his colleagues, characterized the crèche "as a recreation of an event that lies at the heart of the Christian faith." Given this perception, he objected to "the Court's less-than-vigorous application" of establishment clause standards. Even if incorporated into a secular context, Justice Brennan believed that the nativity scene's "singular religiosity" was not diluted. From his perspective, the display was inconsistent with "our remarkable and precious religious diversity as a Nation, which the Establishment Clause seeks to protect." Justice Brennan added that "it blinks reality to claim, as the Court does, that by including such a distinctively religious object as the crèche in its Christmas display," the city had purged its meaning.

Justice Brennan doubted whether non-Christians, when viewing "the chief symbol" of the Christian belief in a divine savior, would perceive anything other than a religious meaning. Contrary to being "a mere representation" of a certain historic religious event, the crèche struck Justice Brennan as a central aspect of Christian dogma—that "God sent His Son into the world to be a Messiah." Equating the crèche with traditional secular symbols such as Santa Claus, from Justice Brennan's viewpoint, insulted those who view "the story of Christ" in religious terms. He thus urged recognition of the city's action "for what it is: a coercive, though perhaps small, step toward establishing the sectarian preferences of the majority at the expense of the minority, accomplished by placing public facilities and funds in support of the religious symbolism and theological tidings that the crèche conveys."

The Court's reliance on accommodation premises to reconcile tension between the establishment clause and free exercise clause has not eliminated doctrinal uncertainty or resulted in a consensus with respect to its utility or application. The primary challenge is drawing a line between accommodation (which is permissible) and endorsement (which is impermissible). This difficulty was evidenced in the next Supreme Court case concerning a holiday display with mixed secular and religious themes. The Court, in *County of Allegheny v. American Civil Liberties Union, Greater Pittsburgh Chapter* (1989), determined that the display of a crèche in a county courthouse endorsed rather than accommodated religion. The positioning of a menorah outside the building, however, was found to be a permissible "recognition of cultural diversity." Critical to the different outcomes were the placement and context of the displays. The crèche was set up by itself on the grand staircase of the government building. The menorah was placed next to a Christmas tree and sign saluting liberty.

Justice Anthony Kennedy, joined by three of his colleagues, dissented. The dissenters objected to the Court's detail-based oversight of the display. They also questioned whether the traditional focus on purpose, effect, and excessive entanglement should continue as the "primary guide" for establishment clause review. In the dissenters' view, "[s]ubstantial revision of Establishment Clause doctrine may be in order."

Dissatisfaction with establishment clause standards, evidenced in the dissenting opinion, has been a continuing but unresolved phenomenon. Among the most vocal critics has been Justice Antonin Scalia. Dissenting from the Court's decision in *Lee v. Weisman* (1992), which prohibited student-led prayers at high school graduation ceremonies, Justice Scalia observed that establishment clause "jurisprudence has become bedeviled ... by reliance on formulaic abstractions that are not derived from, but positively conflict with, our long-accepted constitutional traditions." In *Lamb's Chapel v. Center Moriches Union Free School District* (1993), he and Justice Clarence Thomas announced that they were abandoning any further use of the traditional establishment clause standard of review. Although a majority of the Court at one time or another has expressed dissatisfaction with this standard, consensus with respect to a substitute formula has been difficult to achieve. For Justice Scalia and other critics, the Court's continuing deployment of an unsatisfactory standard of review "[l]ike some ghoul in a late-night horror movie that repeatedly sits up in its grave and shuffles abroad, after being killed and buried, [continues to] stalk our Establishment Clause jurisprudence."

Bibliography

Robert S. Alley, ed., *James Madison on Religious Liberty* (Buffalo, NY: Prometheus Books, 1985). Insight into the First Amendment's primary drafter is provided.

Steven D. Smith, *Foreordained Failure: The Quest for a Constitutional Principle of Religious Freedom* (New York: Oxford University Press, 1995). The challenge of developing satisfactory standards of review under the establishment clause is examined.

Willliam Van Alstyne, *Trends in the Supreme Court: Mr. Jefferson's Crumbling Wall—A Comment on Lynch v. Donnelly,* 1984 *Duke Law Journal* 770 (1984). This sets forth the view that the *Lynch* decision reflects a trend toward reestablishing government under religious auspices.

Lee v. Weisman

The First Amendment protects the right to freely exercise religious beliefs. However, the First Amendment also prohibits the government from "establishing" a religion. The dividing line between accommodation of religious beliefs (and religious exercise) and establishment has not always been clear, and the two religion clauses are frequently in tension.

In *Lee v. Weisman*, the tension between the free exercise clause and the establishment clause came into full play in the context of graduation prayer. In

Citation: 505 U.S. 577.

Issue: Whether state sponsored graduation prayers are permissible under the establishment clause of the First Amendment.

Year of Decision: 1992.

Outcome: It is "[no] part of the business of government to compose official prayers for any group [of] American people to recite as a part of a religious program carried on by government."

Author of Opinion: Justice Anthony Kennedy.

Vote: 5-4.

that case, school district rules authorized school principals in Providence, Rhode Island, to invite members of the clergy to offer invocation and benediction prayers at graduation ceremonies for middle schools and high schools. The rules also created "Guidelines for Civic Occasions," which directed that prayers were to be nonsectarian. The Court was asked to determine whether the practice was unconstitutional.

The school district argued that the "Guidelines for Civic Occasions," and the advice given to clergy that prayers should be regarded as nonsectarian, should be treated as a "good-faith attempt by the school to ensure [that] sectarianism which is so often the flashpoint for religious animosity be removed from the graduation ceremony." While the Court was sympathetic to this concern, noting that ideas and images associated with a particular religion may foster "sectarian rivalry," the Court questioned the legitimacy of the State's decision to create guidelines for prayer. Referring to its prior holdings, the Court emphasized that it is "[no] part of the business of government to compose official prayers for any group [of] American people to recite as a part of a religious program carried on by government." In the Court's view, "religious beliefs and religious expression are too precious to [be] prescribed by the State. It must not be forgotten [that] these same Clauses exist to protect religion from government interference...."

The school district tried to characterize its guidelines as a program that offered graduation participants a choice of whether to participate in prayer or to refrain from participation, and that "our constitutional vision of a free society requires confidence in our own ability to accept or reject ideas of which we do not approve." The Court disagreed, noting that it has always been concerned regarding the presence of coercive pressures in the elementary and secondary school context. The Court worried that the prayer would place protestors in the uncomfortable position of participating in the prayer, or of protesting, and concluded that many high school students would feel coerced into participating by peer pressure. The Court held that the "government may no more use social pressure to enforce orthodoxy than it may use more direct means."

The Court also expressed concern regarding the potential for divisiveness. It feared that interest groups might disagree over the choice of a clergy member to conduct the ceremony and argue over content. The Court concluded that "Divisiveness [can] attend any state decision respecting religions, and neither its existence nor its potential necessarily invalidates the State's attempts to accommodate religion in all cases." The Court worried that there was greater potential for divisiveness in this case because the case involved a religious exercise in which students were effectively forced to participate.

The Court rejected the school district's attempt to characterize its sectarian prayer as a permissible accommodation of religion. The Court recognized that many people regard prayer as an essential part of graduation because "for many persons an occasion of this significance lacks meaning if there is no recognition," and because they believe that "human achievements cannot be understood apart from their spiritual essence." However, the Court held that the school could not "exact religious conformity from a student as the price of attending her own high school graduation." As Justice David Souter, concurring, noted, students could arrange a "privately sponsored baccalaureate if they desire the company of likeminded students."

Justice Harry Blackmun, joined by Justices John Paul Stevens and Sandra Day O'Connor, concurred: "[W]hen the government 'compose[s] official prayers,' selects the member of the clergy to deliver the prayer, has the prayer delivered at a public school event that is planned, supervised and given by school officials, and pressures students to attend and participate in the prayer, there can be no doubt that the government is advancing and promoting religion. [I]t is not enough that the government restrain from compelling religious practices: It must not engage in them either." Justice Souter, joined by Justices Stevens and O'Connor, also concurred, rejecting the notion that the establishment clause permits "nonpreferential" state promotion of religion or allows the government to support a "diversity" of religious beliefs. He argued that such an approach would require the government, and the courts, to "make wholly inappropriate judgments about the number of religions the State should sponsor and the relative frequency with which it should sponsor each."

Justice Scalia, joined by Chief Justice Rehnquist and Justices White and Thomas dissented, arguing that the "history and tradition of our Nation are replete with public ceremonies featuring prayers of thanksgiving and petition." He noted that "From our Nation's origin, prayer has been a prominent part of governmental ceremonies and proclamations." He offered specific examples including the Declaration of Independence (which "appeal[ed] to the Supreme Judge of the world for the rectitude of our intentions" and avowed "a firm reliance on the protection of divine Providence"), President Washington's first inaugural address (which made prayer a part of his first official act as President), our national celebration of Thanksgiving with religiously themed Thanksgiving Proclamations issued by almost every President, the fact that congressional sessions have opened with a chaplain's prayer ever since the First Congress, and the Court's own sessions have opened with the invocation "God save the United States and this Honorable Court." In addition, Justice Scalia argued that there is "a more specific tradition of invocations and benedictions at public school graduation exercises." The majority responded that "religious invocations in Thanksgiving Day addresses and the like, rarely noticed, ignored without effort, conveyed over an impersonal medium, and directed at no one in particular, inhabit a pallid zone worlds apart from official prayers delivered to a captive audience of public school students and their families." Justice Souter, concurring, agreed, noting that, to "be sure, the leaders of the young Republic engaged in some of the practices that separationists like Jefferson and Madison criticized. The First Congress did hire institutional chaplains, and Presidents Washington and Adams unapologetically marked days of 'public thanksgiving and prayer.'" However, in his view, those practices "prove, at best, that the Framers simply did not share a common understanding of the Establishment Clause, and, at worst, that they, like other politicians, could raise constitutional ideals one day and turn their backs on them the next."

Justice Scalia also raised other concerns. For example, he noted that "the present case involves a community's celebration of one of the milestones in its young citizens' lives, and it is a bold step for this Court to seek to banish from that occasion [the] expression of gratitude to God that a majority of the community wishes to make." In addition, he rejected the Court's argument that a student who sits in respectful silence, while others are praying, can be deemed to have joined in the prayer. On the contrary, he argued that maintaining "respect for the religious observances of others is a fundamental civic virtue that government (including the public schools) can and should cultivate." Moreover, he argued that graduation is a milestone because it marks the transition from childhood to adulthood, and graduating students should be treated differently than younger, more impressionable, students. In addition, he argued that attendance at school graduation is voluntary. The majority responded that to "say a teenage student has a real choice not to attend her high school graduation is formalistic. [I]n our society and in our culture high school graduation is one of life's most significant occasions."

The *Lee* opinion is important because it is consistent with the Court's long-standing precedent prohibiting prayer in the public school context. The Court continues to adhere to the proposition that it is not the business of government to compose prayers for people.

Bibliography

R. Collin Mangum, *Shall We Pray? Graduation Prayers and Establishment Paradigms,* 26 *Creighton Law Review* 1027 (1993).

Thomas A. Schweitzer, *The Progeny of Lee v. Weisman: Can Student-Invited Prayer at Public School Graduations Still be Constitutional?,* 9 *Brigham Young University Journal of Public Law* 291 (1995).

Steven H. Shiffrin, *The Pluralistic Foundations of the Religion Clauses,* 90 *Cornell Law Review* 9 (2004).

Russell L. Weaver and Donald E. Lively, *Understanding the First Amendment* (Newark, NJ: LexisNexis, 2004), 278–88.

Agostini v. Felton

The establishment clause was adopted in light of a history of religious persecution in Europe. As Justice Hugo Black stated in *Everson v. Board of Education* (1947), "[a] large proportion of the early settlers of this country came here from Europe to escape the bondage of laws which compelled them to support and attend government favored churches." As a result, when the First Amendment was written, many sought protections for the free exercise of religion and a prohibition against governmental establishments of religion.

Citation: 521 U.S. 203.

Issue: Whether a state's provision of remedial education at parochial schools violates the establishment clause.

Year of Decision: 1997.

Outcome: The establishment clause does not preclude the state from providing in-kind remedial education at parochial schools.

Author of Opinion: Justice Sandra Day O'Connor.

Vote: 5-4.

Because of widespread acknowledgment of the need for the religion clauses, the First Amendment was simply stated: "Congress shall make no law respecting an establishment of religion." Although the establishment clause refers only to "Congress," the Supreme Court in *Everson* held that it is binding on the states. As a result, neither the federal government nor the states are allowed to "establish" a religion.

Despite the establishment clause's seeming simplicity, there has been considerable disagreement regarding its meaning and application. The establishment clause clearly prohibits certain types of governmental activities that were commonplace in Europe and some of the early American colonies: e.g., the establishment of a national (or, for that matter, a state) church; laws requiring individuals to go to or remain away from church against their will; laws forcing individuals to profess a belief or disbelief in any religion. The difficulty is that few establishment clause cases fit this mold. In the history of the United States, for example, there have been no attempts to declare a "national religion."

Given the absence of any formal establishment, modern establishment clause cases have focused on whether certain lesser types of governmental conduct (e.g., school prayer or the posting of the Ten Commandments in public places) constitute an "establishment" of religion. Because these "lesser" acts are not so clearly within the ambit of the First Amendment, the courts have struggled to apply the term "establishment" in these contexts. A frequent source of establishment clause litigation involves governmental attempts to provide financial benefits to religion or religious organizations, and the Court's decisions in these cases have not always been consistent.

Agostini v. Felton concerned long-running establishment clause litigation that arose in New York City. Under Title I of the *Secondary Education Act of 1965,* Congress authorized the states to provide remedial education, guidance, and job counseling to students who were failing or at risk of failing. In the Court's prior decision in *Aguilar v. Felton* (1985), New York City's method of distributing Title I funds was struck down. Since 90 percent of all private school students were in sectarian schools, the Board initially arranged to transport children to public schools for after-school Title I instruction. Attendance was poor because the teachers and children were tired, as well as because parents were concerned about safety issues. As a result, the Board decided to conduct the Title I instruction at the private schools themselves during regular school hours, but to place restrictions designed to keep the teachers from inculcating religion. In *Aguilar,* the Court struck the New York City program down, applying the so-called *Lemon* test. Under that test, a Court must examine three criteria in deciding whether governmental action passes muster under the establishment clause: "First, the action must have a secular legislative purpose; second, its principal or primary effect must be one that neither advances nor inhibits religion; finally, the action must not foster 'an excessive government entanglement with religion.'" *Lemon v. Kurtzman* (1971). On remand, the trial court permanently enjoined the Board "from using public funds for any plan or program under [Title I] to the extent that it requires, authorizes or permits public school teachers and guidance counselors to provide teaching and counseling services on the premises of sectarian schools...."

Subsequently, New York City modified its Title I program to revert to its prior practice of providing instruction at public school sites, at leased sites, and in mobile instructional units (essentially vans converted into classrooms) parked near the sectarian school. The Board also offered computer-aided instruction at the private schools because it did not require public employees to be physically present on the premises of a religious school. However, the additional costs of complying with *Aguilar's* mandate in these various ways was significant. After 1986–1987, the Board spent over $100 million providing computer-aided instruction, leasing sites and mobile instructional units, and transporting students to those sites. These expenditures reduced the amount of money that New York had available for remedial education, and forced New York to reduce the number of students receiving Title I benefits.

Agostini arose pursuant to Supreme Court intimations that *Aguilar's* holding might not be good law. Specifically, in *Board of Education of Kiryas Joel Village School District v. Grumet* (1994), five of the Court's nine justices indicated that *Aguilar* should be overruled. Relying on these statements, as well as on statements made by individual justices in other cases, petitioners filed motions seeking relief from the permanent injunction on the basis that the "decisional law [had] changed...." As a result, *Agostini* presented a clear question regarding whether the Court should alter its approach to establishment clause issues. The Court decided to do so.

In *Agostini,* the Court reaffirmed the first two parts of the *Lemon* test. However, the Court indicated that it had altered its approach for determining "whether aid to religion has an impermissible effect." The Court specifically abandoned its prior presumption that the "placement of public employees on parochial school grounds inevitably results in the impermissible effect of state-sponsored indoctrination or constitutes a symbolic union between government and religion." The Court also abandoned its presumption that all government aid that directly aids the educational function of religious schools is invalid. Relying on its new understanding of the law, the Court decided to lift the injunction. It noted that "there is no reason to presume that, simply because she enters a parochial school classroom, a full-time public employee [will] depart from her assigned duties and instructions and embark on religious indoctrination." The Court also held that it could not find that a program placing full-time public employees on parochial campuses would lead to religious indoctrination.

In addition, the Court doubted that the Title I program would impermissibly finance religion. In *Agostini,* the Court concluded that no "Title I funds ever reach the coffers of religious schools, and Title I services may not be provided to religious schools on a school-wide basis." On the contrary, Title I funds are provided to a governmental agency that "dispenses services directly to the eligible students within its boundaries, no matter where they choose to attend school." The Court refused to find that the Title I instruction supplants the remedial instruction and guidance counseling already provided in New York City's sectarian schools. Indeed, the Court expressed doubt about whether all sectarian schools provide such services. The Court went on to note that, if it were to find that the provision of Title I services could be regarded as financing religion, the establishment clause concerns would exist whether the services were provided on-site (as New York City was requesting) or off-site (as demanded by *Aguilar*).

The Court ultimately moved toward a "neutrality" test for evaluating governmental programs. Under that test, a "financial incentive to undertake religious indoctrination [is] not present [where] the aid is allocated on the basis of neutral, secular criteria that neither favor nor disfavor religion, and is made available to both religious and secular beneficiaries on a nondiscriminatory basis." In applying this new criteria to New York City's program, the Court concluded that "it is clear that Title I services are allocated on the basis of criteria that neither favor nor disfavor religion. The services are available to all children who meet the Act's eligibility requirements, no matter what their religious beliefs or where they go to school. The Board's program does not, therefore, give aid recipients any incentive to modify their religious beliefs or practices in order to obtain those services."

The Court also rejected the argument that New York City's Title I program resulted in an excessive entanglement between church and state. In *Aguilar,* the Court found excessive entanglement for a variety of reasons: "(i) the program would require "pervasive monitoring by public authorities" to ensure that Title I employees did not inculcate religion; (ii) the program required 'administrative cooperation' between the Board and parochial schools; and (iii) the program might increase the dangers of 'political divisiveness.' " In *Agostini,* the Court rejected the last two ideas as the basis for finding an "excessive" entanglement on the basis that those concerns would be present "no matter where Title I services are offered." In addition, the Court concluded that it no longer placed as much emphasis on the first factor. "[W]e no longer presume that public employees will inculcate religion simply because they happen to be in a sectarian environment. Since we have abandoned the assumption that properly instructed public employees will fail to discharge their duties faithfully, we must also discard the assumption that pervasive monitoring of Title I teachers is required." Finally, the Court expressed less concern regarding the possibility of divisiveness. In conclusion, the Court concluded that its establishment clause jurisprudence had changed significantly since it decided *Aguilar,* and the Court chose to overrule that decision to the extent that it was inconsistent with the Court's present understanding of the establishment clause.

Justice Souter, joined by Justices John Paul Stevens, Ruth Bader Ginsburg, and Stephen Breyer, dissented. He regarded the Title I funds, as construed by *Agostini's* majority, as impermissibly subsidizing religion. He also worried about the potential implications of the decision: "[If] a State may constitutionally enter the schools to [teach, it must be] free to assume [the] entire cost of instruction [in any] secular subject in any religious school." Nevertheless, he would have upheld off-site remedial instruction on the basis that "it is less likely to supplant some of what would otherwise go on inside them and to subsidize what remains." In addition, he worried that the presence of public school teachers in parochial schools might signal state approval of the school's mission. Finally, he contended that, when "aid goes overwhelmingly to one religious denomination, minimal contact between state and church is the less likely to feed the resentment of other religions that would like access to public money for their own worthy projects."

Agostini's implications are far from clear. In a number of recent decisions, the Court has suggested that governments may provide "neutral" subsidies to educational institutions, including religious institutions. These decisions have allowed government to provide increasing amounts of aid to sectarian schools. Whether this line of jurisprudence will be expanded, and potentially result in broad subsidies for religious schools, remains to be seen. Certainly, decisions like *Agostini,* which loosen the Court's approach to issues like entanglement and divisiveness, create the potential for broader subsidies.

Bibliography

R. Collin Mangrum, *State Aid to Students in Religiously Affiliated Schools: Agostini v. Felton,* 31 *Creighton Law Review* 1155 (1998).

Jason M. Waite, *Agostini v. Felton: Thickening the Establishment Clause Stew,* 33 *New England Law Review* 81 (1998).

Ellen M. Wasilausky, *See Jane Read the Bible: Does the Establishment Clause Allow School Choice Programs to Include Sectarian Schools after Agostini v. Felton?,* 56 *Washington and Lee Law Review* 721 (1999).

Russell L. Weaver and Donald E. Lively, *Understanding the First Amendment* (Newark, NJ: LexisNexis, 2003), 258–62.

Zelman v. Simmons-Harris

Much establishment clause litigation has focused on whether government may provide financial aid to parochial schools. This aid has taken many different forms. In some instances, state and local governments have provided direct funding to religious schools through subsidies or the provision of teaching materials. In other instances, they have provided aid indirectly through "vouchers" to parents that can be redeemed at any school, including parochial schools. In addition to being a primary source of establishment clause litigation, cases concerning government aid to religious schools or students also has yielded some of the most unpredictable results.

Citation: 536 U.S. 639.

Issue: Whether the establishment clause is violated when government provides vouchers to the parents of school age children that can be used at both parochial and nonparochial schools.

Year of Decision: 2002.

Outcome: The establishment clause does not prohibit educational vouchers, so long as they are religion neutral and decisions on how to use them are made by the parents themselves (rather than by government).

Author of Opinion: Chief Justice William Rehnquist.

Vote: 5-4.

In *Zelman v. Simmons-Harris,* the State of Ohio established a program designed to provide educational choices to families with children who resided in the Cleveland City School District. The District contained 75,000 children, most of whom were from low-income and minority families, and Cleveland's public schools "were among the worst performing public schools in the Nation," having been declared as suffering a "crisis of magnitude." After a judge placed the district under state control, finding that the district failed to meet state standards for "minimal acceptable performance," Ohio created the Pilot Project Scholarship Program which provided financial assistance to families in any Ohio school district that is or has been "under federal court order requiring supervision and operational management of the district by the state."

The program offered tuition aid (scholarships) for students in kindergarten through eighth grade, allowing them to attend a participating public or private school of their parent's choosing. The program was designed to provide educational choices to parents who resided in the Cleveland school district. All private schools, religious and nonreligious, were allowed to accept students from the program provided that the schools were located within the district and satisfied state educational standards. However, schools that chose to participate could not discriminate on the basis of race, religion, or ethnic background and could not "advocate or foster unlawful behavior or teach hatred of any person or group on the basis of race, ethnicity, national origin, or religion." The program also included public schools located in adjacent school districts, which received a $2,250 tuition grant per student plus per-pupil state funding.

The program provided that vouchers were distributed on the basis of need. Families with incomes below 200 percent of the poverty level received 90 percent of private school tuition up to a maximum of $2,250, and private schools that accepted the vouchers could not impose a copayment higher than $250. For higher-income families, the vouchers paid 75 percent of tuition costs, but no more than $1,875, and the schools could impose a copayment without a cap. However, higher-income families could participate in the program only to the extent that aid money was still available after all low-income children had been accommodated. For participating students, the program made checks payable to the parents who endorsed them to the chosen school.

During the 1999–2000 school year, of the 56 private schools who participated in the voucher program, 82 percent (46) had religious affiliations, and 96 percent of the students who enrolled in private schools attended religiously affiliated schools. During that year, no adjacent public school districts chose to participate. Sixty percent of participating students came from families that were at or below the poverty line. In addition to private schools, the program included "community" and "magnet" schools. "Community schools" were funded by the state, but were operated by independent school boards and retained the freedom to hire their own teachers and set their own curricula. Community schools could have no religious affiliation and were required to accept students by lottery. During the 1999–2000 school year, there were 10 startup community schools, enrolling more than 1,900 students, and they received state funding of $4,518 per student. "Magnet schools" were public schools that emphasized particular subjects, teaching methods, or offered special services to students. For each magnet school student, a school district received $7,746, the same amount received by ordinary public schools. In 1999, there were 23 magnet schools with more than 13,000 students.

In evaluating the validity of the Cleveland voucher program, the Court began by recognizing that the law was supported by the "valid secular purpose" of "providing educational assistance to poor children in a demonstrably failing public school system." In upholding the program, the Court emphasized that it had consistently drawn distinctions "between government programs that provide aid directly to religious schools, and programs of true private choice, in which government aid reaches religious schools only as a result of the genuine and independent choices of private individuals." The Court noted that when a program is neutral towards religion, and aid reaches religious schools only as a result of the "genuine and independent private choice[s]" of a broad class of citizens, the program is more likely to be upheld. The Court placed great emphasis on the fact that aid reached "religious institutions only by way of the deliberate choices of numerous individual recipients."

A critical issue in the case was whether the program had the impermissible effect of "endorsing" religion. The Court rejected the argument that the Cleveland voucher program created a "public perception that the State is endorsing religious practices and beliefs." In doing so, the Court found that no "reasonable observer would think a neutral program of private choice, where state aid reaches religious schools solely as a result of the numerous independent decisions of private individuals, carries with it the *imprimatur* of government endorsement." Moreover, the Court concluded that the program created actual choice for Cleveland parents and children: "They may remain in public school as before, remain in public school with publicly funded tutoring aid, obtain a scholarship and choose a religious school, obtain a scholarship and choose a nonreligious private school, enroll in a community school, or enroll in a magnet school." The mere fact that the overwhelming majority of participating private schools were religious was not enough, in the Court's view, to condemn the program.

Zelman produced a number of concurrences and dissents, and very differing perspectives on how the Court should review voucher programs. Concurring Justice O'Connor argued that the Cleveland voucher program offered Cleveland parents the opportunity to exercise "true private choice." She attached little significance to the fact that some parents enrolled their children in religious schools of a different faith than their own. In her view, the critical point was that the program did not create incentives for students to be enrolled in religious schools. Justice Thomas, who also concurred, quoted Frederick Douglass for the proposition that "[e]ducation … means emancipation. It means light and liberty." He went on to note that "[m]any blacks and other minorities now support school choice programs because they provide the greatest educational opportunities for their children in struggling communities."

The dissents focused on the relationship between the voucher program and the general principles underlying the establishment clause. Justice Stevens emphasized that the vast majority of voucher participants "receive religious indoctrination at state expense." Justice Souter, joined by three other justices, also dissented, arguing that "the overwhelming proportion of large appropriations for voucher money must be spent on religious schools if it is to be spent at all, and will be spent in amounts that cover almost all of tuition." As a result, public funds will be used to pay for a parochial school's entire education, both secular and religious. He expressed concern that the program, as structured, tended to push parents towards private parochial schools, so that 96.6 percent of voucher students who attended private schools ended up enrolling in religious schools. Since most parents sent their children to religious schools with different beliefs than their own, he doubted whether the program actually provided parents with a genuine choice: "the only alternative to the public schools is religious." As a result, he would have struck down the voucher program on the basis that "'[a]ny tax to establish religion is antithetical to the command that the minds of men always be wholly free.' Madison's objection to three pence has simply been lost in the majority's formalism." Justice Souter also expressed concern that the program imposed restrictions on participating schools, including the requirement that schools not "discriminate on the basis of ... religion." As a result, a religious school was precluded from preferring members of its own faith, as well as from "teach[ing] hatred of any person or group on the basis of ... religion," including teaching "traditionally legitimate articles of faith as to the error, sinfulness, or ignorance of others." He worried that, as religious appropriations rise, the tendency for social discord will also rise as groups compete for the money.

Justice Breyer, joined by Justices Stevens and Souter, also dissented, arguing that voucher programs create a significant risk of generating religiously based societal conflict. He noted that "any major funding program for primary religious education will require criteria. And the selection of those criteria, as well as their application, inevitably pose problems that are divisive." However, he viewed voucher programs as creating greater dissent because they differ "in both *kind* and *degree* from aid programs upheld in the past. They differ in kind because they direct financing to a core function of the church: the teaching of religious truths to young children. Vouchers also differ in *degree* because they allow a considerable shift of taxpayer dollars from public secular schools to private religious schools." He expressed concern that taxpayers might object to financing the religious education of children and that parents might "see little real choice between inadequate nonsectarian public education and adequate education at a school whose religious teachings are contrary to his own." Moreover, minority religions may object if they do not have enough students to start their own schools.

Zelman is a very important decision because it recognizes the validity of school voucher programs that offer parents and children educational choice, and it opens the door for future similar programs. As the dissents suggest, *Zelman* creates the possibility that the government will finance religious indoctrination at public expense.

Bibliography

Jesse H. Choper, *The Religion Clauses of the First Amendment: Reconciling the Conflict,* 41 *University of Pittsburgh Law Review* 673 (1980).

Philip B. Kurland, *Of Church and State and the Supreme Court,* 29 *University of Chicago Law Review* 1 (1961).

Alan Schwarz, *No Imposition of Religion: The Establishment Clause Value,* 77 *Yale Law Journal* 692 (1998).

Russell L. Weaver and Donald E. Lively, *Understanding the First Amendment* (Newark, NJ: LexisNexis, 2003), 268–78.

FREE EXERCISE CLAUSE

The free exercise clause safeguards against governmental action that would deny religious liberty. Defining the protected interest, however, is not always easy. Early case law attempted to distinguish between religious belief and action. To the extent that government could burden religion freely to the point that it did not officially prohibit belief, such a distinction created risks to meaningful religious freedom. Over the course of the twentieth century, free exercise clause analysis has evolved into a balancing process. This method of review was demonstrated in *Wisconsin v. Yoder* (1972), when the Court considered whether Amish parents had to comply with a state law requiring children to attend school until the age of 16. The Court in this case determined that religious freedom has been burdened, and the regulatory imposition could not be justified by a compelling governmental interest. The strict scrutiny model embraced in *Yoder* was qualified in subsequent years, as the Court refused to apply it to circumstances where regulation was religion neutral and had an incidental burden on religion. When government targets religion with a direct burden, however, the regulation will be strictly scrutinized. This was the point of the Court's decision in *Church of the Lukumi Babulu Aye, Inc. v. City of Hialeah* (1993), which struck down a city ordinance that prohibited animal sacrifice as a religious practice.

Church of the Lukumi Babalu Aye, Inc. v. City of Hialeah

Citation: 508 U.S. 520.

Issue: May the state discriminate against a religious practice (animal sacrifice)?

Year of Decision: 1993.

Outcome: The free exercise clause prohibits government from discriminating against religion absent a compelling governmental interest.

Author of Opinion: Justice Anthony Kennedy.

Vote: 9–0.

Because of a history of religious persecution in both Europe and the colonies, the American colonists sought protections for religious freedom in the newly formulated United States Constitution. These demands led Congress to adopt the First Amendment, which included protections for the free exercise of religion.

Because there was such widespread agreement regarding the need for religious freedom, Congress left little specific evidence regarding its intent with regard to the free exercise clause. There is widespread agreement that the clause protects "religious thought," but there is uncertainty about the extent to which it protects "religious conduct." Even if the clause protects some "religious conduct," it is clear that the clause does not protect *all* religious conduct (e.g., the state can prohibit a religion that believes in human sacrifice from actually killing people), and therefore there is disagreement regarding the clause's scope.

Most litigation under the free exercise clause has involved legislation that burdens religion by prohibiting individuals from engaging in conduct required by their religious beliefs or requiring conduct prohibited by their religious beliefs (i.e., compulsory school attendance laws for religions like the Amish, who have religious beliefs that require them to terminate formal education after the eighth grade, or laws prohibiting polygamy that adversely affect Mormons). These laws are not directed at religion per se, but rather are designed to deal with some secular problem that incidentally affects religious practices (e.g., an uneducated populace). The issue in these cases is whether the individual's interest in the free exercise of religion requires that the law give way (so that the individual gains an exemption from a governmental requirement or prohibition) or whether the state's interest in compliance prevails over the individual's religious interest. In some cases, the Court has relieved litigants of the regulatory burden, but in other cases it has not. The recent trend has been towards greater deference to government. In *Employment Division v. Smith*, 485 U.S. 660 (1990), the Court held that the free exercise clause is not offended by neutral, generally applicable, laws.

Church of the Lukumi Babalu Aye, Inc. v. City of Hialeah (1993), also involved religious practices, but presented them in a different context. In that case, the Court was not confronted by a neutral generally applicable law, but by a city's attempt to discriminate against religious practices. In that case, the Santeria religion sought to establish a church in Hialeah, Florida, and announced its intention to engage in animal sacrifice as an offering to its "orishas" (entities that are powerful, but not immortal, and depend for their survival on human sacrifice). Because of strong adverse public reaction to the possibility of animal sacrifice, the city council of Hialeah, Florida, quickly passed ordinances prohibiting animal sacrifice. One such ordinance, after declaring that the "sacrificing of animals within the city limits is contrary to the public health, safety, welfare and morals of the community," provided that "[i]t shall be unlawful for any person, persons, corporations or associations to sacrifice any animal within the corporate limits of the City of Hialeah, Florida." The ordinances were unanimously passed and provided for fines not exceeding $500 or imprisonment not exceeding 60 days, or both.

In an opinion by Justice Kennedy, the *Lukumi* Court struck down the Hialeah ordinances. Harkening back to the history of religious persecution that led early settlers to emigrate to the British colonies, and led the colonists to demand protections for the free exercise of religion, the Court held that the First Amendment prohibits the government from discriminating against religion: The "First Amendment forbids an official purpose to disapprove of a particular religion or of religion in general" and also forbids an "attempt to disfavor their religion because of the religious ceremonies it commands."

Referencing *Employment Division v. Smith*, the Court distinguished between laws that are neutral towards religion, but imposes incidental burdens, and those that target religion. The Court recognized that, when a law is neutral and generally applicable, the law need not be subjected to strict scrutiny. However, when a law targets and discriminates against a religion or religious practice, it will be subjected to "the most rigorous of scrutiny." In order to survive, the law "must be justified by a compelling governmental interest and must be narrowly tailored to advance that interest." Applying this heightened standard of review, the Court held that the Hialeah ordinances must be struck down.

The Court relied on a variety of facts in finding that Hialeah had purposely discriminated against the Santeria. The Court noted that the ordinances were discriminatory on their face because they used terms like "sacrifice" and "ritual"—words that it concluded had strong religious overtones. There also was significant public consternation over the practice of animal sacrifice in the Hialeah community. Against this backdrop, the Court concluded that the laws involved "an impermissible attempt to target petitioners and their religious practices." Indeed, "few if any killings of animals are prohibited other than Santeria sacrifice, which is proscribed because it occurs during a ritual or ceremony and its primary purpose is to make an offering to the orishas, not food consumption. Indeed, careful drafting ensured that, although Santeria sacrifice is prohibited, killings that are no more necessary or humane in almost all other circumstances are unpunished." As a result, the Court concluded that "the ordinances by their own terms target this religious exercise; the texts of the ordinances were gerrymandered with care to proscribe religious killings of animals but to exclude almost all secular killings; and the ordinances suppress much more religious conduct than is necessary in order to achieve the legitimate ends asserted in their defense." As a result, the Court concluded that: "We conclude, in sum, that each of Hialeah's ordinances pursues the city's governmental interests only against conduct motivated by religious belief. The ordinances 'ha[ve] every appearance of a prohibition that society is prepared to impose upon [Santeria worshippers] but not upon itself.' This precise evil is what the requirement of general applicability is designed to prevent."

Even though the Court struck down the ordinances, it recognized that the City of Hialeah had a legitimate interest in protecting public health and in preventing cruelty to animals. However, the Court noted that these interests could be served by restrictions that did not discriminate against religion and that fell short of a complete ban on animal sacrifice. For example, if Hialeah were concerned about improper and unsanitary disposal of animal carcasses, the City could enact laws governing the disposal of organic waste. However, as the Court noted, the ordinances in question prohibited Santeria sacrifice regardless of how it was carried out. The Court also recognized that the City had an interest in preventing cruelty to animals. However, the Court concluded that the City could also serve this interest under a neutral generally applicable law that did not specifically target animal sacrifice. For example, the City could have regulated the method of killing directly in nondiscriminatory ways.

A history of religious persecution led to the adoption of the First Amendment's free exercise clause. Even though the Court has not been as protective of free exercise in recent decades, especially with respect to generally applicable laws that incidentally burden religion. *Church of the Lukumi* reaffirms the fundamental principle that government may not discriminate against religions or religious beliefs.

Bibliography

Jesse H. Choper, *The Free Exercise Clause: A Structural Overview and an Appraisal of Recent Developments,* 27 *William and Mary Law Review* 943 (1986).
Douglas Laycock, *Formal, Substantive and Disaggregated Neutrality Toward Religion,* 39 *DePaul Law Review* 993 (1990).
Paul Marcus, *The Forum of Conscience: Applying Standards Under the Free Exercise Clause,* 1973 *Duke Law Journal* 1217 (1973).
Russell L. Weaver and Donald E. Lively, *Understanding the First Amendment* (Newark, NJ: LexisNexis, 2003), 333–40.

RELIGION AND EXPRESSIVE FREEDOM

Although both were designed to account for religious freedom, the establishment clause and free exercise clause of the First Amendment at times are in conflict with each other. Sunday closing laws may be viewed as an establishment clause issue insofar as they may be perceived as reflecting a religious purpose or advancing a religious interest. A state employee who refused to work on a Sunday, because of his or her religious beliefs, may have a free exercise claim if his choice is the basis for reprisal. The work of the courts in assessing these types of problems is to reconcile the competing indications of the two clauses. A similar challenge arises in cases where establishment clause and freedom of speech principles collide. Government generally is prohibited from denying access to a public forum except for content neutral reasons. Insofar as government allows religious speech in public forums, it may be argued that it violates the establishment clause. In *Rosenberger v. University of Virginia* the Court, as noted earlier, determined that a university could not exclude religious groups from a policy that provided for funding of all student publications. This nondiscrimination principle was adhered to in *Good News Club v. Milford* (2003), when the Court held that a religious group must have equal access to public elementary school facilities for speech and association purposes.

Good News Club v. Milford Central School

The First Amendment contains two separate and distinct clauses pertaining to religion that are in tension with each other. The establishment clause, which prohibits government from "establishing" a religion, has been invoked to prevent government from engaging in various religious activities (e.g., proscribing an official prayer, providing financial aid to religion, and posting the Ten Commandments in public school classrooms). By contrast, the free exercise clause gives people the right to freely exercise their religions.

Citation: 533 U.S. 98.

Issue: May a religious group use public school facilities on an equal basis with other community groups?

Year of Decision: 2001.

Outcome: A school may not discriminate against religious groups because of their beliefs.

Author of Opinion: Justice Clarence Thomas.

Vote: 7-2.

In a number of cases, the Court has struggled to reconcile this conflict between the establishment clause and the free exercise clause. For example, in the Court's landmark decision in *Everson v. Board of Education*, 330 U.S. 1 (1947), in a case involving bus subsidies to students attending parochial schools, the Court noted that the state "cannot consistently with the 'establishment of religion' clause of the First Amendment contribute tax-raised funds to the support of an institution which teaches the tenets and faith of any church." But the Court was concerned that neither should the State discriminate against religion. In other words, the State "cannot hamper its citizens in the free exercise of their own religion" and cannot exclude individuals, "*because of their faith, or lack of it,* from receiving the benefits of public welfare legislation." The Court concluded that "[w]e must be careful [that we do not] prohibit New Jersey from extending its general State law benefits to all its citizens without regard to their religious belief."

Good News Club v. Milford Central School involved the question of whether a religious group could use elementary school public facilities on an equal basis with other outside groups. That issue had previously been presented to the Court in *Widmar v. Vincent* (1981), a case involving a state university that made its facilities generally available to registered student groups, but closed them to groups desiring to use the facilities for "religious worship and religious discussion." In *Widmar,* the Court decided the case on free speech grounds and held that a university was required to allow religious groups to use its facilities on the same basis as other groups: "Having created a forum generally open to student groups, the University seeks to enforce a content-based exclusion of religious speech. Its exclusionary policy violates the fundamental principle that a state regulation of speech should be content-neutral...." Justice White dissented: "[This] case involves religious worship only; the fact that that worship is accomplished through speech does not add anything to respondents' argument."

Good News Club presented the same issues in the context of an elementary school. Milford Central School (Milford) enacted a community use policy governing the use of its building during after-school hours. The Good News Club, a private Christian organization for children ages 6 to 12, sought permission to meet in the cafeteria to recite Bible verses, pray, sings songs, and engage in games involving Bible verses. Milford rejected the Club's request because it involved religious instruction and Bible study, and the Court expressed concern that the Club's activities might enmesh the Club in a violation of the establishment clause, especially since the Club's activities involved proselytization.

In deciding the case, the Court noted that the school's access policy created a limited public forum for the discussion of certain topics and held that the school "discriminated against the Club because of its religious viewpoint in violation of the Free Speech Clause of the First Amendment." In particular, the school engaged in "viewpoint discrimination" because it allowed discussion of certain subjects (in this case, the teaching of morals and character) in its public forum, but prohibited discussion of those issues from a religious standpoint. Teaching those views from any other perspective was permissible.

The Court found no establishment clause violation, noting that a "neutral" access policy would not violate the concept of "*neutrality* towards religion." On the contrary, in the Court's view, "neutrality is respected, not offended, when the government, following neutral criteria and evenhanded policies, extends benefits to recipients whose ideologies and viewpoints, including religious ones, are broad and diverse." The Court rejected the plaintiff's claim that the Club might coerce young children into attending its meeting. The Court noted that children cannot attend without their parent's permission.

The Court also rejected the argument that parents or children might perceive that the school was "endorsing religion." The Court discounted this possibility, noting that the school's use policy allowed members of the public to enter the school facility after hours. The Court also found it unlikely that children would perceive that the school was endorsing the Good News Club and feel coerced to participate. "Because allowing the Club to speak on school grounds would ensure neutrality, not threaten it, Milford faces an uphill battle in arguing that the Establishment Clause compels it to exclude the Good News Club. The Club's meetings were held after school hours, not sponsored by the school, and were open to any student who obtained parental consent, not just to Club members."

Justice Stevens dissented, arguing that a public school "[need not open] its forum to religious proselytizing or worship...." While Justice Stevens agreed that the state "may not censor speech about an authorized topic based on the point of view expressed by the speaker," he would have held that the state has discretion to preserve property for the uses to which it has been dedicated. In his view, "[d]istinguishing speech from a religious viewpoint, on the one hand, from religious proselytizing, on the other, is comparable to distinguishing meetings to discuss political issues from meetings whose principal purpose is to recruit new members to join a political organization." In his view, recruiting meetings can be prohibited because they "may introduce divisiveness and tend to separate young children into cliques that undermine the school's educational mission."

Justice Scalia concurred, arguing that the Good News Club's activities are protected under the free speech and free exercise clauses. He agreed with the Court that the government could not create a public forum and then ban religious speakers from that forum: "Lacking *any* legitimate reason for excluding the Club's speech from its forum—'because it's religious' will not do—respondent would seem to fail First Amendment scrutiny regardless of how its action is characterized." Moreover, he noted that the school had opened its building to uses "pertaining to the welfare of the community" and that the Club was attempting to teach values from a Christian perspective. He went on to note that any other group can exhort students to live moral lives and give its reasons for encouraging them for doing so. However, the Club "may only discuss morals and character, and cannot give *its* reasons why they should be fostered—because God wants and expects it, because it will make the Club members 'saintly' people, and because it emulates Jesus Christ. The Club may not, in other words, independently discuss the religious premise on which its views are based—that God exists and His assistance is necessary to morality."

Justice Souter, joined by Justice Ginsburg, dissented, arguing that "[Good News's] exercises blur the line between public classroom instruction and private religious indoctrination, leaving a reasonable elementary school pupil unable to appreciate that the former instruction is the business of the school while the latter evangelism is not...." He would have found a violation of the establishment clause, noting that "Good News intends to use the public school premises not for the mere discussion of a subject from a particular, Christian point of view, but for an evangelical service of worship calling children to commit themselves in an act of Christian conversion." As a result, admission of the Good News Club to the forum would suggest to a reasonable observer that the school was endorsing religion. Justice Scalia responded to Justice Souter, agreeing that the Club's religious speech "may be characterized as proselytizing," but suggesting that the Court has previously rejected the attempt to distinguish worship from other religious speech, saying that "the distinction has [no] intelligible content," and no relevance to the constitutional issue.

The *Good News* decision is important because it recognizes that religious groups have the right to use public fora on the same terms as other groups and may not be discriminated against because of those beliefs. Moreover, by allowing religious groups into the forum, the state does not run afoul of the establishment clause. Combined with other recent decisions, *Good News* established the right of religious groups to participate in society on an equal basis with other groups.

Bibliography

Todd Hagins, *Mother Goose and Father God: Extending the Equal Access Act to Pre-High School Students,* 15 *Regent University Law Review* 93 (Fall 2002).

Louis H. Heilbron, *The Decline of the Establishment Clause: Effect of Recent Supreme Court Decisions on Church-State Relations,* 34 *Golden Gate University Law Review* 217 (2004).

Dan Mbulu, *First Amendment: Extending Equal Access to Elementary Education in the Aftermath of Good News Club v. Milford Central School,* 16 *Regent University Law Review* 91 (2004).

Russell L. Weaver and Donald E. Lively, *Understanding the First Amendment* (Newark, NJ: LexisNexis, 2003).

CHAPTER 16

FOURTH AMENDMENT: SEARCH AND SEIZURE

The Fourth Amendment, like many other provisions of the Bill of Rights, emerged in response to colonial experiences with the abusive police practices. Under English rule, the King's agents were empowered to search dwellings and other places on the basis of mere suspicion or whim. Typically, these searches were conducted for the purposes of finding publications that criticized colonial rule. From this historical experience, the Fourth Amendment emerged as a guarantee against unreasonable searches and seizures. Consistent with the Bill of Rights generally, the Fourth Amendment initially was conceptualized as a safeguard against abuse by the federal government. Eventually, it was incorporated through the Fourteenth Amendment and thus made applicable to the states. The primary remedy for a Fourth Amendment violation is exclusion from trial of any evidence illegally obtained. The Supreme Court adopted the exclusionary rule as a federal remedy in *Weeks v. United States* (1914). Nearly half a century passed, however, before the Court in *Mapp v. Ohio* (1961) extended the exclusionary rule to state violations.

The Court has devoted much attention to defining and evolving key terms of the Fourth Amendment. In *Delaware v. Prouse* (1979), the Court found that police could not stop a motorist for a driver's license and registration check minus some reasonable suspicion that the driver was engaged in criminal activity. The Court's decision in *United States v. Mendenhall* (1980) gave meaning to the term "seizure," which occurs only if a reasonable person would not feel free to leave an encounter with police. The ability of police to conduct a search or seizure, barring exceptional circumstances, is contingent upon a showing of probable cause. Probable cause is a general requirement for obtaining a search warrant. When informants are relied upon to establish probable cause, key factors may be the specificity of relevant facts and credibility of the source. In *Illinois v. Gates* (1983), it rejected the notion that probable cause could not be established on the basis of an anonymous tip. Although the informant's veracity and reliability typically are relevant factors, the Court embraced an analysis that factored the totality of relevant circumstances. Second thoughts about the exclusionary rule led the Court, in *United States v. Leon* (1984) to adopt a "good faith" exception to its operation. Applied technology enables police to investigate and obtain information by methods that are less physically invasive. In *Kyllo v. United States* (1983), the Court determined that thermal imaging constituted a search for purposes of the Fourth Amendment. Although searches and seizures must be conditioned upon a showing of probable cause, pursuant to the Fourth Amendment's explicit command, the Court has developed exceptions to this requirement. Its decision, in *Board of Education of Independent School District No. 92 of Pottawatomie*

County v. Earles (2002), carved out an exception to the probable cause requirement for random drug testing of high school students engaged in extracurricular activities.

Delaware v. Prouse

In the late 1960s, the Supreme Court began developing standards that expanded the authority of police to conduct searches and seizures. A momentum-building decision for this trend was *Terry v. Ohio* (1968). This case presented the question of whether, absent probable cause, "it is always unreasonable for a policeman to seize a person and subject him to a limited search for weapons." Rather than adopt a fixed standard for

> **Issue:** Whether the police may "stop" to check and verify the driver's license and registration.
>
> **Year:** 1979.
>
> **Outcome:** The police may not stop an automobile absent a "reasonable suspicion" that the passengers are involved in criminal activity.
>
> **Author of Opinion:** Justice Byron White.
>
> **Vote:** 8-1.

all circumstances, the *Terry* Court determined that each case needed "to be decided on its own facts." In *Terry* itself, the Court determined that it is reasonable under the Fourth Amendment for an officer "to conduct a carefully limited search of the outer clothing" for weapons when observation and experience leads him or her to conclude that the person may be armed and dangerous. This decision reflected a balancing of the "need" for police action, for purposes of protecting the officer's and public's safety, against the level of "intrusion" caused by the stop and frisk. Using this same test, the Court has articulated detailed rules regarding when the police can bring suspects in for questioning or subject them to fingerprinting or lineups.

Delaware v. Prouse presented the question of whether the police may "stop" automobiles simply to check their licenses and registrations. Prouse was pulled over in what the police officer referred to as a "routine" stop. The officer explained that "I saw the car in the area and wasn't answering any complaints, so I decided to pull them off." Unfortunately, for Prouse, the officer smelled marijuana smoke emanating from the vehicle and found marijuana lying in plain view on the floorboard of the vehicle. When Prouse was indicted for illegal possession of a controlled substance, he moved to suppress on the basis that the marijuana evidence would never have been discovered absent an unconstitutional stop.

In evaluating the constitutionality of the stop, the Court balanced the "need" for the stop against the governmental "intrusion": "[T]he permissibility of a particular law enforcement practice is judged by balancing its intrusion on the individual's Fourth Amendment interests against its promotion of legitimate governmental interests."

In *Prouse*, the state argued that its interest in "promoting public safety upon its roads" outweighed the intrusion caused by the stop. The Court agreed that "the States have a vital interest in ensuring that only those qualified to do so are permitted to operate motor vehicles, that these vehicles are fit for safe operation, and hence that licensing, registration, and vehicle inspection requirements are being observed." The court noted that drivers' licenses "are issued periodically to evidence that the drivers holding them are sufficiently familiar with the rules of the road and are physically qualified to operate a motor vehicle." In addition, the registration and vehicle inspection requirements "are designed to keep dangerous automobiles off the road." The Court also found that automobile insurance requirements are important because they implement the "legitimate interest in seeing to it that its citizens have protection when involved in a motor vehicle accident."

Even though the Court agreed that the state's goals were legitimate, the Court doubted whether discretionary spot checks were "a sufficiently productive mechanism to justify the intrusion upon Fourth Amendment interests which such stops entail." The Court concluded that the state had alternate mechanisms available for ensuring that drivers were carrying valid licenses without conducting random spot checks. The Court held that the police were free to pull motorists over when they observed violations of traffic laws and concluded that the police were free to check a motorist's driver's license and registration during such stops. Moreover, the Court assumed that unlicensed drivers were more likely to commit violations than licensed drivers. As a result, the Court concluded that "it must be assumed that finding an unlicensed driver among those who commit traffic violations is a much more likely event than finding an unlicensed driver by choosing randomly from the entire universe of drivers. [The] contribution to highway safety made by discretionary stops selected from among drivers generally will therefore be marginal at best." In addition, the Court concluded that unlicensed drivers would be deterred by the possibility that they will be involved in accidents, or other violations, at which presentment of their license and registration will be required.

The Court also concluded that the state had alternate mechanisms for ensuring that cars were properly registered. The Court noted that all vehicles were required to have current license plates, and the Court noted that such plates could not be obtained absent compliance with the state's registration requirements. As a result, the Court doubted that random stops would advance the state's interest in keeping unregistered vehicles off the road.

In addition, the Court expressed concern about the police exercising unbridled discretion to stop motorists: "When there is not probable cause to believe that a driver is violating any one of the multitude of applicable traffic and equipment regulations—or other articulable basis amounting to reasonable suspicion that the driver is unlicensed or his vehicle unregistered—we cannot conceive of any legitimate basis upon which a patrolman could decide that stopping a particular driver for a spot check would be more productive than stopping any other driver. This kind of standardless and unconstrained discretion is the evil the Court has discerned when in previous cases it has insisted that the discretion of the official in the field be circumscribed, at least to some extent."

By contrast, the Court found that the "intrusion" caused by a random vehicle stop was significant. The Court noted that an automobile is a basic and necessary method of transportation and noted that many people spend hours per day in their cars. "Were the individual subject to unfettered governmental intrusion every time he entered an automobile, the security guaranteed by the Fourth Amendment would be seriously circumscribed."

The Court concluded by holding that, absent an "articulable and reasonable suspicion that a motorist is unlicensed or that an automobile is not registered, or that either the vehicle or an occupant is otherwise subject to seizure for violation of law," the police may not stop the vehicle simply to check the driver's license and registration.

Justice William Rehnquist authored a dissenting opinion. Because government has the right to require drivers' licenses and vehicle registrations, he determined that it also may take the steps necessary to "enforce compliance." Applying the need versus intrusion test, he argued that the "whole point of enforcing motor vehicle safety regulations is to remove from the road the unlicensed driver before he demonstrates why he is unlicensed. The Court would apparently prefer that the State check licenses and vehicle registrations as the wreckage is being towed away."

The Court has departed from its "reasonable suspicion" requirement in the context of police roadblocks. In *Michigan Department of State Police v. Sitz* (1990), the Court upheld the constitutionality of sobriety checkpoints at which drivers were forced to stop and be checked for signs of intoxication. Drivers found to be intoxicated were arrested. In *Sitz,* the Court upheld the checkpoints, even though they were conducted without reasonable suspicion, because of the great need to apprehend drunk drivers in order to protect highway safety. However, in *City of Indianapolis v. Edmond* (2000), the Court struck down "drug interdiction checkpoints" at which drivers were stopped in an effort to uncover illegal drugs. The Court concluded that the checkpoints were seeking evidence of ordinary criminal wrongdoing, were unrelated to highway safety, and could not be justified absent evidence of reasonable suspicion that the drivers were involved in criminal activity.

Prouse is an important decision because it recognizes the right of automobile drivers and passengers to be free from governmental intrusions absent a reasonable suspicion that they are involved in criminal activities.

Bibliography

George C. Thomas III, *Time Travel, Hovercrafts & the Framers: James Madison Sees the Future and Rewrites the Fourth Amendment,* 80 *Notre Dame Law Review* 451 (2005).

Russell L. Weaver, *Investigation & Discretion: The Terry Revolution at Forty (Almost),* 109 *Penn State Law Review* 1205 (2005).

Russell L. Weaver, Leslie W. Abramson, John M. Burkoff, and Catherine Hancock, *Principles of Criminal Procedure* (St. Paul, MN: Thomson/West, 2004), 132.

United States v. Mendenhall

Police-citizen encounters arise in a variety of contexts and may vary in their potential for intrusiveness. In some instances, the police have advance notice and can obtain a warrant to search or seize individuals. In other instances, the circumstances giving rise to the need to act can arise unexpectedly. For many years, the rules governing police-citizen encounters were vaguely defined and subject only to the Fourth Amendment's general prohibition against "unreasonable" searches and seizures.

In general, the United States Supreme Court tended to impose a "warrant preference" for searches. However, the Court has articulated a number of exceptions to the warrant requirement. By contrast, warrants were not always required for "seizures." For example, the Court has held that the police may arrest a citizen for a felony based only on a showing of "probable cause" to believe that the person to be arrested committed the crime. *United States v. Watson* (1976). In addition, the Court has allowed the police to stop and search vehicles based solely on probable cause. *California v. Carney* (1985).

Citation: 446 U.S. 544.

Issue: Whether a woman was "seized" within the meaning of the Fourth Amendment when she was approached by Drug Enforcement Agents in an airport concourse.

Year of Decision: 1980.

Outcome: No seizure occurs unless a reasonable person in the suspect's position would not feel free to leave.

Author of Opinion: Justice Potter Stewart.

Vote: 5–4.

The Court's approach to street encounters changed significantly with its landmark decision in *Terry v. Ohio* (1968). In that case, the Court held that, when a police officer reasonably concludes, in light of his experience, that criminal activity is afoot and that the suspect is both armed and dangerous, the office may be entitled to conduct a "stop and frisk." *Terry* represented a major break from prior precedent because it seemed to sustain seizures (the stop) and searches (the frisk) based on something less than probable cause. In reaching its decision, the Court balanced the need for the search against the level of intrusion imposed on the suspect's privacy. Because the officer perceived that a robbery was about to take place, the need for action was great. Likewise, given that the officer did nothing more than "stop" and "frisk" the suspects, the intrusion was deemed to be relatively minor compared to the need.

In post-*Terry* cases, the Court has applied the "need-intrusion" test in a number of other contexts to give police greater authority to search and seize. In *Mendenhall*, the Court was asked to apply the *Terry* balancing test to airport investigative stops. Mendenhall arrived at the Detroit Metropolitan Airport early one morning and was approached by Drug Enforcement Agency agents who suspected that she was transporting illegal narcotics. The agents asked Mendenhall for her driver's license and identification. Mendenhall's plane ticket was issued in the name of "Annette Ford," and Mendenhall explained that she "just felt like using that name." After the agent learned that Mendenhall had been in California for only two days, the interviewing officer identified himself as a DEA agent. At that point, Mendenhall became "quite shaken, extremely nervous" and "had a hard time speaking." After returning the airline ticket and driver's license to Mendenhall, the DEA agent asked the respondent if she would accompany him to the airport DEA office for further questions. She did not respond to the request, but followed him to the DEA office. At the office the agent asked the respondent if she would allow a search of her person and handbag and told her that she had the right to decline the search if she desired. She responded: "Go ahead." In the ensuing search, the officers found that Mendenhall was carrying heroin. She was charged and convicted.

The Court first considered whether, when the DEA agent approached Mendenhall, he "seized" her within the meaning of the Fourth Amendment. In resolving that question, the Court began by defining the term "seizure." The Court concluded that "not all personal intercourse between policemen and citizens involves 'seizures' of persons." Indeed, the police are free to speak with citizens on the street and ask them questions, and a seizure occurs only "when the officer, by means of physical force or show of authority, has in some way restrained the liberty of a citizen." In the Court's view, a seizure can exist within the meaning of the Fourth Amendment only if, in view of all of the circumstances surrounding the incident, "a reasonable person would have believed that he was not free to leave." Factors that might enter into a court's analysis regarding the seizure issue are the following: whether the individual is surrounded by threatening police officers; whether the officer displayed a weapon; whether there was some physical touching of the person of the citizen; or whether the use of language or tone of voice indicated that compliance with the officer's request might be compelled.

On the *Mendenhall* facts, the Court held that no "seizure" had occurred. The Court emphasized that Mendenhall was approached in a public concourse by officers who were not wearing uniforms and displayed no weapons. In addition, the officers did not demand, but instead requested, the right to examine Mendenhall's identification and ticket. Such conduct, without more, did not amount to an intrusion upon any constitutionally protected interest. As a result, the Court concluded that "nothing in the record suggests that the respondent had any objective reason to believe that she was not free to end the conversation in the concourse and proceed on her way, and for that reason we conclude that the agents' initial approach to her was not a seizure."

In dicta, the Court recognized that a short investigative stop might be justified based on something less than probable cause. Based on the *Terry* "need-intrusion" test, the Court indicated that such a seizure might be justified based only on a showing of "reasonable suspicion" that the suspect was involved in criminal activity. In later cases, the Court has fleshed out the requirements for other types of investigative encounters. For example, in *Dunaway v. New York* (1979), the Court held that probable cause was required in order for the police to take a suspect to the station house for custodial interrogation. Likewise, in *Davis v. Mississippi* (1969), the Court held that probable cause was required to take a suspect to the station house for fingerprinting. However, in *Hayes v. Florida* (1985), the Court indicated that it might uphold a brief detention for fingerprinting based only on a reasonable suspicion that the suspect is involved in criminal activity.

Justice Byron White, joined by three other justices, dissented, arguing that Mendenhall was "seized" within the meaning of the Fourth Amendment when she was escorted from the public area of the terminal to the DEA office for questioning and a strip search of her person. He doubted that she was free to leave, especially once she arrived at the DEA office. "[Because] Ms. Mendenhall was being illegally detained at the time of the search of her person, her suppression motion should have been granted in the absence of evidence to dissipate the taint."

Mendenhall is important because it helps define the rules applicable to investigative stops. In general, a "seizure" occurs only when a reasonable person in the suspect's position would not feel free to leave. In order to justify the most minimal seizure, an investigative stop, nothing more need be shown than a "reasonable suspicion" that the suspect is involved in criminal activity.

Bibliography

Philip S. Greene and Brian W. Wice, *The D.E.A. Drug Courier Profile: History and Analysis*, 22 *South Texas Law Journal* 261 (1982).

Satoru Morizane, *Initial Encounters Between Police and Citizens: A Comparative Study of the United States and Japan*, 13 *Emory International Law Review* 561 (1999).

Overview of the Fourth Amendment, Thirty-Second Annual Review of Criminal Procedure, 91 *Georgia Law Journal* 5 (2003).

Russell L. Weaver, Leslie W. Abramson, John M. Burkoff, and Catherine Hancock, *Principles of Criminal Procedure* (St. Paul, MN: Thomson/West, 2004), 60–82.

Illinois v. Gates

In drafting the Fourth Amendment prohibition against "unreasonable searches and seizures, congressional framers sought to protect the citizenry against arbitrary police action. The framers were motivated by colonial history, in particular, the fact that British soldiers routinely used "general warrants" (warrants authorizing general searches of houses rather than limited searches for particular items) to search colonists' houses from top to bottom. As a result, the Fourth Amendment prohibits "unreasonable searches and seizures." In addition, it provides that "no Warrants shall issue, but upon probable cause, supported by Oath or [affirmation]."

The probable cause requirement contains two elements: not only must a warrant particularly describe the place to be searched and the things to be seized, but it must be based on probable cause to believe that the searched for items can be found in

Citation: 462 U.S. 213.

Issue: Whether courts can rely on an anonymous tip in establishing probable cause to search.

Year: 1983.

Outcome: An anonymous tip can provide probable cause for the issuance of a warrant.

Author of Opinion: Justice William Rehnquist.

Vote: 6-3.

the place to be searched. In *Draper v. United States,* 358 U.S. 307 (1959), the Court defined probable cause in the following way: "Probable cause exists when 'the facts and circumstances within their [the arresting officers'] knowledge and of which they had reasonably trustworthy information [are] sufficient in themselves to warrant a man of reasonable caution in the belief that 'an offense has been or is being committed.'"

When the police seek a warrant, they frequently do so based on the testimony or affidavits of police officers. However, informants are an integral part of the investigative process and are often relied on by police in their affidavits and testimony. Moreover, the testimony of informants is often used in a "hearsay" way (hearsay being defined as an out-of-court statement offered to prove the truth of the matter asserted in the statement). In criminal and civil trials, the use of hearsay is usually prohibited except when the prosecution can fit the testimony into one of the many exceptions to the hearsay rule. By contrast, in probable cause hearings, hearsay is admissible and usable.

A pair of landmark decisions in the 1960s—*Spinelli v. United States* (1969) and *Aguilar v. Texas* (1964)—established that two prerequisites must be satisfied before informant testimony can be considered in the warrant process. First, the warrant application must set forth the "underlying circumstances" necessary to enable the magistrate independently to judge the validity of the informant's conclusions. Second, the application must demonstrate that the informant is "credible" or his information "reliable." In *Aguilar,* a search warrant was deemed inadequate because it was based upon an affidavit of police officers who swore only that they had "received reliable information from a credible person and [did] believe" that narcotics were being illegally stored on the described premises. The Court concluded that the officer was required to provide the basis for his conclusions.

Illinois v. Gates is important because the Court concludes that the *Aguilar-Spinelli* test need no longer be regarded as a precondition to the admissibility of informant testimony in the warrant process. In *Gates,* the Bloomingdale, Illinois, Police Department received an anonymous handwritten letter suggesting that the Gates were selling illegal drugs out of their Illinois home. The tip went on to state that the Gates would travel to Florida in a few days, and it gave a *modus operandi:* the wife would drive the car to Florida, the husband would fly to Florida to drive the car back, and the wife would fly back to Illinois on her own. The tip promised that "I guarantee if you watch them carefully you will make a big catch. They are friends with some big drug dealers, who visit their house often." The police investigated and determined that Mrs. Gates drove the family car to Florida, and Mr. Gates flew down to meet her. However, the Gates deviated from the modus operandi because the two of them drove back towards Illinois together. As soon as the Gates starting heading North, an Illinois magistrate issued a warrant authorizing a search of the Gates' car and residence.

In upholding the warrant, the United States Supreme Court reevaluated the *Aguilar-Spinelli* test. Since the letter was anonymous, it provided virtually nothing from which one might conclude that its author was either honest or his information reliable. In addition, the letter failed to give the "basis for the writer's predictions regarding the Gates' criminal activities." As a result, if the *Aguilar-Spinelli* test were strictly applied, the trial court would not have had probable cause to issue the warrant.

Instead of summarily rejecting the tip, the Court abandoned the *Aguilar-Spinelli* test as a precondition to consideration of the tip. The Court emphasized that the probable cause standard is a "practical, nontechnical conception" that focuses on "the factual and practical considerations of everyday life on which reasonable and prudent men, not legal technicians, act." Since informants' tips vary dramatically, the Court doubted that it should apply a single rule to all tips and chose instead to apply a "totality of the circumstances" test. Under that approach, while an informant's "veracity," "reliability," and "basis of knowledge" should be considered in determining the value of a tip, the Court was unwilling to conclude that the *Aguilar-Spinelli* factors should be regarded as "entirely separate and independent requirements to be rigidly exacted in every case." Instead, the Court held that "they should be understood simply as closely intertwined issues that may usefully illuminate the common-sense, practical question whether there is 'probable cause' to believe that contraband or evidence is located in a particular place." In other words, the "two-pronged test" should be transformed into relevant considerations to be used in the totality of circumstances analysis. In other words, "a deficiency in one [prong] may be compensated for, in determining the overall reliability of a tip, by a strong showing as to the other, or by some other indicia of reliability."

Applying the "totality of circumstances" test to the *Gates* facts, the Court held that the magistrate had probable cause to issue the warrant. The Court acknowledged that the tip did not contain information regarding the informant's identity, and therefore his credibility, and did not contain information suggesting how he came by the information. Nevertheless, the tip included not only allegations regarding the Gates' past conduct, but also predictions regarding their future conduct. In particular, the tip referred to the Gates' plans to travel to Florida on a specific date in the near future. The Court concluded that the tips' accuracy regarding the Gates' future actions suggested that their other allegations of drug activity were probably accurate as well: "If the informant had access to accurate information of this type a magistrate could properly conclude that it was not unlikely that he also had access to reliable information of the Gates' alleged illegal activities." The Court concluded that probable cause does not require certainty and that "there was a fair probability that the writer of the anonymous letter had obtained his entire story either from the Gates or someone they trusted."

Justice White, concurring in the judgment, would have upheld the warrant under the *Aguilar-Spinelli* framework and objected to the majority's modification of that framework. While he agreed that some lower courts were applying *Aguilar-Spinelli* "in an unduly rigid manner," he felt that the better approach was to clarify the meaning and application of the *Aguilar-Spinelli* test.

Justice William Brennan, joined by Justice Thurgood Marshall, dissented, arguing that the *Aguilar-Spinelli* test serves a useful purpose because it provides crucial information regarding the informant, helps structure a magistrate's probable cause inquiry, and therefore produces greater accuracy. Even if a magistrate cannot rely on a tip because he is unable to conclude that the tip "has been obtained in a reliable way by a credible person," the magistrate can still consider the remaining facts and decide whether probable cause exists. Justice John Paul Stevens, joined by Justice Brennan, also dissented. He doubted that, even considering the evidence under a totality of circumstances test, the magistrate had "probable cause" to believe that the Gates were in possession of illegal drugs.

Gates is an important decision because it redefines the probable cause determination by altering the *Aguilar-Spinelli* test. Under *Gates,* in order to rely on a tip, the police need not show that the informant was "credible" and need not provide information suggesting that the information was reliably obtained. Instead, trial courts and magistrates should apply a "totality of circumstances" test and simply consider the *Aguilar-Spinelli* factors as part of that test.

Bibliography

Joel Jay Finer, *Gates, Leon, and the Compromise of Adjudicative Fairness,* 33 *Cleveland State Law Review* 707 (1984–1985).

Edward G. Mascolo, *Probable Cause Revisited: Some Disturbing Implications from Illinois v. Gates,* 6 *West New England Law Review* 331 (1983).

Russell L. Weaver, Leslie W. Abramson, John M. Burkoff, and Catherine Hancock, *Principles of Criminal Procedure* (St. Paul, MN: Thomson/West, 2004), 60–82.

United States v. Leon

Citation: 468 U.S. 1250.

Issue: Whether the Court should create a "good faith" exception to the exclusionary evidence rule.

Year of Decision: 1984.

Outcome: The Court created a "good faith" exception to the exclusionary evidence rule after balancing the "costs" of exclusion against the "benefits."

Author of Opinion: Justice Byron White.

Vote: 7-2.

Even though various provisions of the Bill of Rights protect the people against governmental intrusions, there has been much debate about how to enforce those rights. One controversial method of enforcement is the so-called exclusionary evidence rule. That rule provides that, when evidence is seized in violation of a defendant's constitutional rights, the evidence should be excluded from the defendant's trial.

In *Wolf v. Colorado,* 338 U.S. 25 (1949), the Court was called upon to decide whether the exclusionary evidence rule constituted a fundamental component of due process and therefore should be imposed on the states by virtue of the Fourteenth Amendment. The Court refused to require the states to apply the rule, noting that there were other, equally effective, mechanisms for enforcing the Fourth Amendment prohibition against unreasonable searches and seizures. In *Wolf,* the Court concluded that police abuse could be checked in the following ways: public opinion, police disciplinary procedures and criminal prosecutions against rogue officers, and the possibility of civilian damage suits.

Wolf was overruled by the Court's decision in *Mapp v. Ohio* (1961). *Mapp* was a landmark decision because it mandated application of the exclusionary evidence rule to state prosecutions. In overruling *Wolf,* the Court emphasized that other remedies for Fourth Amendment violations have proven to be both "worthless and futile" and that "admission of the new constitutional right ... could not consistently tolerate denial of its most important constitutional privilege, namely, the exclusion of the evidence which an accused had been forced to give by reason of the unlawful seizure." The Court went on to note that its decision "founded on reason and truth, gives to the individual no more than that which the Constitution guarantees him, to the police officer no less than that to which honest law enforcement is entitled, and, to the courts, that judicial integrity so necessary in the administration of justice."

After *Mapp*, police officials and prosecutors, who were sometimes embarrassed when the exclusionary evidence rule was used to exclude evidence or to reverse convictions, argued that the rule should be subject to a "good faith" exception. The Court considered that issue in *Leon*. The facts were relatively straightforward. An officer sought and obtained a warrant from a magistrate to search Leon's home. Although the Court concluded that the magistrate lacked probable cause to grant the warrant, the officer claimed to have acted in "good faith" in executing the warrant in reliance on the magistrate's determination.

In recognizing the "good faith" exception to the exclusionary rule, *Leon* held that the exclusionary rule is not constitutionally required, but is instead applied as "a judicially created remedy designed to safeguard Fourth Amendment rights generally through its deterrent effect." As a judicial remedy, the Court concluded that the determination of whether to apply the rule in a given case would not be automatic, but would be resolved by "weighing the costs and benefits of preventing the use in the prosecution's case in chief of inherently trustworthy tangible evidence obtained in reliance on a search warrant issued by a detached and neutral magistrate that ultimately is found to be defective."

In weighing the costs and benefits, the Court recognized that the remedial benefit of the exclusionary rule is that it deters police misconduct and therefore helps protect the people against constitutional violations. However, the Court also recognized that the rule exacts "substantial social costs." In some cases, the rule impedes a trial court's "truth-finding function" by excluding reliable, probative, and trustworthy evidence. Because of this exclusion, some "guilty defendants may go free or receive reduced sentences as a result of favorable plea bargains." In addition, the Court feared that indiscriminate application of the exclusionary rule might cause "disrespect for the law and administration of justice." As a result, the Court concluded that the rule should be restricted "to those areas where its remedial objectives are thought most efficaciously served."

Applying the balancing test, the Court concluded that it should accept the good faith exception to the exclusionary rule in the warrant context. The Court noted that search warrants are issued by neutral and detached magistrates, which the Court regarded as a "more reliable safeguard against improper searches than the hurried judgment of a law enforcement officer 'engaged in the often competitive enterprise of ferreting out crime.'" The Court indicated that it was appropriate to give "great deference" to the magistrate's determination.

The Court rejected the argument that the exclusionary rule should be applied to deter judges and magistrates. The Court noted that the purpose of the exclusionary rule is to deter police misconduct, and there is no evidence that judges and magistrates have shown any tendency to "ignore or subvert the Fourth Amendment or that lawlessness among these actors requires application of the extreme sanction of exclusion." In addition, the Court doubted that application of the exclusionary rule would deter judges or magistrates from making incorrect determinations because "they have no stake in the outcome of particular criminal prosecutions." As a result, if application of the exclusionary rule is to have a deterrent effect, it must focus on deterring police misconduct.

In deciding to recognize the good faith exception, the Court doubted "that the exclusionary rule can have any deterrent effect when the offending officers acted in the objectively reasonable belief that their conduct did not violate the Fourth Amendment." In the Court's view, "an officer cannot be expected to question the magistrate's probable-cause determination or his judgment that the form of the warrant is technically sufficient." As a result, the Court held that "the marginal or nonexistent benefits produced by suppressing evidence obtained in objectively reasonable reliance on a subsequently invalidated search warrant cannot justify the substantial costs of exclusion."

In *Leon*, the Court articulated several preconditions for a finding of "good faith." First, the good faith exception would not generally apply to warrantless searches. Second, it would not apply when the officer has no reasonable grounds for believing that the warrant was properly issued. Third, good faith would not be present if a magistrate or judge knew the affidavit was false or would have known it was false except for his or her reckless disregard of the truth. Fourth, a magistrate's failure to act neutrally would preclude a finding of good faith. Fifth, when an affidavit was so lacking in indicia of probable cause, or the warrant was so facially deficient that it could not reasonably be presumed valid, good faith would be absent.

Justice Brennan, joined by Justice Marshall, dissented, arguing that the exclusionary rule cannot be dismissed as a judicially mandated rule of restraint. In his view, when the judiciary admits unlawfully seized evidence, it involves itself in the illegality. Moreover, he viewed the exclusionary rule as grounded in the Fourth Amendment, which he viewed as designed "to prevent the government from subsequently making use of any evidence so obtained." He also took issue with the Court's cost-benefit analysis, which he believed had drawn the Court into "a curious world where the 'costs' of excluding illegally obtained evidence loom to exaggerated heights and where the 'benefits' of such exclusion are made to disappear with a mere wave of the hand." He viewed the cost-benefit analysis as "a virtually impossible task for the judiciary to perform honestly or accurately." In addition, he noted that the costs of the exclusionary rule are less than the Court suggests with a small number of prosecutions actually being affected by exclusionary evidence problems. Finally, he noted that application of the exclusionary evidence rule encourages police departments to increase officer training and education, and will encourage the police to be more careful. By contrast, the Court's "reasonable mistake" rule will "tend to put a premium on police ignorance of the law." As a result, police departments will not be encouraged to provide additional training to officers. In addition, the "police will now know that if they can secure a warrant, so long as the circumstances of its issuance are not 'entirely unreasonable,' all police conduct pursuant to that warrant will be protected from further judicial review."

Justice Stevens, concurred in the judgment, arguing that the good faith exception would "do grave damage to [the] deterrent function [of the exclusionary rule]." He reasoned that, "even when the police know their warrant application is probably insufficient, they retain an incentive to submit it to a magistrate, on the chance that he may take the bait." He recognized that "the exclusionary rule exerts a high price —the loss of probative evidence of guilt," but he viewed that price as one that "courts have often been required to pay to serve important social goals. That price is also one the Fourth Amendment requires us to pay, assuming as we must that the Framers intended that its strictures 'shall not be violated.'"

Leon is an important decision because it establishes the "good faith" exception to the exclusionary evidence rule. As a result, even if probable cause does not exist, the fruits of an illegal police search need not be excluded if the police acted pursuant to a warrant, and the costs of excluding the evidence exceeds the benefits.

Bibliography

Robert M. Bloom, *United States v. Leon and its Ramifications*, 56 *University of Colorado Law Review* 247 (1985).

Abraham S. Goldstein, *The Search Warrant, the Magistrate, and Judicial Review*, 62 *New York University Law Review* 1173 (1987).

Rosemarie A. Lynskey, *A Middle Ground Approach to the Exclusionary Remedy: Reconciliing the Redaction Doctrine with United States v. Leon*, 41 *Vanderbilt Law Review* 811 (1988).

Russell L. Weaver, Leslie W. Abramson, John M. Burkoff, and Catherine Hancock, *Principles of Criminal Procedure* (St. Paul, MN: Thomson/West, 2004), 236–60.

Kyllo v. United States

When the Fourth Amendment to the United States Constitution was created, the state of technology was dramatically different than it is today. In general, the framers were concerned about British intrusions into citizen's homes and, in particular, the use of "general warrants" that allowed British soldiers to search through a colonist's entire home. As time passed, and technology improved, it became possible to physically invade spaces without actually entering them. New devices were invented that allowed the police to remain outside a house, but nonetheless detect high heat levels emanating from the house. These technological advances raised the possibility that devices might be created that would allow the police to stand outside a house, but nonetheless to listen to conversations inside a house or peer inside the house to ascertain what is happening.

> Citation: 533 U.S. 27.
>
> Issue: Whether a "search" occurs when the police point a thermal imaging device (designed to detect excessive heat levels) at a home.
>
> Year of Decision: 2001.
>
> Outcome: Use of the thermal imaging constitutes a "search" within the meaning of the Fourth Amendment.
>
> Author of Opinion: Justice Antonin Scalia.
>
> Vote: 5-4.

Since the late 1960s, the Court has struggled to accommodate Fourth Amendment jurisprudence to these newer forms of technology. In its early decisions, the Court refused to find a Fourth Amendment search unless the police intruded into a "constitutionally protected area." In its landmark decision in *Katz v. United States* (1967), the Court abandoned the requirement of an "intrusion" into a "constitutionally protected area," and opted instead for a standard that focused on whether the police had violated the defendant's "reasonable expectation of privacy." In *Katz*, the "reasonable expectation of privacy" test had the effect of expanding the scope of constitutionally protected interests. In that case, the police placed an electronic listening device to the outside of a phone booth. Since there was no "intrusion" into the booth, there was no search under the Court's prior approach. Applying the *Katz* test, the Court concluded that the listening device involved a "search" because use of that device violated Katz's "reasonable expectation of privacy."

In the years that followed, the Court struggled to determine what the *Katz* test meant and how it applied. *United States v. Place* (1983), involved the question of whether a canine sniff of luggage in an airport constituted a search. The Court answered that question in the negative. The Court noted that the sniff does not require the owner to open the luggage and does not allow the police to rummage through it. Although the sniff may reveal information about the contents of the luggage, the Court concluded that the canine sniff is *unique* because the sniff does nothing more than ascertain smells emanating from the luggage. As a result, the sniff did not violate the defendant's "reasonable expectation of privacy."

In *Kyllo v. United States*, the Court addressed the question of whether the police could aim a thermal-imaging device at a private home to detect heat within the home without constituting a "search" within the meaning of the Fourth Amendment. In that case, a police officer suspected that Kyllo was growing marijuana in his house using high-intensity lamps. In an effort to determine whether his suspicions were well-founded, the officer used a thermal imaging device (an Agema Thermovision 210) to scan the building. Such imagers detect infrared radiation that is not otherwise observable through the naked eye. The device is a nonintrusive device because it "emits no rays or beams and shows a crude visual image of the heat being radiated from the outside of the house"; it "[cannot] penetrate walls or windows to reveal conversations or human activities"; and "[n]o intimate details of the home were observed." The scan of Kyllo's home lasted only a few minutes and was conducted from across the street. The scan revealed that the garage roof and a side wall were "hot" compared to the rest of the home and were much warmer than nearby homes. Based on the scan, the officer concluded that Kyllo was using halide lights to grow marijuana in his house. He took that information, along with tips from informants and utility bills, to a magistrate who issued a search warrant for Kyllo's home. The search uncovered more than 100 marijuana plants.

In an opinion by Justice Antonin Scalia, the Court held that police use of the thermal imaging device constituted a search within the meaning of the Fourth Amendment. The opinion placed great emphasis on the Fourth Amendment's underlying objective to allow citizens to "retreat" into their homes and "there be free from unreasonable governmental intrusion." At the same time, the police need not avert their eyes from homes, and that there is no "search" within the meaning of the Fourth Amendment when the police simply observe activities that are otherwise viewable by the general public. Nevertheless, the Court expressed concern about the effect of advancing technology, which has altered the "degree of privacy secured to citizens by the Fourth Amendment" and "exposed to public view uncovered portions of the house and its curtilage that once were private."

The opinion concluded that, despite the advance of technology, use of the thermal imaging device constituted a search within the meaning of the Fourth Amendment: "We think that obtaining by sense-enhancing technology any information regarding the interior of the home that could not otherwise have been obtained without physical "intrusion into a constitutionally protected area" constitutes a search—at least where (as here) the technology in question is not in general public use." The Court was obviously concerned about the impact of advancing technology on individual privacy. The Court specifically noted that powerful new devices were being created, such as extremely sensitive microphones and satellites. Had it sanctioned the use of thermal imaging devices, it would have been harder to reject other comparable devices: "just as a thermal imager captures only heat emanating from a house, so also a powerful directional microphone picks up only sound emanating from a house—and a satellite capable of scanning from many miles away would pick up only visible light emanating from a house." The Court refused to "leave the homeowner at the mercy of advancing technology—including imaging technology that could discern all human activity in the home."

The Court's opinion rejected any distinction between devices that "detect private activities occurring in private areas" and those that do not. The opinion noted that Fourth Amendment "protection of the home has never been tied to measurement of the quality or quantity of information obtained" and recognized that, in "the home, all details are intimate details, because the entire area is held safe from prying government eyes." In addition, the Court expressed concern that there is "no necessary connection between the sophistication of the surveillance equipment and the 'intimacy' of the details that it observes." The Court noted that a thermal imaging device might reveal "at what hour each night the lady of the house takes her daily sauna and bath—a detail that many would consider 'intimate'; and a much more sophisticated system might detect nothing more intimate than the fact that someone left a closet light on." As a result, the Court concluded that the Fourth Amendment draws "a firm line at the entrance to the house." This "line," as the court observed, not only must be "firm but also bright—which requires clear specification of those methods of surveillance that require a warrant." Because "Government use[d] a device that [was] not in general public use, to explore details of the home that would previously have been unknowable without physical intrusion, the surveillance [was] a 'search' and [was] presumptively unreasonable without a warrant."

Justice Stevens, joined by three other justices, dissented, arguing for a distinction between "'through-the-wall surveillance' that gives the observer or listener direct access to information in a private area, on the one hand, and the thought processes used to draw inferences from information in the public domain, on the other hand." He regarded the thermal imaging device as "off-the-wall" surveillance because it examines only the exterior of the home, and is therefore governed by the principle that "What a person knowingly exposes to the public, even in his own home or office, is not a subject of Fourth Amendment protection." He noted that the device obtained "[n]o details regarding the interior of petitioner's home" and did not result in a "physical penetration into the premises" or allow the police to "obtain information that it could not have obtained by observation from outside the curtilage of the house." He concluded that the "countervailing privacy interest is at best trivial. The interest in concealing the heat escaping from one's house pales in significance to 'the chief evil against which the wording of the Fourth Amendment is directed,' the 'physical entry of the home,' and it is hard to believe that it is an interest the Framers sought to protect in our Constitution."

Kyllo is an extraordinarily important decision because it involves an attempt to deal with the impact of advancing technology on the privacy of citizens in their homes and creates a strong barrier between the police and the citizenry. By drawing "a firm line at the entrance to the house," *Kyllo* limits the ability of the police to intrude on citizens through the use of new technologies.

Bibliography

Stephen E. Henderson, *Nothing New Under the Sun? A Technologically Rational Doctrine of Fourth Amendment Search*, 56 *Mercer Law Review* 507 (2005).

Orin S. Kerr, *The Fourth Amendment and New Technologies: Constitutional Myths and the Case for Caution*, 102 *Michigan Law Review* 801 (2004).

Daniel McKenzie, *What Were They Smoking? The Supreme Court's Latest Step in a Long Strange Trip Through the Fourth Amendment*, 93 *Journal of Criminal Law and Criminology* 153 (2001).

Russell L. Weaver, Leslie W. Abramson, John M. Burkoff, and Catherine Hancock, *Principles of Criminal Procedure* (St. Paul, MN: Thomson/West, 2004), 82–92.

Board of Education of Independent School District No. 92 of Pottawatomie County v. Earles

During the colonial period, Britain subjected Americans to general search warrants that allowed British soldiers to search colonists' homes from top to bottom without

194   Individual Rights and Liberties

Citation: 536 U.S. 822.

Issue: Whether a school district may impose random drug testing, without suspicion, of students participating in extracurricular activities.

Year of Decision: 2002.

Outcome: Under the "special needs" exception to the warrant requirement, public school districts may (under appropriate circumstances) subject students involved in extracurricular activities to suspicionless drug testing.

Author of Opinion: Justice Clarence Thomas.

Vote: 5-4.

any evidence of probable cause. Because of the revulsion against general warrants, the colonists demanded that the United States Constitution contain provisions prohibiting "unreasonable searches and seizures" and providing that no search warrant shall issue except on probable cause and particularly describing the place to be searched and the things to be seized. These protections were ultimately incorporated into the Fourth Amendment to the Constitution.

The United States Supreme Court has generally interpreted the Fourth Amendment as requiring some showing of "reasonableness" before a search can be maintained. In addition, for many types of searches, a warrant is required. However, the Court has struggled to define the Fourth Amendment's application to students. Should students be treated like adults and given full Fourth Amendment protections? Alternatively, do students have more limited rights in the school context? In *Board of Education of Independent School District No. 92 of Pottawatomie County v. Earles,* 536 U.S. 822 (2002), the Court dealt with a Tecumseh, Oklahoma, school district Student Activities Drug Testing Policy that required all middle and high school students to consent to drug testing as a condition of participation in extracurricular activities. The Policy was applied to competitive extracurricular activities, including the Academic Team, Future Farmers of America, Future Homemakers of America, band, choir, pompon, cheerleading, and athletics. Under the Policy, students were required to submit to a drug test before participating, must agree to random drug testing while participating, and must submit to testing at any time based on a reasonable suspicion. The drug tests, conducted by urinalysis, were designed to detect only illegal drugs (e.g., amphetamines, marijuana, cocaine, opiates, and barbiturates) and were not designed to reveal medical conditions or the presence of authorized prescription medications. The Policy was challenged by two students, one of whom was involved in the show choir, the marching band, the Academic Team, and the National Honor Society, and the other who participated in the Academic Team.

The question was whether a constitutional policy must include a showing of probable cause, or at least individual suspicion, as a predicate to testing. In an opinion by Justice Clarence Thomas, the Court upheld the drug testing program relying heavily on the so-called "special needs" exception to the warrant requirement. The Court concluded that school searches need not be based on probable cause because the school was not conducting criminal investigations. In addition, the Court held that the drug testing need not be based on a finding of individualized suspicion of wrongdoing by the student being tested.

The *Earles* Court held that the "reasonableness" of searches must be determined by balancing the nature of the intrusion on individual privacy against the governmental interests promoted by the policy. In recent decisions, the Court has not always required individualized suspicion as a predicate to a search. Indeed, in a number of cases, the Court has held that, if the Government's need to search is sufficiently compelling, it can justify a search without any showing of individualized suspicion. In the context of safety and administrative regulations, the Court has upheld searches not based on probable cause "when 'special needs, beyond the normal need for law enforcement, make the warrant and probable-cause requirement impracticable.'"

In the school context, the Court had previously applied this so-called "special needs" exception. Even though the Court has not held that school age children "shed their constitutional rights when they enter the schoolhouse," the Court has treated schoolchildren differently at school "because of schools' custodial and tutelary responsibility for children." For example, in *Vernonia School District 47J v. Acton,* 515 U.S. 646 (1995), the Court upheld a drug testing program for high school athletes. In doing so, the Court recognized that the collection of urine samples for testing involve "searches" within the meaning of the Fourth Amendment. Nevertheless, even though most searches in the criminal context require a showing of probable cause (and, sometimes, a warrant), the Court held that the probable-cause standard "is peculiarly related to criminal investigations" and may be unsuited to determining the reasonableness of administrative searches where the "Government seeks to *prevent* the development of hazardous conditions." *Treasury Employees v. Von Raab,* 489 U.S. 656, 667–668 (1989). The *Vernonia* Court found that athletics present a situation where the presence of drugs could be dangerous, and the Court found that the requirement of probable cause was unnecessary because that requirement "would unduly interfere with the maintenance of the swift and informal disciplinary procedures [that are] needed."

In *Earles,* the Court also upheld the drug testing requirements as applied to students who participate in extracurricular activities. In its prior decisions, the Court had held that "[s]ecuring order in the school environment sometimes requires that students be subjected to greater controls than those appropriate for adults." The Court rejected the argument that because youth who participate in nonathletic extracurricular activities are not subject to regular physicals and do not participate in communal undress, they have a stronger expectation of privacy than athletes. On the contrary, in the Court's view, students who participate in competitive extracurricular activities "voluntarily subject themselves to many of the same intrusions on their privacy as do athletes." Some of these students are involved in "off-campus travel and communal undress." Moreover, all extracurricular activities have rules and requirements for participation that do not apply to the rest of the student body. As a result, the Court concluded that the students had "a limited expectation of privacy."

The Court then focused on "character of the intrusion imposed by the Policy." Even though the Court recognized that urination is "an excretory function traditionally shielded by great privacy," the Court held that the "degree of intrusion" caused by collecting a urine sample depends upon the manner in which the sample is collected. The Court noted that the faculty monitor was required to wait outside the closed restroom stall for the student to produce a sample and was required to listen for the normal sounds of urination only "in order to guard against tampered specimens and to insure an accurate chain of custody." The monitor then pours the sample into two bottles that are sealed and placed into a mailing pouch along with a consent form signed by the student. The Court found that this method of collection involved a "negligible" intrusion on privacy. In addition, the policy requires that the test results "be kept in confidential files separate from a student's other educational records and released to school personnel only on a 'need to know' basis." Given that there had been only one example of carelessness, the Court found the policy sufficiently protective of student rights. Moreover, the school did not reveal test results to law enforcement authorities and did not use them to impose disciplinary or academic consequences within the institution except in regard to the student's participation in extracurricular activities. Indeed, a student could test positive for drugs twice and still be allowed to participate in extracurricular activities. The Court concluded that, given "the minimally intrusive nature of the sample collection and the limited uses to which the test results are put, we conclude that the invasion of students' privacy is not significant."

Having found the intrusion not undue, the Court balanced the intrusion against "the nature and immediacy of the government's concerns and the efficacy of the Policy in meeting them." The Court began by recognizing the governmental interest in preventing drug use by schoolchildren, and it took notice of the fact that the drug problem had "grown worse." Noting that the schools had a "special responsibility of care and direction" of schoolchildren, the Court concluded that "the nationwide drug epidemic makes the war against drugs a pressing concern in every school." Even though the school district's evidence of a drug epidemic was limited, the Court declined to "second-guess" the School District's judgment. In the Court's view, "it would make little sense to require a school district to wait for a substantial portion of its students to begin using drugs before it was allowed to institute a drug testing program designed to deter drug use."

A significant issue in the case is whether the school district's interest in subjecting students who participate in extracurricular activities to drug testing was as significant as its interest in participating in athletic competitions in *Vernonia.* In *Earles,* the students had argued that "the testing of nonathletes does not implicate any safety concerns, and that safety is a 'crucial factor' in applying the special needs framework." While the Court concluded that "safety factors into the special needs analysis," it held that the "safety interest furthered by drug testing is undoubtedly substantial for all children, athletes and nonathletes alike. We know all too well that drug use carries a variety of health risks for children, including death from overdose."

Justice Stephen Breyer, concurring, argued that the program seeks to discourage demand for drugs by eliminating the most pressing concern: peer pressure. In his view, the program gave youths "a nonthreatening reason to decline his friend's drug-use invitations, namely, that he intends to play baseball, participate in debate, join the band, or engage in any one of half a dozen useful, interesting, and important activities." He doubted that a requirement of individualized suspicion would be effective in this context, and he argued that such a requirement might result in the use of subjective criteria that might "unfairly target members of unpopular groups or leave those whose behavior is slightly abnormal stigmatized in the minds of others."

Justice Ruth Bader Ginsburg, joined by three other justices, dissented. She argued that the drug testing program was "capricious" because it targeted "for testing a student population least likely to be at risk from illicit drugs and their damaging effects." She viewed participation in athletics as different and more acceptable because competitive sports require communal undress and expose students to physical risks. By contrast, in her view, even though students who participate in extracurricular activities occasionally take out-of-town trips where they share motel rooms, "those situations are hardly equivalent to the routine communal undress associated with athletics." Finally, she questioned whether the drug situation was sufficiently compelling to justify the program. She noted that the school district had recently certified that illegal drug use was not a major problem, and she argued that "students who participate in extracurricular activities are significantly less likely to develop substance abuse problems than are their less-involved peers." As a result, she concluded that "Tecumseh's policy thus falls short doubly if deterrence is its aim: It invades the privacy of students who need deterrence least, and risks steering students at greatest risk for substance abuse away from extracurricular involvement that potentially may palliate drug problems."

The *Earles* decision is very significant because it continues the Court's tradition of upholding suspicionless searches in so-called "special needs" contexts. In addition, for students, the decision represents a further extension of case law upholding the authority of school officials to subject students to random, suspicionless, drug searches. Although such searches have been extended, thus far, only to students involved in competitive sports and extracurricular activities, they may eventually be extended to the student body generally.

Bibliography

Fabio Arcila, Jr., *Special Needs and Special Deference: Suspicionless Civil Searches in the Modern Regulatory State,* 56 *Administrative Law Review* 1223 (2004).

Crystal A. Garcia and Sheila Seuss Kennedy, *Back to School: Technology, School Safety, and the Disappearing Fourth Amendment,* 12 *Kansas Journal of Law and Public Policy* 273 (2003).

Meg Penrose, *Shedding Rights, Shredding Rights: A Critical Examination of Student's Privacy Rights and the "Special Needs" Doctrine After Earles,* 3 *Nevada Law Journal* 411 (2003).

Russell L. Weaver, Leslie W. Abramson, John M. Burkoff, and Catherine Hancock, *Principles of Criminal Procedure* (St. Paul, MN: Thomson/West, 2004), 159–161.

CHAPTER 17

DUE PROCESS: CONFESSIONS AND ENTRAPMENT

Police practices prior to the twentieth century traded significantly upon tactics of intimidation and violence. Such tactics relate back to early English police methods that freely used torture and brutality to obtain confessions. Until the late eighteenth century, such statements were admissible at trial. By then, the law reflected concern that confessions elicited by force or promises were unreliable and thus inadmissible. American courts generally embraced the premise that manipulation of a suspect's fears or hopes compromised the reliability and voluntariness of a confession. This understanding is reflected in interpretations of the Fifth Amendment privilege against self-incrimination that make coerced confessions inadmissible at trial on constitutional grounds. Even as physical means of extracting confessions faded as an investigative practice, psychological pressure continued to be employed as a method for overcoming a suspect's will. In *Miranda v. Arizona* (1966), the Supreme Court formulated rules designed to overcome the inherently coercive nature of police interrogation. Pursuant to *Miranda*, custodial interrogation must be preceded by warnings that the person has the right to remain silent, any information elicited may be used against him or her, he or she has the right to an attorney, and counsel will be provided if he or she is indigent. Although *Miranda* aimed toward preempting coercive interrogation procedures, it does not speak to circumstances in which these methods are employed and confessions are coerced. In *Mincey v. Arizona* (1978), the Court reaffirmed that due process precludes admission of a confession obtained under duress. Due process also was the basis for the Court's conclusion, in *Jacobson v. United States* (1992), that entrapment provided a defense against criminal prosecution.

Mincey v. Arizona

During medieval times, some criminal suspects were subjected to torture, including the rack and torture chamber, until they confessed. Over time, public attitudes rebelled against torture and prohibited the government from compelling criminal defendants to confess. In the United States Constitution, torture techniques are prohibited by both the privilege against self-incrimination and the due process clause. The latter clause protects defendants against deprivations of life, liberty, or property without due process of law. A central component of the due process clause is the idea that convictions should not be based on evidence that has been obtained fraudulently or by means that render the evidence "unreliable." That includes the admission of confessions that have been compelled. Such evidence is "unreliable" and cannot provide the basis for a valid conviction.

In the United States Supreme Court's landmark decision in *Brown v. Mississippi* (1936), the Court held that the constitutional requirement of due process protects defendants against compelled confessions. In *Brown*, confessions were

Citation: 437 U.S. 385.

Issue: Whether a confession obtained under physical duress violates due process.

Year of Decision: 1978.

Outcome: Defendants cannot be convicted based on confessions that were elicited under physical and mental duress.

Author of Opinion: Justice Potter Stewart.

Vote: 8–1.

obtained from several African-American men, but the confessions were later determined to be false. The police interrogated one defendant by hanging him by a rope around his neck, and they interrogated the remaining defendants while whipping them. All were subjected to "intense pain and agony." A day or two later, the defendant was arrested, "severely whipped," and told that the whipping would continue "until he confessed." He confessed. Two other defendants were arrested and taken to jail. The same sheriff, accompanied by others, made the defendants strip, "and they were laid over chairs and their backs were cut to pieces with a leather strap with buckles on it." They were told that the whipping would continue until they confessed. These defendants confessed, too, and "changed or adjusted their confession in all particulars of detail so as to conform to the demands of their torturers." At trial, the sheriff admitted the whippings, as did other witnesses.

In *Brown*, the Court held that admission of the confessions violated due process. The Court noted that, while the state is free to establish its own criminal procedure rules, those rules must conform to the requirements of due process. In addition, the "rack and torture chamber may not be substituted for the witness stand. And the trial equally is a mere pretense where the state authorities have contrived a conviction resting solely upon confessions obtained by violence." The Court concluded that the police action in this case violated due process: "It would be difficult to conceive of methods more revolting to the sense of justice than those taken to procure the confessions of these petitioners, and the use of the confessions thus obtained as the basis for conviction and sentence was a clear denial of due process."

Mincey involves a modern application of the prohibition against interrogation through torture. In this case, Mincey exchanged gunfire with officers entering his house to arrest him for narcotics crimes. An officer died in the shootout, and Mincey was wounded. Mincey was taken to the hospital and placed in intensive care. Around 8:00 PM that evening, a detective gave Mincey a *Miranda* warning, told him that he was under arrest, and sought to interrogate him. Since Mincey could not talk because of a tube in his mouth, he wrote answers to the detective's questions. The interrogation lasted for four hours and produced incriminating statements. At his trial, Mincey argued that the statements should be excluded as "involuntary."

The Court concluded that Mincey was in serious physical shape at the time of the interrogation. He was seriously wounded and arrived at the hospital "depressed almost to the point of coma." In addition, he complained that he was suffering "unbearable" leg pain, and some of his written answers were not "entirely coherent." Finally, Mincey was interrogated while "lying on his back on a hospital bed, encumbered by tubes, needles, and breathing apparatus." In the Court's view, not only was he unable to leave, he was at "the complete mercy" of the interrogating detective. Moreover, even though Mincey asked the detective not to interrogate him, the interrogation continued, and the detective ignored Mincey's repeated requests for a lawyer. The interrogation ceased only when Mincey lost consciousness or received medical treatment and then resumed.

The Court concluded that Mincey's statements were involuntary: "Mincey was weakened by pain and shock, isolated from family, friends, and legal counsel, and barely conscious, and his will was simply overborne." The Court concluded that "[d]ue process of law requires that statements obtained as these were cannot be used in any way against a defendant at his trial."

Justice William Rehnquist dissented, arguing that the Court ignored evidence of voluntariness. He argued that Mincey had not received medication, that he was "alert and able to understand the officer's questions," and that he was "very cooperative with everyone."

Mincey is an important ruling because it reaffirms prior decisions applying due process analysis to confessions. In general, it is fairly difficult for a defendant to prevail in a due process challenge. Nevertheless, as *Mincey* suggests, when a criminal defendant is interrogated under outrageous circumstances suggesting that his confession was involuntarily obtained, due process principles will require exclusion of the confession from evidence.

Bibliography

Albert W. Alschuler, *Constraint Confession, Symposium on Coercion: An Interdisciplinary Examination of Coercion, Exploitation and the Law,* 74 *Denver University Law Review* 957 (1997).

Mark Berger, *Taking the Fifth* (Lexington, MA: Lexington Books, 1980).

R.H. Helmholz, Charles M. Gray, John H. Langbein, Eben Moglen, Henry E. Smith, and Albert W. Alschuler, *The Privilege Against Self-Incrimination* (Chicago: University of Chicago Press, 1997).

Russell L. Weaver, Leslie W. Abramson, John M. Burkoff, and Catherine Hancock, *Principles of Criminal Procedure* (St. Paul, MN: Thomson/West, 2004), 164–219.

Jacobson v. United States

Citation: 503 U.S. 540.

Issue: Whether Jacobson, who was repeatedly solicited by governmental agents to purchase child pornography, was entrapped.

Year of Decision: 1992.

Outcome: Jacobson's conviction should be reversed because of entrapment.

Author of Opinion: Justice Byron White.

Vote: 5-4.

The Bill of Rights includes various rights that protect the citizenry against governmental misuse of power. Although issues of governmental abuse can arise in a variety of contexts, it often comes up in the context of whether the government may itself engage in criminal conduct in an effort to trap criminals.

In *Sherman v. United States* (1958), the Court recognized the entrapment defense but placed it on a statutory rather than a constitutional footing. In *Sherman,* a government informer repeatedly encouraged a recovering narcotics addict to purchase illegal drugs for him. When the addict finally succumbed to the pressure, the Court concluded that he had been "entrapped." Because he was in treatment, and resisted the informer's encouragement to purchase drugs, the Court concluded that Sherman was not "predisposed" to commit the crime. Referencing a prior decision in *Sorrells v. United States* (1932), the Court held that the "function of law enforcement is the prevention of crime and the apprehension of criminals" and "does not include the manufacturing of crime." The Court indicated that the police were free to employ both "stealth and strategy" in trying to ferret out crime, but that a "different question is presented when the criminal design originates with the officials of the government, and they implant in the mind of an innocent person the disposition to commit the alleged offense and induce its commission in order that they may prosecute." The *Sherman* test is regarded as the "subjective" approach to entrapment because it focuses on whether the defendant was "predisposed" to commit the crime.

Justice Felix Frankfurter agreed with the result in the case, but argued for an "objective" approach to entrapment. In his view, the courts should focus on whether "the methods employed on behalf of the Government to bring about conviction" are so objectionable that they "cannot be countenanced." This objective approach would analyze whether the government's conduct falls "below standards, to which common feelings respond, for the proper use of governmental power." In other words, Justice Frankfurter would not inquire regarding the defendant's past record, his predisposition to commit crime, "or the depths to which he has sunk in the estimation of society" that predisposed him to commit this particular crime. Instead, Justice Frankfurter would focus on police methods and ask whether those tactics should not "be tolerated by an advanced society." He argued that "if two suspects have been solicited at the same time in the same manner, one should not go to jail simply because he has been convicted before and is said to have a criminal disposition."

Even though *Sorrells* and *Sherman* recognized the entrapment defense, it was very difficult for subsequent criminal defendants to prevail using that defense. Many targets of police activity were actively engaged in the criminal activity and therefore were regarded as "predisposed" to commit the crime. As a result, as to them, the entrapment defense was unavailing.

Jacobson involved extraordinary facts and important questions regarding whether Jacobson was "predisposed" to order child pornography. Jacobson, a 56-year-old veteran and a Nebraska farmer, had previously ordered two magazines and a brochure from a California adult bookstore in 1984. The magazines were titled *Bare Boys I* and *Bare Boys II* and contained photographs of nude preteen and teenage boys. Jacobson claimed that he had expected to receive magazines with "young men 18 years or older." Regardless, the boys in the magazines were not depicted as engaged in sexual activity, and possession of the magazines was legal at the time.

After the adoption of a federal law making possession of such magazines illegal, postal inspectors found Jacobson's name at the bookstore that had mailed him the magazines. Over the following two and one-half years, undercover government agents repeatedly wrote to Jacobson testing his willingness to order (now illegal) sexually explicit child photographs through the mail. The government used a variety of fictitious identities. Agents portrayed themselves as the fictitious "American Hedonist Society," a group that claimed that citizens had the "right to read what we desire, the right to discuss similar interests with those who share our philosophy, and finally that we have the right to seek pleasure without restrictions being placed on us by outdated puritan morality." Jacobson joined the Society and returned a sexual attitudes questionnaire in which he stated that he liked seeing "pre-teen sex," but was opposed to pedophilia. The government also represented itself as a consumer research company, "Midlands Data Research," looking for those who "believe in the joys of sex and the complete awareness of those lusty and youthful lads and lasses of the neophite [sic] age." The petitioner replied: "Please feel free to send me more information, I am interested in teenage sexuality. Please keep my name confidential." The government also contacted Jacobson through the fictitious "Heartland Institute for a New Tomorrow" (HINT), which depicted itself as "an organization founded to protect and promote sexual freedom and freedom of choice." It believed that "arbitrarily imposed legislative sanctions restricting your sexual freedom should be rescinded through the legislative process." HINT also sent Jacobson a survey, and he responded that he had an "average" interest in "[p]reteen sex-homosexual" material. Jacobson also stated that: "Not only sexual expression but freedom of the press is under attack. We must be ever vigilant to counter attack right wing fundamentalists who are determined to curtail our freedoms." HINT portrayed itself as a lobbying organization that sought to repeal "all statutes which regulate sexual activities, except those laws which deal with violent behavior, such as rape. HINT is also lobbying to eliminate any legal definition of 'the age of consent.'" HINT indicated that it would fund these efforts through a future publication. HINT also provided Jacobson with a list of group members with similar survey responses, but Jacobson did not write to any of them. An undercover agent then wrote to Jacobson as "Carl Long," and attempted to "mirror" Jacobson's perceived interests. Jacobson wrote that "As far as my likes are concerned, I like good looking young guys (in their late teens and early 20's) doing their thing together." Jacobson never mentioned child pornography in his letters to Long.

During the more than two years of fictitious governmental mailings, Jacobson did not order any illegal child pornography. At that point, he was contacted by a governmental sting operation entitled "Operation Borderline" which sent him a brochure portraying young boys engaged in sex. Jacobson placed an order that was never filled. Jacobson was then contacted by the United States Postal Service under the fictitious name "Far Eastern Trading Company Ltd.," which stated: "As many of you know, much hysterical nonsense has appeared in the American media concerning 'pornography' and what must be done to stop it from coming across your borders. This brief letter does not allow us to give much comment; however, why is your government spending millions of dollars to exercise international censorship while tons of drugs, which makes yours the world's most crime ridden country, are passed through easily." The letter also stated: "[W]e have devised a method of getting these to you without prying eyes of U.S. Customs seizing your [mail]. After consultations with American solicitors, we have been advised that once we have posted our material through your system, it cannot be opened for any inspection without authorization of a judge." The letter asked the petitioner to affirm that he was "not a law enforcement officer or agent of the U.S. Government acting in an undercover capacity for the purpose of entrapping Far Eastern Trading Company, its agents or customers." When the petitioner affirmed that he was not, he was sent a catalog from which he ordered *Boys Who Love Boys*. The magazine was a pornographic depiction of young boys engaged in various sexual activities. The petitioner was arrested after he received the magazine. The government then searched Jacobson's home, but did not find any other child pornography except the *Bare Boys* magazines previously ordered.

At trial, Jacobson testified that he placed the order because the government had aroused his curiosity. He stated: "Well, the statement was made of all the trouble and the hysteria over pornography and I wanted to see what the material was. It didn't describe the—I didn't know for sure what kind of sexual action they were referring to in the Canadian letter." Jacobson was convicted.

In evaluating Jacobson's conviction, the United States Supreme Court began by recognizing the "evils of child pornography" and the difficulties that the government has encountered in eliminating it. Relying on prior precedent, the Court reaffirmed the idea that it is permissible for governmental officials to "afford opportunities or

facilities for the commission of the offense" and may also employ "[a]rtifice and strat-
agem [to] catch those engaged in criminal enterprises." However, the Court reaffirmed the notion that the focus remains on whether the defendant was "predisposed"
to commit the crime. In other words, if the government agents had "simply offered
petitioner the opportunity to order child pornography through the mails, and petitioner [had] promptly availed himself of this criminal opportunity," his entrapment
defense would have been rejected.

The government tried to show predisposition based on two types of evidence. First,
it argued that Jacobson's order of the *Bare Boys* magazines showed predisposition.
But the Court rejected this evidence on the basis that possession of those magazines
was not criminal at the time. In addition, regarding the offending magazines, Jacobson claimed that he did not realize that they depicted minors until they arrived. The
Court viewed Jacobson's responses to the questionnaires as "at most indicative of certain personal inclinations, including a predisposition to view photographs of preteen
sex and a willingness to promote a given agenda by supporting lobbying organizations." However, the Court concluded that his responses did not show "that he
would commit the crime of receiving child pornography through the mails." In
the Court's view, "a person's inclinations and 'fantasies [are] his own and beyond
the reach of [government].'"

The Court concluded that the criminal conduct in this case had originated with the
government: "By the time petitioner finally placed his order, he had already been the
target of 26 months of repeated mailings and communications from Government
agents and fictitious organizations." Although Jacobson was "predisposed" to commit the crime by the end of these mailings, the government was unable to show that
he was predisposed before the governmental mailings began. The Court concluded
that the Government "excited petitioner's interest in sexually explicit materials
banned by law" and "exerted substantial pressure on petitioner to obtain and read
such material as part of a fight against censorship and the infringement of individual
rights." The Court noted that HINT described itself as "an organization founded
to protect and promote sexual freedom and freedom of choice" and stated that "the
most appropriate means to accomplish [its] objectives is to promote honest dialogue
among concerned individuals and to continue its lobbying efforts with State Legislators." These efforts were to be financed catalog sales. Other solicitations raised
concerns about censorship and the rights of individuals to view such materials. In
addition, HINT required Jacobson to affirm that he was not a Government agent
attempting to entrap the mail order company or its customers, and both Government
solicitations suggested that receiving this material was something that petitioner
ought to be allowed to do." Jacobson purchased prohibited materials only after a
two and one-half year governmental campaign that was designed to convince him
"he had or should have the right to engage in the very behavior proscribed by law."
Relying on *Sherman,* the Court noted that "the Government [may not] pla[y] on
the weaknesses of an innocent party and beguil[e] him into committing crimes which
he otherwise would not have attempted."

Justice Sandra Day O'Connor dissented in *Jacobson,* arguing that there was sufficient evidence of predisposition because Jacobson "was offered only two opportunities to buy child pornography through the mail. Both times, he ordered. Both times,
he asked for opportunities to buy more. He needed no Government agent to coax,
threaten, or persuade him; no one played on his sympathies or friendship, or suggested that his committing the crime would further a greater good. In fact, no Government agent even contacted him face to face."

Jacobson is important because it reaffirms the entrapment defense and applies it in a situation in which the evidence regarding predisposition is arguable. Some have argued that *Jacobson* represents an implicit acceptance of Justice Frankfurter's "objective" approach to entrapment. Certainly, as Justice O'Connor suggests, there was sufficient evidence of predisposition to convict Jacobson. However, the Court appeared to be offended by the government's tactics.

Bibliography

Fred Warren Bennett, *From Sorrells to Jacobson: Reflections on Six Decades of Entrapment Law, and Related Defenses, in Federal Court,* 27 *Wake Forest Law Review* 829 (1992).

Paul Marcus, *Presenting, Back From the (Almost) Dead, the Entrapment Defense,* 47 *Florida Law Review* 205 (1995).

Ian J. McLoughlin, *The Meaning of Predisposition in Practice,* 79 *Boston University Law Review* 1067 (1999).

Russell L. Weaver, Leslie W. Abramson, John M. Burkoff, and Catherine Hancock, *Principles of Criminal Procedure* (St. Paul, MN: Thomson/West, 2004), 220–25.

CHAPTER 18

FIFTH AMENDMENT: TAKINGS

The Fifth Amendment prohibits government from taking private property without just compensation. A taking occurs in the plainest sense when government exercises its power of eminent domain. More difficult cases arise when property value is diminished pursuant to government action. Land use regulation that eliminates all economically beneficial uses of real estate constitutes a taking. Zoning ordinances that restrict development or use, but do not eliminate all economic value, are subject to review that balances competing private and public interests. The Court, in *Penn Central Transportation Co. v. New York* (1978), examined whether a landmark preservation law resulted in a taking. It found that the loss of value was not significant enough to outweigh the public interest in historical preservation and environmental management. In *Lucas v. South Carolina Coastal Council* (1989), the Court found that a land use restriction denying the owner all economically beneficial use of the land constituted a taking.

Penn Central Transportation Co. v. City of New York

There is inevitable tension between the power of states to regulate property and the rights of citizens to own and possess property. Since the nation's founding, the states have exercised the power to regulate property for the "health, welfare and safety" of their citizens. Despite this power, the Constitution provides special protections for property rights. Both the Fifth Amendment and the Fourteenth Amendment explicitly provide that the state may not deprive anyone of life, liberty, or property without due process of law. Further protections are provided by the Fifth Amendment, which precludes the state from "taking" private property without providing "just compensation."

Citation: 438 U.S. 104.

Issue: Whether the City of New York could designate a building as a historic landmark and thereby prohibit alterations to the property without providing just compensation.

Year of Decision: 1978.

Outcome: In some instances, the government has the right to regulate property without providing compensation for the regulatory taking.

Opinion Author: Justice William Brennan.

Vote: 6-3.

Penn Central involved the conflict between state power to regulate property, and the individual interest in using that property free of regulation. The case involved the question of what constitutes a "taking" within the meaning of the Fifth Amendment. In a number of early cases, the Court had held that the takings clause reached only "direct appropriations" of property, or the functional equivalent of an "ouster of the owner's possession." *Transportation Co. v. Chicago* (1879). When the government physically invades property, the Court has generally required compensation "no matter how minute the intrusion, and no matter how weighty the public purpose behind it." In one case, the Court held that a New York law requiring landlords to allow television cable companies to place cable facilities in their apartment buildings constituted a taking even though the facilities occupied at most only a few feet of the landlords' property.

The Court's decisions have been less clear about when governmental "regulation" of property effects a taking. In *Penn Central*, the City of New York adopted a comprehensive plan to preserve historic landmarks and historic areas or districts. However, rather than acquiring historic properties, the government chose to "regulate" them by limiting what property owners could do with them. The law provided that, when a property was designated as a "landmark," the law imposed a duty to keep the exterior of the building "in good repair" and to seek approval of the Landmarks Commission before making any changes to the exterior architectural features. The goal of the law was to ensure that decisions concerning construction on landmark sites are made with "due consideration of the public interest in the maintenance of the structures and the landowners' interest in use of their properties." In exchange for the limitations, the law gave owners of historic properties a significant benefit by allowing them to transfer development rights to contiguous parcels on the same city block. Later amendments gave the owners of landmark sites additional opportunities to transfer development rights to other parcels. The city believed that the Landmarks Law would "safeguard desirable features of the existing urban fabric" and benefit it "by fostering 'civic pride in the beauty and noble accomplishments of the past'; protecting and enhancing 'the city's attractions to tourists and visitors'; 'supporting and stimulating business and industry'; 'strengthening the economy of the city'; and promoting 'the use of historic districts, landmarks, interior landmarks and scenic landmarks for the education, pleasure and welfare of the people of the city.'"

Grand Central Terminal was designated as a "landmark," for purposes of the New York law, because it provided an ingenious engineering solution to the problems presented by urban railroad stations as well as a magnificent example of the French beaux-arts style. Because of the Terminal's distinctive character, the Landmarks Commission denied the owners permission to build an office tower over the terminal. In concluding that no taking had occurred, the United States Supreme Court began by noting that the Fifth Amendment due process clause prohibits the "Government from forcing some people alone to bear public burdens which, in all fairness and justice, should be borne by the public as a whole." However, the Court recognized that it had not developed any "set formula" for determining when compensation was required, and instead considered a variety of factors including the "economic impact of the regulation on the claimant and, particularly, the extent to which the regulation has interfered with distinct investment-backed expectations" and "the character of the governmental action."

The Court concluded that it was more inclined to find a "taking" when the government physically invades property than "when interference arises from some public program adjusting the benefits and burdens of economic life to promote the common good." The Court emphasized that "Government hardly could go on if to some extent values incident to property could not be diminished without paying for every such change in the general law." In some instances, for example, government seeks to promote "the health, safety, morals, or general welfare" by prohibiting particular contemplated uses of land even though they destroy or adversely affect recognized real property interests. The Court viewed zoning laws as the "classic example" of permissible governmental action even though they may prohibit the most beneficial use of the property. But takings challenges have been rejected even when zoning laws do prohibit "a beneficial use to which individual parcels had previously been devoted and thus caused substantial individualized harm."

The owners of Penn Central argued the New York City law had "taken" their property by depriving them of any gainful use of their "air rights" above the Terminal. The Court disagreed, noting that "takings" jurisprudence does not divide a single parcel into discrete segments and attempt to determine whether rights in a particular segment have been entirely abrogated. In deciding whether a particular governmental action has effected a taking, the Court focused "both on the character of the action and on the nature and extent of the interference with rights in the parcel as a whole —here, the city tax block designated as the 'landmark site.'"

The Court also rejected the argument that compensation was required because New York City's law applied only to individuals who own selected properties. "Agreement with this argument would, of course, invalidate [all] comparable landmark legislation in the Nation. We find no merit in it."

The Court also rejected the argument that compensation is required for a land-use decision that arbitrarily singles out a particular parcel "for different, less favorable treatment than the neighboring ones." The Court found no "singling out," noting that the law included a comprehensive plan for preserving historic structures, wherever they might be found in the city, and the plan extended to more than 400 landmarks and 31 historic districts. The Court concluded that "Legislation designed to promote the general welfare commonly burdens some more than others. Unless we are to reject the judgment of the New York City Council that the preservation of landmarks benefits all New York citizens and all structures, both economically and by improving the quality of life in the city as a whole—which we are unwilling to do— we cannot conclude that the owners of the Terminal have in no sense been benefited by the Landmarks Law...."

The Court downplayed the impact of the Landmarks law on Grand Central Terminal. The law did not interfere with present uses of the Terminal and, in fact, allowed appellants to continue to use the property as it had been used (as a railroad terminal with both office space and concessions). In addition, the Court found that the law allowed Penn Central "to profit from the Terminal and to obtain a 'reasonable return' on its investment." The Court also rejected the appellant's claim that the Landmarks law "took" their airspace above the terminal. The Court found that some uses of the airspace might be permitted if they "would harmonize in scale, material and character with [the Terminal]." As a result, although the Landmarks Commission had rejected the proposed 50 story structure, it might permit a smaller structure. The Court noted that the abrogated air rights were transferrable to other parcels in the city, and that this transfer would mitigate any financial burdens.

Penn Central is an important decision because it establishes the power of government to "regulate" property without treating the regulation as a "taking" and without requiring compensation.

Bibliography

Steven I. Brody, *Rethinking Regulatory Takings: A View Toward a Comprehensive Analysis*, 8 *Northern Illinois University Law Review* 113 (1987).

Calvert G. Chipchase, *From Grand Central to the Sierras: What Do We Do with Investment-Backed Expectations in Partial Regulatory Takings?*, 23 *Virginia Environmental Law Journal* 43 (2004).

D. Lively, P. Haddon, D. Roberts, R. Weaver, and W. Araiza, *Constitutional Law: Cases, History, and Dialogues,* 2nd ed. (Cincinnati: Anderson Publishing Co., 2000), 231–32.

Daniel R. Mandelker, *Investment-Backed Expectations: Is There a Taking?*, 31 *Washington University Journal of Urban and Contemporary Law* 3 (1987).

Lucas v. South Carolina Coastal Council

Citation: 505 U.S. 1103.

Issue: Whether the state may regulate land so extensively as to take away all "economically beneficial or productive uses" without paying compensation.

Year: 1992.

Outcome: When governmental regulation deprives a property owner of all "economically beneficial or productive uses," the government has "taken" the property and must pay compensation.

Author of Opinion: Justice Byron White.

Vote: 7-2.

Government has always exercised broad authority to regulate property in the public interest. In the Court's landmark decision in *Penn Central Transportation Co. v. City of New York,* 483 U.S. 104 (1978), the Court held that government had broad authority to "regulate" real property without providing compensation. In *Penn Central,* the Court held that the City of New York could regulate "landmark" properties and prohibit alterations of them without governmental approval. Left open by the *Penn Central* decision was whether there were effective limits on the government's authority to regulate without paying compensation. In *Lucas v. South Carolina Coastal Council,* 505 U.S. 1103 (1992), the Court was asked to decide whether the *Penn Central* rule would allow the government to "take" all economically beneficial or productive uses" of property without paying compensation.

Lucas paid nearly a million dollars for two residential oceanfront lots in South Carolina, intending to build single-family homes. Following the purchase, South Carolina enacted the Beachfront Management Act which effectively barred Lucas from building any permanent habitable structures on the two parcels. The legislature found that the beach/dune area of South Carolina's shores was an extremely valuable public resource, that the erection of new structures contributes to the erosion and destruction of the beaches/dunes, and that discouraging new construction in close proximity to the beach/dune area was necessary to prevent a great public harm. Prohibiting new construction in some beachfront areas was part of the legislature's solution.

In *Lucas,* the plaintiff claimed that the regulation constituted a taking because it denied Lucas "all economically beneficial or productive use" of his land. The State of South Carolina disagreed, arguing that the state was simply regulating land, for a public purpose, and therefore that it was not required to pay compensation. The Court disagreed: "[R]egulations that leave the owner of land without economically beneficial or productive options for its use [carry] with them a heightened risk that private property is being pressed into some form of public service under the guise of mitigating serious public harm."

Justice Harry Blackmun dissented in *Lucas,* arguing that the "State has the power to prevent any use of property it finds to be harmful to its citizens, and that a state statute is entitled to a presumption of constitutionality." Justice John Paul Stevens also dissented, arguing that the "Court's new rule is wholly arbitrary. A landowner whose property is diminished in value 95% recovers nothing, while an owner whose property is diminished 100% recovers the land's full value."

Lucas was followed by *Tahoe-Sierra Preservation Council v. Tahoe Regional Planning Agency*, 535 U.S. 302 (2002). That case involved a moratorium on land use development, and the Court was asked to decide whether the *Penn Central* or *Lucas* analysis should apply. The case arose when fears regarding environmental degradation at Lake Tahoe, California, led the Tahoe Regional Planning Authority to impose an 8 month moratorium on land use development that was followed by a 32 month moratorium. Relying on *Lucas*, the petitioner claimed that she had been denied all viable economic use of her property, and therefore was entitled to compensation during the moratorium.

The Court concluded that *Lucas* was not dispositive because of the temporary nature of the moratorium and the fact that the "property will recover value as soon as the prohibition is lifted." It also expressed concern with an understanding of takings that included "normal delays in obtaining building permits, changes in zoning ordinances, variances, and the like." As the Court saw it, "[a] rule that required compensation for every delay in the use of property would render routine government processes prohibitively expensive or encourage hasty decisionmaking." "The interest in facilitating informed decisionmaking by regulatory agencies counsels against adopting a *per se* rule that would impose such severe costs on their deliberations. Otherwise, the financial constraints of compensating property owners during a moratorium may force officials to rush through the planning process or to abandon the practice altogether." "While each of us is burdened somewhat by such restrictions, we, in turn, benefit greatly from the restrictions that are placed on others."

Lucas is an extremely important decision because it qualifies *Penn Central's* holding that the government may "regulate" property without providing compensation. *Lucas* holds that the government may not so regulate property as to take away all "economically beneficial or productive uses" without paying compensation. Nevertheless, as the *Tahoe* case demonstrates, *Penn Central's* essential holding remains good law, and the government can impose moratoria without paying compensation.

Bibliography

Steven I. Brody, *Rethinking Regulatory Takings: A View Toward a Comprehensive Analysis*, 8 *Northern Illinois University Law Review* 113 (1987).

Calvert G. Chipchase, *From Grand Central to the Sierras: What Do We Do with Investment-Backed Expectations in Partial Regulatory Takings?*, 23 *Virginia Environmental Law Journal* 43 (2004).

D. Lively, P. Haddon, D. Roberts, R. Weaver, and W. Araiza, *Constitutional Law: Cases, History, and Dialogues*, 2nd ed. (Cincinnati: Anderson Publishing Co., 2000), 231–32.

Daniel R. Mandelker, *Investment-Backed Expectations: Is There a Taking?*, 31 *Washington University Journal of Urban and Contemporary Law* 3 (1987).

CHAPTER 19

SIXTH AMENDMENT: RIGHT TO COUNSEL

A defendant's ability to reckon with the criminal justice system depends not only upon the quality of his case but upon the ability to secure legal representation. Without counsel, the odds increase that innocent persons will be found guilty and the defendant will not receive a fair trial. Because the average person possesses neither an attorney's legal expertise nor understanding of the criminal justice system, legal representation is crucial to the criminal justice system's legitimacy and credibility to the point that the government subsidizes it for persons who cannot afford counsel. The right to counsel is triggered when criminal proceedings have been initiated against the defendant, typically an indictment, complaint or other charging instrumentality. Police interrogation of a defendant without the presence of counsel may abridge the Sixth Amendment and trigger the exclusionary rule. This remedy does not apply, as the Court held in *Nix v. Williams* (1984), when the police demonstrate that they inevitably would have discovered the evidence. The Court found no Sixth Amendment violation, in *Kuhlmann v. Wilson* (1986), when a jailhouse informant obtained but did not deliberately elicit incriminating evidence from a cell mate.

Nix v. Williams

Citation: 467 U.S. 431.

Issue: Whether there should be an "inevitable discovery" exception to the exclusionary rule.

Year of Decision: 1984.

Outcome: When evidence would "inevitably" have been discovered, the exclusionary evidence rule does not apply.

Author of Opinion: Chief Justice Warren Burger.

Vote: 7-2.

The exclusionary evidence rule, which provides for the exclusion of evidence seized in violation of a defendant's constitutional rights, provides an important mechanism for the enforcement of some constitutional rights. However, because the rule results in evidence being excluded from juries, sometimes very damning evidence, the rule has been controversial. At various times, both the police and prosecutors have called for modifications of the rule. The cases discussed here, *Brewer v. Williams* (1977), and *Nix v. Williams,* both of which arose from the same facts, present the exclusionary rule in its most controversial aspect.

The cases arose when a 10-year-old girl turned up missing in Des Moines, Iowa. Robert Williams, a mental hospital escapee, was suspected of having kidnapped the girl, but Williams could not be found. Later that day, a Des Moines lawyer (McKnight) called police and indicated that Williams was prepared to turn himself in to police in Davenport, Iowa. Before the police drove Williams back to Des Moines, McKnight advised Williams by phone that Des Moines police officers would be driving to Davenport to pick him up, that the officers would not interrogate him or mistreat him, and that Williams was not to talk to the officers about the murder until after consulting with McKnight after his return. The officers agreed that they would not question Williams during the trip. In the meantime Williams was arraigned before a judge and given a *Miranda* warning. Before leaving the courtroom, Williams conferred with a local lawyer (Kelly) who advised him not to make any statements until he consulted with McKnight. After the police officers picked Williams up, Detective Leaming repeated the *Miranda* warnings, and told Williams: "[W]e both know that you're being represented here by Mr. Kelly and you're being represented by Mr. McKnight in Des Moines, [and] I want you to remember this because we'll be visiting between here and Des Moines." Kelly reiterated to Detective Leaming that Williams was not to be questioned about the disappearance of the girl until after he had consulted with McKnight back in Des Moines. When Leaming expressed some reservations, Kelly firmly stated that the agreement with McKnight was to be carried out and that there was to be no interrogation of Williams during the automobile journey. The officers refused to allow Kelly to ride with them in the police car.

During the return trip, Williams stated several times that "[w]hen I get to Des Moines and see Mr. McKnight, I am going to tell you the whole story." Detective Leaming knew that Williams was a former mental patient and knew also that he was deeply religious, and he began talking to him about a variety of topics, including religion. After awhile, Detective Leaming delivered what has been referred to [as] the "Christian burial speech." Addressing Williams as "Reverend," the detective said, "I want to give you something to think about while we're traveling down the [road]. Number one, I want you to observe the weather conditions, it's raining, it's sleeting, it's freezing, driving is very treacherous, visibility is poor, it's going to be dark early this evening. They are predicting several inches of snow for tonight, and I feel that you yourself are the only person that knows where this little girl's body is, that you yourself have only been there once, and if you get a snow on top of it you yourself may be unable to find it. And, since we will be going right past the area on the way into Des Moines, I feel that we could stop and locate the body, that the parents of this little girl should be entitled to a Christian burial for the little girl who was snatched away from them on Christmas Eve and murdered. And I feel we should stop and locate it on the way in rather than waiting until morning and trying to come back out after a snow storm and possibly not being able to find it at all." Leaming also told Williams that he knew the body was in the area of Mitchellville, a town that they would pass, and then stated: "I do not want you to answer me. I don't want to discuss it any further. Just think about it as we're riding down the road." At a later point, Williams asked whether the girl's shoes had been found. As the car approached Mitchellville, Williams agreed to show the officers where the body was located. Williams was subsequently indicted for murder, his statements were admitted into evidence at his trial, and he was convicted.

In *Brewer,* the Court held that the evidence should have been excluded because Detective Leaming violated Williams' Sixth Amendment right to counsel by "deliberately and designedly" attempting to elicit information from Williams. The Court noted that the detective was "fully aware before departing for Des Moines that Williams was being represented in Davenport by Kelly and in Des Moines by McKnight. Yet he purposely sought during Williams' isolation from his lawyers to obtain as much incriminating information as possible." The Court flatly rejected the argument that Williams had waived his right to counsel. Chief Justice Warren Burger dissented, arguing that the "result in this case ought to be intolerable in any society which purports to call itself an organized society." He went on to note that "Williams is guilty of the savage murder of a small [child]. [A]fter no fewer than five warnings of his rights to silence and to counsel, he led police to the concealed body of his victim. [Williams] was not threatened or coerced [and] he spoke and acted voluntarily and with full awareness of his constitutional rights."

Even though the Court reversed Williams' conviction in *Brewer,* the case came back to the Court under the name of *Nix v. Williams.* In *Nix,* the question was whether the Court should establish an "inevitable discovery" exception to the exclusionary rule. At Williams' second trial, the prosecution did not offer Williams' statements into evidence, nor did it seek to show that Williams had directed the police to the child's body. However, it did introduce evidence regarding the condition of the body, as well as articles and photographs of her clothing, and the results of post mortem medical and chemical tests on the body. The trial court concluded that, even without Williams' confession, the body would have "been found in short order" in essentially the same condition as it was actually found. The Court noted that freezing temperatures prevailed and tissue deterioration would have been suspended. As a result, the evidence was admitted, and Williams was again found guilty of first-degree murder.

The United States Supreme Court agreed that discovery of the body was inevitable, and therefore that the evidence was admissible. In rendering its decision, the Court emphasized that "[e]xclusion of physical evidence that would inevitably have been discovered adds nothing to either the integrity or fairness of a criminal trial." While the Court recognized that the Sixth Amendment right to counsel is designed to protect criminal defendants "against unfairness by preserving the adversary process in which the reliability of proffered evidence may be tested in cross-examination," the Court noted that Detective Leaming's actions had no bearing on the reliability of the evidence. "No one would seriously contend that the presence of counsel in the police car when Leaming appealed to Williams' decent human instincts would have had any bearing on the reliability of the body as evidence." The Court thus concluded that suppression "would do nothing whatever to promote the integrity of the trial process, but would inflict a wholly unacceptable burden on the administration of criminal justice." Rather, the Court observed, "the evidence in question would inevitably have been discovered without reference to the police error or misconduct, there is no nexus sufficient to provide a taint and the evidence is admissible."

The Court then focused on whether discovery of the girl's body was "inevitable." The Court applied a "preponderance of the evidence" standard and concluded that discovery was inevitable. The Court emphasized that some 200 searchers were systematically searching nearby areas that had been marked off into grids. The police testified that they planned to move on to the place where the body was found and to search it in a similarly systematic manner. The Court concluded that, "[o]n this record it is clear that the search parties were approaching the actual location of the body, and we are satisfied, along with three courts earlier, that the volunteer search teams would have resumed the search had Williams not earlier led the police to the body and the body inevitably would have been found."

Justice John Paul Stevens, concurring, noted that this was a case "in which the police deliberately took advantage of an inherently coercive setting in the absence of counsel, contrary to their express agreement," and he expressed concern regarding the cost "imposed on society by police officers who decide to take procedural short-cuts instead of complying with the law." In assessing those costs, he noted that the case had resulted in "years and years of unnecessary but costly litigation." He concluded that these costs provided "an adequate deterrent to similar violations" and justified admission of the evidence.

Justice William Brennan, dissenting, argued that the "inevitable discovery" exception to the exclusionary rule is consistent with the Constitution, but he would have applied a higher burden of proof (clear and convincing evidence) on the question of whether the discovery was, in fact, inevitable. As a result, he would have remanded the case to the lower court for application of this higher burden of proof.

Nix is an important decision because it establishes the "inevitable discovery" exception to the exclusionary evidence rule. Under that exception, even though evidence is obtained in violation of a defendant's constitutional rights, in this case Williams' Sixth Amendment right to counsel, the evidence can be admitted if it "inevitably" would have been discovered.

Bibliography

Hon. John E. Fennelly, *Refinement of the Inevitable Discovery Exception: The Need for a Good Faith Requirement,* 17 *William Mitchell Law Review* 1085 (1991).

Jessica Forbes, *The Inevitable Discovery Exception, Primary Evidence, and the Emasculation of the Fourth Amendment,* 65 *Fordham Law Review* 1221 (1987).

Stephen E. Hessler, *Establishing Inevitability Without Active Pursuit: Defining the Inevitable Discovery Exception to the Fourth Amendment Exclusionary Rule,* 99 *Michigan Law Review* 288 (2000).

Russell L. Weaver, Leslie W. Abramson, John M. Burkoff, and Catherine Hancock, *Principles of Criminal Procedure* (St. Paul, MN: Thomson/West, 2004), 253–58.

Kuhlmann v. Wilson

The Sixth Amendment to the United States Constitution guarantees criminal defendants the right to counsel. Historically, this right had been regarded as a trial right. Although counsel must be appointed early enough so that counsel can prepare for trial, counsel has not been required for pretrial interrogations. Over time, the Court began to extend the right to counsel backwards so that it encompassed pretrial proceedings, but questions then began to arise about how the right would be applied in jail contexts. Not infrequently, the government plants so-called "jail informants" in jails and asks them to report on statements made by defendants and suspects—individuals who were often represented by counsel.

Citation: 477 U.S. 436.

Issue: Whether a government informer can report statements made by an incarcerated defendant without violating the Sixth Amendment right to counsel.

Year of Decision: 1986.

Outcome: No Sixth Amendment violation occurs so long as the informant does not "deliberately elicit" incriminating statements from the defendant.

Author of Opinion: Justice Louis Powell.

Vote: 7-2.

In the Court's landmark decision in *Massiah v. United States* (1964), the Court extended the right to counsel to pretrial interrogation situations. In that case, Massiah had been indicted for violating federal narcotics laws and retained an attorney. While Massiah was out on bail, a federal agent arranged for Massiah's codefendant to have a conversation with him. The codefendant was wired so that the agent could overhear the conversation. The Court concluded that the agent, through the informer, had "deliberately elicited" incriminating statements from Massiah in violation of the Sixth

Amendment. The Court concluded that, if the right to counsel is to be given effect, "it must apply to indirect and surreptitious interrogations as well as those conducted in the jailhouse."

Following the holding in Massiah, there was doubt about how far the right to counsel might extend, and particularly how it would apply in jailhouse contexts. *Kuhlmann v. Wilson* (1986), involved a jailhouse informer, an inmate who was asked to report incriminating statements made by other inmates to the police or prosecutors. Obviously, if a jailhouse plant sets out to "deliberately elicit" incriminating statements from other inmates, at the behest of government agents, then *Massiah* suggests that the Sixth Amendment right to counsel has been violated. On the other hand, if the jail plant does nothing more than passively listen to other inmates, without prompting or engaging them in conversation, then the evidence is admissible. The government should not be penalized or prohibited from using testimony simply because a defendant suffers from "loose lips." However, the evidence is often unclear about whether a jailhouse plant listened passively or actively encouraged other inmates to make incriminating statements.

Issues related to jailhouse informants have surfaced in a number of cases. In *United States v. Henry* (1980), a jailhouse informant engaged the defendant in conversations and "developed a relationship of trust and confidence" that led to the disclosure of "incriminating information." Even though the informant did not question the defendant, the informant did stimulate conversation with the defendant in an effort to "elicit" incriminating information. Relying on *Massiah,* the Court concluded that the government had engaged in "indirect and surreptitious interrogation" of the defendant in violation of the Sixth Amendment.

Kuhlmann cast doubt on *Henry's* scope. In *Kuhlmann,* the defendant, who had been indicted for a robbery and murder, was placed in a cell that overlooked the crime scene. His cell mate was another prisoner (Lee) who had previously agreed to act as a police informant. Since there was strong evidence of Kuhlmann's participation in the crime, the police were hoping to learn the identity of Kuhlmann's coconspirators. However, a police officer instructed the informant not to ask Kuhlmann any questions, but simply to "keep his ears open" for the names of the other perpetrators. The informant first spoke to the defendant after he saw the defendant looking out the cellblock window at the Star Taxicab Garage, where the crimes had occurred. The discussion was prompted by Kuhlmann's statement that "someone's messing with me." At that point, Kuhlmann began talking about the robbery, and he gave the informant the same story that he had previously given to the police. Even though the informant replied that the story "didn't sound too good," the defendant did not alter his story. However, over the next few days, the defendant did alter his story. After a visit from his brother, who mentioned that members of his family were upset because they believed that the defendant had committed the murder, the defendant admitted that he and two unidentified men had committed the robbery and murdered the dispatcher. The informant passed the information on to a police agent along with notes that he had written while sharing the cell with the defendant.

In ruling on the admissibility of the incriminating statements, the Court held that a defendant who objects to evidence "must demonstrate that the police and their informant took some action, beyond merely listening, that was designed deliberately to elicit incriminating remarks." The Court emphasized that "the Sixth Amendment is not violated whenever—by luck or happenstance—the State obtains incriminating statements from the accused after the right to counsel has attached." In other words, government agents are free to report statements, freely and voluntarily made, to the police.

In admitting Kuhlmann's statements, the Court emphasized that the police already had solid evidence of the respondent's participation. Although an informant was placed in Kuhlmann's cell, he was given instructions not to question the defendant, and the Court concluded that he followed those instructions. In other words, he "only listened" to the respondent's "spontaneous" and "unsolicited" statements. The only remark made by the informant was his comment that the defendant's initial story "didn't sound too good." Even though the defendant was placed in a cell that overlooked the crime scene, the Court regarded this fact as a "sheer coincidence" and concluded that there is no reason "to require police to isolate one charged with crime so that he cannot view the scene, whatever it may be, from his cell window." In the final analysis, the Court held that there was insufficient evidence that the confession had been "deliberately elicited" by the informant.

Justice Brennan, joined by Justice Thurgood Marshall, dissented, arguing that the defendant, as an incarcerated individual, was "susceptible to the ploys of undercover Government agents." He expressed concern that the informant "received consideration for the services he rendered the police, and therefore had an incentive to produce the information which he knew the police hoped to obtain." In Justice Brennan's view, the informant "encouraged" Kuhlmann to talk about the crime by "telling respondent that his exculpatory story would not convince anyone without more work." Although the catalyst for the defendant's incriminating statements was a visitation from his brother, the deliberate-elicitation standard "requires consideration of the entire course of government behavior." In Justice Brennan's view, government agents "intentionally created a situation in which it was foreseeable that respondent would make incriminating statements without the assistance of counsel—it assigned respondent to a cell overlooking the scene of the crime and designated a secret informant to be respondent's cellmate. The informant, while avoiding direct questions, nonetheless developed a relationship of cellmate camaraderie with respondent and encouraged him to talk about his crime. While the coup de grace was delivered by respondent's brother, the groundwork for respondent's confession was laid by the State."

Kuhlmann is significant because it helps define the circumstances under which an incarcerated defendant's statements can be used without violating the Sixth Amendment right to counsel. The decision suggests that the police can take various steps (e.g., place defendant in a cell that overlooks the crime scene, and place a government agent in the cell) without having its conduct being construed as "deliberately eliciting" a confession in violation of the Sixth Amendment provided that the informant takes no steps to "elicit" the confession.

Bibliography

April Leigh Ammeter, *Kuhlmann v. Wilson: "Passive" and "Active" Government Informants, a Problematic Test,* 72 *Iowa Law Review* 1423 (1987).

Maia Goodell, *Government Responsibility for the Acts of Jailhouse Informants Under the Sixth Amendment,* 101 *Michigan Law Review* 2525 (2003).

Louis D. Lappen, *A Reconciliation of Henry and Wilson: The Intersection of Constitutional Rights with Procedural Review,* 1987 *Duke Law Journal* 945 (1987).

Russell L. Weaver, Leslie W. Abramson, John M. Burkoff, and Catherine Hancock, *Principles of Criminal Procedure* (St. Paul, MN: Thomson/West, 2004), 203–15.

CHAPTER 20

FOURTEENTH AMENDMENT: RIGHT OF PRIVACY

Judicial supremacy in interpreting the Constitution was established two centuries ago in the benchmark case of *Marbury v. Madison* (1803). Although the Court had power to review the output of the political branches, it did not define boundaries on what limits the judiciary could set on legislative and executive power. Debate on this point largely has focused upon whether the judiciary may invoke only those rights and liberties specifically enumerated in the Constitution, as a basis for declaring government action unconstitutional, or may identify other guarantees as fundamental. Decisions resting on a right or liberty not specifically articulated by the Constitution typically are characterized as activist. Critics of this model note that federal judges are appointed with lifetime tenure. Because judges have no direct electoral accountability to the people, the concern is that they undermine the will of the people when deciding without a clear constitutional charge. Advocates of judicial restraint typically point to the barriers imposed by the Court to economic and social reform, including New Deal initiatives, during the first part of the twentieth century. These results were driven by interpretation of the Fourteenth Amendment due process clause to establish economic rights that, although not enumerated, became the basis for blunting regulatory initiative in the workplace and other settings. Countering this concern are those who maintain that the Constitution does not provide an exclusive itemization of fundamental rights and liberties, and the principles of free government are served better when courts use reasoned judgment to identify other incidents of liberty. Despite ongoing divisions within the Court and among its observers with respect to this function, modern rights including privacy, interstate travel, and voting owe themselves to the judiciary's willingness to extend beyond the textual limitations of the Constitution.

ABORTION

The right of privacy traces its origins not to constitutional text but to a dissenting opinion by Justice Louis Brandeis in *Olmstead v. United States* (1928). The *Olmstead* case concerned a claim that wiretapping constituted an unreasonable search and seizure and thus abridged the Court Amendment. Although the Court rejected this argument, Justice Brandeis introduced the notion that "the right to be let alone—[was] the most comprehensive of rights and the right most valued by civilized men." Although Justice Brandeis spoke to a specific constitutional context (i.e., the Fourth Amendment), the modern right of privacy operates in a broader and more multidimensional manner. Consistent with this framing, it comprehends reproductive freedom, abortion, family living arrangements, the refusal of unwanted medical care, and sexual orientation. The right of privacy in this sense is grounded in *Griswold v. Connecticut* (1965), a decision that invalidated a state law prohibiting distribution of or use of contraceptives. In *Griswold,* the Court determined that the right was to be found in the "penumbras" of several enumerated constitutional rights. In *Roe v. Wade* (1973), the Court extended the right to include a woman's freedom to obtain an abortion. It also identified the Fourteenth Amendment due process clause as the source of the right. The ruling in *Roe v. Wade* has been a lightning rod for critics who cite it as a leading example of judicial overreaching. Although the target of repeated challenges that have narrowed its range somewhat, the central meaning of *Roe v. Wade* has remained largely intact for three decades. Among the significant decisions that have tightened its boundaries is *Webster v. Reproductive Health Services* (1989) and reaffirmed its central meaning is *Planned Parenthood of South-Eastern Pennsylvania v. Casey* (1992).

Roe v. Wade

Among the landmark cases of the late twentieth century, none has been a source of controversy as extensive and intense as *Roe v. Wade.* Unlike *Brown v. Board of Education* (1954), which generated widespread resistance to and evasion of the desegregation mandate but eventually was ratified by civil rights legislation, the Court's decision recognizing a woman's freedom to obtain an abortion has been consistently challenged and cited as an example of raw judicial power. Consistent with divisions over the Court's proper role, it is a decision that has been hailed and vilified.

Citation: 410 U.S. 113.

Issue: Whether state prohibition of abortion is constitutional.

Year of Decision: 1973.

Outcome: The right of privacy protects a woman's freedom to choose an abortion.

Author: Justice Harry Blackmun.

Vote: 7-2.

Regulation of abortion was not widespread at the time of the republic's founding, but it had become pervasive within the next century. By the twentieth century, abortion had become strictly regulated throughout the nation. As time progressed, numerous states relaxed their laws in response to pressure for political change. Typical grounds for allowing abortion included pregnancies that presented danger to the mother's life, resulted from rape or incest, or carried the likelihood of birth defects. In an effort to establish a woman's freedom to choose as a fundamental national right, advocates of a woman's freedom to choose expanded their agenda from the legislatures to the courts.

In *Roe v. Wade* (1973), the Court reviewed a Texas law prohibiting abortion unless the mother's life was imperiled. The state justified the restriction on grounds that a fetus is a person and thus has a life interest that is protected under the due process clause of the Fourteenth Amendment. Justice Harry Blackmun, writing for the majority, refused to accept this premise. Although acknowledging that a fetus may be a life in some religions or under some moral codes, the majority concluded that it was not so in a constitutional sense. The Court conceded that no general right of privacy is enumerated by the Constitution, but stated that it is of constitutional significance. Finding that the due process clause of the Fourteenth Amendment was the appropriate source for this right, the Court determined that it also "is broad enough to encompass a woman's decision whether or not to terminate her pregnancy."

Like any other constitutional right or liberty, the freedom to elect an abortion is not absolute. The Court pointed out, however, that any regulation of the liberty must be limited. No restriction thus would be permissible unless the state could demonstrate that it accounted for a compelling governmental interest and was narrowly drawn so as not to burden unduly the liberty. With respect to the Texas law itself, the Court determined that the state's theory of life was debatable and thus not compelling enough to override the woman's freedom. Although rejecting Texas's regulatory premise, the Court observed that states had legitimate interests in protecting a woman's health and the potential for life. To balance the competing concerns of the state and the woman, the Court devised a trimester framework that made abortion more readily available during the early months of a pregnancy and less possible during the later months.

Based upon this model, a state may not prohibit abortion during the first three months of pregnancy and may regulate only to protect the mother's health. This balance reflected the Court's sense that, during the first trimester, abortion is less perilous to the mother than childbirth. Examples of permissible regulation include licensing requirements for facilities where abortions are performed and for personnel who perform abortions. Over the course of the second trimester, a woman's freedom remains largely unrestricted. Based upon its sense that a fetus becomes viable at the seventh month, the Court determined that the state's interest in prohibiting abortion became compelling at that point. Given the increased significance in life in the third trimester, the Court determined that the state could prohibit abortion during the final term of pregnancy.

The Court's decision established the proposition that freedom to elect an abortion is an incident of the right of privacy. The woman's interest in this regard, therefore, is constitutional. This determination has roiled critics, who maintain that there is no constitutional foundation for the decision and that unelected judges are imposing their values upon the people. In this regard, the Court's detractors argue that the *Roe v. Wade* decision resurrected the discredited model of due process review. Citing decisions in the early twentieth century that established economic rights as barriers to social and market reform, critics maintained that the Court had reverted to antidemocratic ways. The majority anticipated these concerns by asserting that the right of privacy was not just a favored moral premise but "implicit in the concept of ordered liberty."

This effort to explain the right of privacy in terms other than a mere ideological preference has not converted critics. Judge Robert Bork, a leading detractor, has characterized the Court's principle of review as "pretty vaporous stuff." In his mind, it does not hide what he perceives to be "an exercise in moral and political philosophy" and "assumption of illegitimate judicial power and a usurpation of the democratic authority of the American people." Bork's sentiments, that the ruling represented judicial subjectivism at its worst, were echoed in Justice William Rehnquist's dissenting opinion. Justice Rehnquist noted that, because most states banned abortion, the nation's traditions and history provided no support for the liberty. From his perspective, the only legitimate question for the Court to ask was whether the regulation had a rational relationship to a legitimate state objective. This more deferential line of inquiry was essential, from Justice Rehnquist's perspective, to avoid judicial meddling with the political process on mere policy grounds. Justice Byron White shared Justice Rehnquist's concerns and agreed that abortion was not within the Constitution's ambit of concern. Because the issue was not of constitutional dimension, at least for Justice White, he argued that it should be resolved by the people and their elected representatives.

The decision in *Roe v. Wade* is one of the most controversial rulings in the Court's history. A central theme of criticism is that a woman's liberty to choose an abortion was judicially invented rather than grounded in the Constitution. Among *Roe v. Wade's* detractors are some who, although favoring limited regulation of abortion, believe that the Court stretched and warped the Constitution to achieve a desired result. Despite extensive criticism, the decision has been a generally effective barrier against regulation that would limit a woman's freedom to obtain an abortion. The Court regularly struck down laws it perceived as roadblocks, including regulation that imposed unnecessary licensing requirements, required spousal consent, or established first trimester waiting periods. Regulations that the Court upheld, however, included laws denying public funding for abortions and requiring minors to obtain the approval of a parent or court prior to obtaining an abortion.

Constitutional decisions resolve controversies by reference to the nation's highest law. The ruling in *Roe v. Wade,* however, extended and intensified the debate over abortion. The decision also created an aftermath that includes the Court's centrality to the controversy. The decades since *Roe v. Wade* have been characterized by numerous challenges by states seeking to reclaim control over the availability of abortion. Although later decisions have come close to overturning *Roe v. Wade,* and some have trimmed its reach, a woman's freedom to choose an abortion remains a part of constitutional law.

Bibliography

Robert H. Bork, *The Tempting of America* (New York: Free Press, 1990). A leading critic of *Roe v. Wade* states his case, along with the arguments of other detractors.
John H. Ely, *Democracy and Distrust: A Theory of Judicial Review* (Cambridge, MA: Harvard University Press, 1980). A critical perspective on *Roe v. Wade,* by an exponent of abortion freedom, is provided.
Kenneth Karst, *Belonging to America* (New Haven, CT: Yale University Press, 1989). Support for the Court's decision is provided.

Webster v. Reproductive Health Services

The decision in *Roe v. Wade,* establishing a woman's freedom to choose an abortion, has been a lightning rod for criticism. Arguments against judicial activism typically reference the ruling as one of the primary examples of overreaching. Even among constitutional experts who favor a woman's freedom to choose, there has been misgiving with the Court's decision and underlying thinking. In the words of John Hart Ely, "[t]he problem with *Roe* is not so much that it bungles the question it sets itself, but rather that it sets itself a question the Constitution has not made the

Citation: 492 U.S. 490.

Issue: Whether a state law prohibiting abortions in public hospitals and requiring fetal viability testing after 20 weeks violated a woman's freedom to obtain an abortion.

Year of Decision: 1989.

Outcome: The enactment was upheld and a woman's liberty to choose an abortion, although narrowed, was not overturned.

Author of Opinion: Chief Justice William Rehnquist.

Vote: 5-4.

Court's business." Ely thus maintains that "*Roe* is a very bad decision.... It is bad because it is bad constitutional law, or rather because it is *not* constitutional law and gives almost no sense of an obligation to try to be." Countering the perception of

Roe v. Wade as "bad constitutional law" are the observations of other scholars, like Sylvia Law, who contends that "[n]othing the Supreme Court has ever done has been more concretely important for women."

If *Roe v. Wade* were to be assessed merely on the basis of policy, it actually would approximate closely public views on abortion. Critics argue, however, that it is the role of the legislature to develop policy consistent with the will of the people. The role of the Court, as they see it, is not to engage in policy debate or review but simply to interpret the Constitution when it is relevant.

Mirroring the sense that *Roe v. Wade* was illegitimate, some states enacted laws that flouted it. These regulations consistently were invalidated in the decade following *Roe v. Wade*. Instead of removing abortion from politics, the Court's decision actually intensified the debate in this context. Abortion opponents in some instances became increasingly militant and violent. The major political parties adopted sharply differing positions, with Democrats supporting the freedom to choose and Republicans opposing it. Congress considered but did not enact legislation that would end the courts' jurisdiction over abortion. A proposed constitutional amendment protecting the "right to life" also was contemplated but not passed.

The abortion controversy became a focus of the 1980 presidential campaign, when Ronald Reagan promised to appoint "strict constructionist" federal judges who would support "family values." The political implications of abortion were evidenced further by widespread demonstrations and rallies by both sides and heavy volumes of mail directed to the Supreme Court. With the Court as a target of political activity for and against abortion as a constitutional freedom, critics of the *Roe v. Wade* ruling cited more evidence that the judiciary had strayed too far from its proper function. This point was made with particular force in a concurring opinion by Justice Antonin Scalia who, in *Webster v. Reproductive Health Services,* asserted that the Court's role:

> continuously distorts the public perception of the role of the Court. We can now look forward to at least another Term with carts full of mail from the public, and streets full of demonstrators, urging us—their unelected and life-tenured judges who have been awarded these extraordinary, undemocratic characteristics precisely in order that we might follow the law despite the popular will—to follow the popular will.

Consistent with his pledge when he ran for office, President Reagan in his second term authorized the Department of Justice to challenge the *Roe* decision. The administration submitted an *amicus curiae* brief in the Court's review of a Missouri law prohibiting abortion in state-funded hospitals and requiring fetal viability testing after 20 weeks. In this case, *Webster v Reproductive Health Services,* the government maintained that "*Roe* rests on assumptions not firmly grounded in the Constitution; it adopts an unworkable framework tying permissible state regulation to particular periods of pregnancy; and it has allowed courts to usurp functions of legislative bodies in weighting competing social, ethical and scientific factors in determining how much state regulation is permissible."

The challenged regulation, in addition to its substantive provisions, had a preamble that represented a direct repudiation of *Roe v. Wade*. It set forth legislative findings to the effect that life begins at conception and the unborn have constitutionally protected interests in life and liberty. Despite this frontal assault on the premises of *Roe v. Wade*, the Court responded in a way that minimized the preamble's significance. Although acknowledging that the preamble made "a value judgment favoring childbirth over abortion," the Court found that it "impose[d] no substantive restrictions on abortions." It thus bypassed the need to rule on the preamble's constitutionality.

No significant stretch was required for the Court to uphold the prohibition against abortions in public hospitals. This result was supported by precedent that had upheld restrictions on public funding of abortions. The requirement for viability testing during the second trimester, however, represented a much greater challenge to the trimester framework established in *Roe v Wade*. This requirement effectively enabled the state to regulate abortion more extensively at an earlier stage of pregnancy. The trimester framework assumed that the beginning of the third trimester marked fetal viability. Under state law, viability could commence during the fifth month of pregnancy. Such a requirement might have been viewed as a roadblock to a woman's freedom to elect an abortion, particularly insofar as it may have created a deterrent to abortion providers. Chief Justice William Rehnquist, in a plurality opinion, concluded that viability testing merely and properly accounted for post-*Roe v. Wade* advances in medical technology. Upholding this provision simply evolved the law in a manner that was consistent with the relevance of viability, which the Court in *Roe v. Wade* itself had established as the relevant benchmark.

Despite the government's push to have *Roe v. Wade* overturned, the Court declined. Given the state's utilization of viability as its reference point for when life begins, the Rehnquist plurality determined that the case was not appropriate for reconsidering the constitutional premise of *Roe v. Wade*. Justice Sandra Day O'Connor, in a concurring opinion, agreed that the Missouri law did not present the right case for overruling *Roe v. Wade*. She found no inconsistency between the requirement of viability testing and viability as the point at which the state had a compelling interest in protecting the potential of life. Justice O'Connor indicated support for any enactment that would protect life when viability was a possibility.

Justice Scalia authored a strident concurring opinion in which he agreed with the result but maintained that the Court was ignoring the main issue. He argued that the Court simply should overrule *Roe v. Wade* on grounds it was a mistake. Avoiding the real question, as Justice Scalia saw it, was an exercise in irresponsibility.

Justice Blackmun, who had authored the majority opinion in *Roe v. Wade,* was distressed by the result. He viewed the outcome to be undermining of *Roe v. Wade* but in a less than principled way. Justice Blackmun expressed concern that the Court had relaxed the standard for reviewing abortion regulation by asking not whether the reason for it was compelling but whether it was legitimate. He would have been more comfortable had the Court determined that advances in medical technology provided a "compelling" basis for viability testing. Merely asking whether it was a "legitimate reason" indicated to Justice Blackmun that future review of abortion laws would be more relaxed than in the past.

Justice Blackmun also was concerned that the cost of additional medical testing would impose an undue burden upon a woman's freedom to choose. Noting arguments that the trimester framework of *Roe v. Wade* was not prescribed by the Constitution, he countered with the point that constitutional standards for reviewing laws typically are created by the judiciary. Although Justice Blackmun is correct on this point, it does not respond to the central question of whether the Court should establish a right that is not constitutionally enumerated.

Summarizing his concerns with the direction that the Court was taking, Justice Blackmun warned that a woman's freedom to choose an abortion had become more uncertain. The primary danger he saw was the state's potential ability to make its regulatory interests compelling even before viability was established. Justice Blackmun thus noted that "[f]or today, at least, the law of abortion stands undisturbed. For today, the women of this Nation still retain the liberty to control their destinies. But the signs are evident and very ominous, and a chill wind blows." The Court's ruling left *Roe v. Wade* modified but still intact. It also ensured that future challenges lay ahead.

Bibliography

Dallas Blanchard, *The Anti-Abortion Movement and the Rise of the Religious Right: From Polite to Fiery Protest* (New York: Maxwell Macmillan, 1994). The evolution of the pro-life movement into a significant and sometimes strident force is traced

Laurence H. Tribe, *Abortion: The Clash of Absolutes* (New York: Norton, 1990). The significance of the *Webster* decision in the evolution of *Roe v. Wade* is examined.

Planned Parenthood of Southeastern Pennsylvania v. Casey

Citation: 505 U.S. 833.

Issue: Whether a state law imposing a waiting period, requiring parental consent for minors and spousal consent for married women, and establishing reporting requirements for physicians performing abortions invaded a woman's freedom to obtain an abortion.

Year of Decision: 1992.

Outcome: Except for the spousal notification requirement, which imposed an undue burden upon a women's liberty to choose, the law is constitutionally permissible.

Author of Opinion: Justice Sandra Day O'Connor.

Vote: 5-4.

Two decades after the Court's decision in *Roe v. Wade*, the future of a woman's freedom to choose an abortion was uncertain. Justice Blackmun's dissenting opinion, in *Webster v. Reproductive Systems, Inc.* (1989), suggested that a "chill wind" was blowing against this liberty. Constitutional challenges to the freedom to elect an abortion had become a primary incident of *Roe v. Wade's* aftermath. Three years after the *Webster* Court upheld a law requiring fetal viability testing in the fifth month, the Court in *Planned Parenthood of Southeastern Pennsylvania v. Casey* (1992) reviewed several other restrictions upon abortion.

At issue was a law that (1) required abortion providers to give women information identifying the physical and psychological risks of abortion; (2) prohibited abortion pending a 24 hour waiting period; (3) required minors to obtain the consent of a parent or judge; (4) required a married woman to notify her spouse; and (5) obligated physicians to file reports showing compliance with the law for every abortion they performed. Each provision of the law, except for the reporting requirement, provided an exception in the event of a medical emergency. A trial court had struck down the regulatory scheme on grounds that it violated a woman's freedom to end her pregnancy. The court of appeals reversed much of the lower court's ruling, finding only that the spousal notification provision was unconstitutional. For the Supreme Court, the case presented another opportunity to assess the continuing vitality of *Roe v. Wade*.

Consistent with its fragmented thinking on a woman's freedom to choose an abortion, the Court could not muster a majority opinion. Justices Sandra Day O'Connor, Anthony Kennedy, and David Souter authored a plurality opinion that gained the most attention. In their opinion, the three justices reaffirmed the validity of *Roe v. Wade* but upheld most provisions of the state law. The plurality commenced its analysis with a statement of the central principle of *Roe v. Wade*, which is that the state cannot deny an abortion prior to fetal viability. This determination was consistent with the Court's instruction in *Roe v. Wade*. It also was in line with the Court's thinking in *Webster v. Reproductive Health Services* that advanced the starting point of viability consistent with advances in medical technology.

Despite affirming *Roe's* "central" meaning, the plurality determined that the trimester framework was too "rigid." As a result, state interests had not been given due weight, and laws were struck down even though they did not meaningfully impair a woman's freedom to terminate her pregnancy. Based upon these assessments, the plurality maintained that the assessment of abortion regulations should focus upon whether they "unduly burden" a woman's freedom to choose prior to viability. In measuring the spousal notification requirement against this standard, the plurality determined that it was unconstitutional. The condition effectively transferred power from the woman to a third party that was less affected by the pregnancy and the regulation. The plurality noted that it was especially problematic for women with abusive spouses, some of whom might forego an abortion to avoid harm to themselves or to their children.

The plurality found all other provisions of the state law to be constitutionally permissible. Requiring that patients receive information on the physical and psychological risks of abortion was not viewed as unduly burdensome. Rather, the plurality found it to be an appropriate means of ensuring an informed decision on whether to proceed with an abortion. The 24-hour waiting period also was upheld, albeit with the acknowledgment that it might increase the time and money cost of an abortion. Without evidence indicating that the delay would interfere unreasonably with a woman's freedom to chose, the plurality was satisfied that the waiting period also advanced the objective of informed judgment. The plurality determined that the parental consent requirement was supported by existing case law, so long as it provided minors with the opportunity to bypass their parents and obtain a court order. Insofar as the reporting requirements had been set on the basis of their value to medical research and maternal well-being, they also were found to be acceptable.

The ruling represented a further extension of judicial involvement on an issue that continued to divide the public. The plurality communicated its sensitivity to this reality, and in particular to arguments that resolution should be achieved through the political rather than the judicial process. Replying to critics who maintained that the Court should exit the abortion controversy, the plurality maintained that the greater harm would be to retreat in response to political pressure. It thus drew upon the doctrine of *stare decisis* in support of the proposition that the central meaning of *Roe v. Wade* should be reaffirmed. The principle of *stare decisis* basically provides that courts should not overturn precedent minus a compelling reason for doing so. Examples for departure from this norm are when the law has become obsolete or the original judgment was plainly wrong. Although viewed by critics as a key source of the abortion controversy, the Court determined that the interests of certainty and predictability favored its continuing involvement and maintenance of *Roe v. Wade*. Divisions within the Court were pronounced, with some arguing that the plurality had been excessively deferential to the state and others maintaining that it had perpetuated and compounded the Court's original mistake. Justice John Paul Stevens did not dispute the analytical framework but contended that the plurality understated the magnitude of burden imposed by the Pennsylvania law. He was especially concerned that the information and waiting requirements were subtle means of influencing a woman to change her mind. Although relieved that the Court had embraced *Roe v. Wade's* basic meaning, Justice Harry Blackmun expressed concern with what he perceived as a relaxed standard of review. Justice Blackmun singled out the reporting requirement as particularly burdensome. As he saw it, this demand might deter physicians from performing abortions out of concern that they might be harassed or subject to personal harm. Justice Blackmun reiterated his preference for *Roe v. Wade's* original trimester formula, which he regarded as a more effective source of protection for a woman's liberty to choose.

Both Chief Justice William Rehnquist and Justice Antonin Scalia authored pointed dissents that called for the outright overturning of *Roe v. Wade.* The Chief Justice maintained that the Court missed the point of *stare decisis.* As he saw it, the Court's reputation would be enhanced rather than lessened by a forthright acknowledgment of error. Consistent with his original dissent in *Roe v. Wade,* Chief Justice Rehnquist restated his persistent concern that deep public divisions on abortion demonstrated a lack of consensus necessary to define a fundamental right. To the extent that the Court had any role at all, he favored a standard of review that allowed states to regulate abortion on the basis of any reasonable justification. Pursuant to this criterion, Chief Justice Rehnquist thus would have upheld all provisions of the Pennsylvania law. Even the spousal notification requirement, which the plurality was concerned could be risky for women with abusive spouses, was reasonably justified from Chief Justice Rehnquist's perspective. As he viewed it, the provision reflected the husband's legitimate interests, facilitated marital integrity, and accounted for potential life. Even if the wisdom of the policy might be debated, Chief Justice Rehnquist stressed that the Court's role was not to debate politics but to interpret the Fourteenth Amendment, which does not set forth a comprehensive right of privacy.

Justice Scalia also favored the overturning of *Roe v. Wade* and the Court's self-removal from the abortion controversy. Consistent with his prior opinions, Justice Scalia asserted that the freedom to elect an abortion is not provided for by the Constitution and there is no barrier to prohibiting it. Whether it is prohibited or permitted, Justice Scalia maintained, is a matter for the people to decide through their elected agents. Like Chief Justice Rehnquist, Justice Scalia was especially critical of the Court's use of *stare decisis.* He acknowledged the importance of this doctrine in maintaining the law's certainty and predictability. Justice Scalia pointed out, however, that *stare decisis* does not operate when a court comes to realize that a case was wrongly decided. In his view, *Roe v. Wade* was decided wrongly because it failed to resolve the life status of the fetus and establish a settled principle. Its legacy of persistent criticism and challenge, from Justice Scalia's perspective, was further evidence that the law was anything but settled.

Like other significant decisions since the Court declared a woman's freedom to terminate an unwanted pregnancy, the ruling in *Planned Parenthood of Southeastern Pennsylvania v. Casey* did not end the controversy over abortion or the Court's role in it. The "central meaning" of *Roe v. Wade,* which the Court reaffirmed, is that fetal viability is the factor that determines whether the mother's or state's interest is dominant. No longer is the formal trimester framework the basis for balancing, however, the competing interests of state power and individual liberty. Instead, the focus is upon whether a regulation is "unduly burdensome." Perspective on how this standard operates varies. Justices Stevens and Blackmun viewed it as too relaxed and reference analysis of the Pennsylvania law as proof of their point. Justice Scalia argued that the criterion endangers any abortion regulation merely because a court dislikes it. These mixed readings, coupled with the lessening of abortion cases under review in the following decade, might indicate that the Court has established a midpoint between the poles of the controversy. Continuing debate over and attention to judicial appointments in the early twenty-first century, particularly with respect to a candidate's position on abortion, suggest that the future of a woman's freedom to choose is not entirely under lock and key.

Bibliography

Charles Fried, *Constitutional Doctrine,* 107 *Harvard Law Review* 1140 (1994). This presents
an argument that *stare decisis* was used to perpetuate a decision that by itself was deficient.
Cass Sunstein, *The Partial Constitution* (Cambridge, MA: Harvard University Press, 1994).
The difficulty of squaring the right of privacy, with early but now discredited use of the
due process clause to create fundamental rights, is discussed.

SEXUAL ORIENTATION

A significant limitation on the right of privacy was established in *Bowers v. Hardwick* (1986), when the Court determined that it did not comprehend the right to engage in homosexual sodomy. The *Bowers* decision was the work of a deeply divided Court reflecting profoundly different perspectives upon how the right of privacy should be defined. Not accounting for the freedom to be different, from the dissenters' perspective, undermined the significance of the right to privacy. The Court turned about on this point, in *Lawrence v. Texas* (2003), when it found the right of privacy broad enough to protect sexual orientation. This decision generated an equally intense dissenting response to the effect that the majority was resolving the issue on the basis of personal values rather than constitutional principle.

Bowers v. Hardwick

The right of privacy, as the abortion cases demonstrate, originated and has evolved in a state of controversy. Like many generalities, the concept of privacy as a fundamental right is embraced in the abstract. Case law relating back to the early twentieth century manifests this point. In *Meyer v. Nebraska* (1923), the Supreme Court charted boundaries of personal freedom that extended beyond what the Constitution itself specifically delineated. Within these lines were:

Citation: 478 U.S. 186.

Issue: Whether the right of privacy protects persons who engage in consensual homosexual sodomy.

Year of Decision: 1986.

Outcome: The right of privacy does not extend to homosexual sodomy.

Author of Opinion: Justice Byron White.

Vote: 5-4.

freedom from bodily restraint..., [and] the right of the individual to contract, to engage in any of the common occupations of life, to acquire useful knowledge, to marry, establish a home, and bring up children, to worship God according to the dictates of his own conscience, and generally to enjoy those privileges long recognized at common law as essential to the orderly pursuit of happiness by free men.

A common thread in this matrix of liberties is the sense that there are certain personal decisions that are reserved for the individual. This concept of personal autonomy is central to the modern right of privacy. Identifying the range of choices that cannot be encumbered by the state, however, has proved to be both difficult and controversial.

Even if there is general agreement upon the nature of the right, it is necessary to determine what state interests may justify its limitation. A relatively easy case for the Supreme Court, particularly given the specific indication of *Meyer v. Nebraska,* concerned a state's barrier to marriage for spouses who had neglected their child support obligations. In *Zablocki v. Redhail* (1977), the Court determined that this enactment abridged the right to marry. A more difficult case for the Court concerned a city zoning ordinance that capped the number of family members who could live in a single dwelling. This restriction imposed a significant burden upon extended families. In *Moore v. City of East Cleveland* (1978), the Court concluded that the right of privacy protected the ability of such families to live together. It also found that the city's regulatory interest was not strong enough to defeat the liberty interest.

The right of privacy cases reflects a persistent tension between respect for personal autonomy and state interests that typically cannot be trumped minus a clear constitutional basis. Even as the Court has been criticized for alleged overreaching in the abortion cases, it has expressed caution about its role in developing the right of privacy. In *Whalen v. Roe* (1978), for instance, the Court noted that "[s]tate legislation which has some effect on individual liberty or privacy may not be held unconstitutional simply because a court finds it unnecessary, in whole or in part." The Court at times has demonstrated not just reserve but resistance to expanding the dimensions of the right of privacy. Exemplifying this reaction was its decision in *Bowers v. Hardwick* (1986), which concerned what the Court characterized as "the right of homosexuals to engage in acts of sodomy."

The case concerned an arrest and prosecution based upon acts of same-sex oral sodomy that were prohibited by Georgia law. These acts occurred in the privacy of the bedroom that an earlier case, *Griswold v. Connecticut* (1965), had characterized in the marital context as "sacred precincts." Because charges were dropped prior to trial, there was no conviction. The charged individual nonetheless brought an action that challenged the law's constitutionality.

The state law at issue provided that "[a] person commits the offense of sodomy when he performs or submits to any sexual act involving the sex organs of one person and the mouth or anus of another." It was challenged on grounds that the sex was consensual, was within the context of a private association, and thus was within the protected realm of the right of privacy. Although the law on its face did not differentiate between homosexual and heterosexual sodomy, the Court focused its attention on the same sex aspect. The narrowed concern made the decision particularly relevant to the issue of sexual orientation.

Writing for the majority, Justice Byron White described the issue as "whether the Federal Constitution confers a fundamental right upon homosexuals to engage in sodomy and hence invalidates the laws of the many States that still make such conduct illegal and have done so for a very long time." The Court's analysis was framed within a restrictive rather than expansive sense of the right of privacy. It commenced with a reference to prior privacy decisions that comprehended child rearing and education, family relationships, procreation, marriage, contraception, and abortion. None of these interests, the Court observed, "bears any resemblance to the claimed right of homosexuals to engage in acts of sodomy." In this regard, it saw no connection between homosexuality and family or marriage. The Court also saw no basis for concluding that consensual sex was constitutionally immune from state regulation.

Despite arguments that the right of privacy must account for diverse and not just mainstream realities, if it is to be meaningful, the Court was "quite unwilling" to recognize "a fundamental right to engage in homosexual sodomy." Identifying such a right as fundamental would disregard the rules of judicial restraint that the Court must respect "to assure itself and the public that announcing rights not readily identifiable in the Constitution's text involves much more than the imposition of the Justices' own choice of values." Pursuant to these norms, the Court may identify rights as fundamental only to the extent that they may be understood as "implicit in the concept of ordered liberty, such that neither liberty nor justice would exist if [they] were sacrificed" or which "are deeply rooted in this Nation's history and traditions." In the

Court's view, a right to engage in acts of consensual homosexual sodomy met neither criterion. To the contrary, it found that antisodomy provisions have "ancient roots." The Court noted that every state prohibited sodomy from the time the Constitution was framed and ratified through the mid-twentieth century. Nearly half of them, moreover, still banned it at the time the action under review was brought. Viewing history and tradition in this light, the Court dismissed the "claim that a right to engage in such conduct is 'deeply rooted in this Nation's history and tradition' or 'implicit in the concept of ordered liberty' [a]s, at best, facetious."

In rejecting an expanded understanding of the right of privacy in this case, the Court expressed its unease in using its authority "to discover new fundamental rights imbedded in the Due Process Clause." Consistent with Justice White's views in *Roe v. Wade* (1973), echoed by many critics of the decision, the Court observed that it "is most vulnerable and comes nearest to illegitimacy when it deals with judge-made constitutional law having little or no cognizable roots in the language or design of the Constitution." The risk of the judiciary becoming an antidemocratic force increases particularly when it "redefine[s] the category of rights deemed to be fundamental."

Chief Justice Warren Burger authored a concurring opinion that repudiated the right of privacy case even more bluntly. Building upon the Court's observation that "proscriptions against sodomy have very 'ancient roots,'" Chief Justice Burger stated that condemnation of homosexuality as being "firmly rooted in Judeo-Christian moral and ethical standards," "a capital crime under Roman law," under English law "an offense of 'deeper malignity' than rape, a heinous act 'the very mention of which is a disgrace to human nature,' and a 'crime not fit to be named.'" For the Court to recognize a right of homosexual sodomy, from Chief Justice Burger's perspective, would "cast aside millennia of moral teaching."

Forceful as the majority and concurring opinions were, the Court was narrowly divided in its thinking and outcome. Justice Harry Blackmun, joined by three of his colleagues, authored a dissent that questioned the Court's grasp of the issue. Justice Blackmun asserted that the Court had mischaracterized it as "a fundamental right to engage in homosexual sodomy." The real issue, from his perspective, was "about 'the most comprehensive of rights and the right most valued by civilized men,' namely, 'the right to be let alone.'" By framing the controversy and reaching the decision that it did, the Court from Justice Blackmun's perspective had done more than deny a right to engage in homosexual sodomy; it had refused "to recognize a fundamental interest all individuals have in controlling the nature of their intimate associations." Even if sodomy had been condemned "for hundreds of years, if not thousands" of years, Justice Blackmun maintained that neither long history nor intensity of conviction could shield a law from meaningful judicial review. Citing to *West Virginia Board of Education v. Barnette* (1943), a case concerning a student's freedom not to salute the flag, he noted that "freedom to differ is not limited to things that do not matter much. That would be a mere shadow of freedom." Building upon this point, Justice Blackmun maintained that the Court should be particularly "sensitive to the rights of those whose choices upset the majority." Accordingly, he believed that "we must analyze Hardwick's claim in the light of the values that underlie the constitutional right to privacy."

The Court's ruling marked a significant boundary to the right of privacy and a strong statement for judicial restraint. The same self-stated concern with overreaching its authority was manifested a few years later in *Michael H. v. Gerald D.* (1989). Writing for a four-justice plurality, Justice Antonin Scalia maintained that the risk of judicial activism could be managed by defining fundamental rights at a level of specificity rather than generality. Stated generally, the issue in *Michael H.* was whether a natural father could be denied visitation rights with his daughter. Using Justice Scalia's narrowing premise as the starting point for analysis, however, the question became whether a father's visitation rights could be denied because the child was conceived from an extramarital affair. Even if the general proposition was consistent with the nation's history and traditions, they did not support the interests of the "father of a child conceived within, and born into, an extant marital union that wishes to embrace the child." In Justice Scalia's words, "[t]his is not the stuff of which fundamental rights qualifying as liberty interest are made."

The analysis employed by the Scalia plurality is consistent with how the Court characterized the issue in *Bowers v. Hardwick*. Faced with the descriptive choice between a "fundamental right to engage in homosexual sodomy," and a more general "right to be let alone," the Court chose the narrower framing. In doing so, and unlike in *Roe v. Wade,* it resisted pressure to expand the boundaries of the right of privacy into an area where significant societal divisions existed. The Court also demonstrated how definition of the issue is a critical and even determinative factor in shaping the ultimate outcome.

Bibliography

Lord Patrick Devlin, *The Enforcement of Morals* (New York: Oxford University Press, 1965). This sets forth the idea that the majority's position is reflective of a moral philosophy.

H.L.A. Hart, *Law, Liberty and Morality* (London: Oxford University Press, 1965). A challenge to Devlin's theory and arguments that is consistent with Justice Blackmun's dissent is raised.

Donald E. Lively, *Foreshadows of the Law* (Westport, CT: Praeger, 1992). The right of privacy's evolution, and the Court's role in developing it, is discussed.

Lawrence v. Texas

Citation: 539 U.S. 558.

Issue: Whether the right of privacy protects consenting adult sexual behavior including activity between members of the same sex.

Year of Decision: 2003.

Outcome: The right of privacy protects consenting adults in their sexual activity, and the prior contrary decision in Bowers v. Hardwick (1986) was overturned.

Author of Opinion: Justice Anthony Kennedy.

Vote: 5-4.

When the Supreme Court decides highly controversial issues, history indicates that its ruling may feed rather than dampen the controversy. The aftermath of its decision upholding slavery in *Dred Scott v. Sandford* (1857), for instance, was intensified polarization of the North and South. The aftermath of rulings on segregation and abortion in the mid-twentieth century likewise included resistance and challenges to their legitimacy. A similar result followed the Court's decision, in *Bowers v. Hardwick* (1986), finding that there was "no fundamental right to engage in homosexual sodomy."

The primary criticism of the *Bowers* holding was that it framed the fundamental rights issue as a matter of homosexual sodomy rather than as a matter of intimate personal choice incident to a general right of privacy. The Court itself left open the question of whether discrimination on the basis of sexual orientation might constitute an equal protection violation. It addressed this issue in *Romer v. Evans* (1996), when it struck down a Colorado constitutional amendment prohibiting the state and municipalities from extending the protection of antidiscrimination laws to homosexuals. From the Court's perspective, the law was so unrelated to a legitimate state interest that it could be understood only as a reflection of "animus" toward homosexuals. The Court did not indicate whether sexual orientation provided the basis for a heightened standard of review.

In *Lawrence v. Texas* (2003), the Court revisited the underlying premise of *Bowers v. Hardwick*. The factual circumstances of *Lawrence* paralleled those of *Bowers*. Police had been sent to a private residence in response to reports of a weapons related disturbance. Once on the scene, they observed two men engaged in a sexual act. Both were charged with and convicted of a crime under a law prohibiting "deviate sexual intercourse." The defendants were adults, and the conduct was private and consensual.

Justice Anthony Kennedy commenced the majority's opinion with one of the Court's most sweeping statements on personal liberty. He spoke first to the traditional understanding of an especially strong liberty interest in the privacy of the home. He then observed that:

> there are other spheres of our lives and existence, outside the home, where the State should not be a dominant presence. Freedom extends beyond spatial bounds. Liberty presumes an autonomy of self that includes freedom of thought, belief, expression, and certain intimate contact. The instant case involves liberty of the person both in its spatial and more transcendent dimension.

Against this backdrop, the Court reconsidered its holding in *Bowers v. Hardwick* and determined that it had "misapprehended the claim of liberty there presented to it." In particular, it maintained that the *Bowers* inquiry into "whether the Federal Constitution confers a fundamental right upon homosexuals to engage in sodomy" represented a "failure to appreciate the extent of liberty at stake." Because the laws relevant in both cases "touch[ ] upon the most private human conduct, sexual behavior, and in the most private places, the home," the Court found that they reached unacceptably into "the liberty of persons to choose without being punished as criminals."

In repudiating the *Bowers* decision, the Court also separated itself from its contro versial historical analysis. Particularly with respect to the premise that there was a long-standing history in the United States of law directed against homosexual conduct, the Court noted that prohibitions against same-sex relations were more recent and limited. Nearly half of the states that had antisodomy laws when *Bowers* was decided had since repealed them. Several more had a pattern of nonenforcement regarding consenting adults whose interaction was in private. Even if there may be a long history of condemnation of homosexuality from some quarters, the Court reasoned that the moral convictions of some do not empower the state to impose them on society as a matter of criminal law.

The Court further buttressed its holding with a reference to its abortion decisions. It thus cited *Planned Parenthood of Southeastern Pennsylvania v. Casey* (1992) for the proposition that "[a]t the heart of liberty is the right to define one's own concept of existence, of meaning, of the universe, and of the mystery of human life." Adding to this premise, the Court concluded that "[p]ersons in a homosexual relationship may seek autonomy for these persons, just as heterosexual persons do." Because the *Bowers* ruling would deny this right, and was neither "correct when it was decided ... [nor] today," the Court overruled it. In so doing, it distinguished the result from a case that might concern a minor, coercion, public activity, or prostitution. The majority concluded its opinion with the expansive observation that the meaning of constitutional liberty is not locked into any time in history and "persons in every generation can invoke its principles in their own search for greater freedom."

Justice Sandra Day O'Connor concurred in the judgment but disagreed with the majority's overruling of *Bowers*. She would have found the law unconstitutional under the equal protection clause. As she saw it, moral disapproval by itself was not a legitimate basis for discriminating among groups of persons. Because the state criminalized "deviate sexual intercourse" in the context of same-sex relationships, but not opposite-sex relationships, Justice O'Connor maintained that the law could not stand. By relying upon the equal protection clause, she would have provided space for the state to enact an antisodomy law that applied both to heterosexual and homosexual relationships.

In a dissenting opinion joined by Chief Justice William Rehnquist and Justice Clarence Thomas, Justice Antonin Scalia challenged the majority's opinion as essentially hypocritical, driven by irrelevant considerations, and the product of a "law-profession culture." With respect to the first point, Justice Scalia noted the Court's "sententious response" a decade ago to critics of *Roe v. Wade* (1973). This observation referred to the point made in *Planned Parenthood of Southeastern Pennsylvania v. Casey*, in support of maintaining precedent, that "[l]iberty finds no refuge in the jurisprudence of doubt." The Court's disinterest in "stability and certainty" in *Lawrence* thus was striking enough to Justice Scalia for him to raise it disapprovingly at the beginning of his dissent. With the Court having deferred to precedent in *Casey*, but departed from it in overruling *Bowers*, Justice Scalia perceived an outcome that was merely a "result-oriented expedient."

Justice Scalia in more expansive terms criticized what he viewed as a departure from settled norms that reserved constitutional accounting only for fundamental rights that are "deeply rooted in this Nation's history and tradition." Although acknowledging that the *Bowers* decision had been a source of continuing criticism, he noted that the same legacy characterized the Court's rulings on abortion. Without the power to enact legislation based upon moral choices, state laws against a range of behavior including incest, prostitution, bestiality, and obscenity could be called into doubt. Justice Scalia thus viewed the overruling of *Bowers* as a source of "massive disruption of the current social order."

What Justice Scalia found "most out of accord" in the majority's holding was its finding that there was "no rational basis for the law." The state's interest in acting upon its citizens' belief that certain sexual behavior is "immoral and unacceptable," Justice Scalia noted, provides the basis for numerous sex crimes. The determination that the state has no legitimate interest that justifies intrusion into personal and private lives, as Justice Scalia saw it, "decrees the end of all morals legislation." Against this backdrop, he perceived the majority's opinion as the extension of an "agenda promoted by some homosexual activists directed at eliminating the moral opprobrium that has traditionally attached to homosexual conduct." Justice Scalia also accused the Court of "tak[ing] sides in the culture war, departing from its role of assuring, as neutral observer, that the democratic rules of engagement are observed."

Central to Justice Scalia's reasoning was the notion that some people view homosexuality as "immoral and destructive," and that it is a "lifestyle" rather than "immutable characteristic." Consistent with this premise, he contended that the issue of homosexuality and its incidents should be resolved by "normal democratic means," which give every person and group "the right to persuade its fellow citizens that its view ... is the best." It is another matter, Justice Scalia observed, when matters move beyond attempts at persuasion to imposing one's views without a democratic majority.

Justice Scalia, in closing, observed that the Court's opinion had far-reaching consequences that were inevitable. Of particular concern to him was the Court's sweeping statement on liberty, as it relates to personal decisions including marriage, coupled with its point that "persons in a homosexual relationship may seek autonomy for these purposes." This observation, from Justice Scalia's perspective, "dismantles the structure of constitutional law that has "enabled states to deny recognition of same-sex marriage. The Court had addressed this point with the observation that its holding did not address this question. Justice Scalia found no comfort in it minus the ability to believe "that principle and logic have nothing to do with the decisions of this Court."

One significant loose end in the Court's decision relates to the standard of review. Typically, when accounting for fundamental rights, the Court engages in strict scrutiny. In *Lawrence,* the Court used its lowest standard of review in finding that the law merely lacked rationality. The *Lawrence* decision also continues the historic debate over the role of the judiciary in competing against the will of the people as reflected through its elected representatives. Regardless of the outcome in this instance and future cases, it is a debate that is destined to endure.

Bibliography

Richard Posner, *Sex and Reason* (Cambridge, MA: Harvard University Press, 1992). An argument for decriminalizing sodomy is advanced.

RIGHT TO REFUSE MEDICAL TREATMENT

A person's freedom to resist unwanted medical care predates modern understanding of the right to privacy. In *Jacobson v. Massachusetts* (1905), the Court determined that the government's interest in disease prevention did not outweigh an individual's freedom to decline a smallpox vaccination. When medical treatment is essential to maintain life, but refused, personal autonomy conflicts with societal values and laws that disfavor suicide and criminalize its facilitation. In *Cruzan v. Director, Missouri Department of Health* (1990), the Court examined whether the right of privacy comprehended an individual's freedom to refuse unwanted medical treatment.

Cruzan v. Director, Missouri Department of Health

The right of privacy is a multifaceted concept. In a series of decisions over the final decades of the twentieth century, this right of privacy was defined in a manner that included the freedom to terminate an unwanted pregnancy, marry, and live as an extended family. These developments were not a steady progression, however, as evidenced by decisions in the 1980s when the Court raised questions about its own role and legitimacy with respect to fundamental rights development.

Despite the Court's own stated apprehensions regarding the use of its power to declare rights not specifically enumerated

Citation: 497 U.S. 261.

Issue: Whether medical treatment may be refused even if death is the consequence.

Year of Decision: 1990.

Outcome: The right of privacy includes the right to decline unwanted medical treatment, but the state has a compelling interest in verifying the individual's intent.

Author of Opinion: Chief Justice William Rehnquist.

Vote: 8-1.

by the Constitution, the Court has not abandoned this function altogether. The continuing willingness of the Court to add new dimensions to the right of privacy was evidenced in *Cruzan v. Director, Missouri Department of Health* (1990). In this case, the Court reviewed the claim of parents that they had the right to end medical treatment of their daughter. Their child, Nancy Cruzan, had suffered severe brain damage in an automobile accident and had been placed on life support. Medical experts concluded that she was unlikely ever to regain consciousness. Her parents requested a court order directing the hospital to remove her from the life maintenance system. The state opposed the order on grounds state law required "clear and convincing evidence" of their daughter's own wishes. The Missouri Supreme Court determined that such evidence was lacking, and the parents had insufficient authority to make the decision for their daughter.

The United States Supreme Court, in upholding the state court's decision, stated first that "a competent person has a constitutionally protected liberty interest in refusing unwanted medical treatment." This premise was inferred from prior decisions that acknowledge a person's freedom to decline the administration of vaccines and drugs. The Court's identification of a protected liberty under the due process clause, however, did "not end the inquiry." Writing for the majority, Chief Justice William Rehnquist observed that the right to refuse life support hinges in part upon whether a person is competent or incompetent. Given her state of incompetence, the Court observed, her right to refuse life support was not the same as if she had been competent. As the Court saw it, "[a]n incompetent person is not able to make an informed and voluntary choice to exercise a hypothetical right to refuse treatment or any other right." Under such conditions, the right "must be exercised for her, if at all, by some sort of surrogate."

Under Missouri law, a third party could make a decision to end life support if sufficient safeguards were in place to ensure that it reflected the wishes of the patient to the best extent possible. Compliance with this prerequisite depended upon a showing that "the incompetent's wishes as to the withdrawal of treatment [were] proved by clear and convincing evidence." For the Court, the key question was whether the right to refuse unwanted medical treatment outweighed the state's interest in a procedural safeguard. In making this assessment, the Court found that the Missouri law was based "on its interest in the protection and preservation of human life, and there can be no gainsaying this interest." It viewed the state's concern as being even more significant when a person was incompetent. As the Court put it, a state need not "remain neutral in the face of an informed and voluntary decision by a physically able adult to starve to death." Because choosing between life and death represents "a deeply personal decision of obvious and overwhelming finality," the Court concluded that the state's concern with the integrity of the decision was legitimate.

Among the risks that the Court noted was the possibility that an incompetent person might be taken advantage of by a third party not dedicated to his or her best interests. Given this potential for abuse, the state's interest in procedural safeguards seemed a logical and legitimate concern. Even with respect to close family members, the Court emphasized that "the Due Process Clause requires the State to repose judgment on these matters with ... the patient herself." Although acknowledging that family members may have strong feelings about a loved one's condition, it noted too that their concerns may not be "entirely disinterested." Family membership by itself, as the Court noted, does not provide "automatic assurance that the view of close family members will necessarily be the same as the patient's."

The state's "clear and convincing evidence" requirement imposed a higher standard of proof than the "preponderance of the evidence" requirement that typically governs civil proceedings. The Court found that the enhanced standard was appropriate when life was the issue, and that it was "self-evident that the interests at stake ... are more substantial, both on an individual and societal level, than those involved in a run-of-the-mill civil dispute." The higher standard of proof helped ensure that the consequences of a bad court decision would fall more likely upon the third party. Because an order to withdraw life support would result in death, in the most practical sense it "is not susceptible to correction." A misconceived ruling in favor of life support might result in burdens for the third party. They might be offset or mitigated, however, by medical discoveries, new evidence regarding the patient's intent, or eventual death. The Court noted that the state, if it chose, could "assert an unqualified interest in the preservation of human life to be weighed against the constitutionally protected interests of the individual." Viewed thusly, a procedural safeguard of the life interest follows logically.

Justice Scalia agreed with the outcome but, in his concurring opinion, objected to basing it upon the due process clause. Consistent with his concern that due process analysis is too freewheeling, he "would have preferred that we announce, clearly and promptly, that the federal courts have no business in this field; that American law has always accorded the State the power to prevent, by force if necessary, suicide" by any means. Restating this sense that the Court should steer clear of developing rights not set forth specifically in the Constitution, Justice Scalia maintained:

> that the point at which life becomes "worthless," and the point at which the means necessary to preserve it become "extraordinary" or "inappropriate," are neither set forth in the Constitution nor known to the nine Justices of this Court any better than they are known to nine people picked at random from the Kansas City telephone directory.

Because the Constitution did not address the matter directly, Justice Scalia maintained that the people through their elected representatives had exclusive authority to determine what the law should be. Noting that the Constitution does not prohibit any number of "horribles," he contended that the "Court need not, and has no authority to, inject itself into every field of human activity where irrationality and oppression may theoretically occur; and if it tries to do so it will destroy itself."

Justice William Brennan, in a concurring opinion, asserted that "no state interest could outweigh the rights of an individual in Nancy Cruzan's position." From Justice Brennan's perspective, the state had "no legitimate general interest in someone's life completely abstracted from the interest of the person living that life." The state regulatory interest, as he saw it, extended no further than ensuring and protecting the integrity of her will. The key inquiry for Justice Brennan was "whether the incompetent person would choose to live in a persistent vegetative state on life support or to avoid this medical treatment." He disputed the Court's premise that the state could compel life support absent clear and convincing evidence of the patient's own express will. On this point, Justice Brennan argued that the state must respect the choice of the person to whom the person most likely would have delegated it.

In a separate concurrence, Justice John Paul Stevens also disagreed with the "clear and convincing evidence" standard. From his perspective, the conflict between life and liberty was an "artificial consequence of Missouri's effort, and this Court's willingness, to abstract Nancy Cruzan's life from Nancy Cruzan's person." Insofar as the state declared a policy in favor of life in the abstract, he found the state's responsibility for protecting life to be "desecrate[d]" rather than "honored."

The diverging opinions illuminate a difficult question. The willingness of some justices to identify a right of privacy, despite their traditional opposition to it, also reflects the Court's persistent challenge in determining its role in identifying fundamental rights. Since *Roe v. Wade* (1973), Chief Justice Rehnquist persistently and often stridently criticized decisions establishing and evolving the right of privacy. He was the author of the majority opinion, however, in the *Cruzan* decision and thus led the way in recognizing a right to refuse unwanted medical treatment. Results like these are why some constitutional scholars have observed that demands for judicial restraint "are most insistent when it is most obvious that they are being honored in the breach rather than in the observance."

Bibliography

Ronald Dworkin, *Life's Dominion* (New York: Knopf, 1993). Life's value in the context of abortion and life support is examined.

Seth Kreimer, *Does Pro-Choice Mean Pro-Kevorkian? An Essay on Roe, Casey, and the Right to Die*, 44 *American University Law Review* 803 (1995). Whether the freedom to elect an abortion necessarily leads to support for a right to die is discussed.

APPENDIX

THE CONSTITUTION OF THE UNITED STATES

We the People of the United States, in Order to form a more perfect Union, establish Justice, insure domestic Tranquility, provide for the common defense, promote the general Welfare, and secure the Blessings of Liberty to ourselves and our Posterity, do ordain and establish this Constitution for the United States of America.

ARTICLE I

Section 1. All legislative Powers herein granted shall be vested in a Congress of the United States, which shall consist of a Senate and House of Representatives.

Section 2. [1]The House of Representatives shall be composed of Members chosen every second Year by the People of the several States, and the Electors in each State shall have the Qualifications requisite for Electors of the most numerous Branch of the State Legislature.

[2]No Person shall be a Representative who shall not have attained to the Age of twenty five Years, and been seven Years a Citizen of the United States, and who shall not, when elected, be an Inhabitant of that State in which he shall be chosen.

[3]Representatives and direct Taxes shall be apportioned among the several States which may be included within this Union, according to their respective Numbers, which shall be determined by adding to the whole Number of free Persons, including those bound to Service for a Term of Years, and excluding Indians not taxed, three fifths of all other Persons. The actual Enumeration shall be made within three Years after the first Meeting of the Congress of the United States, and within every subsequent Term of ten Years, in such Manner as they shall by Law direct. The Number of Representatives shall not exceed one for every thirty Thousand, but each State shall have at Least one Representative; and until such enumeration shall be made, the State of New Hampshire shall be entitled to chuse three, Massachusetts eight, Rhode-Island and Providence Plantations one, Connecticut five, New-York six, New Jersey four, Pennsylvania eight, Delaware one, Maryland six, Virginia ten, North Carolina five, South Carolina five, and Georgia three.

[4]When vacancies happen in the Representation from any State, the Executive Authority thereof shall issue Writs of Election to fill such Vacancies.

[5]The House of Representatives shall chuse their Speaker and other Officers; and shall have the sole Power of Impeachment.

Section 3. [1]The Senate of the United States shall be composed of two Senators from each State, chosen by the Legislature thereof for six Years; and each Senator shall have one Vote.

[2]Immediately after they shall be assembled in Consequence of the first Election, they shall be divided as equally as may be into three Classes. The Seats of the Senators of the first Class shall be vacated at the Expiration of the second Year, of the second Class at the Expiration of the fourth Year, and of the third Class at the Expiration of the sixth Year, so that one third may be chosen every second Year; and if Vacancies happen by Resignation. or otherwise, during the Recess of the Legislature of any State, the Executive thereof may make temporary Appointments until the next Meeting of the Legislature, which shall then fill such Vacancies.

[3]No Person shall be a Senator who shall not have attained to the Age of thirty Years, and been nine Years a Citizen of the United States, and who shall not, when elected, be an Inhabitant of that State for which he shall be chosen.

[4]The Vice President of the United States shall be President of the Senate, but shall have no Vote, unless they be equally divided.

[5]The Senate shall chuse their other Officers, and also a President pro tempore, in the Absence of the Vice President, or when he shall exercise the Office of President of the United States.

[6]The Senate shall have the sole Power to try all Impeachments. When sitting for that Purpose they shall be on Oath or Affirmation. When the President of the United States is tried, the Chief Justice shall preside: And no Person shall be convicted without the Concurrence of two thirds of the Members present.

[7]Judgment in Cases of Impeachment shall not extend further than to removal from Office, and disqualification to hold and enjoy any Office of honor, Trust or Profit under the United States: but the Party convicted shall nevertheless be liable and subject to Indictment, Trial, Judgment and Punishment, according to Law.

Section 4. [1]The Times, Places and Manner of holding Elections for Senators and Representatives, shall be prescribed in each State by the Legislature thereof; but the Congress may at any time by Law make or alter such Regulations, except as to the Places of chusing Senators.

[2]The Congress shall assemble at least once in every Year, and such Meeting shall be on the first Monday in December, unless they shall by Law appoint a different Day.

Section 5. [1]Each house shall be the Judge of the Elections, Returns and Qualifications of its own Members, and a Majority of each shall constitute a Quorum to do Business; but a smaller Number may adjourn from day to day, and may be authorized to compel the Attendance of absent Members, in such Manner, and under such Penalties as each House may provide.

[2]Each House may determine the Rules of its Proceedings, punish its Members for disorderly Behaviour, and, with the Concurrence of two thirds, expel a Member.

[3]Each House shall keep a Journal of its Proceedings, and from time to time publish the same, excepting such Parts as may in their Judgment require Secrecy; and the Yeas and Nays of the Members of either House on any question shall, at the Desire of one fifth of those Present, be entered on the Journal.

[4]Neither House, during the Session of Congress, shall, without the Consent of the other, adjourn for more than three days, nor to any other Place than that in which the two Houses shall be sitting.

Section 6. [1]The Senators and Representatives shall receive a Compensation for their Services, to be ascertained by Law, and paid out of the Treasury of the United States. They shall in all Cases, except Treason, Felony and Breach of the Peace, be privileged from Arrest during their Attendance at the Session of their respective Houses, and in going to and returning from the same; and for any Speech or Debate in either House, they shall not be questioned in any other Place.

[2]No Senator or Representative shall, during the Time for which he was elected, be appointed to civil Office under the Authority of the United States, which shall have been created, or the Emoluments whereof shall have been encreased during such time; and no Person holding any Office under the United States, shall be a Member of either House during his Continuance in Office.

Section 7. [1]All Bills for raising Revenue shall originate in the House of Representatives; but the Senate may proprose or concur with Amendments as on other Bills.

[2]Every Bill which shall have passed the House of Representatives and the Senate, shall, before it become a Law, be presented to the President of the United States: If he approve he shall sign it, but if not he shall return it, with his Objections to that House in which it shall have originated, who shall enter the Objections at large on their Journal, and proceed to reconsider it. If after such Reconsideration two thirds of that House shall agree to pass the Bill, it shall be sent, together with the Objections, to the other House, by which it shall likewise be reconsidered, and if approved by two thirds of that House, it shall become a Law. But in all such Cases the Votes of both Houses shall be determined by yeas and Nays, and the Names of the Persons voting for and against the Bill shall be entered on the Journal of each House respectively. If any Bill shall not be returned by the President within ten Days (Sundays excepted) after it shall have been presented to him, the Same shall be a Law, in like Manner as if he had signed it, unless the Congress by their Adjournment prevent its Return, in which Case it shall not be Law.

[3]Every Order, Resolution, or Vote to which the Concurrence of the Senate and House of Representatives may be necessary (except on a question of Adjournment) shall be presented to the President of the United States; and before the Same shall take Effect, shall be approved by him, or being disapproved by him, shall be repassed by two thirds of the Senate and House of Representatives, according to the Rules and Limitations prescribed in the Case of a Bill.

Section 8. [1]The Congress shall have Power To lay and collect Taxes, Duties, Imposts and Excises, to pay the Debts and provide for the common Defence and general Welfare of the United States; but all Duties, Imposts and Excises shall be uniform throughout the United States;

[2]To borrow Money on the credit of the United States;

[3]To regulate Commerce with foreign Nations, and among the several States, and with the Indian Tribes;

[4]To establish an uniform Rule of Naturalization, and uniform Laws on the subject of Bankruptcies throughout the United States;

[5]To coin Money, regulate the Value thereof and of foreign Coin, and fix the Standard of Weights and Measures;

[6]To provide for the Punishment of counterfeiting the Securities and current Coin of the United States;

[7]To establish Post Offices and post Roads;

[8]To promote the Progress of Science and useful Arts, by securing for limited Times to Authors and Inventors the exclusive Right to their respective Writings and Discoveries;

[9]To constitute Tribunals inferior to the supreme Court;

[10]To define and punish Piracies and Felonies committed on the high Seas, and Offences against the Law of Nations;

[11]To declare War, grant Letters of Marque and Reprisal, and make Rules concerning Captures on Land and Water;

[12]To raise and support Armies, but no Appropriation of Money to that Use shall be for a longer Term than two Years;

[13]To provide and maintain a Navy;

[14]To make Rules for the Government and Regulation of the land and naval Forces;

[15]To provide for calling forth the Militia to execute the Laws of the Union, suppress Insurrections and repel Invasions;

[16]To provide for organizing, arming, and disciplining, the Militia, and for governing such Part of them as may be employed in the Service of the United States, reserving to the States respectively, the Appointment of the Officers, and the Authority of training the Militia according to the discipline prescribed by Congress;

[17]To exercise exclusive Legislation in all Cases whatsoever, over such District (not exceeding ten Miles square) as may, by Cession of particular States, and the Acceptance of Congress, become the Seat of the Government of the United States, and to exercise like Authority over all Places purchased by the Consent of the Legislature of the State in which the Same shall be, for the Erection of Forts, Magazines, Arsenals, dock-Yards, and other needful Buildings; –And

[18]To make all Laws which shall be necessary and proper for carrying into Execution the foregoing Powers, and all other Powers vested by this Constitution in the Government of the United States, or in any Department or Officer thereof.

Section 9. [1]The Migration or Importation of such Persons as any of the States now existing shall think proper to admit, shall not be prohibited by the Congress prior to the Year one thousand eight hundred and eight, but a Tax or duty may be imposed on such Importation, not exceeding ten dollars for each Person.

[2]The Privilege of the Writ of Habeas Corpus shall not be suspended, unless when in Cases of Rebellion or Invasion the public Safety may require it.

[3]No Bill of Attainder or ex post facto Law shall be passed.

[4]No Capitation, or other direct, Tax shall be laid, unless in Proportion to the Census or Enumeration herein before directed to be taken.

[5]No Tax or Duty shall be laid on Articles exported from any State.

[6]No Preference shall be given by any Regulation of Commerce or Revenue to the Ports of one State over those of another; nor shall Vessels bound to, or from, one State, be obliged to enter, clear, or pay Duties in another.

[7]No Money shall be drawn from the Treasury, but in Consequence of Appropriations made by Law; and a regular Statement and Account of the Receipts and Expenditures of all public Money shall be published from time to time.

[8]No Title of Nobility shall be granted by the United States: And no Person holding any Office of Profit or Trust under them, shall, without the Consent of the Congress, accept of any present, Emolument, Office, or Title, of any kind whatever, from any King, Prince, or foreign State.

Section 10. [1]No State shall enter into any Treaty, Alliance, or Confederation; grant Letters of Marque and Reprisal; coin Money; emit Bills of Credit; make any Thing but gold and silver Coin a Tender in Payment of Debts; pass any Bill of Attainder, ex post facto Law, or Law impairing the Obligation of Contracts, or grant any Title of Nobility.

[2]No State shall, without the Consent of the Congress, lay any Imposts or Duties on Imports or Exports, except what may be absolutely necessary for executing its inspection Laws: and the net Produce of all Duties and Imposts, laid by any State on Imports or Exports, shall be for the Use of the Treasury of the United States; and all such Laws shall be subject to the Revision and Controul of the Congress.

[3]No State shall, without the Consent of Congress, lay any Duty of Tonnage, keep Troops, or Ships of War in time of Peace, enter into any Agreement or Compact with

another State, or with a foreign Power, or engage in War, unless actually invaded, or in such imminent Danger as will not admit of delay.

ARTICLE II

Section 1. [1]The executive Power shall be vested in a President of the United States of America. He shall hold his Office during the Term of four Years, and, together with the Vice President, chosen for the same Term, be elected, as follows:

[2]Each State shall appoint, in such Manner as the Legislature thereof may direct, a Number of Electors, equal to the whole Number of Senators and Representatives to which the State may be entitled in the Congress: but no Senator or Representative, or Person holding an Office of Trust or Profit under the United States, shall be appointed an Elector.

[3] [Superseded by Twelfth Amendment.]

[4]The Congress may determine the Time of chusing the Electors, and the Day on which they shall give their Votes; which Day shall be the same throughout the United States.

[5]No Person except a natural born Citizen, or a Citizen of the United States, at the time of the Adoption of this Constitution, shall be eligible to the Office of President; neither shall any Person be eligible to that Office who shall not have attained to the Age of thirty five Years, and been fourteen Years a Resident within the United States.

[6]In Case of the Removal of the President from Office, or of his Death, Resignation, or Inability to discharge the Powers and Duties of the said Office, the Same shall devolve on the Vice President, and the Congress may by Law provide for the Case of Removal, Death, Resignation or Inability, both of the President and Vice President, declaring what Officer shall then act as President, and such Officer shall act accordingly, until the Disability be removed, or a President shall be elected.

[7]The President shall, at stated Times, receive for his Services, a Compensation, which shall neither be increased nor diminished during the Period for which he shall have been elected, and he shall not receive within that Period any other Emolument from the United States, or any of them.

[8]Before he enter on the Execution of his Office, he shall take the following Oath or Affirmation: "I do solemnly swear (or affirm) that I will faithfully execute the Office of President of the United States, and will to the best of my Ability, preserve, protect and defend the Constitution of the United States."

Section 2. [1]The President shall be Commander in Chief of the Army and Navy of the United States, and of the Militia of the several States, when called into the actual Service of the United States; he may require the Opinion, in writing, of the principal Officer in each of the executive Departments, upon any Subject relating to the Duties of their respective Offices, and he shall have Power to grant Reprieves and Pardons for Offences against the United States, except in Cases of Impeachment.

[2]He shall have Power, by and with the Advice and Consent of the Senate, to make Treaties, provided two thirds of the Senators present concur; and he shall nominate, and by and with the Advice and Consent of the Senate, shall appoint Ambassadors, other public Ministers and Consuls, Judges of the supreme Court, and all other Officers of the United States, whose Appointments are not herein otherwise provided for, and which shall be established by Law: but the Congress may by Law vest the Appointment of such inferior Officers, as they think proper, in the President alone, in the Courts of Law, or in the Heads of Departments.

[3]The President shall have Power to fill up all Vacancies that may happen during the Recess of the Senate, by granting Commissions which shall expire at the End of their next Session.

Section 3. He shall from time to time give to the Congress Information of the State of the Union, and recommend to their Consideration such Measures as he shall judge necessary and expedient; he may, on extraordinary Occasions, convene both Houses, or either of them, and in Case of Disagreement between them, with Respect to the Time of Adjournment, he may adjourn them to such Time as he shall think proper; he shall receive Ambassadors and other public Ministers; he shall take Care that the Laws be faithfully executed, and shall Commission all the Officers of the United States.

Section 4. The President, Vice President and all civil Officers of the United States, shall be removed from Office on Impeachment for, and Conviction of, Treason, Bribery, or other high Crimes and Misdemeanors.

ARTICLE III

Section 1. The judicial Power of the United States shall be vested in one supreme Court, and in such inferior Courts as the Congress may from time to time ordain and establish. The Judges, both of the supreme and inferior Courts, shall hold their Offices during good Behaviour, and shall, at stated Times, receive for their Services a Compensation, which shall not be diminished during their Continuance in Office.

Section 2. [1]The judicial Power shall extend to all Cases, in Law and Equity, arising under this Constitution, the Laws of the United States, and Treaties made, or which shall be made, under their Authority; to all Cases affecting Ambassadors, other public Ministers and Consuls; to all Cases of admiralty and maritime Jurisdiction; to Controversies to which the United States shall be a Party; to Controversies between two or more States; between a State and Citizens of another State; between Citizens of different States; between Citizens of the same State claiming Lands under Grants of different States, and between a State, or the Citizens thereof, and foreign States, Citizens or Subjects.

[2]In all Cases affecting Ambassadors, other public Ministers and Consuls, and those in which a State shall be Party, the supreme Court shall have original Jurisdiction. In all the other Cases before mentioned, the supreme Court shall have appellate Jurisdiction, both as to Law and Fact, with such Exceptions, and under such Regulations as the Congress shall make.

[3]The Trial of all Crimes, except in Cases of Impeachment, shall be by Jury; and such Trial shall be held in the State where the said Crimes shall have been committed; but when not committed within any State, the Trial shall be at such Place or Places as the Congress may by Law have directed.

Section 3. [1]Treason against the United States, shall consist only in levying War against them, or in adhering to their Enemies, giving them Aid and Comfort. No Person shall be convicted of Treason unless on the Testimony of two Witnesses to the same overt Act, or on Confession in open Court.

[2]The Congress shall have Power to declare the Punishment of Treason, but no Attainder of Treason shall work Corruption of Blood, or Forfeiture except during the Life of the Person attainted.

ARTICLE IV

Section 1. Full Faith and Credit shall be given in each State to the public Acts, Records, and judicial Proceedings of every other State. And the Congress may by general Laws prescribe the Manner in which such Acts, Records and Proceedings shall be proved, and the Effect thereof.

Section 2. [1]The Citizens of each State shall be entitled to all Privileges and Immunities of Citizens in the several States.

[2]A person charged in any State with Treason, Felony, or other Crime, who shall flee from Justice and be found in another State, shall on Demand of the executive Authority of the State from which he fled, be delivered up, to be removed to the State having Jurisdiction of the Crime.

[3]No Person held to Service or Labour in one State, under the Laws thereof, escaping into another, shall, in Consequence of any Law or Regulation therein, be discharged from such Service or Labour, but shall be delivered up on Claim of the Party to whom such Service or Labour may be due.

Section 3. [1]New States may be admitted by the Congress into this Union; but no new State shall be formed or erected within the Jurisdiction of any other State; nor any State be formed by the Junction of two or more States, or Parts of States, without the Consent of the Legislatures of the States concerned as well as of the Congress.

[2]The Congress shall have power to dispose of and make all needful Rules and Regulations respecting the Territory or other Property belonging to the United States; and nothing in this Constitution shall be so construed as to Prejudice any Claims of the United States, or of any particular State.

Section 4. The United States shall guarantee to every State in this Union a Republican Form of Government, and shall protect each of them against Invasion; and on Application of the Legislature, or of the Executive (when the Legislature cannot be convened), against domestic Violence.

ARTICLE V

The Congress, whenever two thirds of both Houses shall deem it necessary, shall propose Amendments to this Constitution, or, on the Application of the Legislatures of two thirds of the several States, shall call a Convention for proposing Amendments, which, in either Case, shall be valid to all Intents and Purposes, as Part of this Constitution, when ratified by the Legislatures of three fourths of the several States, or by Conventions in three fourths thereof, as the one or the other Mode of Ratification may be proposed by the Congress; Provided that no Amendment which may be made prior to the Year One thousand eight hundred and eight shall in any Manner affect the first and fourth Clauses in the Ninth Section of the first Article; and that no State, without its Consent, shall be deprived of its equal Suffrage in the Senate.

ARTICLE VI

[1]All Debts contracted and Engagements entered into, before the Adoption of this Constitution, shall be as valid against the United States under this Constitution, as under the Confederation.

[2]This Constitution, and the Laws of the United States which shall be made in Pursuance thereof; and all Treaties made, or which shall be made, under the Authority of the United States, shall be the supreme Law of the Land; and the Judges in every

State shall be bound thereby, any Thing in the Constitution or Laws of any State to the Contrary notwithstanding.

[3]The Senators and Representatives before mentioned, and the Members of the several State Legislatures, and all executive and judicial Officers, both of the United States and of the several States, shall be bound by Oath or Affirmation, to support this Constitution; but no religious Test shall ever be required as a Qualification to any Office or public Trust under the United States.

ARTICLE VII

The Ratification of the Conventions of nine States, shall be sufficient for the Establishment of this Constitution between the States so ratifying the Same.

AMENDMENT I

Congress shall make no law respecting an establishment of religion, or prohibiting the flee exercise thereof; or abridging the freedom of speech, or of the press; or the right of the people peaceably to assemble, and to petition the Government for a redress of grievances.

AMENDMENT II

A well regulated Militia, being necessary to the security of a free State, the right of the people to keep and bear Arms, shall not be infringed.

AMENDMENT III

No Soldier shall, in time of peace be quartered in any house, without the consent of the Owner, nor in time of war, but in a manner to be prescribed by law.

AMENDMENT IV

The right of the people to be secure in their persons, houses, papers, and effects, against unreasonable searches and seizures, shall not be violated, and no Warrants shall issue, but upon probable cause, supported by Oath or affirmation, and particularly describing the place to be searched, and the persons or things to be seized.

AMENDMENT V

No person shall be held to answer for a capital, or otherwise infamous crime, unless on a presentment or indictment of a Grand Jury, except in cases arising in the land or naval forces, or in the Militia, when in actual service in time of War or public danger; nor shall any person be subject for the same offence to be twice put in jeopardy of life or limb; nor shall be compelled in any criminal case to be a witness against himself, nor be deprived of life, liberty, or property, without due process of law; nor shall private property be taken for public use, without just compensation.

AMENDMENT VI

In all criminal prosecutions, the accused shall enjoy the right to a speedy and public trial, by an impartial jury of the State and district wherein the crime shall have been committed, which district shall have been previously ascertained by law, and to be informed of the nature and cause of the accusation; to be confronted with the witnesses against him; to have compulsory process for obtaining witnesses in his favor, and to have the assistance of counsel for his defence.

AMENDMENT VII

In Suits at common law, where the value in controversy shall exceed twenty dollars, the right of trial by jury shall be preserved, and no fact tried by a jury, shall be otherwise re-examined in any Court of the United States, than according to the rules of the common law.

AMENDMENT VIII

Excessive bail shall not be required, nor excessive fines imposed, nor cruel and unusual punishments inflicted.

AMENDMENT IX

The enumeration in the Constitution, of certain rights, shall not be construed to deny or disparage others retained by the people.

AMENDMENT X

The powers not delegated to the United States by the Constitution, nor prohibited by it to the States, are reserved to the States respectively, or to the people.

AMENDMENT XI

The Judicial power of the United States shall not be construed to extend to any suit in law or equity, commenced or prosecuted against one of the United States by Citizens of another State, or by Citizens or Subjects of any Foreign State.

AMENDMENT XII

The Electors shall meet in their respective states and vote by ballot for President and Vice-President, one of whom, at least, shall not be an inhabitant of the same state with themselves; they shall name in their ballots the person voted for as President, and in distinct ballots the person voted for as Vice-President, and they shall make distinct lists of all persons voted for as President, and of all persons voted for as Vice-President, and of the number of votes for each, which lists they shall sign and certify, and transmit sealed to the seat of the government of the United States, directed to the President of the Senate; the President of the Senate shall, in the presence of the Senate and House of Representatives, open all the certificates and the votes shall then be counted; The person having the greatest number of votes for President, shall be the President, if such number be a majority of the whole number of Electors appointed; and if no person have such majority, then from the persons having the highest numbers not exceeding three on the list of those voted for as President, the House of Representatives shall choose immediately, by ballot, the President. But in choosing the President, the votes shall be taken by states, the representation from each state having one vote; a quorum for this purpose shall consist of a member or members from two-thirds of the states, and a majority of all the states shall be necessary to a choice. And if the House of Representatives shall not choose a President whenever the right of choice shall devolve upon them, before the fourth day of March next following, then the Vice-President shall act as President, as in case of the death or other constitutional disability of the President. The person having the greatest number of votes as Vice-President, shall be the Vice-President, if such number be a majority of the whole number of Electors appointed, and if no person have a majority, then from the two highest numbers on the list, the Senate shall choose the Vice-President; a quorum for the purpose shall consist of two-thirds of the whole number of Senators, and a majority of the whole number shall be necessary to a choice. But no person constitutionally ineligible to the office of President shall be eligible to that of Vice-President of the United States.

AMENDMENT XIII

Section 1. Neither slavery nor involuntary servitude, except as a punishment for crime whereof the party shall have been duly convicted, shall exist within the United States, or any place subject to their jurisdiction.

Section 2. Congress shall have power to enforce this article by appropriate legislation.

AMENDMENT XIV

Section 1. All persons born or naturalized in the United States, and subject to the jurisdiction thereof, are citizens of the United States and of the State wherein they reside. No State shall make or enforce any law which shall abridge the privileges or immunities of citizens of the United States; nor shall any State deprive any person of life, liberty, or property, without due process of law; nor deny to any person within its jurisdiction the equal protection of the laws.

Section 2. Representatives shall be apportioned among the several States according to their respective numbers, counting the whole number of persons in each State, excluding Indians not taxed. But when the right to vote at any election for the choice of electors for President and Vice-President of the United States, Representatives in Congress, the Executive and Judicial officers of a State, or the members of the Legislature thereof, is denied to any of the male inhabitants of such State, being twenty-one years of age, and citizens of the United States, or in any way abridged, except for participation in rebellion, or other crime, the basis of representation therein shall be reduced in the proportion which the number of such male citizens shall bear to the whole number of male citizens twenty-one years of age in such State.

Section 3. No person shall be a Senator or Representative in Congress, or elector of President and Vice President, or hold any office, civil or military, under the United States, or under any State, who, having previously taken an oath, as a member of Congress, or as an officer of the United States, or as a member of any State legislature, or as an executive or judicial officer of any State, to support the Constitution of the United States, shall have engaged in insurrection or rebellion against the same, or given aid or comfort to the enemies thereof. But Congress may by a vote of two-thirds of each House, remove such disability.

Section 4. The validity of the public debt of the United States, authorized by law, including debts incurred for payment of pensions and bounties for services in suppressing insurrection or rebellion, shall not be questioned. But neither the United States nor any State shall assume or pay any debt or obligation incurred in aid of insurrection or rebellion against the United States, or any claim for the loss or emancipation of any slave; but all such debts, obligations and claims shall be held illegal and void.

Section 5. The Congress shall have the power to enforce, by appropriate legislation, the provisions of this article.

AMENDMENT XV

Section 1. The right of citizens of the United States to vote shall not be denied or abridged by the United States or by any State on account of race, color, or previous condition of servitude.

Section 2. The Congress shall have the power to enforce this article by appropriate legislation.

AMENDMENT XVI

The Congress shall have power to lay and collect taxes on incomes, from whatever source derived, without apportionment among the several States, and without regard to any census or enumeration.

AMENDMENT XVII

[1]The Senate of the United States shall be composed of two Senators from each State, elected by the people thereof, for six years; and each Senator shall have one vote. The electors in each State shall have the qualifications requisite for electors of the most numerous branch of the State legislatures.

[2]When vacancies happen in the representation of any State in the Senate, the executive authority of such State shall issue writs of election to fill such vacancies: *Provided,* That the legislature of any State may empower the executive thereof to make temporary appointments until the people fill the vacancies by election as the legislature may direct.

[3]This amendment shall not be so construed as to affect the election or term of any Senator chosen before it becomes valid as part of the Constitution.

AMENDMENT XVIII

Prohibition of Liquor [Repealed]

AMENDMENT XIX

[1]The right of citizens of the United States to vote shall not be denied or abridged by the United States or by any State on account of sex.

[2]Congress shall have power to enforce this article by appropriate legislation.

AMENDMENT XX

Section 1. The terms of the President and Vice President shall end at noon on the 20th day of January, and the terms of Senators and Representatives at noon on the 3d day of January, of the years in which such terms would have ended if this article had not been ratified; and the terms of their successors shall then begin.

Section 2. The Congress shall assemble at least once in every year, and such meeting shall begin at noon on the 3d day of January, unless they shall by law appoint a different day.

Section 3. If, at the time fixed for the beginning of the term of the President, the President elect shall have died, the Vice President elect shall become President. If a President shall not have been chosen before the time fixed for the beginning of his term, or if the President elect shall have failed to qualify, then the Vice President elect shall act as President until a President shall have qualified; and the Congress may by law provide for the case wherein neither a President elect nor a Vice President shall have qualified, declaring who shall then act as President, or the manner in which one who is to act shall be selected, and such person shall act accordingly until a President or Vice President shall have qualified.

Section 4. The Congress may by law provide for the case of the death of any of the persons from whom the House of Representatives may choose a President whenever the right of choice shall have devolved upon them, and for the case of the death of any of the persons from whom the Senate may choose a Vice President whenever the right of choice shall have devolved upon them.

Section 5. Sections l and 2 shall take effect on the 15th day of October following the ratification of this article.

Section 6. This article shall be inoperative unless it shall have been ratified as an amendment to the Constitution by the legislatures of three-fourths of the several States within seven years from the date of its submission.

AMENDMENT XXI

Section 1. The eighteenth article of amendment to the Constitution of the United States is hereby repealed.

Section 2. The transportation or importation into any State, Territory, or Possession of the United States for delivery or use therein of intoxicating liquors, in violation of the laws thereof, is hereby prohibited.

Section 3. This article shall be inoperative unless it shall have been ratified as an amendment to the Constitution by conventions in the several States, as provided in the Constitution, within seven years from the date of the submission hereof to the States by the Congress.

AMENDMENT XXII

Section 1. No person shall be elected to the office of the President more than twice, and no person who has held the office of President, or acted as President, for more than two years of a term to which some other person was elected President shall be elected to the office of President more than once. But this Article shall not apply to any person holding the office of President when this Article was proposed by Congress, and shall not prevent any person who may be holding the office of President, or acting as President, during the term within which this Article becomes operative from holding the office of President or acting as President during the remainder of such term.

Section 2. This article shall be inoperative unless it shall have been ratified as an amendment to the Constitution by the legislatures of three-fourths of the several States within seven years from the date of its submission to the States by the Congress.

AMENDMENT XXIII

Section 1. The District constituting the seat of Government of the United States shall appoint in such manner as Congress may direct:

A number of electors of President and Vice President equal to the whole number of Senators and Representatives in Congress to which the District would be entitled if it were a State, but in no event more than the least populous State; they shall be in addition to those appointed by the States, but they shall be considered, for the purposes of the election of President and Vice President, to be electors appointed by a State; and they shall meet in the District and perform such duties as provided by the twelfth article of amendment.

Section 2. The Congress shall have power to enforce this article by appropriate legislation.

AMENDMENT XXIV

Section 1. The right of citizens of the United States to vote in any primary or other election for President or Vice President, for electors for President or Vice President, or for Senator or Representative in Congress, shall not be denied or abridged by the United States or any State by reason of failure to pay poll tax or other tax.

Section 2. The Congress shall have power to enforce this article by appropriate legislation.

AMENDMENT XXV

Section 1. In case of the removal of the President from office or of his death or resignation, the Vice President shall become President.

Section 2. Whenever there is a vacancy in the office of the Vice President, the President shall nominate a Vice President who shall take office upon confirmation by a majority vote of both Houses of Congress.

Section 3. Whenever the President transmits to the President pro tempore of the Senate and the Speaker of the House of Representatives his written declaration that he is unable to discharge the powers and duties of his office and until he transmits to them a written declaration to the contrary, such powers and duties shall be discharged by the Vice President as Acting President.

Section 4. Whenever the Vice President and a majority of either the principal officers of the executive departments or of such other body as Congress may by law provide, transmit to the President pro tempore of the Senate and the Speaker of the House of Representatives their written declaration that the President is unable to discharge the powers and duties of his office, the Vice President shall immediately assume the powers and duties of the office as Acting President.

Thereafter, when the President transmits to the President pro tempore of the Senate and the Speaker of the House of Representatives his written declaration that no inability exists, he shall resume the powers and duties of his office unless the Vice President and a majority of either the principal officers of the executive department or of such other body as Congress may by law provide, transmit within four days to the President pro tempore of the Senate and the Speaker of the House of Representatives their written declaration that the President is unable to discharge the powers and duties of his office. Thereupon Congress shall decide the issue, assembling within forty-eight hours for that purpose if not in session. If the Congress, within twenty-one days after receipt of the latter written declaration, or, if Congress is not in session, within twenty-one days after Congress is required to assemble, determines by two-thirds vote of both Houses that the President is unable to discharge the powers and duties of his office, the Vice President shall continue to discharge the same as Acting President; otherwise, the President shall resume the powers and duties of his office.

AMENDMENT XXVI

Section 1. The right of citizens of the United States, who are eighteen years of age or older, to vote shall not be denied or abridged by the United States or by any State on account of age.

Section 2. The Congress shall have power to enforce this article by appropriate legislation.

AMENDMENT XXVII

No law, varying the compensation for the services of the Senators and Representatives, shall take effect, until an election of Representatives shall have intervened.

GLOSSARY

Actual malice A standard requiring a public official or public figure suing for defamation to demonstrate that an alleged falsehood was made with knowledge that it was untrue or with reckless disregard of the truth.

Affirmative action Governmental action that establishes a preference for a traditionally disadvantaged group, typically on the basis of race or gender, to compensate for past discrimination or to achieve diversification of an institution or program.

Association The constitutionally protected ability to organize and interact with other persons for purposes of facilitating expressive freedom and aims. The right of association is not specifically mentioned by the First Amendment, but the Supreme Court has determined that it is essential to the facilitation and exercise of freedom of speech.

Commercial speech Expression that pertains to the economic interests of the speaker and audience or invites an economic transaction.

Concurring opinion An opinion by one or more justices that agrees with the judgment of the Court but offers separate reasons in support of that outcome.

De facto segregation A condition of segregation that is attributable to factors other than the law and not constitutionally significant.

Defamation A false statement that injures a person's reputation either by slander (the spoken word) or libel (the published word).

De jure segregation A condition of segregation that intentionally was created by law and is illegal.

Dissenting opinion An opinion disagreeing with the Court's judgment and typically its reasoning.

Dormant commerce clause A reference to Congress's power under Article I, Section 8[3], which, even if not used to enact a law, may preclude states from regulating in ways that burden interstate commerce or discriminate on the basis of a product's or service's place of origin.

Due process A guarantee secured by the Fifth and Fourteenth Amendments that, respectively, applies to federal and state governments. The due process originally was understood as an assurance that government, through the judicial process, could not deprive an individual of life, liberty, or property without fair procedures. Such fairness consists at a minimum of notice and a hearing. Contrasting with procedural due process is the concept of substantive due process, which is a product of case law that has developed since the mid-nineteenth century. Substantive due process review is typified by the judiciary's identification of a fundamental right that it reads into the due process clause and uses as a basis for striking down legislation.

Equal protection A guarantee secured by the Fourteenth Amendment that generally prohibits classification of or discrimination against persons on the basis of a particular group status. As interpreted, the equal protection clause is particularly intolerant of distinctions on the basis of race. Officially imposed burdens on the basis of gender, alienage, and illegitimacy also have been carefully reviewed and often found unconstitutional.

Establishment Government aid to, support of, or preference for a particular religion or religion generally. Such action or policy violates the First Amendment.

Executive privilege A protection extended to communications within the executive branch that is recognized for purposes of ensuring full and frank discussion of policy alternatives.

***Ex post facto* law** A law that retroactively punishes or penalizes an individual. Article I, Sections 9 and 10, prohibits enactment of criminal laws that operative retroactively.

Federalism A principle that requires accommodation of state policies, which may differ from those of the national government and other states, unless they conflict with a constitutional power or prohibition or a valid federal law. This concept responds to and respects the diversity and sovereignty of states within the national union.

Fighting words Expressions that by their very utterance inflict injury or tend to incite an immediate breach of the peace. Fighting words are assigned slight value and, although viewed as a very narrow class of speech, are excluded from the protective scope of the First Amendment.

***In camera* review** Judicial proceedings, such as the review of documents claimed to be privileged, in private session.

Injunction A court order requiring performance of a particular act or, more typically, prohibiting a person from engaging in a specified activity. Violation of an injunction may result in a contempt citation.

Judicial Review The power of the judiciary to determine the constitutionality of laws enacted or actions taken by the legislative or executive branches of federal or state governments.

Natural law A theory of law grounded in the premise that basic rights and freedoms exist that are fundamental to human nature, even if not constitutionally enumerated, and the judiciary may refer to them as a basis for striking down legislation.

Necessary and proper A standard, set forth in Article I, Section 8, of the Constitution, enabling Congress to enact all laws that are reasonably necessary to achieve an enumerated constitutional power. So long as the legislative objective is legitimate and within the scope of the Constitution, means that are appropriate, plainly adapted toward that end, and consistent with the letter and spirit of the Constitution are permissible.

Obscenity Sexually explicit expression that fails to meet specific state and community standards of acceptability and thus is not protected by the First Amendment.

Overbreadth   A status defining a law that regulates so indiscriminately that it reaches constitutionally protected activity in addition to whatever legitimate focus it may have.

Parens patriae   The interest of government in regulating to account for the well being of children that operates as a basis, among other things, for a diminished level of constitutional freedoms for minors.

Penumbra   A zone, extension, or radiation of an enumerated constitutional right or liberty, or collection thereof, which houses a right or freedom that although not specified by the Bill of Rights is found to be fundamental.

Police power   The authority of states to regulate matters of local concern, such as health, safety, and morality. This power preceded the framing and ratification of the Constitution and was reaffirmed by the Tenth Amendment.

Per curiam   An opinion authored by the entire court rather than under the name of a particular judge or justice.

Plurality opinion   An opinion that attracts support from more than one justice but falls short of a majority.

Preemption   The displacement of state regulation by federal law when the former undermines congressional objectives.

Prior restraint   A system of official censorship or prepublication review that prohibits expression, unlike a system of subsequent punishment that imposes penalties for speech that generates a legal claim.

Privileges and immunities   Rights and protections afforded to citizens by government. Article IV, Section 2, of the Constitution requires states to treat residents and nonresidents similarly, absent a persuasive justification, with respect to interests that are essential to a viable national union. The Fourteenth Amendment secures the privileges and immunities of national citizenship, which do not include the Bill of Rights.

Public figure   A person who, because of pervasive fame or notoriety or having injected himself or herself into a public controversy in an attempt to influence the outcome, must prove actual malice to recover in a defamation action.

Separate but equal   The doctrinal premise of official segregation that, in theory, required provision for and maintenance of racially separate facilities, programs, accommodations, and services. This system of racial management was established in the late nineteenth century, upheld in *Plessy v. Ferguson* (1896), and began to crumble when the Supreme Court declared official segregation of public schools "inherently unequal" and thus unconstitutional in *Brown v. Board of Education* (1954).

Stare decisis   A doctrine requiring courts to follow principles of law that have been established in preceding cases that are factually similar, even if a different result might be achieved if the issue was being heard for the first time. This policy accounts for society's interest in the law's certainty and predictability, and may be departed from when overriding considerations are identified.

Subpoena duces tecum   A judicial order requesting production of documents and other materials that must be complied with unless successfully resisted on grounds of privilege or some other legal basis.

Suspect classification   The official categorization of persons on the basis of a trait, such as race or gender, that suggests an invidious and unconstitutional motive. Judicial review of such classifications thus is characterized by searching inquiry.

Symbolic speech   Expression that communicates a point of view in a nonverbal way, typically through the use of symbols or by action.

Vagueness   The state of a law that is not precise enough to provide adequate notice of the activity that is regulated or subject to prohibition.

GENERAL BIBLIOGRAPHY

Adler, Amy. *Girls! Girls! Girls! The Supreme Court Confronts the G-String*, 80 *New York University Law Review* 1108 (2005).

Adler, Jonathan A. *Waste and the Dormant Commerce Clause–A Reply*, 3 Green Bag 353 (2000).

Alley, Robert S., ed. *James Madison on Religious Liberty*. Buffalo, NY: Prometheus Books, 1985.

Alschuler, Albert W. *Constraint Confession, Symposium on Coercion: An Interdisciplinary Examination of Coercion, Exploitation and the Law*, 74 *Denver University Law Review* 957 (1997).

Ammeter, April Leigh. *Kuhlman v. Wilson: "Passive" and "Active" Government Informants, a Problematic Test*, 72 *Iowa Law Review* 1423 (1987).

Arcila, Fabio, Jr. *Special Needs and Special Deference: Suspicionless Civil Searches in the Modern Regulatory State*, 56 *Administrative Law Review* 1223 (2004).

Baker, C. Edwin. *Advertising and a Democratic Press*. Princeton, NJ: Princeton University Press, 1994.

Baker, C. Edwin. *Scope of the First Amendment Freedom of Speech*, 25 *UCLA Law Review* 964 (1978).

Beery, Ryan H. *Modern Use of Military Tribunals: A Legal "Can" and a Political "Should"?* 28 *Ohio Northern University Law Review* 789 (2002).

Bell, Jeannine. *O Say Can You See: Free Expression by the Light of Fiery Crosses*, 39 *Harvard Civil Rights-Civil. Liberties Law Review* 335 (2004).

Bennett, Fred Warren. *From Sorrells to Jacobson: Reflections on Six Decades of Entrapment Law, and Related Defenses, in Federal Court*, 27 *Wake Forest Law Review* 829 (1992).

Berger, Mark. *Taking the Fifth*. Lexington, MA: Lexington Books, 1980.

Berger, Raoul. *Executive Privilege: A Constitutional Myth*. Cambridge, MA: Harvard University Press, 1974.

Berkowitz, Peter. *Terrorism, the Laws of War, and the Constitution: Debating the Enemy Combatant Cases*. Stanford, CA: Hoover Institution, 2005.

Bernabe-Riefkohl, Alberto. *Another Attempt to Solve the Prior Restraint Mystery: Applying the Nebraska Press Standard to Media Disclosure Attorney-Client Communications*, 18 *Cardozo Arts and Entertainment Law Journal* 307 (2000).

Blanchard, Dallas. *The Anti-Abortion Movement and the Rise of the Religious Right: From Polite to Fiery Protest*. New York: Maxwell Macmillan, 1994.

Bloom, Robert M. *United States v. Leon and its Ramifications*, 56 *University of Colorado Law Review* 247 (1985).

Bollinger, Lee. *The Tolerant Society*. New York: Oxford University Press, 1986.

Bork, Robert H. *The Tempting of America*. New York: Free Press, 1990.

Brandeis, Louis D., and Samuel D. Warren. *The Right to Privacy*, 4 *Harvard Law Review* 193 (1890).

Brennan, William, Jr. *State Constitutions and the Protection of Individual Rights*, 90 *Harvard Law Review* 489 (1977).

Brenner, Daniel. *Cable Television and the Freedom of Expression*, 1988 *Duke Law Journal* 329 (1988).

Brest, Paul. *Palmer v. Thompson: An Approach to the Problem of Unconstitutional Legislative Motive*, 1971 *Supreme Court Review* 95 (1971).

Brody, Steven I. *Rethinking Regulatory Takings: A View Toward a Comprehensive Analysis*, 8 *Northern Illinois University Law Review* 113 (1987).

Brownmiller, Susan. *Against Our Will: Men, Women and Rape.* New York: Simon and Schuster, 1976.

Carter, Stephen L. *From Sick Children to Synar: The Evolution and Subsequent De-Evolution of the Separation of Powers,* 1987 *Brigham Young University Law Review* 719 (1987).

Carter, Stephen L. *Reflections of an Affirmative Action Baby.* New York: BasicBooks, 1991.

Caughlan, Susan G. *Private Possession of Child Pornography: The Tensions Between Stanley v. Georgia and New York v. Ferber,* 29 *William and Mary Law Review* 187 (1987).

Chafee, Zechariah. *Government and Mass Communications.* Chicago: University of Chicago Press, 1947.

Chemerinsky, Erwin. *The Deconstitutionalization of Education,* 36 *Loyola University of Chicago Law Journal* (2004).

Chipchase, Calvert G. *From Grand Central to the Sierras: What Do We Do with Investment-Backed Expectations in Partial Regulatory Takings?* 23 *Virginia Environmental Law Journal* 43 (2004).

Choper, Jesse H. *The Free Exercise Clause: A Structural Overview and an Appraisal of Recent Developments,* 27 *William and Mary Law Review* (1986).

Choper, Jesse H. *The Religion Clauses of the First Amendment: Reconciling the Conflict,* 41 *University Pittsburgh Law Review* 673 (1980).

Colker, Ruth. *Anti-Subordination Above All: Sex, Race and Equal Protection,* 61 *New York University Law Review* 1003 (1986).

Coons, John, William Clune, and Stephen Sugarman. *Private Wealth and Public Education.* Cambridge, MA: Belknap Press, 1970.

Cox, Archibald. *Executive Privilege,* 122 *University of Pennsylvania Law Review* 1383 (1974).

Craig, Tracy S. *Abortion Protest: Lawless Conspiracy or Protected Free Speech?* 72 *Denver University Law Review* 445 (1995).

Days, Drew. *Fullilove,* 96 *Yale Law Journal* 453 (1987).

De Figueiredo, John M., and Elizabeth Garrett, *Paying for Politics,* 78 *Southern California Law Review* (2005).

de Sola Pool, Ithiel. *Technologies of Freedom.* Cambridge, MA: Belknap Press, 1983.

Devlin, Patrick. *The Enforcement of Morals.* New York: Oxford University Press, 1965.

Drake, St. Clair, and Horace R. Clayton. *Black Metropolis.* New York: Harper and Row, 1945.

Dworkin, Ronald. *Life's Dominion.* New York: Knopf, 1993.

Ely, John Hart. *The Constitutionality of Reverse Discrimination,* 41 *University of Chicago Law Review* 723 (1974).

Ely, John Hart. *Democracy and Distrust: A Theory of Judicial Review.* Cambridge, MA: Harvard University Press, 1980.

Emery, Edward. *The Press and America.* Englewood Cliffs, NJ: Prentice-Hall, 1962.

Engel, Kirsten. *Reconsidering the National Market in Solid Waste: Trade-Offs in Equity, Efficiency, Environmental Protection and State Autonomy,* 73 *North Carolina Law Review* 1481 (1995).

Epstein, Richard A. *Was New York Times v. Sullivan Wrong?* 53 *University of Chicago Law Review* (1986).

Epstein, Richard A. *Waste and the Dormant Commerce Clause,* 3 Green Bag 29 (1999).

Farber, Daniel A. *Civilizing Public Discourse: An Essay on Professor Bickel, Justice Harlan, and the Enduring Significance of Cohen v. California,* 1980 *Duke Law Journal* 283 (1980).

Fee, John. *Speech Discrimination,* 85 *Boston University Law Review* 1103 (2005).

Fennelly, John E. *Refinement of the Inevitable Discovery Exception: The Need for a Good Faith Requirement,* 17 *William Mitchell Law Review* 1085 (1991).

Finer, Joel Jay. *Gates, Leon, and the Compromise of Adjudicative Fairness,* 33 *Cleveland State Law Review* 707 (1984–1985).

Fisher, Louis. *Constitutional Conflicts between the Congress and the President.* Princeton, NJ: Princeton University Press, 1997.

Fletcher, George. *Loyalty.* New York: Oxford University Press, 1993.

Foley, Edward B. *"Smith for Congress" and its Equivalents: An Endorsement Test under Buckley and MCFL,* 2 *Election Law Journal* 3 (2003).

Forbes, Jessica. *The Inevitable Discovery Exception, Primary Evidence, and the Emasculation of the Fourth Amendment,* 65 *Fordham Law Review* 1221 (1987).

Frantz, John P. *The Reemergence of the Commerce Clause as a Limit on Federal Power: United States v. Lopez,* 19 *Harvard Journal of Law and Public Policy* 161 (1995).

Freedman, Warren. *Press and Media Access to the Criminal Courtroom.* New York: Quorum Books, 1988.

Fried, Charles. *Constitutional Doctrine,* 107 *Harvard Law Review* 1140 (1994).

Garcia, Crystal A., and Sheila Seuss Kennedy. *Back to School: Technology, School Safety, and the Disappearing Fourth Amendment,* 12 *Kansas Journal of Law and Public Policy* 273 (2003).

Gates, Henry Louis, Jr., Anthony P. Griffin, Donald E. Lively, Robert C. Post, William R. Rubinstein, and Nadine Strossen. *Speaking of Race, Speaking of Sex.* New York: New York University Press, 1994.

Gedid, John L. *History and Executive Removal Power: Morrison v. Olson and Separation of Powers,* 11 *Campbell Law Review* 175 (1989).

Gilligan, Carol. *In a Different Voice: Psychological Theory and Women's Development.* Cambridge, MA: Harvard University Press, 1982.

Goldstein, Abraham S. *The Search Warrant, the Magistrate, and Judicial Review,* 62 *New York University Law Review* 1173 (1987).

Goodell, Maia. *Government Responsibilty for the Acts of Jailhouse Informants Under the Sixth Amendment,* 101 *Michigan Law Review* 2525 (2003).

Goodman, Frank I. *De Facto Segregation: A Constitutional and Empirical Analysis,* 60 *California Law Review* 275 (1972).

Green, William. *Children and Pornography: An Interest Analysis in System Perspective,* 19 *Valparaiso University Law Review* 441 (1985).

Greene, Abner S. *Checks and Balances in an Era of Presidential Lawmaking,* 61 *University of Chicago Law Review* 123 (1994).

Greene, Philip S., and Brian W. Wice. *The D.E.A. Drug Courier Profile: History and Analysis,* 22 *South Texas Law Journal* 261 (1982).

Hagins, Todd. *Mother Goose and Father God: Extending the Equal Access Act to Pre-High School Students,* 15 *Regent University Law Review* 93 (2002).

Hart, H.L.A. *Law, Liberty and Morality.* Stanford, CA: Stanford University Press, 1965.

Hartley, Roger C. *Cross Burning-Hate Speech as Free Speech: A Comment on Virginia v. Black,* 54 *Catholic University Law Review* 1 (2004).

Heilbron, Louis H. *The Decline of the Establishment Clause: Effect of Recent Supreme Court Decisions on Church-State Relations,* 34 *Golden Gate University Law Review* 217 (2004).

Helmholz, R.H., Charles M. Gray, John H. Langbein, Eben Moglen, Henry E. Smith, and Albert W. Alschuler. *The Privilege Against Self-Incrimination.* Chicago: University of Chicago Press, 1997.

Henderson, Stephen E. *Nothing New Under the Sun? A Technologically Rational Doctrine of Fourth Amendment Search,* 56 *Mercer Law Review* 507 (2005).

Hentoff, Nat. *The First Freedom.* New York: Delacorte Press, 1980.

Hersch, Charles. *Five Tellings of an Abortion Clinic Protest: Madsen v. Women's Health Center and the Limits of Legal Narrative,* 19 *Legal Studies Forum* 395 (1995).

Jacobs, Paul. *Prelude to Riot: A View of Urban America from the Bottom.* New York: Vintage Books, 1967.

Kalven, Harry, Jr. *The Concept of the Public Forum,* 1965 *Supreme Court Review* 1 (1965).

Kalven, Harry, Jr. *The New York Times Case: A Report on "The Central Meaning of the First Amendment,"* 1964 *Supreme Court Review* 191 (1964).

Karst, Kenneth L. *Belonging to America.* New Haven, CT: Yale University Press, 1989.

Karst, Kenneth L. *Freedom of Intimate Association,* 89 *Yale Law Journal* 624 (1980).

Karst, Kenneth L. *Not One Law at Rome and Another at Athens: The Fourteenth Amendment in Nationwide Application,* 1972 *Washington University Law Quarterly* (1972).

Katsch, Ethan M. *The Electronic Media and the Transformation of Law.* New York: Oxford University Press, 1989.

Kennedy, Randall. *Persuasion and Distrust: A Comment on the Affirmative Action Debate,* 99 *Harvard Law Review* 1327 (1986).

Kerr, Orin S. *The Fourth Amendment and New Technologies: Constitutional Myths and the Case for Caution,* 102 *Michigan Law Review* 801 (2004).

Krause, Patricia A., ed. *Anatomy of an Undeclared War: Congressional Conference on the Pentagon Papers.* New York: National Universities Press, 1972.

Kreimer, Seth. *Does Pro-Choice Mean Pro-Kevorkian? An Essay on Roe, Casey, and the Right to Die,* 44 *American University Law Review* 803 (1995).

Kurland, Philip B. *Of Church and State and the Supreme Court,* 29 *University of Chicago Law Review* 1 (1961).

Kurland, Philip B. *Equal Educational Opportunity: The Limits of Constitutional Jurisprudence,* 35 *University of Chicago Law Review* 583 (1968).

Kurland, Philip B. *The Religion Clauses and the Burger Court,* 34 *Catholic University Law Review* 1 (1984).

LaFave, Wayne R., Jerold H. Israel, and Nancy J. King. *Criminal Procedure.* St. Paul, MN: Thomson/West, 2004.

Lappen, Louis D. *A Reconciliation of Henry and Wilson: The Intersection of Constitutional Rights with Procedural Review,* 1987 *Duke Law Journal* 945 (1987).

Law, Sylvia. *Rethinking Sex and the Constitution,* 132 *University of Pennsylvania Law Review* 955 (1984).

Lawrence, Charles R. III. *The Id, the Ego, and Equal Protection: Reckoning with Unconscious Racism,* 39 *Stanford Law Review* 317 (1987).

Laycock, Douglas. *Formal, Substantive and Disaggregated Neutrality Toward Religion,* 39 *DePaul Law Review* 993 (1990).

Lessig, Lawrence, and Cass R. Sunstein. *The President and the Administration,* 94 *Columbia Law Review* 1 (1994).

Levy, Leonard W. *Emergence of a Free Press.* New York: Oxford University Press, 1985.

Linder, Douglas. *Freedom of Association after Roberts v. United States Jaycees,* 82 *Michigan Law Review* 1878 (1984).

Lively, Donald E. *Foreshadows of the Law.* Westport, CN: Praeger, 1992.

Lively, Donald E., William D. Araiza, Phoebe A. Haddon, John C. Knechtle, and Dorothy E. Roberts. *First Amendment Law.* Cincinnati, OH: Anderson Publishing Co., 2003.

Lively, Donald E., Phoebe A. Haddon, Dorothy E. Roberts, Russell L. Weaver, and William D. Araiza. *Constitutional Law: Cases, History, and Dialogues.* Cincinnati, OH: Anderson Publishing Co., 2000.

Lively, Donald E., Allen S. Hammond IV, Blake D. Morant, and Russell L. Weaver. *Communications Law.* Cincinnati, OH: Anderson Publishing Co., 1997.

Lynskey, Rosemarie A. *A Middle Ground Approach to the Exclusionary Remedy: Reconciliing the Redaction Doctrine with United States v. Leon,* 41 *Vanderbilt Law Review* 811 (1988).

MacKinnon, Catharine A. *Toward a Feminist Theory of the State.* Cambridge, MA: Harvard University Press, 1991.

Mandelker, Daniel R. *Investment-Backed Expectations: Is There a Taking?* 31 *Washington University Urban and Contemporary Law* 3 (1987).

Mangrum, R. Collin. *Shall We Pray? Graduation Prayers and Establishment Paradigms,* 26 *Creighton Law Review* 1027 (1993).

Mangrum, R. Collin. *State Aid to Students in Religiously Affiliated Schools: Agostini v. Felton,* 31 *Creighton Law Review* 1155 (1998).

Marcus, Paul. *The Forum of Conscience: Applying Standards Under the Free Exercise Clause,* 1973 *Duke Law Journal* 1217 (1973).

Marcus, Paul. *Presenting, Back From the (Almost) Dead, the Entrapment Defense,* 47 *Florida Law Review* 205 (1995).

Martinez, Jenny S. *Availability of U.S. Court to Review Decision to Hold U.S. Citizen as Enemy Combatant—Executive Power in War on Terror,* 98 *American Journal of International Law* 782 (2004).

Mascolo, Edward G. *Probable Cause Revisited: Some Disturbing Implications from Illinois v. Gates*, 6 *Western New England Law Review* 331 (1983).

Matsuda, Mari, Charles R. Lawrence III, Richard Delgado, and Kimberle Crenshaw. *Words That Wound*. Boulder, CO: Westview Press, 1993.

McKenzie, Daniel. *What Were They Smoking? The Supreme Court's Latest Step in a Long Strange Trip Through the Fourth Amendment*, 93 *Journal of Criminal Law and Criminology* 153 (2001).

McLoughlin, Ian J. *The Meaning of Predisposition in Practice*, 79 *Boston University Law Review* 1067 (1999).

Meiklejohn, Alexander. *Free Speech and Its Relation to Self-Government*. New York: Harper, 1948.

Morizane, Satoru. *Initial Encounters Between Police and Citizens: A Comparative Study of the United States and Japan*, 13 *Emory International Law Review* 561 (1999).

Nelson, Grant S., and Robert J. Pushaw, Jr. *Rethinking the Commerce Clause: Applying First Principles to Uphold Federal Commercial Regulations but Preserve State Control over Social Issues*, 85 *Iowa Law Review* 1 (1999).

Nourse, V.F. *Toward a New Constitutional Anatomy*, 56 *Stanford Law Review* 835 (2004).

Nowak, John E., and Ronald D. Rotunda. *Principles of Constitutional Law*. St. Paul, MN: Thomson/West, 2004.

Ortiz, Daniel R. *The Myth of Intent in Equal Protection*, 41 *Stanford Law Review* 1105 (1989).

Overton, Spencer. *Restraint and Responsibility*, 61 *Washington and Lee Law Review* 663 (2004).

Overview of the Fourth Amendment, Thirty-Second Annual Review of Criminal Procedure, 91 *Georgetown Law Journal* 5 (2003).

Penrose, Meg. *Shedding Rights, Shredding Rights: A Critical Examination of Student Privacy Rights and the "Special Needs" Doctrine After Earles*, 3 *Nevada Law Journal* 411 (2003).

Posner, Richard. *Breaking the Deadlock: The 2000 Election, the Constitution, and the Courts*. Princeton, NJ: Princeton University Press, 2001.

Posner, Richard. *The DeFunis Case and the Constitutionality of Preferential Treatment of Racial Minorities*, 1974 *Supreme Court Review* 1 (1974).

Posner, Richard. *Sex and Reason*. Cambridge, MA: Harvard University Press, 1992.

Post, Robert. *Between Governance and Management: The History and Theory of the Public Forum*, 34 *UCLA Law Review* 1713 (1987).

Post, Robert. *The Constitutional Concept of Public Discourse: Outrageous Opinion, Democratic Deliberation, and Hustler Magazine v. Falwell*, 103 *Harvard Law Review* 603 (1990).

Powe, Lucas A., Jr. *American Broadcasting and the First Amendment*. Berkeley: University of California Press, 1987.

Raggi, Reena. *An Independent Right to Freedom of Association*, 12 *Harvard Civil Rights-Civil Liberties Law Review* 1 (1977).

Redish, Martin. *Freedom of Thought as Freedom of Expression: Hate Crime Sentencing Enhancement and First Amendment Theory*, 1992 *Criminal Justice Ethics* 29 (1992).

Redish, Martin, and Daryl Kessler. *Government Subsidies and Free Expression*, 80 *Minnesota Law Review* 543 (1996).

Redlich, Norman. *Separation of Church and State: The Burger Court's Tortuous Journey*, 60 *Notre Dame Law Review* 1094 (1985).

Report of the Attorney General's Commission on Pornography. Washington, DC: U.S. Department of Justice, 1986.

Report of the Commission on Obscenity and Pornography. Washington, DC: U.S. Department of Justice, 1970.

Rosen, Mark D. *The Surprisingly Strong Case for Tailoring Constitutional Principles*, 153 *University of Pennsylvania Law Review* 1513 (2005).

Rosenthal, Albert J. *Conditional Federal Spending and the Constitution*, 39 *Stanford Law Review* 1103 (1987).

Rossiter, Clinton, ed. *The Federalist No. 45*. New York, NY: New American Library, 1961.

Schauer, Frederick. *Causation Theory and the Cases of Sexual Violence,* 1987 *American Bar Foundation Research Journal* 737 (1987).

Schauer, Frederick. *Codifying the First Amendment: New York v. Ferber,* 1982 *Supreme Court Review* 285 (1982).

Schwarz, Alan. *No Imposition of Religion: The Establishment Clause Value,* 77 *Yale Law Journal* 692 (1998).

Schweitzer, Thomas A. *The Progeny of Lee v. Weisman: Can Student-Invited Prayer at Public School Graduations Still be Constitutional?* 9 *Brigham Young University Public Law Review* 291 (1995).

Shiffrin, Steven H. *The Pluralistic Foundations of the Religion Clauses,* 90 *Cornell Law Review* 9 (2004).

Skolnick, Jerome K. *The Sociological Tort of Defamation,* 74 *California Law Review* 677 (1986).

Smith, Steven D. *Foreordained Failure: The Quest for a Constitutional Principle of Religious Freedom.* New York: Oxford University Press, 1995.

Smolla, Rodney A. *Information, Imagery, and the First Amendment: A Case for Expansive Protection of Commercial Speech,* 71 *Texas Law Review* 777 (1993).

Smolla, Rodney A. *Jerry Falwell v. Larry Flynt: The First Amendment on Trial.* Urbana: University of Illinois Press, 1990.

Sowell, Thomas. *Race and Culture.* New York: Basic Books, 1994.

Spitzer, Matthew. *Seven Dirty Words and Six Other Stories.* New Haven, CT: Yale University Press, 1986.

Steele, Shelby. *The Content of Our Character.* New York: St. Martin's Press, 1990.

Straus, David A. *Discriminatory Intent and the Taming of Brown,* 56 *University of Chicago Law Review* 935 (1989).

Strossen, Nadine. *Defending Pornography.* New York: Scribner, 1995.

Sullivan, Kathleen M. *Unconstitutional Conditions,* 102 *Harvard Law Review* 1413 (1989).

Sunstein, Cass R. *Democracy and the Problem of Free Speech.* New York: Free Press, 1993.

Sunstein, Cass R. *The Partial Constitution.* Cambridge, MA: Harvard University Press, 1994.

Sunstein, Cass R. *Why the Unconstitutional Conditions Doctrine is an Anachronism (with Particular Reference to Religion, Speech and Abortion),* 70 *Boston University Law Review* 593 (1990).

Sunstein, Cass R., and Richard Epstein, eds. *The Vote: Bush, Gore, and the Supreme Court.* Chicago: University of Chicago Press, 2001.

Taylor, Jared. *Paved with Good Intentions.* New York: Carroll and Graf, 1992.

Thomas, George C., III. *Time Travel, Hovercrafts & the Framers: James Madison Sees the Future and Rewrites the Fourth Amendment,* 80 *Notre Dame Law Review* 451 (2005).

Thomas, Tracy S. *The Prophylatic Remedy: Normative Principles and Definitional Parameters of Injunctive Relief,* 52 *Buffalo Law Review* 301 (2004).

Tribe, Laurence H. *Abortion: The Clash of Absolutes.* New York: Norton, 1990.

Tribe, Laurence H. *American Constitutional Law.* Mineola, NY: Foundation Press, 1988.

Tuttle, William, Jr. *Race Riot: Chicago in the Red Summer of 1919.* New York: Atheneum, 1971.

Van Alstyne, Willliam. *Trends in the Supreme Court: Mr. Jefferson's Crumbling Wall—A Comment on Lynch v. Donnelly,* 1984 *Duke Law Journal* 770 (1984).

Volokh, Eugene. *Speech as Conduct: Generally Applicable Laws, Illegal Courses of Conduct, "Situation-Altering Utterances," and the Uncharted Zones,* 90 *Cornell Law Review* 1277 (2005).

Waite, Jason M. *Agostini v. Felton: Thickening the Establishment Clause Stew,* 33 *New England Law Review* 81 (1998).

Warren, Charles. *The Making of the Constitution.* Boston: Little, Brown and Company, 1937.

Wasilausky, Ellen M. *See Jane Read the Bible: Does the Establishment Clause Allow School Choice Programs to Include Sectarian Schools after Agostini v. Felton?* 56 *Washington and Lee Law Review* 721 (1999).

Weaver, Russell L. *Investigation & Discretion: The Terry Revolution at Forty (Almost),* 109 *Pennsylvania State Law Review* 1205 (2005).

Weaver, Russell L., Leslie W. Abramson, John M. Burkoff, and Catherine Hancock. *Principles of Criminal Procedure*. St. Paul, MN: Thomson/West, 2004.

Weaver, Russell L., and Donald E. Lively, *Understanding the First Amendment*. Newark, NJ: LexisNexis, 2003.

Werhan, Keith. *The Liberalization of Freedom of Speech on a Conservative Court*, 80 *Iowa Law Review* 51 (1994).

Wiecek, William. *The Sources of Antislavery Constitutionalism in America, 1760–1848*. Ithaca, NY: Cornell University Press, 1977.

Williams, Patricia J. *Metro Broadcasting, Inc. v. Federal Communications Commission*, 104 *Harvard Law Review* 525 (1990).

Wright, Robert. *The Moral Animal: Why We Are the Way We Are*. New York: Pantheon Books, 1994.

Yudof, Mark G. *Politics, Law, and Government Expression in America*. Berkeley: University of California Press, 1983.

INDEX

ABOUT THE AUTHORS

DONALD E. LIVELY is Vice President for Program Development for InfiLaw, the parent company of Florida Coastal School of Law, Phoenix International School of Law, and Charlotte School of Law. He has two decades of experience as a legal educator and is the founding dean of Florida Coastal School of Law and Phoenix International School of Law. Dean Lively has written numerous books and articles, has won book awards, and has spoken and lectured to national and international audiences on constitutional law and law and policy.

RUSSELL L. WEAVER has published numerous books and articles about the United States Constitution including the First Amendment and various aspects of criminal procedure. In addition, he has spoken at conferences around the world and regularly teaches in various foreign countries including France, Germany, Canada, and Australia. He has also served as a consultant to the constitutional commissions in both Belarus and Kyrgyzstan, and he was asked to submit written comments on the Russian Constitution.